KARL MARX AND
WORLD LITERATURE

KARL MARX AND WORLD LITERATURE

S. S. PRAWER

I am a citizen of the world
(*Marx to Paul Lafargue*)

OXFORD
AT THE CLARENDON PRESS
1976

Oxford University Press, Ely House, London W. 1

GLASGOW NEW YORK TORONTO MELBOURNE WELLINGTON

CAPE TOWN IBADAN NAIROBI DAR ES SALAAM LUSAKA ADDIS ABABA

DELHI BOMBAY CALCUTTA MADRAS KARACHI DACCA

KUALA LUMPUR SINGAPORE HONG KONG TOKYO

ISBN 0 19 815745 2

© *Oxford University Press, 1976*

*Printed in Great Britain
at the University Press, Oxford
by Vivian Ridler
Printer to the University*

77-2074

FOR

PROFESSOR ELIZABETH M. WILKINSON

TEACHER, GUIDE, AND FRIEND

Preface

THIS is not a book about Marxism nor an attempt to construct yet another Marxist theory of literature. It seeks, instead, to present to the English reader, as fairly and fully as the author's own orientation allows, what Marx said about literature at various times in his life; what use he made of the many novels, poems, and plays which he read for enjoyment, recreation, or instruction; and how he introduced, into works not overtly concerned with literature, the terminology and concepts of literary criticism. The task seems necessary because mountains of commentary and elaboration are beginning to hide Marx's own words from view; because the standard compilations of his utterances on aesthetic matters tend to create confusion by mixing up pronouncements made at various times of his life, as well as pronouncements by Marx and by Engels;* and because only a small proportion of Marx's references to literary works has so far been recognized and made available in English. The present chronological scrutiny of Marx's dealings with literature hopes to make a modest contribution to the understanding of a mind that has helped—for good or ill—to shape our world; of the history of literary taste in the nineteenth century; of the genesis of Marxist literary theory and criticism; and of the way in which literature may be 'used' by men of great stature who are not, professionally and in the first instance, literary critics. Through full quotation, in English, from the entire corpus of Marx's work it hopes also to advance the debate about Marx's literary theories, tastes, and attitudes among English-speaking

* 'What is so very strange', Marx complains, in a letter to Engels, about a contemporary commentator, 'is to see how he treats the two of us as a singular: "Marx and Engels *says*" etc.' (1 Aug. 1856; *MEW* XXIX, 68). I would not deny, of course, that Marx and Engels came to think alike on many points, nor would I assert that it is possible to disentangle neatly what each of them contributed to collaborative works like *The German Ideology*.

readers whose approach differs from mine but who have not, so far, had access to more than a fraction of the relevant material.

In making my translations from Marx's German works I have profitably and gratefully consulted existing versions by Bottomore, McLellan, Nicolaus, Livingstone, Milligan, Hook, Baxandall, Dona Torr, and many others—including, of course, Engels and the anonymous translators of the *Selected Works* published in Moscow. Of the *Collected Works* in English (*MECW*) only volume I had appeared when my manuscript went to press. I am also grateful to Dr. M. W. H. Schreuder of the Internationaal Instituut voor Sociale Geschiedenis, Amsterdam, Professor Dr. R. Dlubek of the Institut für Marxismus-Leninismus beim ZK der SED, Berlin, Mr. R. S. Livingstone, as well as the staffs of the Library of the Freie Universität, Berlin, and the Taylorian Library, Oxford, for assistance in finding out-of-the-way material; to the Faculty Board of Medieval and Modern Languages, Oxford University, for two travel-grants; and—especially—to Professor Roy Pascal, Mr. T. J. Reed, Mr. Paul Foote, Mr. James Bolton, and Mr. T. F. Eagleton for helpful criticism and advice.

Contents

Contents

List of Abbreviations

The following abbreviations have been used in notes and references:

BM   *Marx and Engels on Literature and Art. A Selection of Writings*, ed. L. Baxandall and S. Morawski (St. Louis, Milwaukee, 1973).

BR   Karl Marx, *Selected Writings in Sociology and Social Philosophy*, ed. T. Bottomore and M. Rubel (Harmondsworth, 1963).

CM   *Karl Marx on Colonialism and Modernization. His Despatches and Other Writings on China, India, Mexico, The Middle East and North Africa*, ed. S. Avineri (Anchor Books, New York, 1969).

EPM   *Economic and Philosophic Manuscripts of 1844*, trans. M. Milligan, ed. D. J. Struik (London, 1973).

ET   *Karl Marx: Early Texts*, trans. and ed. D. McLellan (Oxford, 1972).

G   Karl Marx, *Grundrisse der politischen Ökonomie* (Rohentwurf) (Berlin, 1953).

Gespräche   *Gespräche mit Marx und Engels*, ed. H. M. Enzensberger (Frankfurt, 1973).

GI   Karl Marx and Frederick Engels, *The German Ideology*, ed. C. J. Arthur (London, 1970).

GM   D. McLellan, *Marx's Grundrisse* (Paladin, London, 1973).

GN   Karl Marx, *Grundrisse. Foundations of the Critique of Political Economy* (Rough Draft), trans. M. Nicolaus (The Pelican Marx Library) (Harmondsworth, 1973).

K   Karl Marx, *Das Kapital. Kritik der politischen Ökonomie* (vols. XXIII–XXV of *MEW*).

KMP   *Karl Marx privat. Unbekannte Briefe*, ed. W. Schwerbrock (Munich, 1962).

L   Karl Marx, Friedrich Engels, *Über Kunst und Literatur. Eine Sammlung aus ihren Schriften*, ed. M. Lifshits (Berlin, 1948).

Manuskripte   *Manuskripte über die polnische Frage (1863–1864)*, ed. W. Conze and D. Hertz-Eichenrode (The Hague, 1961).

MECW   Karl Marx and Frederick Engels, *Collected Works* (Moscow, New York, and London, 1975 ff.).

MEGA	Karl Marx, Friedrich Engels, *Historisch-kritische Gesamt-ausgabe*, ed. D. Ryazanov and V. Adoratski (Frankfurt, Berlin, Moscow, 1927–35).
METEC	*Marx and Engels through the Eyes of their Contemporaries* (Progress Publishers, Moscow, 1972).
MEW	Karl Marx, Friedrich Engels, *Werke*. Herausgegeben vom Institut für Marxismus-Leninismus beim ZK der SED (Berlin, 1956–68).
MEW EB	Supplementary Volumes [*Ergänzungsbände*] of *MEW*.
Nachlaß	*Aus dem literarischen Nachlaß von Karl Marx, Friedrich Engels, und Ferdinand Lassalle*, I: *Gesammelte Schriften von Karl Marx und Friedrich Engels von März 1841 bis März 1844*, ed. F. Mehring (Stuttgart, 1902).
NOZ	*Neue Oder-Zeitung*.
NRZ	*Neue Rheinische Zeitung*.
NYDT	*New-York Daily Tribune*.
OB	Karl Marx and Frederick Engels, *Articles on Britain* (Progress Publishers, Moscow, 1971).
PP	*The People's Paper*.
PS	Karl Marx, *Politische Schriften*, ed. H. J. Lieber (Stuttgart, 1960).
R	*Neue Rheinische Zeitung: Politisch-ökonomische Revue*, redigiert von Karl Marx, ed. K. Bittel (Berlin, 1955).
RZ	*Rheinische Zeitung*.
SDH	Karl Marx, *Secret Diplomatic History of the Eighteenth Century* and *The Story of the Life of Lord Palmerston*, ed. L. Hutchinson (London, 1969).
SW	Karl Marx and Frederick Engels, *Selected Works in Three Volumes* (Moscow, 1969).
TM	*Theorien über den Mehrwert*. Vierter Band des *Kapitals* (vols. XXVI i, ii, iii of *MEW*).
ÜKL	Karl Marx, Friedrich Engels, *Über Kunst und Literatur*, ed. M. Kliem (Berlin, 1967).

1 · Prometheus

'Prometheus is the foremost saint and martyr in
the philosopher's calendar'
(*MEW EB* I, 265)

(i)

THERE is much in Marx's early life which might have seemed
to predestine him for a literary career. As his daughter Eleanor
recalled in later years:

He was a unique, an unrivalled story-teller. I have heard my aunts
say that as a little boy he was a terrible tyrant to his sisters, whom
he would 'drive' down the Markusberg at Trier full speed, as his
horses, and worse, would insist on their eating the 'cakes' he made
with dirty dough and dirtier hands. But they stood the 'driving' and
ate the 'cakes' without a murmur, for the sake of the stories Karl
would tell them as a reward for their virtue.[1]

His fellow pupils at school feared him because of the ease with
which he composed satirical verses and lampoons. He was introduced to Ovid, Cicero, and Tacitus at school, as well as to
Homer, Sophocles, Plato, and Thucydides; a gifted teacher,
Vitus Loers, who had published commentaries on Ovid, succeeded in arousing in his pupil an enthusiasm for that poet
which brought in its wake attempts to translate the *libri tristium*
into German verse, and admiring references to the same work
in later life. A taste for the eighteenth-century German classics
was nourished by his father (who held up Schiller, in particular,
for his son's admiration); while the Marx family's neighbour at
Trier, Karl Marx's later father-in-law Ludwig von Westphalen,
induced him to share his own admiration for Shakespeare. 'He
never tired', Eleanor told Wilhelm Liebknecht, 'of telling us

[1] *BM* 147.

about old Baron von Westphalen and his wonderful knowledge
of Shakespeare and Homer. He could recite whole cantos of
Homer from beginning to end, and most of Shakespeare's plays
he knew by heart in English and in German alike.' Marx's
father, on the other hand, Eleanor adds, 'was a proper "French-
man" of the eighteenth century. He knew his Voltaire and his
Rousseau by heart as old von Westphalen knew his Homer and
Shakespeare.'[2] The young Marx's school reports praise his performance in literary subjects and his ability as a translator,
though his German essays are said to be 'marred by an exaggerated striving after unusual picturesque expression'.[3]

In an essay he wrote for his school-leaving examination, Marx
addressed himself, in 1835, to the subject: 'A Young Man's
Reflections on the Choice of a Career'; and among the careers
there envisaged that of a *Dichter*, a writer of imaginative literature, figures at least in passing. The career a young man should
choose, the young Marx declares in 1835, should be

one that is most consonant with our dignity, one that is based on
ideas of whose truth we are wholly convinced, one that offers us
largest scope in working for humanity and approaching that general
goal towards which each profession offers only one of the means:
the goal of perfection . . . If he works only for himself he can become
a famous scholar, a great sage, an excellent imaginative writer
[*Dichter*], but never a perfected, a truly great man.[4]

Two related themes are here lightly touched which will recur
in Marx's later work. The first of these is the urge to become
more than just a professional man, even if the profession chosen
be that of a poet—the urge to work for others, to benefit humanity at large. This connects with a second theme, familiar to the
age of Goethe, a theme given memorable expression in Goethe's
Wilhelm Meister novels, in Schiller's *Aesthetic Education of Man*,
and in Hölderlin's *Hyperion*: the yearning for fullness of development, for overcoming the limitations imposed by that division
of labour without which no modern society can function. There
is nothing highly original in such sentiments; many boys at the

[2] *Mohr und General. Erinnerungen an Marx und Engels* (Berlin, 1970), pp. 157–8.
[3] D. McLellan, *Marx before Marxism* (Harmondsworth, 1972), pp. 50–2;
P. Demetz, *Marx, Engels und die Dichter* (Frankfurt and Berlin, 1969), p. 52;
MEGA I, 1 (2), 167.
[4] *MEGA* I, 1 (2), 164; *MEW EB* I, 593–4.

end of their school career will have had similar thoughts. The same is true of Marx's reflections, in this same school-leaving essay, on the different kinds of limitation that inevitably circumscribe a man's choice of profession. Some of these are due to individual and physical factors; but Marx also stresses the *social* determinations which force a young man to fit himself into a pre-existent framework: 'To some extent our social relations have already begun before we are in a position to determine them.'[5] By itself this observation too is unremarkable enough. But it was Marx who made it; and if we look at it in the context of his whole career we can at least sympathize with the (often ridiculed) view of Franz Mehring, who thought he saw the germ of Marxism in this one sentence from a school-leaving exercise. Mehring might, in fact, have employed his hindsight further by pointing to the way in which the Latin essay Marx wrote at the same time and for the same purpose sought to explain the Romans' alleged neglect of the arts and education before the Punic wars by their absorption in agriculture. Eloquence, the young Marx goes on to explain, was deemed unnecessary, for men spoke with few words about what had to be done, and regarded the content of their speech rather than elegance of form; nor did Roman history, in this early time, need rhetorical elaboration, for it only recorded things done, and confined itself to the compilation of annals.[6] Marx was often to speak, in later years, of what linked intellectual and artistic pursuits to a nation's economy; and the place of rhetorical elaboration and polished writing in historiography was to occupy him more than once as he tried to assess the relation of 'belletristic' virtues to the pursuit of truth.

As a university student, first at Bonn and later at Berlin (1835–41) Marx spent a good deal of time on the study not only of history, philosophy, and law, but also of literature. He heard lectures by A. W. Schlegel on Homer and Propertius, by F. G. Welcker on Greek and Latin mythology, and by Bruno Bauer on Isaiah; he copied out extracts from the aesthetic writings of Lessing, Solger, and Winckelmann; he tried to keep up with

[5] *MEW EB* I, 592.
[6] *MEW EB* I, 595 and *MECW* I, 640. The school-leaving exercises are reprinted in their original languages and with teachers' comments and corrections in *MEGA* I, 1 (2), 164–82.

what was new in literature (*alles Neueste der Literatur*);[7] he schooled his style by translating from Tacitus and Ovid; he joined a rhymers' club to which the poets Emanuel Geibel and Karl Grün also belonged; and he wrote a good deal of poetry. In a letter to his father, dated 10 November 1837, in which he drew the sum of his experiences so far, Marx noted a natural affinity between moments of change and the lyric mood: 'At such moments . . . an individual becomes lyrical, for every metamorphosis is partly a swansong, partly the overture of a great new poem that is trying to find its right proportions amid brilliant colours that are not yet distinct.'[8] Here all the arts are impressed to yield metaphors that help the young Marx to convey his feelings: literature ('lyrical', 'a great new poem'), music ('overture'), the visual arts ('brilliant colours').

Among the poems Marx wrote in the mood on which he here looks back there are some that reflect directly on the processes of artistic inspiration. The second of two dedicatory poems to his father (*Widmung. An den Vater*) provides a characteristic example:

Dichtung

Schöpferähnlich strömten Flammen
Rieselnd mir aus Deiner Brust,
Hochweit schlugen sie zusammen,
Und ich nährt' sie in der Brust.
Strahlend stand Dein Bild, wie Aeolsklingen,
Deckt die Gluten sanft mit Liebesschwingen.

Rauschen hört' ich's, sah es blinken,
Ferne Himmel zogen hin,
Tauchten auf, hinabzusinken,
Sanken, höher aufzufliehn.
Als der innre Kampf sich nun geschlichtet,
Blickt' ich Schmerz und Lust im Lied verdichtet.

Schmiegend an der Formen Milde,
Steht die Seele festgebannt,
Aus mir schwollen die Gebilde,
Aus Dir waren sie entbrannt.
Geistig lösen sie die Liebesglieder,
Sprühn sie voll im Schöpferbusen wieder.

---

[7] *MEW EB* I, 8.   [8] *MEW EB* I, 3.

Poetry

Creator-like, flames streamed,
Purling, from your breast to mine,
High, wide, they tongued together
And I nourished them in my breast.
Your image stood bright, like Aeolian sound;
Gently it covered the glow with pinions of love.

I heard murmuring sounds, I saw a gleam,
Faraway skies drifted along,
Emerged to sight, sank down again,
Sank only to rise higher still.
When the inner struggle came to rest
I saw pain and joy concentrated in song.

Nestling against gentle forms
The soul stands rapt,
These forms grew out of me,
Your fire quickened them.
In spirit they unbend loving limbs,
They scintillate again, brightly, in their creator's
                                        bosom.[9]

From this fantastic compliment to a father four thoughts
emerge: (*a*) that the 'flames' of inspiration come to the poet
from outside, but that he has to nourish them; (*b*) that the
poetic process begins as turmoil from which, at last, a concentrated poem emerges; (*c*) that in the finished work of art, pain
and pleasure are alike contained; (*d*) that the finished poem
fascinates the soul through the gentle power of form, and that
this is a *sensual* fascination (conveyed by the sexual imagery of
the final stanza).

The young Marx here tries to speak of poetry from the inside,
as a poet who has himself experienced inspiration. But the
evidence of the poem itself, with its cliché images deriving from
Schiller[10] and German Romantic poetry, with its mechanical,
inert rhythms, and with its clumsy formulations, brands this as
a delusion. Nor do we find anything in the thoughts conveyed

[9] *MEW EB* I, 603. My prose-translations aim at reproducing the literal sense
of the words as closely as possible. Verse-translations, which sometimes improve
on the original, may be found in *MECW* I, 517–615.

[10] The Schillerian strain in Marx's early poetry is described and illustrated in
M. Lifshits's *The Philosophy of Art of Karl Marx*, trans. R. B. Winn (reprinted London,
1973), p. 17.

which is not familiar aesthetic currency. These impressions are confirmed by a sonnet sequence addressed to the poet's future wife (*Schlußsonette. An Jenny*). Here the 'lyric I' sees his poems as inspired by love, as speaking of that love to its object, as exciting a reflection of the beloved which, in its turn, inspires him to deed and word (though also to feelings of tender sadness):

Dann darf ich kühner ringen, streiten,
Dann klingt mein Lied verklärt und freier,
Dann wagt sich höher mein Gesang,
Dann weint vor Wehmut meine Leier.

Then I may strive and battle more boldly,
Then my song rings out, transfigured and more free,
Then my singing dares to take higher flights,
Then my lyre weeps with tender sadness.[11]

The young poet is aware that neither his feelings nor his expressions are sufficiently clear and defined:

Doch wie sollen Worte richtig zwängen,
Selber Nebelrauch und Schall.
Was unendlich ist, wie Geistesdrängen,
Wie du selber und das All.

But how can words—themselves but
Misty smoke and sound—force into shape
What is infinite, like the thrust of the spirit,
Like yourself, like the universe.[12]

What such love-poems *can* do, however, is help to bridge the distance between those who are physically apart, and form a link between them; their moving appeal to one beloved reader, the final compliment has it, is the one reason why they exist:

Doch ach! ich will ja nichts als Tränen,
Will nur, Du sollst dem Sange lauschen,
Verklärung ihm verleihn und Zier,
Dann mag er dumpf im Nichts verrauschen.

But alas! all I want is tears;
All I want is that *you* should listen to this song,
That you should transfigure and adorn it—
Then it may darkly die away into nothingness.[13]

[11] *MEW EB* I, 614.   [12] *Nachlaß* I, 27.   [13] *MEW EB* I, 615.

These conventional compliments (Petrarchism via the gentle, melancholy purlings of the eighteenth-century *Göttinger Hain* poets) have proved prophetically true: Marx's early poetry *has* remained a family affair, of little interest to the wider world outside.

There are other, more romantic images of wild-eyed minstrels, inspired singers in these early verses: the dialogue-poem 'The Minstrel' (*Der Spielmann*), for instance, which shares with 'Night-Love' (*Nachtliebe*) the distinction of having been actually published in Marx's lifetime, though only in a very obscure journal:

> „Spielmann, zerreiß't dir das Herz mit Spott,
> Die Kunst, die lieh Dir ein lichter Gott,
> Sollst ziehn, sollst sprühn auf Klangeswellen,
> Zum Sternentanz hinanzuschwellen!"

> „ ‚Was, was! Ich stech', stech' ohne Fehle
> Blutschwarz den Säbel in deine Seele,
> Gott kennt sie nicht, Gott acht' nicht der Kunst;
> Die stieg in den Kopf aus Höllendunst . . .' "

'Minstrel, your mockery tears your very heart,
Your art was bestowed on you by a god of light;
You must roam the world, must scintillate on waves of sound,
Must strive upwards to the dance of the stars.'

' "What are you saying? Without fail I thrust
My sabre, black with blood, into your soul.
God does not know it; God thinks nothing of art;
Art ascended to the head from the fumes of hell." '[14]

Here we meet the two conflicting views of inspiration familiar to the German Romantics, from Wackenroder to E. T. A. Hoffmann: art as the gift of heaven, leading upwards; art as the gift of hell, dragging down into madness, alienation, death. The mockery and self-division which characterize the minstrel of Marx's poem ('Spielmann, zerreiß't dir das Herz mit Spott') recall Heine more than any other German poet—in particular the *Dream-Picture* section (*Traumbilder*) which opens Heine's *Book of Songs*.[15]

---

[14] *MEW EB* I, 604.

[15] Cf. N. Reeves, 'Heine and the Young Marx', *Oxford German Studies*, vii (1973), 47–52. W. M. Johnston has seen in this poem 'Marx's sharpest expression of the

Two poems have been preserved, however, which show the young Marx playing a significant variation on a theme familiar from Brentano, Eichendorff, and Heine. The first of these is the ballad 'Song of the Sirens' (*Sirenengesang*) in which a romantic minstrel figure, sounding his lyre, is lured by the sirens as the heroes of earlier poems are lured by the Lorelei. In Marx's poem the hero is able to charm nature and the water-nymphs, and the sirens cannot harm him:

> Mich könnt ihr nimmer fassen,
> Mein Lieben und mein Hassen,
> Und meine Sehnsuchtsglut;
> Sie schlägt wie Blitz nach oben,
> Von zarter Kraft gehoben,
> In Melodienflut.

> Me you can never seize—
> My loving and my hating,
> And the longing that burns in me—
> That strikes upward like lightning,
> Raised up by gentle power
> In a flood of melodies.[16]

That tribute to the gentle strength of poetry—a poetry of hate as well as one of loving and longing—does seem to ring true and clear through the inert rhythms and hackneyed images. Another poem on the same theme, entitled 'Song of a Boatman on the Sea' (*Lied eines Schiffers auf der See*) begins and ends with a stanza of similar self-confidence:

> „Ihr möget spielen, ihr möget schlagen,
> Und hüpfen um meinen Kahn,
> Ihr müßt ihn zum Ziele tragen,
> Ihr seid mir untertan!"

artist's isolation', and has called attention to the fact that the minstrel is made to carry a sabre as well as a violin: 'It is not far-fetched to say that out of this minstrel a revolutionary is waiting to be born.' It should be remembered, however, that the armed minstrel is a familiar figure in nineteenth-century German literature. Johnston has also commented on the dramatic form of this poem: 'As in so many of his lyrics, [Marx] uses a dialogue form, in which an unnamed interlocutor challenges the principal figure.' ('Karl Marx's Verse of 1836–1837 as a Foreshadowing of his Early Philosophy', *Journal of the History of Ideas*, xxviii (1967), 266–7.)

[16] *MEGA* I, 1 (2), 14.

'You may play, you may sound your lyre,
You may leap about my boat,
Yet you must bear it to its goal,
You are subject to me.'

Here the self-confident boatman of Marx's poem contrasts
instructively with the drifting, helpless victims of natural and
supernatural forces that people Romantic 'Rhine'-poems from
Brentano to Heine; though it is worthy of remark, in view of
later developments, that Marx's persona is made to draw part
of its strength from a prayer to God:

„Und ich kämpfe mit Wind und Wellen,
Und bete zu Gott, dem Herrn,
Und laß die Segel schwellen,
Und halt' mich an sichern Stern."

'And I battle with wind and waves,
And pray to the Lord,
And let the sails swell,
And navigate by a safe star.'[17]

In Bonn Marx had attended lectures by A. W. Schlegel, one
of the founding fathers of German Romanticism; and during
his stay in Berlin he came into personal contact with another—
somewhat less eminent—representative of that movement. This
was Bettina von Arnim, the wife of Achim von Arnim and
sister of Clemens Brentano, who had been admitted in her
early years, to the friendship of Goethe, and who had just
erected a monument to that friendship in her book *Goethe's
Correspondence with a Child* (*Goethes Briefwechsel mit einem Kinde*,
1835). In 1839 Bettina even paid a visit to Jenny von Westphalen and Karl Marx in Trier—but that visit proved a strain
and served only to confirm the sceptical view Marx had taken
of Bettina in a satirical poem entitled 'Newfangled Romanticism' (*Neumodische Romantik*).[18] This contact with an actual
member of the German Romantic school, one who had, by
her writings and her life-style, added a significant nuance to
Romanticism in Germany, helped to diminish still further the
young Marx's already waning allegiance to Romantic modes
of writing and thinking.

[17] *MEW EB* I, 613.   [18] *MEGA* I, 1 (2), 11.

In some of these early verses poetry is said to adumbrate a higher life:

> „Glaubst, Sänger, wohl ich fasse nicht
> Den Seelenkampf, das Busenlicht,
> Die Bilder, die aufwärts streben?
> Sie schimmern rein, wie Sternenland,
> Sie brausen hoch, wie Flutenbrand,
> Die deuten ein höheres Leben."

> 'Perhaps you think, poet, that I cannot grasp
> The battles in your soul, the light within your bosom,
> The images that strive upwards?
> They shine, pure like the realm of the stars,
> They billow up like a burning flood,
> They point towards a higher life';

others convey the realization that life as actually lived, life not warmed and enriched by love, may be felt as a cold and poor affair:

> Zu kalt war ihr das Leben,
> Zu arm das Erdenland.

> Life was too cold for her,
> The earth too poor.[19]

These last lines come from a poem entitled *Die Zerrissene* (a term indicating self-conflict and inner division which was fashionable in the earlier nineteenth century); it is one of a number of poems in which Marx shows an interest in those frontier situations of madness and despair which have so often fascinated young poets.[20]

Among these early lyrics one remains of special interest: a poem entitled 'Human Pride' (*Menschenstolz*) which begins with an evocation of the huge buildings and bewildering confluence of people characteristic of a modern city. The young poet finds the oppressiveness of this city—his sense of what he would later learn to call 'alienation' and 'reification'—lightened by the thought that these buildings did not create themselves, that it was human ingenuity which brought them into being, and by

---

[19] *MEGA* I, 1 (2), 37, 48.
[20] Others are *Des Verzweiflenden Gebet* and *Die Wahnsinnige* (*MEGA* I, 1 (2), 30–1 and 25–6).

a related feeling that the human soul (particularly the soul of
a man in love) could raise itself above bricks, mortar, marble,
and thronging feverish activity through becoming conscious of
its inexhaustible riches and power. The poet feels God-like now,
superior to a man-made world which he can presently address,
with contemptuous mockery, as a 'giant-dwarf':

> Jenny! Darf ich kühn es sagen,
>   Daß die Seelen liebend wir getauscht,
>   Daß in eins sie glühend schlagen,
>   Daß ein Strom durch ihre Wellen rauscht,
>
> Dann werf' ich den Handschuh höhnend
>   Einer Welt ins breite Angesicht,
>   Und die Riesenzwergin stürze stöhnend,
>   Meine Glut erdrückt ihr Trümmer nicht.
>
> Götterähnlich darf ich wandeln,
>   Siegreich ziehn durch ihr Ruinenreich,
>   Jedes Wort ist Glut und Handeln,
>   Meine Brust dem Schöpferbusen gleich.

> Jenny—if I may boldly say
> That we have lovingly exchanged hearts,
> That our glowing hearts beat as one,
> That one and the same stream agitates their waves,
>
> Then I fling my gauntlet disdainfully
> Into the world's broad face.
> Let the giant-dwarf collapse and groan—
> Its fall will not stifle my ardour.
>
> Like to the gods I can then wend my way
> Victoriously through its ruined realm;
> Every word is ardour and activity,
> My breast is like that of the Creator.[21]

In speaking of his love, in writing this very poem, the poetic
persona or 'lyric I' feels akin at once to Prometheus and to
Jove.
  The note struck at the end of this poem, with its paean to
activity and creativity, is one heard more than once in these

early poems. Marx is clearly most himself when speaking of an overpowering drive to action:

> Darum laßt uns alles wagen,
> Nimmer rasten, nimmer ruhn,
> Nur nicht dumpf so gar nichts sagen,
> Und so gar nichts woll'n und tun.

> Nur nicht brütend hingegangen
> Ängstlich in dem niedern Joch,
> Denn das Sehnen und Verlangen
> Und die Tat, sie blieb uns doch.

> Therefore let us dare all,
> Never pause, never rest,
> Let us never sink into dull silence,
> Into willing nothing and doing nothing.

> Let us not walk, in brooding anxiety,
> Under the yoke that weighs us down:
> For longing and desire
> And action—these remain to us in spite of all.[22]

This urge towards activity, towards *Praxis*, includes the desire to conquer the realms of poetry and art:

> Nimmer kann ich ruhig treiben
> Was die Seele stark erfaßt,
> Nimmer still behaglich bleiben,
> Und ich stürme ohne Rast.

> Alles möcht' ich mir erringen,
> Jede schöne Göttergunst,
> Und im Wissen wagend dringen
> Und erfassen Sang and Kunst.

> I can never pursue calmly
> What seizes the soul so powerfully,
> I can never remain comfortably at rest:
> Ceaselessly, tempestuously, I rush on.

> I would like to conquer everything for myself,
> Every fair favour of the gods,
> Daringly advance in knowledge
> And seize song and art.[23]

[22] *Nachlaß* I, 28; cf. *MECW* I, 526–7.
[23] *Nachlaß* I, 27–8; cf. *MECW* I, 525.

Marx had enough taste, however, to see that the conquest of poetry and art *as an artist* was denied to him. 'I must tell you', his daughter Laura wrote to Franz Mehring after Marx's death, 'that my father treated these verses with very little respect. Every time my parents came to speak of them they laughed heartily at such youthful follies.'[24]
Literature and its creators figure in Marx's early poetry in another way too: through mockery of what he considers to be inadequate estimates of great writers by philosophers and critics from Hegel to Pustkuchen. How absurd, we are meant to feel, to ask of great writers precisely what *their* peculiar genius forbids them to give!

> So war an dem Schiller auszusetzen,
> Er könne nicht menschlich genug ergetzen,
> Er treibe die Dinge auch gar zu hoch,
> Und zieh' nicht gehörig am Werkeltagsjoch.
> Er spiele wohl sehr mit Donner und Blitz,
> Doch fehle ihm gänzlich der Straßenwitz.

> Thus it was to be objected that Schiller
> Cannot give enough human enjoyment:
> He pushes everything on to too exalted a plane,
> He does not labour as he should under the work-
> aday yoke.
> He plays a good deal with thunder and lightning,
> But the wit of the streets he lacks altogether.[25]

How much more absurd to ask them to conform to religious and moral orthodoxy!

> Goethe sei für Frauen ein Grauen,
> Denn er passe nicht grad' für alte Frauen,
> Er habe ja nur die Natur ergriffen,
> Sie nicht mit Moral zurechtgeschliffen,
> Hätt' Luthers Katechete sollen studieren,
> Daraus dann Verse fabrizieren.
> Zwar das Schöne hat er manchmal gedacht,
> Doch vergaß er zu sagen: „Gott hab' es gemacht."

> Goethe (it is objected) inspires horror in women:
> He does not suit old women at all:

[24] *Nachlaß* I, 26.   [25] *MEW EB* I, 609.

All he has done is to seize hold of nature,
Without polishing it into moral shape.
He should have studied Luther's catechism
And put *that* into verse.
True, he sometimes considered the beautiful,
But he forgot to say: 'God made it'.[26]

This is a vein Marx will exploit later: the exposure of 'false consciousness', of sloppy thinking, and philistine expectations, through a sharp look at the way in which philosophers and men of letters deal with the literature of past and present. He also satirizes, in these early poems, the way in which art is received by the ordinary public: a Heinesque poem, 'Armida von Ritter Gluck', ridicules the foolish chatter of a young lady sitting next to the poet at a performance of Gluck's opera *Armida*, and contrasts the poet's absorption in the world of beautiful sounds with the young lady's pretensions:

Sie rief: „Ist das Ballet nicht schön gewesen?"
„Gott", sprach ich, „was gibt's im Intelligenzblatt zu lesen?"

Dann sank ich in die Töne stumm.
Sie lächelte höhnisch: „Der Kerl ist dumm!"

She cried: 'Was not the ballet beautiful?'
'My God', said I, 'what's new in the papers?'

Then, silently, I submerged myself in the music.
She smiled derisively: 'the fellow is stupid!'[27]

This description of the poet turning away from pretentious chatter about art to the news of the day, and then to art itself which he receives in silence, continues a line of anti-bourgeois satire familiar from Heine's *Pictures of Travel*.

One last poem is worth a passing glance, in view of the later development of Marx's views on the arts. It is entitled 'Viennese Monkey-Play in Berlin' (*Wiener Affentheater in Berlin*):

Ich saß und blickt' in guter Ruh
Dem reinen Spiel der Bestien zu,
Natur, die war nicht zu vermissen,
Hätt'n nur noch solln an die Wände — — —

---

[26] *MEW EB* I, 610.   [27] *MEGA* I, 1 (2), 9.

I sat (in the theatre) and calmly watched
The beasts' pure play:
There was no lack of nature here—
All that was lacking, was to see them piss on the walls.[28]

It may well be felt, after this poem, that Marx would not be favourably inclined to sordid naturalism on the stage, or to 'happenings' which carve out a raw slice of nature and then ask to be regarded as art.

The fragment of a novel Marx began in 1837 (*Scorpion und Felix. Ein humoristischer Roman*) is heavily dependent on Sterne's *Tristram Shandy* and Heine's *Pictures of Travel* in its over-all construction, the cadences of its prose, its sudden, deliberate letdowns, and its verbal cartoons.[29] It also drags in, at every opportunity, allusions to the Bible, to Ovid's *libri tristium*, to Winckelmann, to Goethe's Mignon, to the famous opening passage of Goldsmith's *The Vicar of Wakefield*, to Hoffmann's *The Devil's Elixirs*, and to many other literary works and characters. Shakespeare figures prominently, with a parody of *Richard III* and an allusion (the first of many!) to the character of Thersites in *Troilus und Cressida*.[30] Chapters 29 and 30 strike up, parodistically, a theme made popular by Hegel which was later to inspire one of Marx's most famous pronouncements on the arts: 'An epic . . . can no longer be written in our day';[31] and a strongly Heinesque later chapter comments with heavy wit and not always appropriate imagery on the decline of politics, philosophy, and literature in the nineteenth century:

Every giant, and thus every chapter twenty lines long, presupposes a dwarf, every genius a dry philistine, every rising of the seas mud; as soon as the former disappear, the latter take their place at the table and arrogantly sprawl out their long legs. The former are too great for this world, and are therefore thrown out. The latter, however, take root and stay, as one may see from the facts: for champagne leaves a lasting unpleasant aftertaste, on the hero Caesar follows the showman Octavius, on the Emperor Napoleon the bourgeois king Louis-Philippe, on the philosopher Kant the carpet-knight Krug, on the poet Schiller the court-councillor Raupach, on the

[28] *MEGA* I, 1 (2), 8.
[29] Reeves, op. cit., pp. 49–51; Demetz, op. cit., p. 57.
[30] *MEGA* I, 1 (2), 77.
[31] *MEGA* I, 1 (2), 83.

heaven Leibniz the schoolroom Wolff, and on the dog Boniface this
chapter . . .[32]

From Leibniz to Christian Wolff, from Kant to W. T. Krug,
from Napoleon to Louis-Philippe, from Schiller to one of
Heine's favourite butts, the playwright Ernst Raupach—the
way is uniformly downwards. Since only a fragment of *Scorpion
und Felix* survives, it is hard to say how far the whole novel
would have borne out, in its humorous context, this dark
diagnosis.

Scorpion und Felix is chiefly remarkable, perhaps, as an attempt
to speak of political matters in a literary form borrowed from
Sterne and Heine. It contains a first attack, in chapter XXIX,
on the laws of entail and primogeniture which Hegel had
defended in his *Philosophy of Right*, and which the Prussian
government wanted to apply to the Rhine-provinces.[33] The
clumsy anti-bourgeois satire that pervades the whole fragment
also has political implications.

Another fragment of these early years, comprising a few
scenes from the fate-tragedy *Oulanem*, is as dependent on Goethe
and Adolph Müllner (such names mingled: but these are the
facts) as *Scorpion und Felix* had been on Sterne and Heine. The
dominant figure in the scenes we have is Pertini, who is a pale
but recognizable reflection of Mephistopheles in Goethe's *Faust*.
Pertini himself, in fact, is made to comment on the resemblance,
if only to play it down.[34] Into his mouth Marx puts all the
adverse comment that German Romantic poetry and poets are
apt to excite in the cynical:

> Ein Deutscher ist's, er wirft aus allen Ecken
> Mit Melodie und Seele um sich her . . .

> He is a German, lavishly throws about
> 'Melody' and 'soul' at every opportunity;

Or again:

> . . . Das klingt romantisch, klingt,
> Doch lieber junger Herr, es ist nur Klang . . .

[32] *MEGA* I, 1 (2), 85–6.
[33] Cf. A. Cornu, *Karl Marx et Friedrich Engels: Leur vie et leur œuvre*, vol. 1 (Paris,
1955), p. 95.
[34] *MEGA* I, 1 (2), 63.

or yet again:

> That *sounds* romantic,
> But dear young sir, it is *only* sound;

> Nicht wahr, es gibt 'nen wundersamen Dichter,
> So 'ne ästhet'sche, finstre Blindekuh,
> Die selt'ne Grübeleien hat und Stunden,
> Das Leben zu 'nem Reime machen will,
> Und gern das Leben selbst gedichtet hätte?

> There is a wondrous poet, is there not,
> Who plays aesthetic blind-man's buff in the dark,
> Who knows rare ruminations and strange hours,
> Who wants to turn life into a rhyme
> And transform life itself into poetry?[35]

It is no accident, surely, that so much of what has been preserved from Marx's abortive play is given over to this anti-Romantic character: his assertions of the reality principle against German Romantic dreaming clearly corresponds to something strongly present in Marx's own way of thinking.
A valid point has recently been made by Ian Birchall about a passage in *Oulanem* which compares an eternally existing universe to a work of art or a piece of artifice (*Kunstwerk*):

> Ha, Ewigkeit! Das ist ein ew'ger Schmerz
> Ein unaussprechlich unermeß'ner Tod!
> Schnöd' Kunstwerk, uns zum Hohn ersonnen,
> Wir Uhrwerk, blindmechanisch aufgezogen,
> Des Zeitenraums Kalendernarr zu sein,
> Zu sein, damit doch irgendwas geschieht,
> Zerfall'n, damit doch irgendwas zerfällt!

> Ha! eternity! that is an eternal pain,
> An unspeakably immeasurable death.
> Vile artifice, invented to our scorn,
> We are clockwork, blindly, mechanically, wound up
> To be the calendars, the fools of time,
> To be, so that something happens,
> Decay, so that something decays![36]

---

[35] *MEGA* I, 1 (2), 70, 61, 65.
[36] *MEGA* I, 1 (2), 68; I. Birchall, 'The Total Marx and the Marxist Theory of Literature', in *Situating Marx*, ed. Walton and Hall (London, 1972), p. 136.

This passage, Birchall suggests, may serve to show that some of Marx's ideas came to him first in the form of images—for in these lines, it would seem, the hero of *Oulanem* is made to express a premonition of Marx's later key-idea of 'reification'.[37] A study of Marx's poems bears this out; we have already seen how in 'Human Pride' (*Menschenstolz*) the Promethean ardours of its final stanza are preceded by an extended presentation of man's inability to feel at home in the nineteenth-century city (see above, p. 10). It should be pointed out, however, that in the context of German literature the imagery Marx uses is conventional enough—its play on the ideas connected with anguish, death, time, eternity, art, artifice, and clockwork may be paralleled in many a Romantic work. With different emotional connotations such images may also be found in the writers of the Enlightenment and the Baroque. But Marx *chose* such imagery from the rich store of German literature; his choice remains significant even though he added little of his own.

After toying with the idea of publishing a volume of his poems —a project happily frustrated by the advice of his father and the reluctance of publishers—Marx turned the force of his critical intelligence on these products of his Muse. Not that he had any doubt about the important function they fulfilled in his life. At significant turning-points, he explained to his father, men compose lyric poetry in order to 'erect a monument to what we have lived through. This is to regain in the imagination the place it has lost in action.'[38] Such poems, such crystallizations of past experiences, are then sent into the world to be taken into the hearts of well-disposed readers. Steeped as he was, however, in other, greater poetry, Marx could not long retain any illusions he might once have had about the aesthetic value of what he had written:

Considering the state of my mind at that time it was inevitable that lyric poetry should be my first project, it was certainly the pleasantest and readiest to hand; but my attitude and all my previous development made it purely idealistic. My heaven and my art became a world beyond, as remote as my love. Everything real

---

[37] 'Man's own deed', Marx writes in *The German Ideology*, 'becomes an alien power opposed to him, which enslaves him instead of being controlled by him' (*MEW* III, 33).
[38] *MEW EB* I, 3.

becomes hazy and loses all bounds. The poems in the first of the three volumes I sent to Jenny are therefore characterized by attacks on the present, feeling without moderation and form, nothing natural, everything built on moonshine—what is and what ought to be are depicted as wholly opposed, rhetorical reflections occupy the place of poetic thoughts; though there is also, perhaps a certain warmth of feeling emotion, an attempted soaring of the imagination. The expansiveness of a longing that sees no bounds expresses itself in many forms and causes poetry to dilate when it should be concentrated. . . . At the end of the term I again sought the dances of the muses and the music of the satyrs; and in the last volume I sent you, forced humour (*Scorpion and Felix*) and a misconceived fantastic drama (*Oulanem*) are shot through with idealism; until idealism changes completely into a purely formal art, mostly without objects to inspire it and with no exciting progression of ideas.

And yet these last poems are the only ones in which suddenly, as at the touch of a magic wand—oh! the touch was shattering at first—the kingdom of true poetry glistened towards me like a distant fairy palace and all my creations crumbled into nothing.[39]

This remarkable passage enunciates a number of critical principles to which Marx was henceforth to remain faithful: that literature should stay close to the realm of the real and actual and not fly off too far into ideal realms; that it should have form, measure, concentration; that there is a quality in great works of literature which can be felt as truly poetic ('the kingdom of true poetry'), and that works of which this can be said provide touchstones by which lesser works may be tried and found wanting; that rhetorical tricks are no substitute for the poetic imagination; and that there is nothing which damns a work of art more surely than the substantiated charge of pure formalism (*reine Formkunst*) which has neither objects to inspire it (*begeisternde Objekte*) nor exciting progression of ideas (*schwunghaften Ideengang*).

Marx's own poetic compositions could not stand up to the critical principles he had evolved while writing them. He now knew that he would never be a true poet. After an illness he burnt such poems and novellistic fragments as he still possessed, 'deluding myself' (as he writes to his father) 'that I could stop writing such things altogether—which I have not, as yet, disproved'. He did not, however, abandon all hope of publishing

[39] *MEW EB* I, 4–8; *ET* 2–6 (letter to Heinrich Marx, 10 Nov. 1837).

his literary work; the very letter to his father from which the passage just quoted has been taken, written on 10 November 1837, expresses annoyance with Adalbert von Chamisso, who had refused to accept contributions Marx had sent him for a literary almanac.[40]

What, then, of Jenny von Westphalen, that eager and grateful recipient of so many products of the young Marx's muse? She was not to be wholly deprived of poetic love-tokens. In lieu of his own poems, however, Marx now sent her a tribute of a slightly different kind: a collection of folk-poems, culled, for the most part, not from the most obvious source, *The Boy's Magic Horn* (*Des Knaben Wunderhorn*) by Arnim and Brentano, but from a less altered and reworked collection made by Erlach, Kretschmer, and Zuccalmaglio. These folk-poems Marx copied out (occasionally substituting the names 'Karl' and 'Jenny' for 'Hans' and 'Rosa') and sent to his fiancée, letting the anonymous poets who created or revised the texts of German folk-songs speak for him. In a note that accompanied these copies he gave Jenny to understand that he was here in very respectable poetic company: for one song of Albanian origin, he explained, had already figured in Byron's *Childe Harold's Pilgrimage*.[41]

The letter to his father, from which so much of our evidence for Marx's early development comes, has at its centre the story of Marx's conversion to Hegel whose philosophy had earlier been abhorrent to him. This story is told in imagery which clearly derives from German Romantic poetry:

... dies mein liebstes Kind, beim Mondschein gehegt, trägt mich wie eine falsche Sirene dem Feind in den Arm.

... This, my favourite child, tenderly nursed by moonlight, bears me like a false Siren into the arms of my enemy.[42]

In annoyance at being borne towards Hegel rather than away from him, he tells his father, he rushed through the gardens beside the River Spree with its dirty water 'that washes souls and weakens tea'. The words in inverted commas are a quotation from Heine's *North Sea* cycle, from a section of the poem 'Peace' (*Frieden*) which Heine later omitted as being too bitterly satirical. Marx is clearly beginning to make use of his splendidly

[40] *MEW EB* I, 9, 10.   [41] *MEGA* I, 1 (2), 96.   [42] *MEW EB* I, 9.

ready memory to reinforce the expression of his own views with phrases coined by greater masters of language. As Nigel Reeves plausibly suggests,

This quotation is tiny but eloquent, for *Frieden* is probably the most biting work in Heine's entire early lyric production . . . The poet's serene vision of the Saviour walking on the waters in the first part is crassly contrasted [with] the hypocritical use to which such pious thoughts could be put in the social rat-race . . . This poem anticipates Heine's later critique of Christianity as the handmaiden of the social and political establishment.[43]

Marx's early allusion to *Frieden* may thus be seen as a pointer to some of the things which attracted him to Heine after the period in which he wrote his own poems; to some of the ways in which Heine's ideas and their expression were to influence, or confirm, Marx's later social criticism together with its formulation.

The distinction between the outward obscurity of German classical philosophy including Hegel and its hidden revolutionary content; the interpretation of German philosophy since Kant as an intellectual equivalent to the French revolution; the belief that ideas shape the world and that the philosophical revolution would bring in its train a German political and social revolution; the view that a philosophy is not valuable in itself but in its effect on reality, in *Praxis*; the claim that Christianity was allied to despotism and the source of men's inner self-division; the declaration that an age of subjectivism was in the ascendant . . . [44]

—these were but some of the ideas which Marx, and the Young Hegelians, could find in Heine before they formulated them for themselves. Heine's cherished notion that it is *ideas* which most effectively shape the world became, however, increasingly unacceptable to Marx as his own views evolved—his later conception of the processes of history would not allow him to follow Heine in seeing Robespierre, for instance, as no more than the 'bloody hand' which drew from the womb of time a body whose soul had been created by Rousseau.[45]

[43] Reeves, op. cit., pp. 52–3. In the course of a description of Berlin philistines masquerading as heroes of liberty Marx quotes the same line again (letter to Ruge, 30 Nov. 1842; *MEW* XXVII, 412).

[44] Reeves, op. cit., p. 57.

[45] Heine, *Zur Geschichte der Religion und Philosophie in Deutschland*, Book III.

One of Marx's early epigrammatic poems mentions Hegel's aesthetics in a humorous context:

> Verzeiht uns Epigrammendingen,
> Wenn wir fatale Weisen singen,
> Wir haben uns nach Hegel einstudiert,
> Und sein' Ästhetik noch nicht — abgeführt.

> Pardon us creatures of epigram
> If we sing unpleasant tunes;
> We have learnt our lesson of Hegel
> And are not purged of his aesthetic.[46]

Mikhail Lifshits, who quotes this passage, opines that in the course of his translation to Hegelianism 'Marx made a thorough study of Hegel's *Aesthetik*, read, no doubt, during the summer of 1837'.[47] There can be no doubt that Marx was well informed about Hegel's views on art and literature; but his notes and writings afford little evidence of first-hand acquaintance with those lectures on aesthetics which were first published in 1835, and which are usually known as Hegel's *Aesthetik*. Most of the Hegelian notions that reappear in Marx's own occasional aesthetic statements were either the common currency of German aesthetics in the late eighteenth and early nineteenth centuries,[48] or had already been enunciated in other works by Hegel (notably the *Phenomenology of the Spirit*) which we know Marx to have studied intensively.[49]

(ii)

After the collapse of his hopes that he might be a poet, Marx thought for a time of combining literature and philosophy. He sketched a Platonic dialogue, *Cleanthes, or Reflections on the Starting-point and Necessary Progress of Philosophy*, but found that this, instead of carrying him back to poetry, bore him more

---

[46] *MEGA* I, 1 (2), 42. W. M. Johnston's commentary is once again relevant: 'Here Marx speculates on the practical applications of Hegel's aesthetic. If it will not help poets to write better, what use is it?' ('Karl Marx's Verse of 1836–1837', pp. 261–2.)

[47] M. Lifshits, *The Philosophy of Art of Karl Marx*, p. 12.

[48] Cf. S. Pazura, *Marks a klasyczna estetyka niemiecka* (Warsaw, 1967).

[49] Cf. G. Hillmann, *Marx und Hegel. Von der Spekulation zur Dialektik* (Frankfurt, 1966).

firmly than ever towards Hegel and philosophy: 'The last sentence [of my dialogue] was the beginning of Hegel's system...'[50] A few years later, in the early 1840s, he was to have the idea of writing a farce, to be entitled *Fischer vapulans*, against K. P. Fischer's attempt to justify theism in his book *The Idea of the Divinity* (*Die Idee der Gottheit*); this came to nothing, however.[51] Nor did anything come of his plan to found a journal of dramatic criticism. Instead, Marx devoted himself with greater application to his philosophical studies, and, between the end of 1839 and 1841, to the composition of his doctoral dissertation on *The Difference between Democritus' and Epicurus' Philosophy of Nature*. The Preface to the completed dissertation shows clearly one of the most important functions which, at this stage, Marx saw fulfilled by literature:

As long as a single drop of blood pulses in her world-conquering, absolutely free heart, philosophy will continually cry out to her opponents, with Epicurus: 'The truly impious man is not he who destroys the gods worshipped by the multitude, but he who affirms of the gods what the multitude believes about them.'

Philosophy makes no secret of this. The confession of Prometheus: 'In a word, I detest all the gods' is her own confession, her own watchword against all the gods of heaven and earth who do not recognize man's self-consciousness as the highest divinity. It will have none other beside.

But to the pitiful March hares who rejoice at the apparently worsened civil position of philosophy, she repeats what Prometheus said to Hermes, the servant of the gods:

'Be sure of this, I would not change my evil plight for your servility. It is better to be slave to the rock than to serve Father Zeus as his faithful messenger.'

Prometheus is the foremost saint and martyr in the philosopher's calendar.

Berlin, March 1841[52]

The great literature of the past, then, speaks across the ages to all men, as the lines here quoted from Aeschylus' *Prometheus Bound* are meant to speak to readers of a doctoral thesis in nineteenth-century Germany. The figures at the centre of Greek

[50] *MEW EB* I, 9.   [51] *MEGA* I, 1 (2), 237; McLellan, op. cit., p. 94.
[52] *MEW EB* I, 262-3; *ET* 13-14.

drama, especially the titanic rebel Prometheus, can serve as spokesmen for the aspirations of men who live in quite different times and societies. What had been generalized Promethean titanism in Marx's early poems—in 'Human Pride', for instance, or, especially, in 'The Despairing Man's Prayer' (*Des Verzweiflenden Gebet*)—has now embodied itself in a literary symbol.[53] But although Prometheus here speaks the words Aeschylus put into his mouth (Marx quotes his lines in the original Greek), Aeschylus himself could hardly have acknowledged the thought that man's self-consciousness is to be the highest divinity as the thought of *his* Prometheus. The Prometheus of the German Storm and Stress, and in particular Goethe's famous poem of defiance, together with neo-Hegelian philosophy, form a prism through which the original myth, and Aeschylus' words, have been refracted.

The link between Aeschylus and Hegel is, in fact, quite consciously made in the notes which Marx did not incorporate in the final version of his thesis:

As Deucalion, according to the legend, threw stones over his shoulder at the creation of mankind, so philosophy casts its regard behind it (its mother's bones are shining eyes), when its heart has grown strong enough to create a world; but just as Prometheus, having stolen fire from heaven, begins to build houses and settle on the earth, so philosophy, having extended itself to comprehend the whole world, turns against the phenomenal world. So it is now with Hegelian philosophy.[54]

With clear reference to lines 453–4 of Aeschylus' *Prometheus Bound*, Marx here transforms the Prometheus myth, like that of Deucalion, into a symbol for the state of philosophy in his own day. In the myths moulded by the greatest poets of antiquity he sees configurations which can serve as analogies for the experiences of men in later ages. Through such analogies Marx hopes to make us see our own world more clearly and, at the same time, convey an attitude, an intellectual and emotional reaction, to it.

In the same spirit he chose as the central subject of his doctoral thesis a period of Greek philosophy—that which fol-

---

[53] *MEGA* I, 1 (2), 30–1 and 48–50; cf. R. Sannwald, *Marx und die Antike* (Zürich, 1957), pp. 70–2.
[54] *MEW EB* I, 215.

lowed on what he called the 'total' philosophies of Plato and
Aristotle—which in his view offered remarkable parallels with
the situation of German philosophy after Hegel, and which
might, therefore, be expected to illuminate that situation. The
point of the parallel has been brought out particularly well by
A. C. MacIntyre:

> Marx's thesis for his doctorate . . . is . . . part of his study of what
> happened to Greek philosophy after Aristotle. What happened to
> Greek philosophy is that it became practical. It turned from specu-
> lative metaphysics to ethics. This suggests the solution of Marx's
> problem. Hegel has in principle completed the task of speculative
> philosophy. But Hegel's philosophy remains in the realm of specula-
> tion, of the ideal. What has to be done is to realise the ideal in the
> world, not simply of thought, but of material reality. Hegel's theory
> must be converted into Marx's practice. This is Marx's problem.[55]

Different cultures, different periods, may have stages that correspond to one another. Such correspondences may and should be
recognized no less than the features which make each culture,
each period, unique. They may even suggest important lessons
for the present and the future.

It is not surprising, therefore, that Marx should experiment,
in his doctoral thesis, with a kind of literary superimposition
technique that brings old and new intimately together. Epicurus,
whom Lucretius praised for freeing men from the burdens religion imposed on them, is thus called 'the greatest of the Greek
Enlighteners' (*der größte griechische Aufklärer*);[56] this flashes before
the reader's eyes simultaneously the ancient world and the more
recent *Aufklärung*, that European Enlightenment which had
inspired his father and in whose traditions Marx increasingly
felt himself to stand. Nor was he the only one to feel this:
'imagine Rousseau, Voltaire, Holbach, Lessing, Heine, and
Hegel fused into one person—I say fused, not juxtaposed—and
you have Dr. Marx', Moses Hess wrote about him at this time.[57]

In speaking of post-Aristotelian philosophy in ancient Greece,
Marx speaks indirectly of post-Hegelian philosophy in Germany; in speaking of Epicurus' relation to Greek polytheism,
he speaks indirectly of his own relation to the Judaeo-Christian

[55] A. C. MacIntyre, *Marxism. An Interpretation* (London, 1953), p. 39.
[56] *MEW EB* I, 305.
[57] *MEGA* I, 1 (2), 261 (letter to Berthold Auerbach, 2 Sept. 1841).

faith of modern Europe. But beyond the likenesses he would have us see the differences; parallels and isomorphisms must throw into relief what distinguishes the new situation from the old.[58]

Marx's doctoral thesis thus offers a subtly dialectical view of uniqueness and recurrence in history. It accepts as a truism the biological-organic scheme of history which had proved congenial to so many historians of ideas: 'Genesis, flowering, decline—that is the iron circle in which everything human is confined and which it must traverse.' Marx censures this scheme, however, as too vague and general, as one in which everything can be accommodated and through which nothing can be really understood. Even decline and fall are different in each historical case. He therefore proposes to bring out the particularity of the phenomena he has undertaken to scrutinize: epicureanism, stoicism, and scepticism in the ancient world. But particularity, in its turn, is also not enough. Epicureanism, stoicism, and scepticism must be seen as 'the form in which Greece migrated to Rome'; as 'basic types' (*Urtypen*) of the Roman spirit; and as characteristic, concentrated, eternal 'essences' which have acquired full rights of citizenship in the modern world.[59]

N. D. Livergood has convincingly shown that Marx exalted the atomism of Epicurus over the related materialist philosophy of Democritus because he could see in it the possibility of a measure of 'free activity' to alleviate the mechanical materialism which he always abhorred. 'It was', Livergood comments, 'in Epicurus' concept of the declination (swerve) of the atoms that he found a partial answer to his problem. This "swaying" of the atoms in their downward path could serve as the basis for free motion within a materialist scheme.'[60] And the change in conceptions of the world observed in philosophy has its counterpart for Marx, in literature and the arts. Homer's beautiful, integrated world is as clearly pre-Epicurean as that of Lucretius is post-Epicurean; and Epicurus' gods, 'who, though they resemble men, inhabit the intermundane spaces of the real world, who have a *quasi* body instead of a body and *quasi* blood instead of blood, and who, being frozen in blissful calm, hearken to no

[58] Cf. G. Hillmann, op. cit., pp. 357–8.
[59] *MEW EB* I, 266–7.
[60] N. D. Livergood, *Activity in Marx's Philosophy* (The Hague, 1967), p. 44.

prayer, worry about neither us nor the world, and are worshipped for their beauty, majesty and perfect nature'—these are
not just figments of the philosopher's imagination. 'They
existed. They are the sculptured gods of Greek art.'[61]
That last-quoted passage is doubly revealing. It shows, first
of all, how steeped the young Marx was in the aesthetics and
art-history of eighteenth-century Germany—for what he here
says about Epicurus' gods clearly echoes J. J. Winckelmann's
paean to the 'divine self-containment' of Greek sculpture. Such
self-containment, Winckelmann had said in his *History of the Art
of Classical Antiquity* (*Geschichte der Kunst des Altertums*, Dresden,
1767), 'throws light on Epicurus' opinion on the shape of the
gods—he gives them a body which is *like* a body, blood which
is *like* blood; Cicero finds this obscure and inconceivable.'

The same passage also suggests, however, a potent—perhaps
the principal—reason why Epicurus and Lucretius should be
at the centre of Marx's doctoral thesis. He saw in their work a
lever that might help to dislodge simplistic religious beliefs; a
task he came to believe, with Feuerbach and the Hegelian Left,
to be among the most pressing of his own time. Had not Lucretius in fact proclaimed, in *On the Nature of Things*, that Epicurus
had sought to demonstrate 'what are the elements out of which
everything is formed, and how everything comes to pass *without
the intervention of the gods*'? [my italics].[62]

The doctoral thesis shows beyond doubt that even at this
early stage Marx could not conceive of philosophy as something
which belongs solely to the realm of the mind. The inward
illumination of philosophers enkindle flames in the outside
world:

Was innerliches Licht war, wird zur verzehrenden Flamme, die sich
nach außen wendet.

What was inward illumination becomes a consuming flame that
turns outward.[63]

Latent within this Promethean image, the last of Marx's later
'Theses on Feuerbach' may already be discerned.

---

[61] *MEW EB* I, 283; cf. Livergood, op. cit., p. 82, and *MECW* I, 51, 736.
[62] Quoted by Maurice Cornforth in *Materialism and the Dialectical Method* (vol. i
of *Dialectical Materialism. An Introduction*), rev. edn. (London, 1968), p. 30.
[63] *MEW EB* I, 328.

The notes Marx made while he was composing his doctoral thesis also show quite clearly, however, that he was still very much a disciple of Hegel. Thus he sees the age of the ancient Greeks as that of nature and art, the modern age as that of the spirit and philosophy:

The premise of the ancients is the act of nature, that of the moderns the act of the spirit. The struggle of the ancients could only end by the visible heaven, the substantial nexus of life, the force of gravity of political and religious life being shattered, for nature must be split in two for the spirit to be one in itself. *The Greeks broke it up with the Hephaestan hammer of art,* broke it up in their statues; the Roman plunged his sword into its heart and the peoples died, but modern philosophy unseals the word, lets it pass away in smoke in the holy fire of the spirit, and as fighter of the spirit fighting the spirit . . . [my italics].[64]

Marx's phrase about the 'Hephaestan hammer of art' breaking up the unity of nature demonstrates once again how powerfully his mind was affected by Greek mythology and how constantly he sought to enlist its help in describing the processes of history and the workings of art.

The doctoral thesis and the notes he made for it also show Marx looking to literature for insight into the feelings and the thoughts of the vanished nations whose philosophy he had set himself to investigate. By juxtaposing works written at different times and in different countries he tried to bring out the salient characteristics of representative writers and thinkers, and of the peoples to which they belonged. Thus Lucretius is set against Homer and against Plutarch:

Lucretius is the true heroic poet of the Romans, for he sings of the substance of the Roman spirit [*er besingt die Substanz des römischen Geistes*]; instead of the serene, powerful, integral characters of Homer we have here firm heroic figures in impenetrable armour who lack all other qualities; Lucretius gives us war, *omnium contra omnes,* the rigid form of being-for-oneself, a nature bereft of god and a god bereft of the world.[65]

The passage just quoted shows the young Marx attempting to define the way in which great writers represent and convey the

---

[64] *MEW EB* I, 75 (*MECW* I, 431).   [65] *MEW EB* I, 171.

'spirit' of the world in which they live. At the same time it reformulates the classical ideal, made up of gay serenity, power, full development, and an undivided self—[*die*] *heitern, kräftigen, totalen Gestalten des Homer*—in a way which would not have seemed strange to Winckelmann, or Herder, or Goethe. Here attention rests firmly on the works themselves, as indicators of a Homeric-Greek and a Lucretian-Roman way of apprehending the world; other passages in these same notes, however, concentrate rather on the *effect* such works are likely to have on different readers:

Just as in spring-time Nature lays herself bare and (sure, as it were, of her conquest) exhibits all her charms, while in winter, she covers her shame and nakedness with snow and ice: so Lucretius, that lively, bold, poetic master of the world differs from Plutarch, who covers his paltry ego with the ice of morality . . . Whose spirit is more moral and more free—that of the man who emerges from Plutarch's schoolroom ruminating on the injustice which makes the good lose the fruit of their life in death; or that of the man who sees the promise of eternity fulfilled in Lucretius' bold, thundering song . . . ?[66]

Discussion of the philosophy of the ancients, Marx finds, merges constantly with discussion of poetry; and in modern times, too, he finds that he cannot treat Hegel's view of Socratic irony without glancing at the theories Friedrich Schlegel evolved out of, and for, literature.[67]

Yet another of the uses of literature, prominent in Marx's later works, is suggested in his doctoral dissertation whose very first section opens with the words: 'Greek philosophy seems to exhibit what no good tragedy must ever be allowed to have: a lame conclusion.'[68] It is as though Marx's thwarted aspirations towards editing a journal of dramatic criticism were being absorbed into his philosophy. Dramatic literature provided metaphors, or structural analogies, which can clarify problems that lie quite outside the literary domain.

Lastly: the doctoral dissertation shows Marx going to admired writers, both ancient and modern, for formulations he can either adopt to express what he wants to say or adapt to his own

---

[66] *MEW EB* I, 155.   [67] *MEW EB* I, 221.
[68] *MEW EB* I, 266.

purposes. What attracts him to Epicurus can best be said in the words of Lucretius:

> Quem neque fama deum nec fulmina nec minitanti
> Murmure compressit caelum . . .

> Fables of the gods did not crush him, nor the
> lightning flash and growling menace of the sky . . .

what he feels about the decline of Greek philosophy can best be conveyed by opposing an image from Act III, scene ii, of Schiller's *The Robbers* to one from the fables of Aesop:

> But the death of the hero resembles the setting sun, not the bursting of an inflated frog;

and what he feels about 'Christianizing' Greek philosophers can best be expressed in the language of Heine: 'Chaste monks', Heine had written in his book on the Romantic movement in Germany (*Die romantische Schule*, 1833), 'have tied an apron around the Venus of antiquity'; and Marx, in the Preface of his doctoral dissertation, echoes him:

> Gassendi . . . seeks to reconcile his Catholic conscience with his heathen knowledge, and Epicurus with the Church—a vain endeavour, indeed. It is as though someone had tried to cast a Christian nun's habit around the gaily luxuriant body of the Greek Lais.[69]

'. . . als wollte man der griechischen Lais einen christlichen Nonnenkittel um den heiter blühenden Leib werfen'—even the adverb and adjective, *heiter* and *blühend*, are those which Heine liked to apply to a Greek world whose 'sensualism' he contrasted so often with the ascetic attitudes of Christianity.[70]

Between 1835 and 1841 Marx showed an urge to literary composition not matched by native talent; a tendency to work out his own attitudes to life and letters in the process of criticizing the attitudes of others; an interest in the *effect* of works of literature as well as in the way they represented their authors and their times; a growing predilection for transferring the terms of literary criticism to other spheres of human activity;

[69] *MEW EB* I, 305, 267, 261; cf. Sannwald, op. cit., p. 70, and *MECW* 73.

[70] For an account of the philosophical implications of Marx's doctoral thesis, and of the way in which its interpretation of Greek sculpture marks a step in the direction of a denial of Hegelian idealism, see M. Lifshits, op. cit., pp. 21–32.

and a developing view of cultural history which embraced at once its particularities and its recurrences. We saw, too, his love for the poetry of the ancient world—particularly that of Aeschylus and Lucretius, who seemed to Marx to express their own cultural ambience while also giving voice to aspirations that later generations could recognize as their own; delight in Greek myth; respect for the poetry of Goethe and Schiller, together with contempt for their nineteenth-century critics; attraction to certain aspects of German Romanticism (its concern with folk-poetry as well as many of its themes) soon counterbalanced by suspicion and dislike; a strong affinity with Heine, and an ability to find in the literary works he loved and respected formulations, images, and symbols that helped him to express his own thoughts more forcefully than he could have done without their aid. The most prominent and significant of such symbols is that of Prometheus: a Prometheus who speaks words Aeschylus had put into his mouth in *Prometheus Bound,* but who is clearly to be seen through the eyes of the young Goethe and the writers of the German Storm and Stress.

2 · The Lantern of Diogenes

> 'As for literature in the Rhineland . . .—one could
> have searched through all its five administrative
> districts with Diogenes' lantern and never have
> met "such a man"'
>
> *(MEW* I, 36)

AFTER taking his doctorate in April 1841, Marx thought for a
while of becoming a university lecturer. It soon became obvious,
however, that there would be no opening for him at any German
university. He planned a number of books, several of them on
aesthetic subjects: one of these, on religion and art, seems to
have reached the stage of a sizeable manuscript, but Marx grew
dissatisfied with its Hegelian tendencies, and it was never published.[1] His preliminary studies for this work were to stand him
in good stead, however. A book by Charles Debrosses on fetish-
gods introduced him to a subject on which his later analysis of
'commodity-fetishism' was to play a most original variation,
while books by K. A. Böttiger, J. J. Grund[2], and C. F. von
Rumohr were to mould his views on the art of ancient Greece
and Rome. The following excerpt, copied by Marx from
Rumohr's *Italian Studies (Italienische Forschungen)* in the first half
of 1842, is wholly characteristic:

If we approach the heroes and gods of Greek art . . . without
religious or aesthetic superstition, we will surely not find there
anything which had not developed, or could not still develop,

---

[1] See Marx's letters to Arnold Ruge, *MEW* XXVII, 400 ff.

[2] M. Lifshits (*The Philosophy of Art of Karl Marx*, p. 58) has drawn particular
attention to one passage among Marx's notes on his reading of J. J. Grund's
Greek Painting (Malerei der Griechen): 'It has been observed that great men appear
in surprising numbers at certain periods which are invariably characterized by the
efflorescence of art. Whatever the outstanding traits of this efflorescence, its
influence upon men is undeniable; it fills them with its vivifying force. When this
one-sided culture is spent, mediocrity follows.'

within the general life of nature. For what belongs to art in these shaped images is the depiction of beautiful human ways (*menschlich schöner Sitten*) in glorious organic forms.[3]

There is nothing here with which Marx could not, at this stage of his life, have wholeheartedly agreed.

Marx's readings in aesthetics, in the 1830s and 40s as well as later in the 1850s, have been well documented by scholars from Lifshits to Lukács and Pazura; and a beginning has been made in tracing the influences that may have gone to the making of Marx's own outlook on art. Kant, Winckelmann, Lessing, Goethe, Schiller, A. W. Schlegel, and (of course) Hegel have all been adduced; so have Georg Forster's and Fichte's thoughts on 'alienated' art; so have ideas on literature and society expressed by non-German thinkers and littérateurs from Plato and Aristotle to Rousseau, Diderot, and Mme de Staël.[4] Marx need not —indeed could not—have read all the works and authors which in some degree anticipate his own thoughts; but he was, as we shall have occasion to see in the course of this book, a voracious reader who could reconstruct the tree from a casually found leaf. He was also unusually sensitive to ideas that were in the air—ideas he could adopt and (more frequently) ideas he could react against.

In 1842 Marx took his first plunge into journalism. An article on the new Prussian censorship regulations, written in February of that year, was intended for Arnold Ruge's Young-Hegelian *German Yearbooks* (*Deutsche Jahrbücher*), but could not appear there because the censors would not let it pass. Ruge therefore published it in Switzerland a year later (February 1843), in a volume entitled *Anekdota* which brought together a number of essays on questions of the day that had incurred the German censor's displeasure.[5] In March 1842 Marx joined the staff of a new liberal newspaper, the *Rheinische Zeitung* (*Rhenish Gazette for Politics, Commerce, and Industry*); he became its editor-in-chief in October of the same year. Under his editorship the paper increased its circulation dramatically—but his policies were too

[3] *MEGA* I, 1 (2), xxvii, 114 ff.; cf. Lifshits, op. cit., p. 35.
[4] An excellent summary can be found in *BM* 40–5.
[5] The full title of Ruge's book was *Anekdota zur neuesten deutschen Philosophie und Publizistik*. It also contained another article by Marx, dealing with the relation of Feuerbach and D. F. Strauß to Martin Luther.

radical for the Prussian censors whose vigilance had been allowed to relax for a brief moment during the hopeful time which followed the accession of King Frederick William IV in 1840. In March 1843 the *Rheinische Zeitung* was suppressed.

Marx's first contribution to journalism, then, was an article on censorship—a question of great importance to literature. One of the strongest points he makes, in his analysis of the muddled thinking behind the new Prussian edict on that question, is that censorship sets mediocrities to judge men of talent and deprives writers of an essential right: the right to express themselves fully, the *right to their own style* which will necessarily differ from that of even the most enlightened censor.

Truth, furthermore, is common to all—it does not belong to me, it belongs to everybody, it possesses me, I do not possess it. What is my property is a form, my mental and spiritual individuality. *Le style c'est l'homme.* Indeed! The law permits me to write, but I am to write a style that is not mine! I may show the profile of my mind, but I must first imprint on it the prescribed expression! What man of honour will not blush at such an unreasonable demand . . .?[6]

Marx therefore feels himself to be fighting a battle for literature, not just for journalism.

Even more significant, however, for Marx's approach to literature and literary criticism is his passionate assertion, in this same essay on censorship, that a writer's 'truth' is not something given and invariable; that all 'objects produced by a writer's activity' cannot be usefully subsumed under some general idea of 'truth'. One and the same object of perception, Marx argues, is differently refracted in the minds of different individuals; and in the different aspects it assumes in different minds its genuine many-sidedness reveals itself. But each literary object also imposes, by its specific nature, a specific mode of approach appropriate to it. Those who ignore such complications, who demand of literary products an abstract and invariant 'truth', are therefore told by the young Marx: 'You are infringing the right of the object as well as that of the subject. You conceive truth as an abstraction and transform the mind into an examining magistrate who drily takes down a deposition.'[7] 'Zur Wahrheit', he proclaims in a phrase of Lessingian incisiveness, 'gehört nicht

[6] *MEW* I, 6.   [7] *MEW* I, 7.

nur das Resultat, sondern auch der Weg'—truth is a matter, not only of results, but also of the way in which they are reached.[8]

One passage in the Prussian instruction to censors roused Marx's especial ire. The censors were there told to watch, not only for treasonable sentiments, but also for offensiveness of tone. They were to forbid the publication of any writings which tended to corrupt through 'vehemence, over-intensity, and arrogance'. The Prussian censors, in other words, were to become arbiters of style. But, Marx objects, it is well known that this would operate only against writers in opposition—that writers supporting the government could get away with any amount of crudity however 'vehement' their advocacy. 'Thus the censor must sometimes judge the content by the form, sometimes the form by the content. First content ceased to serve as a criterion for censorship; and then, in turn, form vanished.'[9] The censor is enabled to deprive an author not only of his subject but also of the form through which his personality asserts itself. He is enabled to impose the rule of mediocrity on the writers who have to submit their work to his scrutiny.

There are other ways in which the young Marx tries to link the concerns of the journalist with those of the literary critic. 'The depiction of an institution of the state', he assures the readers of *Rheinische Zeitung* on 11 December 1842, 'is not identical with that institution. Polemic against the depiction is not, therefore, polemic against the institution itself. The conservative Press, which constantly reminds its readers that the views of the critical Press are unacceptable because they are nothing but individual opinion and distort reality, always forgets that it does not itself constitute its subject but represents only an opinion about that subject, and that, therefore, an attack on its views does not invariably imply an attack on the subject of those views. Every object which is introduced into the Press, whether in praise or in blame, becomes thereby a literary object, an object, that is, for literary discussion.' 'What makes the Press into the most powerful lever of culture and the intellectual education of the people', Marx concludes, 'is precisely that it transforms material battles into ideal battles, the battle of flesh and blood into that of the spirit and intellect, the battle of

[8] *MEW* I, 7.   [9] *MEW* I, 23; cf. Lifshits, op. cit., p. 56.

necessity, cupidity, and empiricism into one of theory, under-standing, and form.'[10]

Marx clearly feels that the battle he is waging against censor-ship and against the attitudes which produce it and which it, in turn, reinforces, is of the greatest importance for the future of literature. It therefore seems appropriate that he should call on the support of the world's great writers from the very first sentence onwards. 'We do not belong to those malcontents', his 'Remarks on the latest Prussian Instruction on the Censorship' begin, 'who exclaim even before the new Prussian censorship edict has appeared: *Timeo Danaos et dona ferentes.*'[11] The tag from Virgil, whose application to the present case is called in question only to be emphatically confirmed, is soon joined, in the same article, by others from Buffon, Goethe, Schiller, Laurence Sterne, and Voltaire. In literature, in quotations from the world's authors supplied at appropriate times by his wide reading, catholic taste, and ready memory Marx finds con-firmation, sanction, and incisive formulations of passionately held views whose truth he tries to impress upon his readers.

There are other functions, however, which literary quota-tions serve in these early essays. In another article on the question of censorship, published in the *Rheinische Zeitung* of 5 May 1842, Marx writes:

Goethe says somewhere that a painter will succeed in depicting only those types of female beauty which he has once loved in some living individual. Freedom of the Press is such a beauty (even if not a female one) which one must have loved if one wants to be able to defend it. The existence of what I truly love I feel to be necessary: that I must have, without it my being cannot be fulfilled, satisfied or complete.[12]

Even Goethe-specialists will have some difficulty in placing Marx's allusion—he is probably thinking of a sentence in Goethe's *Miscellaneous Thoughts on Art* (*Verschiedenes über Kunst*) which reads 'What an artist has not loved, what an artist does not love, he should not, he cannot, depict.' But what Marx is doing here is not difficult to fathom. He is directing into political channels energies that had previously flowed into aesthetic investigations and into love-poetry. He is projecting an image of wholeness: the artist, the lover, the fighter for freedom from political interference are one and the same person. Nor are the energies that had flowed into Marx's early satires and epigrams less evident in this same newspaper article. Directing his scorn at the way the *Prussian State Gazette*, the *Preußische Staatszeitung*, had commented on the new censorship edict, he seems, for a moment, to be turning away from his main concerns:

> But, our reader will object, we wanted to debate the proceedings of the Rhenish parliament; and here, instead, we find ourselves invited to meet that *'innocent angel'* [den *'unschuldsvollen Engel'*], that superannuated Press-child, the *Prussian State Gazette*, and we are forced to hear again those precocious lullabies with which she tries, again and again, to soothe herself and her sisters into health-giving winter-sleep.

But does not Schiller say:

> Und was kein Verstand der Verständigen sieht,
> Das übet in *Einfalt* ein *kindlich* Gemüt?

And what the understanding of the wise fails to fathom,
A childlike spirit will practise in its simplicity.

The *Prussian State Gazette* has reminded us, 'in all simplicity', that we in Prussia, like the English, have representative local government, and that the daily Press is permitted to discuss the proceedings of these provincial Diets *if it can*. The *State Gazette*, in its classic self-confidence, thinks that what the Prussian newspapers lack is not permission, but ability . . .[13]

The phrase *'innocent angel'*, italicized and in inverted commas, conflates two descriptions of Gretchen in Goethe's *Faust* Part I —Mephistopheles' 'ein gar unschuldig Ding' and Faust's 'ahnungsvoller Engel'.[14] Gretchen's 'Ahnung', her suspicions of Mephistopheles and divination of ills to come, is thus removed, and only guilelessness remains. To this image of heavenly innocence, deliberately incongruous in its context, Marx adds another, related one: Schiller's invocation, in his poem 'Words of Faith' (*Die Worte des Glaubens*), of a childlike soul whose intuitively directed conduct puts understanding to shame. By

[13] *MEW* I, 32.   [14] Goethe, *Faust* Part I, 'Straße' and 'Marthens Garten'.

shamming innocent guilelessness, Marx's incongruous juxta-
positions would seem to suggest, the *State Gazette* wants to keep
Prussia's subjects 'innocent' too; it wants to foster the kind of
'childlike simplicity' which will accept paternal authority without uncomfortable questioning.

Schiller's lines about the childlike spirit surpassing, in practice, the understanding of men of reason, will henceforth belong
to the basic stock of Marx's literary quotations. The context in
which he quotes it will always be ironical.

If the article of 5 May from which I have been quoting stood
under the aegis of Goethe and Schiller, that of 30 November is
dominated by Shakespeare. Its epigraph comes from *Othello*, I.
iii—Iago's 'It is merely a lust of the blood and a permission of
the will'—and its attack on another journal of the day, the
Augsburg Gazette (Augsburger Zeitung), is peppered with quotations from *King Lear*, IV. iv.[15] Marx thus attributes to the *Augsburg Gazette* a concern with political 'indecency' which parallels
the obsession with sexual 'indecencies' in the heads of evil Iago
and mad Lear. Having made this point, he goes on to use other
quotations from *King Lear* as ironical applause at one of the
Augsburg Gazette's more obvious misses ('That fellow handles his
bow like a crow-keeper . . .'), or as oblique comment on its
blindness to the obvious ('Were all the letters suns, I could not
see one'). The *Augsburg Gazette*, it is pleasing to report, took up
the Shakespearian challenge by comparing the *Rheinische Zeitung*
to Ancient Pistol; the *Rheinische Zeitung* in its turn responded on
12 January 1843 by leaving its Augsburg contemporary the
choice of being compared to Doll Tearsheet, to Mistress Quickly,
or to the Falstaff of the speech on honour.[16] Marx is here taking
part in a spirited game, played by journalists who could be sure
that their readers would catch Shakespearian allusions without
difficulty and would refer them to their original context. Nor is
the use of great literature for the purposes of this game entirely
frivolous. What Shakespeare's plays provide here is a repertoire
of attitudes, of types of response to recurring human situations;
these are embodied in great characters, the very mention of
whose names can conjure up a whole complex of such attitudes
and responses from which judicious quotation can then select
the appropriate ones.

[15] *MEW EB* I, 399 ff.   [16] *MEW EB* I, 403–4.

The same is true of another great writer: Miguel de Cervantes. In his *Anekdota* article on censorship in Prussia, Marx had commented on the absurdity of hoping to bring about a future improvement in the tone and matter of the Press by depriving it of its present rights and possibilities. 'Its fate', Marx wrote, 'is that of poor Sancho Panza, whose court physician removed all food from his sight in order that no stomach-upset should make him incapable of discharging the duties enjoined on him.'[17] Henceforward *Don Quixote* is never absent for long from Marx's polemical writings.

Nor is it only the great authors' fictional creations that can bring before us typical attitudes to life and experience. An author's name, conjuring up remembrances of his work as a whole or of certain aspects of that work, can serve the same purpose. An article on the 'historical school of law' (*Rheinische Zeitung*, 9 August 1842) attempts this in the course of a discussion devoted to Gustav Hugo, an eminent professor of jurisprudence:

Hugo misinterprets his master Kant in saying that since we cannot know what is true, we must, for consistency's sake, let pass as entirely valid what is untrue, if only it exists. Hugo is a sceptic towards the necessary essence of things only to become a Hoffmann in respect of their contingent existence.[18]

---

[17] *MEW* I, 19.

[18] *MEW* I, 79. The same essay once again shows Marx building up his arguments in such a way that they culminate in a Shakespearian quotation his readers would instantly recognize. The passage just quoted continues as follows: 'He does not, therefore, seek to prove that the positive [institutions and law] is *reasonable*; he seeks to prove, rather, that it is *not reasonable*. He drags together evidence from all parts of the world with the most self-congratulatory industry, to arrive at a climax of evidence that positive institutions, property for instance, forms of the state, marriage etc. are animated by no rational necessity, that in fact they even *contradict* reason, that they can serve, at best, as occasions for idle chatter. One cannot attribute this *method* to the accidental fact of Hugo's own personality; it is, rather, the method which logically derives from his principles, it is the *openly acknowledged, naive, ruthless* method of the historical school. If the positive is to be valid merely because it exists, then I must prove that the positive does not derive its validity from its being rational and reasonable. And how can I prove that more conclusively than by showing that what is unreasonable is positive, and what is positive is not reasonable; that the positive exists, not *through* reason, but *in spite of* reason? If reason were the touchstone of the positive, the positive could not be the touchstone of reason. "Though this be madness, yet there is method in't".' (*MEW* I, 79; cf. *Hamlet*, II. ii.)

Ein Hoffmann—Marx here bids his reader recollect E. T. A. Hoffmann's ghostly tales, and the willing suspension of disbelief these imposed on him. 'A Hoffmann', someone who can make us see supernatural beings walking the streets of recognizable German cities in broad daylight, is therefore the very opposite of a 'sceptic'. By mentioning this author Marx is making another point too, very important in his context: he is stressing, unobtrusively, but none the less firmly, the well-attested connection between the 'historical school of law' and German Romanticism.

Marx's growing suspicion and dislike of Romanticism cannot be missed. 'Romanticism', he declares bluntly in his *Anekdota* essay on censorship, 'is always poetry that has a palpable design on us [*Tendenzpoesie*]';[19] and he leaves his readers in no doubt of his belief that the *Tendenz* of Romanticism, its drift and design, boded little good for Germany and the world. The article on the 'historical school of law' has clear anti-Romantic implications—but it also casts a sceptical eye at pre-Romantic fictions. Foremost among these is the eighteenth-century notion of a 'natural state' of man.

A fiction current in the eighteenth century viewed the state of nature as the true state of human nature. People wanted to see the Idea of Man with their own eyes and created *natural men, Papagenos*, whose naïvety extended even to their feathered skins. In the last decades of the eighteenth century people imagined that primal wisdom might be found among peoples in a state of nature and on all sides we heard bird-catchers twitter in imitation of the songs of the Iroquois Indians etc., thinking by these arts to lure the birds themselves into the trap. At the back of all these eccentricities lay the correct idea that the *primitive* state was a naïve Dutch picture of the *true* state. The natural man of the historical school, not yet licked into shape by any romantic culture, is Gustav Hugo.[20]

Clearly, eighteenth-century notions of a 'natural state' are not entirely rejected; Marx allows them a kernel of truth—but they are ridiculed. To convey his sense of the ridiculous Marx has recourse to a literary-musical creation: Papageno, the fantastic bird-man from *The Magic Flute*, created by the combined genius of Mozart and Emanuel Schikaneder.

[19] *MEW* I, 22.   [20] *MEW* I, 78 (*ET* 31–2).

We have just heard Marx voicing suspicion of Romantic *Tendenzpoesie*. As editor of the *Rheinische Zeitung* he also, however, kept an eye open for 'palpable designs' of another kind. Ludwig Börne had made it fashionable, in Germany, to slip political views and arguments past the censor by disguising them as literary criticism—particularly criticism of plays and their performances. Marx found several would-be contributors to his feuilleton anxious to follow Börne's example. Here Marx put his foot down. 'I declared', he writes to Ruge on 30 November 1842, 'that I thought it unfitting, immoral even, to smuggle in communistic or socialistic dogmas, i.e. a new way of looking at the world, by way of incidental dramatic criticism.'[21] Marx himself, though clearly left of centre, did not, at this time, subscribe to the 'communistic and socialistic dogmas' some of his associates tried to smuggle into the paper; nor had he, as yet, formulated the doctrines of class-struggle and the historic mission of the proletariat with which posterity will always associate his name.

His work as an editor taught Marx to appreciate the value of a good literary section. On its very front page, below the thick line which divided news and political commentaries from the feuilleton, the *Rheinische Zeitung* carried poems by Robert Prutz and other popular writers of the day who were sympathetic to liberal causes. The star contributor whom Marx managed to attract to his feuilleton was Georg Herwegh, whose poem proclaiming (in overt contradiction of Ferdinand Freiligrath) that it was a poet's right and duty to engage himself in political struggles[22] was soon joined by others which demanded freedom in vague and general but stirring terms:

> Raum, ihr Herrn, dem Flügelschlag
> Einer freien Seele!

> Lords and gentlemen make way
> For the soaring flight of a free soul![23]

Herwegh was the first—but by no means the last—among contemporary German poets whom Marx valued as allies, but

[21] *MEGA* I, 1 (2), 286.
[22] Cf. Herwegh's poem 'Die Partei. An Ferdinand Freiligrath'.
[23] *RZ* Sept. 1842; cf. H. Gemlow (and others), *Karl Marx. Eine Biographie* (Berlin, 1968), p. 51.

whose later development and career proved a sad disappointment to him.

Wherever one looks in his early journalistic work one finds Marx trying out different ways of bringing his literary and his political concerns together. The one article bearing his name which was actually printed in the chief organ of the Young Hegelians, the *German Yearbooks* (*Deutsche Jahrbücher für Wissenschaft und Kunst*), is an interesting case in point. It berates an unfortunate publicist and philosopher named Otto Friedrich Gruppe, who tried to justify the measures the Prussian government had seen fit to take against Bruno Bauer:

If the comedy of dilettantism were to be written in Germany, Dr. O. F. Gruppe would be the one character indispensable to it. Fate has furnished this man with that iron tenacity which great men cannot do without—least of all the great men of dilettantism. Even if most of his adventures end, like those of Sancho Panza, with the receipt of ambiguous signs of favour, the monotony of such triumphs is elevated and varied in many ways by the comic lack of self-consciousness and the touching *naïveté* with which Herr Gruppe receives his laurels. It is even impossible not to recognize a kind of greatness of soul in the logical consistency which teaches Herr Gruppe to draw his conclusions: 'Because I have been thrown out of the schoolroom of Philology', he seems to argue, 'it will be my calling in life to be thrown out of the ballroom of Aesthetics and the halls of Philosophy too. But though that is much, it is not everything. My role will not be played out until I have been thrown out of the temple of Theology'; and Herr Gruppe is conscientious enough to play his role to the very end.[24]

What is happening here should not surprise those who have read Marx's doctoral thesis. Here too, in the *Rheinische Zeitung*, the young Marx is trying out ways in which the vocabulary and concepts of literary and dramatic criticism—'comedy', 'character', 'adventures . . . of Sancho Panza', 'role', 'elevated and varied'—can be applied to polemics that have only a remote connection with literature, but a very close connection with philosophy, politics, and social thought. And from there it is only a step to the procedures illustrated in the last issue of the *Rheinische Zeitung* to be published under Marx's editorship—in an article that shows Marx applying techniques of literary

24 *MEW EB* I, 381.

criticism and stylistic analysis to material which had appeared in the columns of a rival and antagonistic journal, the *Rhine and Moselle Gazette* (*Rhein- und Mosel-Zeitung*). The result of these analyses, which strikingly parallel procedures Nietzsche was to apply to D. F. Strauß in *Thoughts out of Season*, are hammered home with an irony that once again makes liberal use of literary allusions:

Truly Homeric! Just look at this epic breadth. And that deep insight into bestial psychology is Aesopian, I suppose . . .[25]

Homer and Aesop provide a measure at once of the rival journalists' pretensions and of the extent of their failure.

The serious context in which this stylistic scrutiny of contemporary journalism must be seen has been clearly provided by Marx himself, in an earlier article (*Rheinische Zeitung*, 8 May 1842). His chief exhibit is the Dresden *Evening News* (*Abendzeitung*), edited for many years by one K. G. T. Winkler who adopted the pseudonym 'Theodore Bright' (*Theodor Hell*).

In the time which saw the strict application of censorship, the years 1819–1830 . . . our literature went through its *Evening-News*-period. This may be called 'true and noble and spiritual and progressive' with the same right with which the editor of the *Evening News*, whose original name was Winkler, humorously assumed the pseudonym 'Bright' [*Hell*], although it would be difficult to ascribe to him as much brightness as can be found in the marshes at midnight. This provincial philistine [*Krähwinkler*, a pun on Winkler's name], trading under the name 'Bright', is the prototype of the literature of those days; and that lenten period will convince a later age that if few saints can go for forty days without food, the whole of Germany (which wasn't even in a state of sanctity!) was able to go for over twenty years without intellectual consumption and production. The Press had become *base*; the only doubt that remains is whether its lack of intelligence exceeded its lack of character, whether its lack of form exceeded its lack of content, or the other way round. Criticism would bestow its greatest benefit on Germany if it could prove that period never existed. The only part of literature which was still informed, at that time, by a vital spirit—philosophy —ceased speaking German, because the German language had ceased to be the language of thought. The spirit spoke in incomprehensible, mysterious words, because comprehensible words were no longer allowed to be reasonable.

[25] *MEW EB* I, 435.

As for literature in the Rhineland . . .—one could have searched through all its five administrative districts with Diogenes' lantern and never have met 'such a man'. We regard this, not as a deficiency in the Rhineland province, but rather as a proof of its practical political sense. The Rhineland can father a *free Press*; but it lacks the agility, and the illusions, necessary to produce an *unfree* one. The literary period which has just come to an end, and which we may call 'the literary period of strict censorship' is thus self-evident historical proof of the contention that censorship has indeed retarded the development of the German mind and spirit in a disastrous and irresponsible way.[26]

'Literature', in Marx's use of the term, embraces not only belles-lettres but philosophy too—and also popular reading-matter, including the feuilletons of Theodor Hell. Obscurities of style, Marx tells his readers, allow one to draw conclusions about the political and social climate in which their perpetrators live. Such conclusions resemble those suggested by Heine in his verbal caricature of Hegel, whom he shows anxiously looking around when he had said something comprehensible, for fear that he might have compromised himself in the eyes of the authorities.[27] Analyses of deficiencies in form and expression can lead to a recognition of deficiencies in thought and spirit. The style of popular reading-matter can become, to the initiated, an index of the political and social health of those for whom it is intended. Repressive politics have literary consequences of which total silence is one of the most respectable.

In the account of his quest for good, plain, honest writing in Germany which has just been quoted, the young Marx sees himself as Diogenes, who carried his lantern about in broad daylight declaring that he was searching for an honest man. The image is an apt one; and there was no place into which he carried his lantern more often than the Rhenish Diet or parliament. He found there an oratory whose character derived less from the individual actually making the speech than the 'estate' (*Stand*) the speaker represented. The young Diogenes thus had his first practice in the analysis of what he was later to call 'class' interests:

The polemics against freedom of the Press which the debates show us are those of the princely estate, the knightly estate, the estate of

[26] *MEW* I, 36.　　　[27] See Heine's *Geständnisse* (1854).

the cities—it is not the individual who polemicizes, but the estate [*Stand*]. What mirror, therefore, could reflect the inmost character of the Diet more faithfully than its debates about the Press?[28]

Before long Marx was to find a different answer to his rhetorical question than the one he suggests here; he was to find the class-character of parliamentary oratory reflected even more clearly in debates about *wood-theft* in which men of property asserted their rights against the poor. What always remained with him, however, from his early days as a parliamentary reporter and critic, was an interest in oratorical style, which was further fostered by his reading:

The greatest orator of the French Revolution, whose ever thundering voice sounds yet into our own time, the lion whose roaring one had to hear oneself in order to join the people in calling out to him: 'Well roar'd, lion!'—*Mirabeau*, in short, trained himself in prisons. Does that make prisons academies of oratory?[29]

One notices here Marx's own stylistic sophistication (his playing of a complex sentence, which keeps the reader in suspense by withholding Mirabeau's name until near the end, against the simple interrogative sentence that follows it); his application of standards—standards already derived from the oratory of the French revolutionary period which he was later to study in much greater detail; his critique of illogical argument, proceeding by way of a *reductio ad absurdum*; and his use of a famous tag from Act v of *A Midsummer Night's Dream* as a sign of humorous approbation.

In our context Marx's articles in the *Rheinische Zeitung* occupy a special place because they represent his first attempt to formulate, publicly, the relation in which the professional writer stands to the social economy within which he has to work.

In order to defend, and even to understand, freedom in any given sphere, I must seize on its essential character, not just its external relations. But can the Press be true to its character, can it act in accord with the nobility of its nature, can the Press be *free*, if it stoops to being nothing but a trade? A writer, it is true, must earn his living if he is to be able to exist and write; but by no means

must he exist and write in order to earn his living. When Béranger
sings:

> Je ne vis que pour faire des chansons,
> Si vous m'ôtez ma place, Monseigneur,
> Je ferai des chansons pour vivre,

then his threat contains the ironic admission that the poet descends
from his proper sphere as soon as his poetry becomes a means to
an end.

A writer does *not* regard his works as means to an end. They are
an end in themselves; so little are they 'means', for himself and
others, that he will, if necessary, sacrifice his own existence to their
existence. He is, in another way, like the preacher of religion who
makes it a principle 'to obey God more than men' (among which
'men' he includes himself, with all his human needs and desires).
But just imagine a tailor coming to me, when I have asked him to
make me a frock-coat in the Parisian fashion, and bringing me a
toga, on the grounds that it was more in keeping with the eternal
law of beauty!

The first freedom of the Press consists in this: that it is not a trade. The
writer who degrades it to a material means deserves as punishment
for this internal constraint the external constraint of censorship; or
rather: his very existence *is* his punishment.

True, the Press does exist as a trade; but that aspect is of no
concern to the writer; that concerns only printers and book-sellers.
What is at issue here, however, is not the freedom of printers and
book-sellers to pursue their trade, but freedom of the Press.[30]

As a contribution to a debate about freedom of the Press, this
is clear and forceful; and in the context of Marx's thinking
about literature it is memorable as a first attempt to present the
work of the poet as an unalienated activity—not free from commercial pressures, of course, but free from subservience to
commercial values. It raises, however, more questions than it
answers. What is the place of the writer in a society dedicated,
like that of nineteenth-century Europe, to complex commercial
transactions of various kinds? How dependent is his work on
economic lines of force, on the very conditions of production,
even when he lives to write instead of writing to live? How far
does the community of interests between poets and journalists
really extend? And lastly: in what sense is it legitimate to speak,

[30] *RZ* 19 May 1842—*MEW* I, 70–1.

as Marx here makes his absurd tailor do, of an '*eternal* law of beauty'?

One problem, however, Marx could not leave without at least attempting an answer: he had to address himself, in the context of the censorship debate, to a distinction which must crop up whenever censorship laws are discussed. Should one not—*must* one not—distinguish between great writers (to whom the censor should grant full privileges) and venal scribblers (who are entitled to no such consideration)? Who—Marx asks, pertinently—is to make such distinctions? Who is to sort writers into the 'authorized' and the 'unauthorized', the privileged and the unprivileged? An established author, even if his greatness is widely acknowledged, will not do, for he is not likely to favour those who are totally different from himself. Kant would not have testified whole-heartedly to Fichte's competence as a philosopher, Ptolemy to Copernicus's competence as an astronomer, Bernard of Clairvaux to Luther's competence as a theologian. Or is one to leave judgement to those who have not, themselves, made outstanding contributions to the field in question? So many answers, so many absurdities.

Inasmuch as *reading* is just as important as writing, there must also be 'authorized' and 'unauthorized' readers. The full consequences of this argument were accepted in ancient Egypt, where the priests, the only 'authorized' writers, were also the only 'authorized' readers.[31]

In fact, Marx concludes, the German writers recognized as competent, 'authorized', by official leaders of taste among their contemporaries, have frequently proved a national disaster:

When a German looks back on his history, he may find *one* reason among those principally responsible for the slowness of political development, and for the miserable state of German literature before Lessing, in the activity of 'authorized' writers. The savants by trade, by profession and by privilege, the doctors and proctors, the characterless university wits of the seventeenth and eighteenth centuries with their stiff pigtails, their superior pedantry, and their microscopic-micrological dissertations, have interposed themselves between the people and the spirit, between life and science, between freedom and man. It is the 'unauthorized' writers who have made our literature. Gottsched and Lessing—there you have your choice between an 'authorized' and an 'unauthorized' writer![32]

[31] *MEW* I, 72.   [32] *MEW* I, 73-4.

Lessing, the dedicated searcher for truth, the embattled pamph-
leteer, the fearless, witty, and impassioned champion of reason,
whose powers of dramatic construction went hand in hand with
an understanding of social tensions and an ability to convey an
image of contemporary life in the very rhythms of contemporary
speech—he clearly has a place at the very top of Marx's literary
pantheon. A later article in the *Rheinische Zeitung* (13 January
1843) culminates in fact in a quotation from one of Lessing's
pamphlets against Pastor Melchior Goeze with which the young
Marx throws down the gauntlet to his own adversaries: 'Write,
Herr Pastor, and get others to write, as much as you can and like.
If I leave unchallenged the slightest item in which you are
wrong—then, you may be sure, I can no longer move my pen.'[33]
Lessing's opponent, on the other hand, the Leipzig Professor
Johann Christoph Gottsched, Marx would have us see through
Lessing's eyes as an officially sanctioned pedantic purveyor of
obsolescent rules.

The articles Marx wrote for the *Rheinische Zeitung* bristle
with literary quotations and allusions. Such allusions may be
generalized:

Ignorance is a demon which will, we fear, be responsible for many a
tragedy yet; the greatest Greek dramatists were right when they
depicted it, in the terrible dramas that deal with the royal families
of Mycene and Thebes, as tragic fate.[34]

More often, however, Marx refers his readers to particular
authors and works. There are acknowledged citations from the
Bible, Lucretius, Lucian, Shakespeare, Molière, Lessing, Goethe,
Uhland, and from the Persian poet Hariri in Rückert's translation;[35] and there are many incidental allusions calculated to
arouse in German readers precise literary associations:

What could philosophy say about religion or about itself which
would be worse and more frivolous than the imputations in your
loud-mouthed newspapers? It need only repeat what you unphilo-
sophical *capuchins* have *preached* in thousands upon thousands of
controversial addresses, and it has said the worst [my italics].[36]

That passing allusion to preaching capuchins could not fail to
remind German readers of the *Kapuzinerpredigt*, the coarsely

---

[33] *MEW* I, 169.   [34] *MEW* I, 104.
[35] e.g. *MEW* I, 87, 96, 162, 131; 50 (*Die Rache*), 66, 67.   [36] *MEW* I, 99.

vigorous, popular, obscurantist, punning sermon preached by the friar in the opening play of Schiller's *Wallenstein* trilogy. And Marx's own sermon, his own exhortations which ring through these articles, is a call not only to think and feel, but to read and study: 'read your Cicero', he calls to his readers, *Leset den Cicero*, or again: 'Read St. Augustine's *De Civitate Deo*, study the church fathers and the spirit of Christianity, and then come back and tell me whether the church and state we know are "the Christian state".'[37] The tone of these early essays is that of a man in love with reading who appeals to the knowledge of the German and foreign classics he shares with his educated audience, and who challenges his opponents to acquire not only better logic, but also more of the experience and insight that books can give.

In his articles for the *Rheinische Zeitung*, and in the maturer works that were to follow, Marx exhibits the vivacity of an intelligence that constantly associates many diverse contexts. He needs to quote from, and allude to, literary works in order to suggest the complex relationships and interconnections which he sees between the different activities of men. His habit of literary quotation and allusion thus helps to make his social philosophy a true anthropology. This did not mean, however, that he wanted to confuse and confound the various realms in which man's creative aspirations and abilities can find expression. In the course of a polemic with two other journalists about a philosophical poem by Friedrich von Sallet entitled 'Gospel for Laymen' (*Laien-Evangelium*), Marx berates his opponents for failing to notice that Sallet was not only incompetent as a theologian and philosopher, but that he was also a bad poet: 'The passages quoted by the *Rhine and Moselle Gazette* [*Rhein- und Mosel-Zeitung*] . . . suffer from a fundamental defect: that of being *unpoetical*. And what an altogether mistaken idea it is to want to treat theological controversies poetically! Has it ever occurred to a composer to set dogma to music?'[38] Only when he has discussed what he calls 'this heresy against art' does Marx feel ready to analyse Sallet's defects as a thinker.

Looking back on his year with the *Rheinische Zeitung* at a later date, in 1859, Marx pointed to a series of articles on wood-theft and on the problems faced by wine-growers in the Moselle

[37] *MEW* I, 91, 101.   [38] *MEW EB* I, 432.

region as a watershed in his way of thinking. Here, he said in the Preface which opens *Towards a Critique of Political Economy*, he first experienced 'the embarrassment of having to take part in speaking on so-called material interests'; here, he claimed, he was first led to occupy himself with economic questions.[39] But here too Marx called in literature as an important auxiliary. The very first article on the wood-theft question (25 October 1842) begins by drawing out the parallels implied in such expressions as 'the social and political *scene*':

Up to now we have depicted two great *Haupt- und Staatsaktionen* of our Rhenish parliament: its confusion about freedom of the Press, and its lack of freedom in respect of these confusions. Now we act on the level ground. Before we pass to the real, worldly question in full life-size—the question of the parcelling-out of landed property—we will let our readers see some genre-pictures [*Genrebilder*] in which the spirit and even more, we would say, the physical make-up of that parliament will mirror itself in many ways.[40]

Haupt- und Staatsaktionen are plays dealing with affairs of state and the lives of kings and princes; they are acted on a raised stage from which Marx's second sentence asks us to descend to something more down-to-earth. The analogy is carried on, and varied, by the allusion to 'genre-pictures' in the sentence that follows. Although primarily a term from the visual arts, *Genrebilder* could also be used, in Marx's day, to describe literary depictions of everyday life, depictions of aspects ignored or pushed aside in *Haupt- und Staatsaktionen*. Images from theatrical, literary, artistic activity—grandiloquent plays, raised platform, acting on level ground, 'full life-size', 'genre-pictures', holding up a 'mirror' to nature—are used by Marx to relate political to literary experience and to suggest attitudes or valuations while purporting to describe.

The creations of great dramatists—notably Shakespeare—appear in these wood-theft articles in two distinct ways. Marx finds in them, firstly, a repository of incisive formulations irrespective of their original context: thus Cornwall's description, in *King Lear*, ii. ii, of the man who parades his 'bluntness' as a cover for craft and corrupt ends is quoted without reference to the vile nature of the character who utters it or the situation of

[39] *MEW* XIII, 7. [40] *MEW* I, 109.

tyranny and injustice in which it is spoken.[41] On other occasions, however, Marx clearly wants to draw on his readers' knowledge of the original context of his quotations:

Self-interest is practical, and there is nothing in the world more practical than striking down an enemy. 'Hates any man the thing he would not kill?'—that lesson was already taught by Shylock.[42]

Here the character of Shylock and the union of greed and cruelty in the action of the *Merchant of Venice* are unmistakably relevant. Marx drives the point home by extended quotations from Act IV, scene i, of that play: from the exchange between Portia, Shylock, and Gratiano in which Shylock finds himself discomfited. 'Is that the law?', he asks, to be answered by Portia's 'Thyself shalt see the act'. 'And you *shall* see the act', Marx echoes triumphantly, as he concludes his demonstration of the inhumanity and, ultimately, the illegality of the claims made by landowners against those who gathered firewood in their forests. The implied identification of Gentile, feudal landowners with Shylock the Jew no doubt gave Marx, and readers attuned to him, a malicious species of pleasure.

Works in the epic rather than the dramatic mode can, of course, be used in the same way—as Marx demonstrates, in the wood-theft articles, by a juxtaposition of arguments used by those who championed landowners' rights with a quotation from Goethe's *Reynard the Fox* (*Reineke Fuchs*).[43] This poem was to retain a special interest for Marx because of its cynicism about politicians of all shades, and because beneath its courtly or politically sophisticated French, Flemish, and Low German originals (*Roman de Renart, Van den Vos Reinaerde, Reinke de Vos*) its origin in folk-art, in popular animal fables, is still clearly discernible. If there was one endeavour of the German Romantics with which he sympathized whole-heartedly it was their attempt to preserve and study German folk-literature. A telling aside in Marx's *Rheinische Zeitung* article of 1 January 1843 speaks of 'a *true* fairy-tale' (*ein* wahres *Märchen*) as an expression of the essence of a given people, an embodiment of its thoughts, fears, and hopes.[44]

Literature does not, however, appear invariably as the ally

[41] *MEW* I, 96.   [42] *MEW* I, 121.   [43] *MEW* I, 131.
[44] *MEW* I, 153.

of truth in Marx's articles for the *Rheinische Zeitung*. In his essay
on 'The Historical School of Law' (*Das philosophische Manifest
der historischen Rechtsschule*), for instance, Marx blames Gustav
Hugo for making no distinction between evidence from works
of the imagination, and evidence from other kinds of authority:

Hugo's argumentation is as *positive*, i.e. *uncritical*, as his principles.
He knows of no distinction. Any existing thing is an authority for
him, and any authority he considers sufficient. So in a single
paragraph he will quote Moses and Voltaire, Richardson and
Homer, Montaigne and Ammon, Rousseau's *Contrat Social* and St.
Augustine's *De Civitate Dei* . . .[45]

The critical spirit, the historical spirit, the spirit that makes distinctions, has to be exercised as vigilantly when making use of
literary allusions as everywhere else. Hugo's failure to make the
right use of such authority as Homer and Richardson may be
said to possess is paralleled, in Marx's eyes, by his failure to
distinguish between higher and lower forms of morality, between
'the rash on the skin' and 'the skin itself'.

In the work of Gustav Hugo, then, literary references help to
obfuscate rather than enlighten. This theme is pursued in a
different key by several passages in the 'wood-theft' articles.
Marx tells the readers of the *Rheinische Zeitung*:

The owner of a forest is not content with forcing the thief to make
good just the plain value [of the wood he has taken]; he goes
further and endows that value with a character of its own and bases
his demand for additional compensation *on this poetic, individual
character* [my italics];

or again, dramatically addressing landowners and those who
champion their cause:

With a nebulous notion of your personal excellence, *poetically self-
enraptured*, you offer those who have dealings with you your individual character as a protection against your laws. I must confess that
I do not share this *novelistic notion* of what a forest-owner is [my
italics].[46]

Notions derived from literature, *poetisch* and *romanhaft*, may be
used to veil the harsh realities of oppression and injustice—they
may create a deceptive self-image and give sentimental sanction

[45] *MEW* I, 79–80.   [46] *MEW* I, 114, 128.

to brutal conduct. Literature may be used, consciously or unconsciously, as a tool of self-interest:

Self-interest ... has two kinds of weights and measures with which to
weigh and measure men, two kinds of spectacles, one black and the
other rose-coloured. When what is required is . . . to lend a fair
appearance to dubious means, then Self-interest can lull himself
and others into the unpractical and charming enthusiasms of a
tender, trusting soul. He can press an opponent's hand until it is
sore, and do so in a pure excess of trust. But suddenly one's own
advantage is at stake; that requires a careful testing of the utility of
one's tools and one's means *behind the scenes, where the illusions of the
stage disappear* [my italics].[47]

Marx clearly sees it as his task to dispel illusions derived from,
or tricked out with, notions found in poetry, in the novel, in the
drama—a task which is part of that wider purpose he described
to Arnold Ruge in September 1843:

If it is not for us to construct the future and give final shape to
something which will last for all time, then our present task is all the
more certain: I mean *the merciless critique of all that exists* which will
not let itself be deflected by fear of its own results any more than by
fear of coming into conflict with existing powers.[48]

Literature too, its reception and its uses, was to come under the
scrutiny of Marx's *rücksichtslose Kritik*.

In this connection it is particularly significant that Marx's
articles on wood-theft in the *Rheinische Zeitung* first introduce a
notion which was soon to play a central part in his thinking:
the notion of 'ideology'.[49] 'How', he writes, ironically, about
those who invoke individual free will when the rights of landowners are to be safeguarded, 'are we to understand this sudden
appearance of ideology—for in respect of ideas we have only
followers of Napoleon before us?'[50] Napoleon, one remembers,
had picked up the word *idéologues* (used, before his time, to
denote a school of philosophy that derived ideas from sensations)
to mock what he considered 'unpractical' thinkers—men who
lived in a cloud-cuckoo-land of ideas and failed to understand

---

[47] *MEW* I, 127.   [48] *MEW* I, 344.
[49] A brief history of this term, from Destutt de Tracy and Condillac to Marx and
Engels, will be found in Henri Lefebvre's *The Sociology of Marx*, trans. N. Guterman
(Harmondsworth, 1972), pp. 59 ff.
[50] *MEW* I, 153.

reality.[51] Such suggestions of 'false consciousness' were to inform the term *Ideologie* in Marx's works too, particularly in *The German Ideology* on which he collaborated with Engels. He was to add, however, the notion that such 'ideologies' reflected material conditions and class-interests, and that it was their social function—whatever the amount of truth they contained, and whatever the intentions and illusions of their authors and propagators may have been—'to protect the privileges or justify the pretensions of some class or group in society'.[52]

One other important point emerges clearly from Marx's articles in the *Rheinische Zeitung*. He realizes, he tells us, that there is a rough, even coarse colouration in his descriptions of the economic plight of wine-growers in the Moselle region:

Whoever hears, directly and frequently, the inconsiderate voice of distress among the population of our region, easily loses that aesthetic tact which knows how to choose the most delicate and modest images; he may even think it his political duty to adopt for a moment, in public, the speech of popular distress which he never had occasion to learn in his homeland.[53]

Marx is here primarily concerned with the absurdity of applying the criterion of 'aesthetic tact' to journalistic works designed to stir up the public conscience. At the same time, however, he is voicing something like the discontent with 'delicate and modest images' felt, in the same period, by such different authors as Heine and Georg Büchner. To convey the realities of the nineteenth century one may need a stronger, coarser language than that of those *Göttinger Hain* poets whose diction had influenced Marx's own early poems.

In his first year as a journalist, then, Marx had discovered how literary quotations and allusions could bring him into cultural communion with his readers. On the basis of shared literary experiences the journalist could play games with his readers and use figures and phrases from the great writers of the past for emotional charge, rapid characterization, and ridicule through comparison or contrast. He had, in his own phrase, roamed through the realm of literature with the lantern of

[51] Cf. P. Stadler, *Karl Marx. Ideologie und Politik*, 2nd edn. (Göttingen, 1971), p. 49, and J. Plamenatz, *Ideology* (London, 1970), p. 15.

[52] J. Plamenatz, *German Marxism and Russian Communism* (London, 1954), p. 313.

[53] *MEW* I, 172.

Diogenes in search of honest men. Such honesty was difficult
to achieve in his own day, he had found, because of censorship,
and because of social conditions which were forcing too many
authors to write in order to live, instead of living in order to
write. He had asserted the complexity of literary 'truths': the
way the same work refracted itself differently in different
readers, and the way in which each literary 'object' called
for a specific and appropriate mode of approach. He had
raised the question of social recognition by contemporaries:
which authors were 'authorized' or 'competent' (*befugt*),
entitled to speak for their age and society, and which were not?
And what about 'authorized' or 'competent' *readers*? He had
deepened his suspicions of Romanticism, while continuing
to share the German Romantics' respect for the spirit of
the common people, the *Volksgeist*,[54] and its literary expression. He had voiced his first suspicions of aestheticism, the attitude which made the comfortably placed turn away from the
rough-and-tumble of human life and which led to a mode of
writing so fine and smooth that it could slide over reality almost
without touching it. He had conceived a new interest in parliamentary oratory and had tried to relate the manner and
matter of individual speeches to the social interests that lay
behind them. He had learnt to look for the misuse of literary
sources: as a repertoire of false self-images, as a disguise for lack
of real evidence. Literature had helped him in his self-imposed
task of letting the light of reason play on heavenly and earthly
authority. Lucretius' *On the Nature of Things*, Lucian's *Dialogues*,
Molière's *Les Fâcheux*, Voltaire's *L'Enfant prodigue*, Lessing's
Anti-Goeze, Goethe's *Reynard the Fox*—these were some of the
allies he had found in the literature of the past. As editor of the
Rheinische Zeitung he sought allies among contemporary men of
letters too; and while he kept his distance from those who
wanted to use his literary columns for covert communist or
socialist propaganda, he was glad to avail himself of the stirring
poems of Georg Herwegh. Here, it seemed, the lantern of
Diogenes had discovered an honest man.

[54] *MEW* I, 153.

3 · Shylock, Timon, Mephistopheles

'Money . . . is the visible godhead, the transformation of all human and natural qualities into their
opposites, the general confusion and inversion of
things; it makes impossibilities fraternize.'

(MEW EB I, 565)

(i)

MARX resigned his editorship of the *Rheinische Zeitung* in March
1843, and after spending some time with relatives in Holland
he moved to Kreuznach, where he married Jenny von Westphalen in June 1843. His Young-Hegelian friend Arnold Ruge
tried in the meantime to set up a new political journal outside
the frontiers of Germany, and he persuaded Marx to collaborate
with him. While waiting for these plans to mature, Marx engaged in intense study of history and political theory. Five
notebooks have been preserved which show him reading and
excerpting works dealing with the history of England, France,
Germany, Italy, Sweden, and the United States of America. He
displays particular interest in the history of the French Revolution of 1789. Among the political theorists he studies at this time
are Machiavelli, Montesquieu, Rousseau, and Justus Möser,
as well as a Romantic author who was to become one of his
bêtes noires: François-René de Chateaubriand.[1]

Above all Marx occupied himself, in the spring and summer
of 1843, with a critique of Hegel's views on law and politics.
His approach to Hegel was influenced in no small way by
Ludwig Feuerbach, who had suggested, in the very volume of
Anekdota which contained two essays by Marx, that Hegel had
failed to see the true relationship between 'thought' and 'being'.

---

[1] L. I. Golman (and others), *Karl Marx. Biographie* (Berlin, 1973), pp. 56–7.

'Being', Feuerbach had written, 'is the subject, thought the predicate. Thought arises from being—being does not arise from thought.' 'The only point in Feuerbach's aphorisms that does not satisfy me', Marx commented, 'is that he gives too much importance to nature and too little to politics. Yet *an alliance with politics affords the only means for contemporary philosophy to become truth*' [my italics]. If Feuerbach helped him towards a critique of Hegel, Moses Hess, in his turn, was helping him towards a critique of Feuerbach.[2]

The manuscript commentary on Hegel's *Philosophy of Right* on which Marx worked from March to August 1843 shows him engaged in the activity, not just of exegesis, but of *translation*. He tried, as he himself puts it, to 'translate' the 'logical, pantheistic mysticism' of Hegel's text[3] into something more down-to-earth and therefore nearer the truth—though it should be stressed, as George Lichtheim has rightly pointed out, that for Marx as for Hegel reality 'is not as it appears to empirical perception, but as it is revealed by philosophical reflection'.[4] 'If we translate this sentence into prose', Marx says, for instance, with a fine irony, of § 262 in the *Philosophy of Right*, 'then it follows . . .'.[5] With this concern Marx merges a close philological attention to Hegel's text which expresses itself in grammatical analysis. He divides his page into columns: where the left-hand column quotes a sentence from Hegel the right-hand columns add a 'translation' and expansion together with comments of the following kind:

It is evident that Hegel connects his further predicates to two subjects: 'different sides of the organism' and 'organism'. In the third sentence the 'sides between which a distinction has been made' are defined as 'different powers'. The interposition of the word 'thus' [*so*] then produces the illusion that these 'different powers' have been derived from the interposed clause which speaks of the organism as the development of the Idea . . .[6]

The conclusion Marx draws from a series of such logical and grammatical analyses is one which had already been anticipated by Feuerbach: 'Hegel has turned into a product, a

[2] D. McLellan, *Marx before Marxism*, p. 142; P. Demetz, *Marx, Engels und die Dichter*, p. 64.   [3] *MEW* I, 206.
[4] G. Lichtheim, *Marxism. An Historical and Critical Study*, 2nd edn. (London, 1964), p. 8.   [5] *MEW* I, 205.   [6] *MEW* I, 211–12.

predicate of the Idea, what is in reality its subject. Instead of developing his thought from an object [*Gegenstand*], he develops the object in accordance with a manner of thinking which is predetermined, which has reached its finished form in the abstract sphere of logic.'[7]

In looking anew at the philosophy of right that Hegel works out in this way Marx again finds literary analogies springing to mind. Hegel's conception of the power of a ruling sovereign, for instance, which appears in one place as a mediating one, in another as an extreme itself in need of mediation, reminds him of *A Midsummer Night's Dream*: 'It is like the lion in the *Midsummer Night's Dream*, who calls out: "I am a lion", and "I am not a lion, but Snug". Thus every extreme is here at one time the lion of contradiction, at another the Snug of mediation.'[8] He charges Hegel's views on inheritance with being influenced by 'the romantic titillation of the seignorial glories of entail'.[9] *Der romantische Kitzel der Majoratsherrlichkeit*—Marx's punning phrase reminds us that these laws of entail, so dear to the historical school of law, appear in the very title of two well-known works by German Romantic writers, Arnim's *Die Majoratsherren* and Hoffmann's *Das Majorat*. And in expressing his opposition to inherited private property, Marx again finds the familiar terms of literary theory flowing readily from his pen:

Held against the uncouth stupidity of independent private property the uncertainty of trade is elegiac, the passion for gain pathetical or dramatic, the mutability of possessions a stern fate (tragic), dependence on state funds ethical. In short, in all these qualities the *human heart* may be felt beating in and through property—man is here dependent on man.[10]

The literary genres and modes, especially as Schiller and Hegel had classified them, are here seen as so many ways of expressing essential human relations. They show how men come to terms with the world they are helping to fashion, and with each other. They can be used as shorthand symbols of human attitudes:

Your letter, my dear friend, is a good elegy, a breath-taking threnody; but it is not at all political . . .,[11]

[7] *MEW* I, 213.   [8] *MEW* I, 292.   [9] *MEW* I, 306.
[10] *MEW* I, 307.
[11] *MEW* I, 338 (letter to Ruge, May 1843). This letter responds to one from Ruge in which the latter quotes Hölderlin's famous lament at the condition of

or as ways of grading the dignity of different societies and systems of government:

The comedy of despotism which is being performed with us is as dangerous to [Frederick William IV of Prussia] as its tragedy was once for the Stuarts and the Bourbons. And even if, for a long time, people should fail to recognize this comedy for what it is, it would yet constitute a revolution. The state is too serious a matter to be made into a harlequinade.[12]

The *topos* to which Marx here appeals—the state as theatre—was to recur in his work with many variations in the years to come. It is joined, in the letters to Ruge written while Marx was composing his critique of Hegel's *Philosophy of Right*, by two other *topoi* familiar from European literature:

One could, perhaps, allow a ship full of fools to drift a good long while before the wind; but it would move towards its predestined end for the very reason that the fools do not believe it is doing so. This fate is the revolution which awaits us;

and again:

I will not take it upon myself to underwrite the ship of fools like an insurance company; but I maintain that the King of Prussia will be the man of his age for as long as the topsy-turvy world is the real one.[13]

The allusion, here, is to the central image of Sebastian Brant's sixteenth-century *Ship of Fools*, and to a *topos* which had been used by Hegel and applied to contemporary Prussia by Heine in 1842: the topsy-turvy world, *die verkehrte Welt*.[14] That last image had an obvious appeal for Marx at a time when he thought himself engaged, as he himself was to put it, in turning philosophy the right way up after Hegel had left it upside down.

The passages just quoted come from a series of letters between

Germany in the penultimate chapter of his novel *Hyperion*. Marx objects to the use Ruge makes of this quotation: 'No people despairs; and even if for many years it is only stupidity that bids it hope, after many years it will suddenly grow wise and fulfil all its pious wishes.' There is no evidence that Marx himself ever read any of Hölderlin's works.

[12] *MEW* I, 337–8 (letter to Ruge, Mar. 1843).   [13] *MEW* I, 338, 340.

[14] J. Höppner, in his edition of the *German–French Yearbooks* (*Deutsch–Französische Jahrbücher*, herausgegeben von Arnold Ruge und Karl Marx, 1844 (Leipzig, 1973, p. 401), points out that Fourier had used the same image in a socio-critical context.

Feuerbach, Bakunin, Ruge, and Marx that Ruge edited and published in the *German–French Yearbooks* (*Deutsch–Französische Jahrbücher*) for which he and Marx assumed joint responsibility. The very title was a programme: Germans and Frenchmen were to collaborate, to help bring about a juster world, in the teeth of that Francophobia which so many nineteenth-century Germans regarded as inseparable from German patriotism. After leaving Germany in October 1843 and joining Ruge in Paris, Marx threw himself with his customary vigour into the task of editing, and writing for, the *Yearbooks*. Among the eminent Frenchmen whom he and Ruge approached with a request for literary contributions was Alphonse de Lamartine. Lamartine held out hope of a contribution;[15] but in the event neither he nor any other French writer sent anything. When, therefore, the first (and, as it was to turn out, the last) issue of the *Yearbooks* appeared in February 1844, it contained only the work of *German* authors. There was to be found a programmatic statement by Ruge; a hilarious political poem by Heine and a rhetorical one by Herwegh; letters by Feuerbach, Bakunin, Ruge, and Marx; glosses on German newspaper articles by F. C. Bernays (to which Marx seems to have added some Attic salt);[16] documents concerning Johann Jacoby's trial for treason and *lèse-majesté* in Prussia; a critique of political economy and a discussion of Carlyle's *Past and Present* by the young Engels; and two important articles by Marx. The first of these was an essay on the Jewish question, couched in the form of a review of two works by Bruno Bauer. The second bore the title 'Towards a Critique of Hegel's *Philosophy of Right*. Introduction', and turned out to be Marx's most important and influential statement of political principles before *The Communist Manifesto* of 1848.

---

[15] Cf. *MEW EB* I, 437.

[16] D. Ryazanov (*MEGA* I, 1 (2), pp. xxviii–xl) has pointed out that the last of these glosses, comparing articles by two newspaper-correspondents and skilfully showing that one of them uses words and constructions in a way which implies the very opposite of what the loyal journalist thinks he is saying, has many of the hallmarks of Marx's own style. Readers of the present book may well be reminded of Marx's use of literary and mythological allusions by the following passage from the final gloss: 'If the correspondent of the *Bremer Zeitung* is rough like Achilles, that of the *Augsburger Zeitung* is cultivated like Ulysses. He has the style of a Cicero and the invention of a pupil in a convent-school. He is the prosaic Klopstock of the new royal Messiah.' Cf. J. Höppner, ed. cit., pp. 360, 460.

In the letters to Ruge printed in the *German–French Yearbooks*,[17] Marx painted the picture of a world dominated by philistines. Appealing to Goethe for confirmation,[18] he showed up this world as a 'political animal-world' (*politische Tierwelt*), a 'dehumanized world' (*entmenschte Welt*),[19] which could only be improved by a 'ruthless critique of the whole *status quo*' (*rücksichtslose Kritik des Bestehenden*).[20] This would include, Marx's letters show, the critique of Romantic obfuscations: when he attacks the 'liberal speeches and outpourings of the heart'[21] characteristic of Frederick William IV of Prussia, he uses a term which could not but remind his German readers of the title of one of the key works of German Romanticism, the *Herzensergießungen eines kunstliebenden Klosterbruders* (*Outpourings from the Heart of an Art-loving Friar*) by Wackenroder and Tieck. It would also include a critique of ready-made Utopias, such as that embodied in Etienne Cabet's recently published novel *Voyage to Icaria* (*Voyage en Icarie. Roman philosophique et social*, Paris, 1842). The over-all programme of the new *Yearbooks* could therefore be summed up by Marx as 'critical philosophy which leads the age to understand its own struggles and desires'.[22]

Marx's essay 'On the Jewish Question' must be seen as part of his critique of the 'political animal-world', the 'dehumanized world', of his own time. Its analysis of Judaism and Jewishness is dangerously misleading: he adopts the common prejudice of identifying the Jew with gross and unrelieved commercialism and chooses to overlook the Jewish traditions of spirituality, intellectual adventurousness, altruism, and prophetic fervour whose heir he himself unwillingly was. In this respect Marx contrasts strikingly with Freud, who once declared, in a lecture to fellow Jews, that he found the attraction of Jewry and Jews 'irresistible':

Whenever I felt an inclination to national enthusiasm I strove to suppress it as being harmful and wrong, alarmed by the warning

---

[17] In a letter to Wilhelm Liebknecht (18 Dec. 1890) Engels reports: 'Marx said to me more than once that Ruge edited him about and added all sorts of nonsense' (quoted J. Höppner, ed. cit., pp. 368–9).

[18] 'All they want is to live and reproduce (and no one, says Goethe, gets farther than this)'—*MEW* I, 338.

[19] *MEW* I, 339.   [20] *MEW* I, 334.

[21] *MEW* I, 341 ('seine liberalen Reden und Herzensergießungen').

[22] *MEW* I, 346.

examples of the people among whom we Jews live. But plenty of other things remained over to make the attraction of Jewry and Jews irresistible—many obscure emotional forces, which were the more powerful the less they could be expressed in words, as well as a clear consciousness of inner identity, the safe privacy of a common mental construction. And beyond this there was a perception that it was to my Jewish nature alone that I owed two characteristics which had become indispensable to me in the difficult course of my life. Because I was a Jew I found myself free from many prejudices which restricted others in the use of their intellect; and as a Jew I was prepared to join the Opposition and to do without agreement with the 'compact majority' . . .[23]

Marx's essay 'On the Jewish Question' is important, however, not only as an illustration of his ability to overlook facts which did not suit his argument, but also as his most sustained analysis so far of the power of money to transform everything into mere commodity. Contemporary society, he had grown to believe, was coming to be dominated more and more by 'the man of money'; and among the 'virtues' of this *Geldmensch* Marx listed (besides contempt for theory, for history, for the notion of man as an end in himself) contempt for art, *Verachtung . . . der Kunst.*[24] This is the first brief occurrence of a theme to be sounded many times afterwards in Marx's writings. The modern age is not favourable to art; nineteenth-century capitalism alienates men from their artistic (and hence their literary) heritage as it alienates them from so many other products of human labour.

The essay 'On the Jewish Question' also shows something of the importance which Marx attached to the contemporary documentary novel. In the course of his argument he describes the state of religion in North America, and he draws on three main sources for his information: the writings of de Tocqueville; Thomas Hamilton's *Men and Manners in America*; and a novel entitled *Marie or Slavery in the United States* (*Marie ou l'Esclavage aux États-Unis*, Brussels, 1835) by Gustave-Auguste Beaumont de la Bonninière. Marx quotes freely from Beaumont without ever indicating that his work differs in kind from that of informants like Hamilton and de Tocqueville.[25]

[23] Standard Edition of the *Complete Works of Sigmund Freud* (London, 1964), vol. xx, p. 274.
[24] *MEW* I, 375.   [25] *MEW* I, 351–2, 361, 362–3, 374.

Since Marx's analysis of the role and power of money occurs in the context of his reflections on the Jewish question, it is not surprising that Shylock should once again appear on his stage. Characteristically, however, he does so not in the course of Marx's discussion of what he misleadingly labels 'the Jewish spirit', but in his discussion of Hegel and German law. Shylock is called before us to help sustain an attack on the *historische Rechtsschule*, that arch-conservative, proudly and consciously Germanic, 'historical school' of German jurists which he had already attacked in the *Rheinische Zeitung*:

A school which justifies today's baseness by pointing to the baseness of yesterday, a school which brands as rebellion the cry of the serf against the lash as soon as that lash can be shown to be an ancient, historical, inherited lash, a school to which history (like the God of Israel to his servant Moses) shows only its *a posteriori*, the *historical school of law*—that school would have invented history if it were not itself an invention made by the history of Germany. Shylock, but Shylock the lackey, it appeals, at every pound of flesh cut from the heart of the people, to its bond, its historical bond, its Christian-Germanic bond.[26]

That conveys directly what was also the argument of the essay 'On the Jewish Question': qualities attributed to Jews by their enemies are, in the nineteenth century, by no means confined to Jews. Marx no doubt hoped to rile the 'historical school' by the pointedly Jewish parallels (Shylock is reinforced by the God of Israel and his servant Moses) much as Heine liked to rile anti-Jewish opponents by the same device. At the same time, however, Marx turns the screw of polemic with a conscious variation on the character Shakespeare had created in *The Merchant of Venice*. The 'historical school' is said to lack that very quality which great interpreters of the role have always tried to bring out, a quality also stressed by Heine in the eloquent passages he devotes to Shylock in his book on Shakespeare: dignity, the dignity of suffering, the dignity of pride. Whatever Shakespeare's Shylock may be, he is not a 'lackey'. His appearance in Marx's context therefore provides, not just an illustrative parallel, but a standard by which his modern 'counterparts' are judged.

[26] *MEW* I, 380.

The essay from which I have now begun to quote, entitled 'Towards a Critique of Hegel's Philosophy of Right. Introduction' (*Zur Kritik der Hegelschen Rechtsphilosophie. Einleitung*) is one of the key documents of Marx's intellectual and political development. It begins with a tribute to Feuerbach and those who followed where he had led: 'As far as Germany is concerned, the criticism of religion is essentially complete, and the criticism of religion is the presupposition of all criticism.' It proclaims the vital importance of *Praxis*. It culminates in the invocation of a new class with whose fortunes Marx will henceforth identify himself and which will play the dominant part in a German 'resurrection'— a 'resurrection' to be heralded by 'the crowing of the Gallic cock':

When the proletariat proclaims the dissolution of the world-order which has existed hitherto, it only proclaims the secret of its own existence—for it is in fact the dissolution of this order . . . As philosophy finds in the proletariat its material weapons, so the proletariat finds in philosophy its intellectual weapons.[27]

In this essay Marx skilfully uses the vocabulary of the Bible and of religious tradition to attack religion: 'The criticism of religion is therefore the germ of the criticism of that vale of tears whose halo is religion';[28] and he uses the vocabulary of literary theory and criticism to convey his conception of the course of history. He expresses his feeling that contemporary Germany lacks revolutionary ardour by saying that there the relationship of the social classes to one another is 'not dramatic but epic', and adapts to his own purposes Hegel's views on the historical sequence and relationship of tragedy and comedy:

For the peoples of modern times it is instructive to see the *ancien régime*, that experienced its tragedy in their midst, play out its comedy as a German *revenant* . . . The *ancien régime* of modern times is only the comedian of a world-order whose true heroes are dead. History is thorough and passes through many phases when it carries an old form to its grave. The last phase of a world-historical form is its comedy.[29]

Here Marx introduces once again the character his doctoral thesis had called the 'patron saint' of philosophy: the fettered Prometheus of Aeschylus:

[27] *MEW* I, 378, 385, 391 (*ET*, 115, 122, 128).   [28] *MEW* I, 379.
[29] *MEW* I, 389, 381.

The gods of Greece, who had already been mortally wounded in the tragedy of Aeschylus' *Prometheus Bound*, had to die again, comically, in the *Dialogues* of Lucian. Why does history choose this course? So that humanity should leave its past behind in a cheerful spirit. This cheerful historical destiny we claim for the authorities who at present control Germany.[30]

The sequence of tragedy and comedy which may be observed (with Hegel's help) in the history of literature can clarify similar sequences in political history. It can do so because the two kinds of history are so intimately intertwined that they are ultimately one. Aeschylus and Lucian have represented, in their masterpieces, important aspects of their age, different ways in which the ancients regarded their gods. Comparison between them can therefore illuminate significant differences in a significant sequence. Comparative literature can become a tool of historical understanding.

What is particularly interesting about Marx's comment on Aeschylus, in view of a later and more famous statement on the relation of Greek literature to Greek mythology, is that he does not see Aeschylus as naïvely dependent on myth. The over-statement that in *Prometheus Bound* the Greek gods have been 'mortally wounded' implies that Aeschylus' play constitutes, in Marx's view, a critique of mythology, of the Greek pantheon, even while it treats, with entire seriousness, a mythological sub-ject. As for that subject itself: Marx makes clear, in this same essay on Hegel, what he now thinks the function of mythology to be. 'The peoples of antiquity', he writes, 'lived their pre-history in imagination, in their mythology.'[31]

The editorship of the *German–French Yearbooks*—of which a good deal landed on Marx's shoulders because his co-editor, Arnold Ruge, fell ill during the final stages—brought Marx into personal contact with two of the most celebrated German poets of the day: Georg Herwegh, whose sybaritic way of life he now loyally defended against Ruge as the privilege of a man of talent; and Heinrich Heine, who not only allowed the *German–French Yearbooks* to reprint his hilariously irreverent poem sequence about King Ludwig I of Bavaria but who also tried to recruit other contributors during his journey through Germany

[30] *MEW* I, 381–2 (*ET*, 119).
[31] *MEW* I, 383; cf. C. Prévost, *Littérature, politique, idéologie* (Paris, 1973), p. 16.

in December 1843.[32] Marx and Heine contributed to the same
short-lived periodicals; Marx read Heine's satiric poems in
proof; the Marx family and Heine were on friendly visiting
terms; and Marx felt warmly enough about Heine to say, when
he finally had to leave Paris, that he would have liked to take
Heine away with him in his luggage.[33] There are two later
accounts of their association at this time. One comes from a
letter by Ruge to E. Kapp, dated 18 February 1870, in which
Ruge complains, mildly, that Heine never acknowledged how he
came to write his most effective and celebrated political satires:
'This turn he owed to Marx and me. We said to him: "Leave
your eternal love-plaints and show the poetical [Ruge probably meant to write: 'political'] lyricists, how these things
are properly done—with a whip!"'[34] The other derives from
some notes Eleanor Marx made for the use of Karl Kautsky in
1895: 'It is no exaggeration to say that Mohr [= Marx] not
only admired Heine as a poet, but had a sincere affection for
him. He would even make all sorts of excuses for Heine's
political vagaries. Poets, Mohr maintained, were queer kittle-
cattle, not to be judged by the ordinary, or even the extraordinary, standards of conduct.'[35] Eleanor then goes on to
relate how Heine asked Marx's opinion about his verses and
talked possible alterations and improvements over with him;
how hard Marx found it to bear with Heine's morbid sensitivity
to criticism, even when such criticism came from those he held
in profound and justified contempt; and how Heine once, by
his presence of mind, saved the life of Marx's baby daughter
Jenny. She concludes: 'Politically, so far as I understand, they
seldom discussed things. But certainly Mohr judged Heine very
tenderly, and he loved not only the man's work, but also the
man himself.' Marx's own later letters, and the testimony of
Franziska Kugelmann, give reason to doubt that Marx always
loved the man as much as his works; but there can be no doubt
that the association had its effect on both men. It encouraged
Heine to make his satiric and political poetry more radical
than it had ever been before; and it stimulated Marx to

---

[32] Cf. J. Höppner, ed. cit., p. 37.
[33] Letter to Heine, 12 Jan. 1845—*MEW* XXVII, 434.
[34] H. H. Houben (ed.), *Gespräche mit Heine*, 2nd edn. (Potsdam, 1948), p. 506.
[35] *BM* 148–50.

continue reading Heine in a way which has left tangible traces on his own style. Heine reminiscences abound in the essays published in the *German–French Yearbooks*. They range from individual coinages (*Menschenkehricht*, 'human garbage', from the last poem in Heine's *New Spring* cycle) to the recollection of a sentence from Heine's *Ludwig Börne* which ends Marx's programmatic Hegel essay:

The Gallic cock has now crowed for the second time, and in Germany too the day is beginning to break. (Heine)

When all inward conditions have been fulfilled, the day of German resurrection will be heralded by the crowing of the Gallic cock.
(Marx)[36]

Nigel Reeves, who has traced many parallels in the way the thoughts of Marx and Heine were evolving at this time, justly comments that these 'plainly reveal the extent to which Heine and Marx were working along the same lines in 1844 but that it would be vain to try to determine who influenced whom'.[37] In expression and formulation, however, it was clearly Marx who gained from Heine. It should go without saying, after all we now know of Marx, that his Paris essays bristle with allusions to other writers too—notably Goethe, whose *Faust* provides the polar terms 'superman' and 'non-man', *Übermensch* and *Unmensch*, with which the Hegel critique in the *German–French Yearbooks* opens.[38]

(ii)

One literary production of 1844 appeared to Marx of special significance. This was a poem written during the revolt of the Silesian weavers in that year and sung by those weavers on their marches. Such a poem, it seemed to Marx, justified his faith in the creative power, class-consciousness, and, ultimately, the revolutionary will, of proletarian 'Cinderellas' to whom he prophesied an 'athletic stature' in the not too distant future:

Not a single one of the French and English workers' revolts possessed so theoretical and conscious a character as the revolt of the Silesian

[36] *MEW* I, 359, 391.   [37] N. Reeves, 'Heine and the Young Marx', p. 63.
[38] *MEW* I, 378; cf. P. Demetz, op. cit., p. 60.

weavers. Remember, first of all, the *Weavers' Song*, that bold call to
battle in which domestic hearth, factory, district are not so much as
mentioned; in which, rather, the proletariat shouts its opposition to
a society based on private property in a striking, trenchant, ruthless, and violent way. The Silesian revolt begins with the very thing
with which the French and English workers' revolt ends: with
conscious understanding of what the proletariat is.[39]

The Weavers' Song (whose German title, *Das Blutgericht*, may
be roughly translated as 'Bloody Assize') thus occupies an important place in Marx's literary gallery. It signifies, in his eyes,
the transition from old folk-song to new proletarian poetry. In
his anxiety to see the German working class enter modern
literature he has, however, overestimated—or at least over-
stated—the ideological self-consciousness of the doomed
Silesian weavers. Nor can he have known the French equivalent
of 'Bloody Assize', the 'Song of the Silk-Weavers from Lyons'
(*Chant des canuts*) which had appeared some thirteen years
earlier and had shown at least as much 'conscious understanding of what the proletariat is'. Heine, significantly enough,
chose this same *Chant des canuts* as the model for his own famous
poem on the plight and the fury of the Silesian weavers.

Both Marx's commentary on 'Bloody Assize' and Heine's
poem 'The Poor Weavers' (later renamed 'The Silesian
Weavers') appeared in a radical German journal started in
Paris at the beginning of 1844. It was entitled *Forwards!*
(*Vorwärts*); its executive editor was Heinrich Börnstein, and its
contributors included Marx, Engels, Heine, Herwegh, Georg
Weerth, and Bakunin. Marx's connection with this journal was
fourfold. He frequently discussed the political situation with
Börnstein and thus left his mark on editorials and political
commentaries. He induced the editor to print extracts from
books which he, Marx, had been reading and which he deemed
calculated to reinforce desirable attitudes and tendencies—
these ranged from eighteenth-century Enlighteners to Feuerbach. He mediated between Börnstein and Heine—the proofs of
Heine's *Germany. A Winter's Tale*, for instance, passed through
Marx's hands before they were allowed to reach Börnstein. Last
but not least: Marx himself contributed to *Vorwärts* two signed

[39] *MEW* I, 404.

'Marginal Glosses' (*Kritische Randglossen*) and an unsigned commentary on a Prussian order in council which occupy themselves, in various ways, with questions of style.[40]

Marx's 'Marginal Glosses' (*Kritische Randglossen zu dem Artikel 'Der König von Preußen und die Sozialreform. Von einem Preußen'*) are directed against an article by Ruge and take up the question of what happens when a writer concentrates on polishing his style instead of thinking hard about what he has to say. Aestheticism of this kind, Marx proclaims, is self-defeating; it leads to vulgarity, *Gemeinheit*: 'Those who seek in every subject an occasion for stylistic exercises in public will be led, by this purely formal activity, to a perverted content; and such perverted content, in its turn, will impress the stamp of vulgarity on this form.'[41] Ruge, who prompted these reflections, is said by Marx to have been led away from the truth by his love of stylistic antitheses, and by his use of a 'ready-made phraseology dipped into hollow self-love'. That clearly develops two themes first heard in the *Rheinische Zeitung*. The first of these is Marx's belief—proclaimed, in respect of German property laws, in the article dated 3 November 1842—that 'form is of no value unless it is the form of its content' (*Die Form hat keinen Wert, wenn sie nicht die Form des Inhalts ist*).[42] The second is that distrust of aestheticism which has already been noted—a distrust, permanent from now on, of fine phrases, of excessive concern with stylistic excellence. At the same time, however, Marx takes pleasure in beating the stylist at his own game; at showing, through close analysis, how defects of thinking lead to concomitant defects of style.[43]

This kind of examination, incidental in 'Marginal Glosses', completely dominates the second of Marx's contributions to *Vorwärts*: 'Illustrations of the latest stylistic cabinet-exercise of Frederick William IV' (*Illustrationen zu der neuesten Kabinettsstilübung Friedrich Wilhelm IV.*). Here Marx subjects the style adopted by the Prussian King and his advisers in an address to the Prussian people to an analysis so trenchant, amusing, and effective that it could bear comparison with the work of Karl Kraus.

---

[40] The story of *Vorwärts* is fully told in Jacques Grandjonc's *Marx et les communistes allemands à Paris, 1844. Contribution à l'étude de la naissance du marxisme* (Paris, 1974).

[41] *MEW* I, 405. [42] *MEW* I, 146. [43] *MEW* I, 406–9.

The essay on Frederick William IV takes off from an Order in Council which the King had issued in August 1844, after escaping a would-be assassin's attempt on his life. In this stiffly worded message the King thanks God for preserving him, and thanks the Prussian people for their many expressions of loyalty. Marx reprints the King's missive in full, and begins his ironic comment as follows:

Passion, immediately felt, makes for ill-composed letters. A letter written by an excited lover to his beloved does not set a good stylistic example; but the very confusion of its expression is the clearest, most obvious, most moving indication of the power that love has over the writer. Love's power over the writer is the power the beloved exerts on him. Passionate lack of clarity and boundless confusion of style therefore flatter the beloved's heart, since the indirect, generally accessible, and therefore unreliable nature of language has taken on an immediate, individual, sensuous, and compelling character which makes it a wholly reliable index of feeling. Unsuspicious belief in the truth of the passion the lover declares for her becomes the beloved's supreme self-enjoyment, an expression of her belief in herself.

It follows from these premises that we are rendering an inestimable service to the Prussian people by removing any shadow of doubt about the inner truthfulness of its King's expressions of gratitude. We can raise this truthfulness above all doubt by showing the power with which feelings of gratitude have seized on the royal writer; and we can prove that power by demonstrating the stylistic confusion that characterises the Order in Council in which the King's gratitude has found expression. The purpose our patriotic analysis is intended to serve cannot, therefore, be open to misinterpretation.[44]

The close analysis that follows this ironic introduction shows up stylistic and grammatical failings in a way well calculated to make the King and his advisers appear ridiculous. At the same time Marx attempts to 'translate' the actual wording of the Order in Council into the thoughts that may have been at the back of the royal writer's mind but to which it would have been imprudent to give direct expression. The King's final sentence, for instance, unhappily constructed, had come to a halt on the words *und meines Volkes Liebe verdient*—words clearly meant to

[44] *MEW EB* I, 438–9.

conclude a sentence ('and deserves the love of my people') but giving the unfortunate impression of needing an additional phrase to complete it ('and my people's love deserves . . .'). Marx therefore comments:

The isolated final clause, thrust back upon itself by a comma, seems to point to an unexpressed, hidden, complementary phrase; something like this, perhaps: 'deserves the knout of brother-in-law Nicholas and the policies of cousin Metternich'; or perhaps: 'deserves the derisory constitution [*das Konstitutiönchen*] offered by Baron Bunsen'.[45]

In the guise of ironic praise Marx's analysis offers suggestions of stupidity coupled with ill will. His stylistic criticism seeks to expose, not only thick-headedness, but also cunning designs to manipulate and to deceive.

(iii)

Like the *German–French Yearbooks*, which never got beyond their first double number, *Vorwärts* proved short-lived. During the year he worked for these journals, however, Marx deepened his understanding of the French Revolution of 1789 by studying examples of political oratory (notably the speeches of Saint-Just and Robespierre), of memoirs (like those of R. Levasseur), of political pamphlets (the works of Babeuf), of official reports, and of French historiography.[46] His interest in all these modes of writing was henceforth to continue unabated and was to influence the style as well as the subject-matter of his own work. At the same time he now embarked on a first systematic course of reading in classical economics; and this too has had its effect on a series of essays, never published in Marx's own lifetime, which contain some of his deepest and most enduring insights. These Paris Manuscripts (*Ökonomisch-philosophische Manuskripte*) took their lead from an essay by Engels which made a great impression on Marx: an essay entitled 'Outlines of a Critique of Political Economy' (*Umrisse zu einer Kritik der Nationalökonomie*). It was chiefly this essay which stimulated Marx to read the standard works on political economy written in England and France, and to join the insights thus derived, in a historically fruitful alliance, with communistic ideas absorbed from Moses

[45] *MEW EB* I, 441.
[46] *MEGA* I, 3, 419–34; cf. A. Cornu, *Karl Marx et Friedrich Engels: Leur vie et leur œuvre*, vol. 3 (Paris, 1962), p. 11.

Hess as well as various French writers and modes of thinking
derived, directly and indirectly, from Hegel. And it was again
Engels who, through a review of Carlyle's *Past and Present* in the
German–French Yearbooks, directed Marx's attention to Carlyle's
denunciations of a 'gospel of mammonism' that makes 'cash-
payment . . . the sole nexus of man with man'. Carlyle thus
became a powerful if unacknowledged presence in the Economic
and Philosophic Manuscripts Marx composed in 1844. Three
years later, when trying to clarify his thoughts on the relation of
wages to work, he was to make careful notes on Carlyle's observations on this question in his essay on Chartism.[47]

From the notes Marx kept of his reading in the earlier 1840s
we can see clearly that even when he is engrossed in economic
studies he makes constant mental cross-reference to literature.
Among his jottings on the works of James Mill, for instance
(which he reads, at this period of his life, in French translation)
we find the following characteristic sentences:

> Let us disregard the *content* of such 'confidence', which consists of one
> man's extending credit to another—in the most favourable case,
> when he does not ask payment for such credit, i.e. when he is not a
> usurer—in the 'confidence' that his fellow man is not a 'rascal' but
> a 'good' man. The person who exhibits such confidence equates—
> like Shylock!—a 'good' man with a man who can pay.[48]

Shylock, it would seem, is never far from Marx's thoughts when
he considers the behaviour of nineteenth-century entrepreneurs
and the principles of nineteenth-century economists.

Literature and the arts enter the world of the Paris Manuscripts in many different ways. They appear, first of all, as one
of the 'specifically human acts' (*menschliche Gattungsakte*) whose
products seem less alien to men than many a more concrete
and utilitarian object, and which have therefore attracted a host
of previous thinkers away from the study of material production
and industry. The old *topos* of the world as a 'book' in which
men might read the works of God is significantly varied in
Marx's image of industry as a book that may teach us to understand man's essential nature:

> . . . the history of industry and the objective existence it has now
> acquired is an open book of man's faculties; it is human psychology

available for inspection by the senses. Hitherto this was not conceived in its inseparable connection with man's essential being, but
only in an external relation of utility, because, moving in the realm
of alienation, people could only apprehend the generalized existence
of man, religion, or history in its abstract and universal form as
politics, art, literature, etc.; only these were apprehended as the
reality of human faculties and powers in specifically human acts.*
In ordinary material industry (which one can consider as part of
that general development just as well as one can consider the general
development as a particular part of industry—for all human
activity has hitherto been labour, i.e. industry, activity alienated
from itself) we have the objectified faculties of man before us as
sensuous, strange, utilitarian objects, in the form of alienation. A
psychology for which this remains a closed book—which has no
access to the part of history that is most fully present to the senses
and most accessible—cannot become a genuine science with a real
content.[49]

Literature must therefore be seen, not in isolation, but in conjunction with other, more 'prosaic' human activities and products. Its study must become part of a 'science of man'.

Literature also has its place in the anti-Romantic polemic
of the Paris Manuscripts—in their attempt to dispel the aura
of poetry which Romantic writers have woven around pre-
capitalist Germany and around feudal conditions still lingering
on in the nineteenth century. In the course of a brilliant passage
Marx confronts the auto- and allo-stereotypes of landowner and
manufacturer in a way which leaves no doubt on which side
Romantic poetry is ranged. The landowner is made to boast of
the 'poetry of reminiscence' (*Poesie der Erinnerung*) that adheres to
feudalism, and is made to reject the manufacturer's view of life
with a phrase adopted from *As You Like It*, II. i: 'sans honour, he
calls it, sans principles, sans poetry, sans everything'. The cap-
tains of industry and commerce are made to counter this
Shakespearian suggestion by calling into service another of the
masterpieces of world literature, Cervantes's *Don Quixote*. The
man of movable property

deplores his opponent as a blockhead who—and this is correct—
has no clear idea of what he really is, who wants to replace moral

---

* or: 'actions characterizing humanity as a species', 'human species-acts'.

[49] *MEW EB* I, 542–3.

capital and a free labour-market by uncouth, immoral force and serfdom. He depicts him as a Don Quixote who hides under a semblance of upright straightforwardness, common interest, and stability, things which are in reality quite different: covetous epicureanism, the interests of one narrow group, evil intent. He declares him an artful monopolist; he deflates his reminiscences, his poetry, his cloudy uplift by narrating, historically and sarcastically, what baseness, cruelty, exclusiveness, prostitution, infamy, anarchy, and rebellion were in fact manufactured in his romantic castles.[50]

Literature, it would seem, can veil in specious beauty things that are ugly when looked at in their nakedness. But literature—the creations of great writers, Shakespeare and Cervantes—can also help to make clear what men, and things, really are. It can help to convey judgements, too: once again we see Marx adopting the 'variation' method he had tried out in the Shylock passage of his Hegel essay (see above, p. 63); the noble Don Quixote of Cervantes helps to 'place' the ignoble nature of men whose prototype he seems, in other respects, to be.

Whatever case the modern capitalist may have against the landowner, however (and Marx concedes that the case is formidable), his self-image is to be shown as no less unjustifiably flattering than that of his opponent. The society of which he is the representative has alienated man from all the results of his labour—and this includes man's artistic creations. He himself, given over to money-making, has no time for anything as 'useless' as books and theatres: 'The less you eat, drink, buy books, go to the theatre, go to the ball, go to the inn, think, love, theorize, sing, paint, fence, etc., the more you save, the larger your treasure grows, the treasure that moths and robbery cannot eat up, your *capital*.'[51] His workmen, on the other hand, have no choice at all: chained to their labour by dire economic necessity, they have no time to cultivate a taste for the arts: 'Music must first awaken man's musical sense . . . for the unmusical ear the most beautiful music is senseless . . . A worried, indigent man has no sense for the most beautiful spectacle.'[52] In such conditions literature becomes, all too easily, corrupt and servile: 'Political economy, the science of wealth . . . is at the same time the science of asceticism, and its true ideal is

[50] *MEW EB* I, 527.   [51] *MEW EB* I, 549.   [52] *MEW EB* I, 541–2.

the ascetic but usurous miser and the ascetic but productive slave. Its moral ideal is the workman who deposits part of his wages in the savings-bank, and to convey this its favourite idea it has even found a servile art. It has been brought, in sentimental fashion, on to the stage.'[53] Plays in the wake of Lillo's *The Merchant of London* may thus be seen, through Marx's eyes, as sentimental expressions of the ideology of a dominant class.

The most memorable pages of the Paris Manuscripts are undoubtedly those which deal with the 'alienation', 'externalizations', and 'reification' (*Entfremdung, Entäußerung,* and *Vergegenständlichung*) of human labour. In the following passage, the link between Marx's socio-economic critique, and Feuerbach's critique of religion, may still be clearly discerned:

The more the worker externalizes himself in his work, the more powerful becomes the alien, objective world that he creates opposite himself, the poorer he becomes himself in his inner life and the less he can call his own. It is just the same in religion. The more man puts into God, the less he retains in himself. The worker puts his life into the object and this means that it no longer belongs to him but to the object. So the greater this activity, the more the worker is without an object. What the product of his labour is, that he is not. So the greater this product the less he is himself. The externalization of the worker in his product implies not only that his labour becomes an object, an exterior existence but also that it exists outside him, independent and alien, and becomes a self-sufficient power opposite him, that the life which he has lent to the object affronts him, hostile and alien.[54]

Marx adds:

The more the worker produces the less he has to consume, the more values he creates, the more valueless and bereft of dignity he himself becomes, the more formed the product, the more deformed the worker, the more civilized the product, the more barbaric the worker, the more powerful the work, the more powerless the worker becomes, the more cultured [*geistreicher*] the work, the more uncultured [*geistloser*] the worker becomes, and more of a slave to nature . . . [Labour] produces beauty, but cripples the worker . . . It produces culture [*Geist*], but also imbecility and cretinism for the worker.[55]

[53] *MEW EB* I, 549.   [54] *ET* 135; *MEW EB* I, 512.
[55] *ET* 136; *MEW EB* I, 513.

In all these denunciations broadly aesthetic antinomies—
'beauty' versus 'deformation', 'civilization' versus 'barbarism'—
play an important part. It is no wonder, therefore, that when
Marx wants to convey his sense of what has been lost, his sense
of what 'alienation' means in practice, he again and again
finds himself driven, in the Paris Manuscripts, to the creations
of great writers:

For the workman even the need for fresh air ceases to be a need.
Man returns to his cave-dwelling which is now, however, tainted
with the mephitic, pestilential odour of civilization, which he
occupies only precariously, as an alien power, from which he can be
driven any day if he does not pay for it. And for this house of death
he must pay. The 'dwelling of light', which Aeschylus' Prometheus
names as one of the great gifts by which he turned savages into
men, ceases to exist for the workman. Light, air etc., the simplest
animal cleanliness ceases to figure among the needs of men.[56]

Aeschylus' vision of a 'dwelling of light', Goethe's vision of
'the firm, well-founded earth',[57] remind men of what they
have lost.

No less, however, can the great artists convey to us, in pity
and memorable form, what it is that makes for 'alienation'
—seen by Marx, as R. J. Bernstein has rightly reminded us,
as 'a social category, a category for understanding "political
economy", not an ontological category rooted in the nature of
man'.[58] Goethe's Mephistopheles is enlisted to explain how
money can 'make up' for gross deficiencies; how, if I can pay
for six horses, I have the power, not only of my own hands,
feet, head, and backside, but also of those horses. As Mephistopheles explains to Faust:

> Was Henker! Freilich Händ' und Füße
> Und Kopf und Hintre,* die sind dein!
> Doch alles, was ich frisch genieße,
> Ist das drum weniger mein?

* Goethe's text reads 'H— —', which Marx expands into 'Hintre' (= 'Hintern',
bottom). Goethe, surely, meant 'Hoden' (= testicles).

---

[56] *MEW EB* I, 548.
[57] *MEW EB* I, 577 (Marx here quotes, inaccurately, from Goethe's poem
Grenzen der Menschheit).
[58] R. J. Bernstein, *Praxis and Action* (London, 1971), p. 49.

Wenn ich sechs Hengste zahlen kann
Sind ihre Kräfte nicht die meine?
Ich renne zu und bin ein rechter Mann
Als hätt' ich vierundzwanzig Beine.

Why, hang it all! Your hands and feet
And head and bottom, they are yours;
But things which I use at my pleasure—
Are they less wholly mine?
If I can pay for six stallions,
Are not their powers mine?
I speed along, a proper man,
As though I had four and twenty legs.

That may seem a *positive* characterization of the power of money, and so, in many ways, it is. Marx is careful to point out, however, that it is Mephistopheles' voice we are hearing, and he draws out implications that are far from admirable. These include the smudging of personality and individuality; the blotting-out of moral and intellectual distinctions; and above all—what is only just implied in Goethe's reference to 'stallions' —the wrenching-awry of the laws of natural attraction between the sexes:

What exists for me through the medium of money, what I can pay for, i.e. what money can buy, is what *I am* as the possessor of money. My power is as great as the power of money. The properties of money are my—the possessor's—properties and essential powers. What I *am* and what I *can do* is, then, not at all determined by my individuality. I am ugly, but I can buy myself the most beautiful woman. Hence, I am not ugly, for the effect of ugliness, its power to repel, has been annihilated by money. In my individuality I am lame, but money procures me four and twenty legs; hence, I am not lame. I am a wicked, dishonest, unscrupulous, dull-witted man, but money is honoured and so is its possessor. Money is the highest good, so its possessor is good. Besides, money saves me the trouble of being dishonest; hence, I am presumed honest. I am dull of mind, but money is the true mind and spirit of all things—how, then, could its possessor be dull-witted? Moreover, he can buy himself intelligent people, and is not he who has power over the intelligent more intelligent than they? When I can perform, through money, everything the human heart desires, do I not possess all human capacities? Does not my money, then, transform all my incapacities into their opposite?[59]

The negative sides of money which this commentary suggests—money's power to pervert everything into its opposite—are brought out more clearly, in Marx's view, by Shakespeare's Timon of Athens in the lowest depths of his disillusion and misanthropy:

> Gold? Yellow, glittering, precious gold? No, gods,
> I am no idle votarist: roots, you clear heavens!
> Thus much of this will make black, white; foul, fair;
> Wrong, right; base, noble; old, young; coward, valiant;
> . . . Why, this
> Will lug your priests and servants from your sides;
> Pluck stout men's pillows from below their heads:
> This yellow slave
> Will knit and break religions; bless th' accurst;
> Make the hoar leprosy adored; place thieves,
> And give them title, knee, and approbation,
> With senators on the bench! this is it
> That makes the wappen'd widow wed again;
> She whom the spittal house and ulcerous sores
> Would cast the gorge at, this embalms and spices
> To th' April day again. Come, damned earth,
> Thou common whore of mankind, that putt'st odds
> Among the rout of nations, I will make thee
> Do thy right nature.

And again:

> O thou sweet king-killer and dear divorce
> 'Twixt natural son and sire! Thou bright defiler
> Of Hymen's purest bed! Thou valiant Mars!
> Thou ever young, fresh, loved and delicate
> Whose blush doth thaw the consecrated snow
> That lies on Dian's lap! Thou visible god!
> That solder'st close impossibilities,
> And mak'st them kiss! That speak'st with every tongue,
> To every purpose! O thou touch of hearts!
> Think, thy slave man rebels; and by thy virtue
> Set them into confounding odds, that beasts
> May have the world in empire![60]

---

[59] *MEW EB* I, 564–5. The translation from *Faust* is that of Bayard Taylor, revised by Stuart Atkins. It comes from Part I of the play; the scene is headed 'Studierzimmer'.   [60] *Timon of Athens*, IV. iii; *MEW EB* I, 563–4.

'Shakespeare portrays the essence of money excellently', Marx comments, without specific ascription to Timon. It is no part of his purpose to discuss how far, if at all, these represent Shakespeare's own views—he takes it for granted (as well he might!) that anyone who read such a passage would know it is the misanthropist Timon who speaks, it is Timon who ironically calls money 'sweet', 'young', 'fresh', 'loved', and 'delicate', it is Timon who gloats over his ability to make the common whore of mankind act according to her nature. Nor does he set out to trace the provenance of the ideas here expressed, to examine how far they were commonplaces in Shakespeare's day and earlier. What he does proceed to do, in the exegesis that follows, is to show how memorably this passage expresses certain aspects of the functions of money in which he himself was then becoming interested: its power to take the place of God, its power to transform, debase and degrade, its power to act as whore and pander among men and nations:

Shakespeare brings out two particular properties of money:
(1) It is the visible Godhead, the transformation of all human and natural qualities into their opposites, the general confusion and inversion of things; it makes impossibilities fraternize.
(2) It is the universal whore, the universal pander between men and peoples.
The inversion and confusion of all human and natural qualities, the fraternization of impossibilities—the *divine* power—of money lies in its being essentially the alienated, externalized and self-externalizing 'species-being' [*Gattungswesen*] of man. It is the externalized capacities of humanity.
What I cannot do as a man, thus what my individual faculties cannot do, that I can do through money. Thus money turns each of these faculties into something that it is not, i.e. into its opposite.[61]

The medieval attitude to money which Timon adopts at the nadir of his fortunes—an attitude which, as Laurence Lerner has said, does not differ in its essentials from that taken up by Chaucer's Pardoner in his sermon on the text: 'Cupidity is the root of all evil'—this attitude is one that remained congenial to Marx even after his economic studies had shown him many of the ways in which a modern money economy serves the cause of progress.

[61] *MEW EB* I, 565.

Literature reminds us of a health we have lost (Aeschylus' 'dwelling of light'); literature diagnoses our corruption (Timon's 'common whore of mankind'); and literature will have its part to play in our cure. Alienation, Marx believes, can be overcome, and it will be overcome with the help of a single, all-embracing science, which he called 'the science of man' and which would include the natural sciences and economics along with aesthetics: 'there will be just one science'.[62]

It is not difficult to see that Marx's analysis of the predicament of modern man has much in common with that of Schiller's *On the Aesthetic Education of Man*, summarized by its greatest English interpreters as an indictment of

the evils of specialization, whether of knowledge or skill, or of one function of the psyche at the expense of the others; the dissociation of what was once united—sensibility and thought, feeling and morality, body and mind; the cleavage between different branches of learning, between the sciences and the arts, between the development of the individual and the welfare of the community, between those who are too exhausted by the struggle for existence to think for themselves and those who are too indolent to make creative use of their leisure; the reduction of man to a mere cog in the wheel of an over-developed society; the de-humanization of the citizen in a State where he is valued for the function he performs rather than the being that he is, treated as a classifiable abstraction and administered by laws which seem irrelevant to him as a person.[63]

Schiller's essay is also relevant, however, to the vision of the 'total', 'all-round' unalienated man of the future which forms the climax of the Paris Manuscripts. In the process of achieving the conquest of alienation and a juster society (which Marx, unlike Schiller, now conceives as necessarily a communist one) literature and the arts have a vital role. They are part of the necessary self-creation of man; they create the very senses by which they are enjoyed:

Music must first awaken man's musical sense . . . Only through the concretely unfolded wealth of the human essence is the wealth of

---

[62] McLellan, op. cit., p. 244.

[63] Friedrich Schiller, *On the Aesthetic Education of Man, in a Series of Letters*, ed. and trans., with Introduction, Commentary, and Glossary of Terms, by E. M. Wilkinson and L. A. Willoughby (Oxford, 1967), p. xii; McLellan, op. cit., 243–4; Reeves, op. cit., p. 72.

subjective human sensuality in part developed, in part created: an ear for music, an eye to see beauty of form, in short all human senses capable of enjoyment, senses which find themselves confirmed as essentially human . . . The concrete unfolding of the human essence, in theoretical and practical regards, is necessary to achieve this end: to make man's senses truly human and to create that human sense which corresponds to the full wealth of the human and natural being.[64]

Behind such reminders of the classical German tradition of *Humanität* lurks an anxiety that rings out powerfully at the end of the section on Money:

Let us assume *man* to be *man*, and his relation to the world a human one. Then love can only be exchanged for love, trust for trust, etc. If you wish to enjoy art you must be an artistically cultivated person; if you wish to influence other people you must be a person who really has a stimulating and encouraging effect upon others. Every one of your relations to man and to nature must be a *specific expression* corresponding to the object of your will, of your *real individual* life.[65]

'"Let us assume man to be man"', Lionel Trilling has commented, '"and his relation to the world a human one." It is an astounding thing to say: in no other epoch of history had it been felt necessary to make the assumption explicit. Throughout the nineteenth century runs the thread of anxiety that man may not be man, that his relation to the world may cease to be a human one. Marx's expression of the anxiety was of singular intensity; but one need not have been of his political persuasion to share the apprehension. The perception that being was threatened by having was characteristic of the bourgeois moralists of the age. "Culture", said Matthew Arnold, "is not a having but a being and becoming." And Oscar Wilde, in his great essay, "The Soul of Man under Socialism", echoed Arnold: "The true perfection of man lies not in what man has but what man is."'[66]

The point here made by Trilling can be put another way. If literature and the arts correspond to specific human needs which they themselves must mould in the act of satisfying them, then it follows that such needs can easily be perverted, or that

[64] *MEW EB* I, 541–2. [65] *MEW EB* I, 567.
[66] L. Trilling, *Sincerity and Authenticity* (London, 1972), pp. 124–5.

false needs may be called into being by those who have a commerical interest in doing so. The Paris Manuscripts therefore include a powerful critique of 'imaginary appetites' in nineteenth-century European society.

Every man speculates on creating a new need in another so as to drive him to a fresh sacrifice, to place him in a new dependence, to tempt him to new modes of pleasure entailing economic ruin. Everyone seeks to call into being, for the satisfaction of his own selfish desires, an *alien* power [*eine* fremde *Wesenskraft*] to which others can be subjected. As the mass of objects increases, the realm of those alien beings to which man is subjected also grows. Every new product is potentially a new means by which men can cheat and rob one another . . . The extension of products and needs makes man become, subjectively, the inventive and ever-calculating slave of inhuman, exquisitely cunning, unnatural, and *imaginary* appetites.[67]

This analysis may well be thought even more apposite today than when Marx first made it over a hundred and thirty years ago.

In the Paris Manuscripts the *Humanität* of Herder, Schiller, and Goethe is in the process of being wedded to a political purpose that derives from French socialists and communists, and to an economic analysis that is beginning to be indebted to the classical economists of England and Scotland. 'Here for the first time', McLellan rightly comments, 'what Engels described as the three constituent elements in Marx's thought—German idealist philosophy, French socialism and English economics—appear together, if not yet united.'[68] He might well have added to his list the classical literature of the Age of Goethe; though it must be remembered, as Lukács has pointed out, that Marx never believed maladies rooted in social conditions could be cured by improving the artistic consciousness.[69]

Three further aspects of the Paris Manuscripts deserve notice in our context. Marx scrutinizes not only books and their authors but also the readers to whom they appeal and who take them to their hearts. A less than classical product of the Age

---

[67] *MEW EB* I, 546–7; cf. I. Mészáros, *Marx's Theory of Alienation* (London, 1970), p. 115.
[68] McLellan, op. cit., p. 265.
[69] G. Lukács, *Goethe and his Age*, trans. R. Anchor (London, 1968), p. 84.

of Goethe, Justus Möser's *Patriotic Fantasies* (*Patriotische Phantasien*, 1775–86), Marx describes as 'distinguished by the fact that they never, for a single moment, go beyond the humdrum, petty-bourgeois, domesticated horizon of the philistines and that they are nonetheless pure fantasies. This contradiction has made them so attractive to the German heart.'[70] Books, we see, have their history; they are not only written *by* men affected by ways of thinking and feeling in their own class and society, but also *for* men living in a definite society and representing strata of that society. The tale of their reception has, therefore, for the Marx of the Paris Manuscripts, its own significance and importance.

The second of these three aspects may be observed in a passage of the Paris Manuscripts which deals, not with a literary, but with a philosophical text—with Hegel's *Phenomenology of the Spirit*: 'The *Phenomenology* is . . . a hidden, mystifying critique, still unclear to itself; but in so far as it steadily grasps man's *alienation*—even if "man" appears in the guise of "mind" or "spirit"—*all* the elements of criticism lie concealed in it, *prepared* already, and *elaborated,* in a way that rises far above Hegel's own standpoint.'[71] The principle here proclaimed—that an author may speak more truly than he knows himself—could easily be transferred from philosophy to literature.

Lastly: the presence of Mephistopheles, acknowledged in one famous and important passage which has already been quoted, can be discerned in other passages too, passages in which Marx has not drawn specific attention to it:

Every product is a bait with which to seduce away the other's very being, his money; every real and possible need is a weakness which will lead the fly to the glue-pot . . .; every need is an opportunity to approach one's neighbour in the semblance of the utmost amiability and to say to him: dear friend, I will give you what you require, but you know the necessary condition; *you know with what kind of ink you have to sign yourself over to me; I dupe you in providing enjoyment for you* [my italics].[72]

The voice of the evil spirit tempting men to a devil's bargain can be clearly heard in the clauses I have italicized. In a money economy man plays *vis-à-vis* his neighbour the role that Mephistopheles plays *vis-à-vis* Faust. Marx's reading, and his

[70] *MEW EB* I, 527. [71] *MEW EB* I, 573.
[72] *MEW EB* I, 547 (*EPM* 148).

early attempts at independent literary creation, achieve a sym-
biosis with his socio-political interests in such narrative and
dramatic passages.

Marx writes in the Paris Manuscripts:

Admittedly animals also produce. They build themselves nests,
dwellings, like the bees, beavers, ants, etc. But an animal only
produces what it needs immediately, for itself or its offspring, it
produces one-sidedly, while man produces universally; it produces
only under the sway of immediate physical need, whilst man
produces even when he is free from physical need—he truly produces, in fact, only when he is free from such need . . . An animal
forms things in accordance with the standard and the need of the
species to which it belongs, while man knows how to produce in
accordance with the standard of every species, and knows how to
apply everywhere the inherent standard of the object. Man therefore also forms things in accordance with the laws of beauty.

And again:

Only through the objectively unfolded richness of man's essential
being is the richness of subjective *human* sensibility—a musical ear,
an eye for beauty of form, in short, *senses* capable of human grati-
fication, senses confirming themselves as essential powers of *man*—
either cultivated or brought into being. For not only the five senses
but also the so-called mental senses, the practical senses (will, love,
etc.)—in a word, *human* sense, the humanity of the senses—comes
to be by virtue of *its* object, by virtue of *humanized* nature. The
formation of the five senses has been the work of the whole history of
the world down to the present day.[73]

Here, as István Mészáros has argued,[74] lies the most lasting
contribution the Paris Manuscripts have made to our understanding of literature: in their demonstration of the way the
arts arise from specifically human needs, which go well beyond
the purely physical and economic; of the way they can create
and strengthen such needs in the very act of gratifying them;
of their place in the *self-creation* of man; of the extent to which,
even in an age Marx sees as one of 'alienation' and 'reification',
they may constitute a realm of comparative freedom, a realm
in which man's creative urges can find an outlet worthy of his
humanity. Even if once again Marx speaks, in the first of the

[73] *MEW EB* I, 517, 541.   [74] I. Mészáros, op. cit., pp. 190–214.

passages just quoted, of 'laws of beauty' without further explanation or elaboration, he does supply one clue to an essential feature of such 'laws': for the word *Maß* rings out again and again, a word which means not only 'standard' but also 'proportion', 'measure', and 'moderation'. An intimate union of form and content is clearly implied in Marx's praise of man's aesthetic sense, of his ability *überall das inhärente Maß dem Gegenstand anzulegen*[75]—'to apply everywhere the inherent standard of the object', 'to keep due proportion in everything'. But to be able to do this, the Paris Manuscripts proclaim, man must be liberated from pressures that force him to appropriate objects only to satisfy his crude physical needs; he must experience aesthetic objects, not only in thought but with all his senses, as *relating* to him, as affirmations of his own essential humanity—and that, for Marx, implies man's self-affirmation as a social, not just an individual, being.

Goethe's Mephistopheles takes a devilish outsider's joy in the perversions that money can bring about; Shakespeare's Shylock and Timon are victims of these perversions even while profiting from or exulting in them. The words of such characters, found and formed by Goethe and Shakespeare, aid Marx in conceiving and formulating his own message. They help him to see his own world more clearly and induce others to share his vision of topsy-turvy disorder—a vision to which he can then oppose that of a future state in which Mephistopheles could not delight, in which Shylock would find neither oppressor nor victim, and in which Timon's misanthropy would wither away for lack of nourishment. The inherent 'measure' or 'proportion' of art is at once an adumbration and a promise of the unalienated state we may hope for in that better and juster future.

[75] The word 'Maß', as has often been pointed out, is a key term in Marx's aesthetic thinking. Stefan Morawski has given an account of some of its meaning in the Paris Manuscripts: '(a) reproduction of the *structures of physical reality* (their shapes mainly . . .); and (b) various specific attributes of symmetry, regularity, proportion, and harmony, which provide an attractive and coherent whole such as differs from—or more exactly, *rivals*—the shapes of material reality. But whatever else "*Maß*" meant for Marx, in aesthetic context this term definitely indicates an *inner compact structure* of the work of art.' (*BM* 15.)

4 · Mysteries of Paris

'"Critical criticism", incarnated in Szeliga-
Vishnu, furnishes an apotheosis of *Les Mystères de
Paris*. Eugène Sue is dubbed a "critical critic".
When he learns of this he may well exclaim, with
Molière's bourgeois gentilhomme: "Par ma foi,
il y a plus de quarante ans que je dis de la prose,
sans que j'en susse rien; et je vous suis le plus
obligé du monde de m'avoir appris cela."'

(*MEW* II, 57)

THE *German–French Yearbooks* collapsed after the very first issue;
and the leading contributors to *Vorwärts*, Marx among them,
incurred such strong displeasure in Prussia that pressure was
put on the French government to expel them from French soil.
The French obliged, and Marx was forced to leave for Brussels
in February 1845. 'Of all the people I leave behind here', he had
written to Heine the previous month, 'Heine is the one I most
regret leaving. I would like to take you with me in my luggage.'[1]
His luggage did not, in the event, contain Heine; but it did hold
the manuscript of a work entitled *The Holy Family* (*Die heilige
Familie, oder Kritik der kritischen Kritik*)—the first of several books
he was to write in close collaboration with Friedrich Engels.
Engels in fact soon joined him in Brussels; the two friends
travelled to England together for a brief look at conditions
there. In England Marx met a number of German political
exiles, including the Communist Wilhelm Weitling, a tailor
turned writer whose work Marx had hailed with enthusiasm in
Vorwärts[2] but with whose views on the necessity of an immediate workers' rebellion, and on ultimate aims, he was soon
to disagree. After his return to Brussels Marx threw himself
once more into his studies, into that 'sea of books' which—as
Ruge had said—was his real element and outside which he

[1] *MEW* XXVII, 434.   [2] *MEW* I, 404–5.

could not live. He also began to speak at socialist meetings;
founded a 'German Workers' Society'; and enlisted correspondents in other European countries to keep himself abreast of
socialist and communist ideas. When a 'Communist League'
was formed in London, which incorporated the old 'League
of the Just', Marx and Engels were at once invited to join.
Both accepted; Engels attended the first congress of the new
League by himself, but he brought Marx with him to the second
congress, held (like the first) in London. At this second congress
in November 1847 the two friends were given the fateful commission to compose a manifesto for the new communist movement—a task they discharged with the brilliance and the
success which all the world now knows.[3]

The Holy Family, composed in 1844, contains a Preface signed
jointly by Engels and Marx and a number of essays, mainly
written by Marx, on aspects of Young Hegelianism. These
essays were prompted for the most part by articles in the
Literary Gazette (Allgemeine Literaturzeitung) whose editor was
the same Young Hegelian, Bruno Bauer, whom Marx had
already taken to task in his essay 'On the Jewish Question'.
The *Literary Gazette* provided Marx with material for a critique
of speculative idealism—of attempts, in the wake of Hegel, to
substitute such concepts as 'self-consciousness' and 'spirit'
(*Selbstbewußtsein* and *Geist*) for what Marx now conceived as
material, economically based realities. As its title indicates,
Bauer's journal was largely a review of books of all kinds; it is
not surprising, therefore, that one of Marx's contributions to
The Holy Family should turn out to be the most elaborate critique
he was ever to devote to a single work of fiction: Eugène Sue's
The Mysteries of Paris (Les Mystères de Paris).

The work so honoured had first seen the light as a *roman
feuilleton*—itself a new and fascinating phenomenon!—and its
successive instalments had kept the readers of the Paris *Journal
des Débats* in suspense from 1842 to 1843. The book edition,
translated into many languages, was an immediate world-wide
success; the editor of *Vorwärts*, the radical German language
paper to which Marx had contributed in Paris, was so enthusiastic about it that he not only advertised it in *Vorwärts*

[3] D. McLellan, *The Thought of Karl Marx* (London and New York, 1971),
pp. 29–30, 41.

and caused a German translation to be made, but even wrote a supplement volume.[4] In Bauer's *Literary Gazette* the novel had been made the occasion, by a bird-brained contributor who wrote under the pen-name 'Szeliga' and whose real name was Franz Zychlin von Zychlinsky, for an exercise in neo-Hegelian exegesis. It is this exegesis which provides the immediate impetus for Marx's critique; but he was clearly fascinated, and repelled, by the way Sue had combined thrilling adventures, improbable coincidences, melodramatic effects, grotesque distortions, and flat characters with a social preaching that becomes more shrill and insistent as the novel goes on.

Marx's examination proceeds on five levels at once. At the first level he holds Szeliga's interpretation against what we actually see happening in the novel—and here he has no difficulty in showing that the critic has (*a*) given simple incidents an absurdly improbable or demonstrably wrong interpretation in order to fit them into his speculative Hegelian scheme; (*b*) misunderstood the implications, and even the plain surface meaning of many passages because he was ignorant of the French metropolitan life from which Sue derived so many of his incidents; (*c*) missed the force of literary conventions like the (almost obligatory) ballroom scene which unites many characters whose fortunes the author has followed; (*d*) proclaimed platitudes as profound insights; (*e*) taken Sue's own obtrusive interpretations of his characters and incidents too much at their face value; (*f*) failed to take up a properly sceptical and critical stance *vis-à-vis* Sue's self-proclaimed social purpose; (*g*) overestimated the literary value of Sue's work; (*h*) couched his over- and mis-interpretations in a language that betrays alike his inability to think clearly and his matching inability to write decent German. In all these respects Szeliga was vulnerable, and Marx's shafts hit home. This analysis demonstrates beyond question the vacuity of at least one contributor to Bauer's journal and serves to show what a caricature speculative idealism could become in lesser hands than Hegel's.

But Marx's analysis works also at a second level, one more important in the present context. Here it is not Szeliga's interpretation that is held against Sue's novel, but Sue's own valua-

[4] Eugène Sue, *Gerolstein*, trans. H. Börnstein (Berlin, 1843).

tions, as they appear in the work itself, are held against what the work actually *shows*. Thus *The Mysteries of Paris* leaves its readers in no doubt that, despite certain well-advertised flaws, the novel's hero, Rodolphe de Gérolstein, is to be thought of as an admirable character and that his actions are considered to further the interests of justice. By closely analysing many strands of the action Marx demonstrates that the tale in fact speaks against the teller: that what the novel *shows* is a petty German prince indulging evil and selfish passions under a cloak of righteousness:

Rudolph* the 'good'! With his feverishly burning lust for revenge, his bloodthirstiness, his calm and considered rage, his hypocritical, casuistic varnishing-over of every vile impulse, he possesses precisely those passions for *evil* for whose sake he deprives others of their eyesight.[5]

Marx here makes an important point: a good part of the success of this sensational novel is due to its ability to let the reader gratify, in imagination, his lower passions while obtaining gratuitous uplift from the moral guise in which the novelist has made them appear. He supplements this with a series of further analyses in which the tale is made to speak against the teller. Are we to admire—as Sue would certainly seem to ask us to do—the moral development of the character known as *Le Chourineur*? Marx shows it up, by reference to the text, as the development of an independent man into a servile dog. Are we to rejoice at Fleur-de-Marie's 'salvation'? Marx shows how, after the initial boldness of his presentation of this centrally important character, Sue panders more and more crudely to moral and religious conventions:

Eugène Sue has raised himself above the horizon of his narrow world-view. He has affronted the prejudices of the bourgeoisie. He then delivered over Fleur-de-Marie to his hero Rudolph in order, no doubt, to atone for such temerity, in order to gain the applause of all old men and women, of the whole Parisian police force, of accepted religion, and of 'critical criticism'.[6]

* The Germanization, or re-Germanization, of the name Sue gave his hero is part of Marx's intended effect, and I therefore retain it in my translation.

---

[5] *MEW* II, 221.   [6] *MEW* II, 181.

Sue's ability to indulge at once the sadism of his readers and
the conventional morality accepted by their society is indeed
an important element in his success, and Marx deserves all
credit for having shown it up so clearly and so soon.

   Ultimately, as Marx demonstrates, Sue's ability to indulge his
readers in this way stems from the fact that he was indulging
himself. Sue satisfies, he says in one place, 'his monkish, bestial
delight in human self-abasement to such an extent . . . that
he makes the Schoolmaster kneel before the old witch Chouette
and the little goblin Tortillard'; and in another, again referring
to the character known as 'the Schoolmaster' (*le Maître d'École*):
'The idea of punishment which Rudolph applies in blinding
the Schoolmaster; the isolation of a man, throwing him back
on his own soul, cutting him off from the outside world—this
combination of judicial punishment with theological torture
finds its most decisive application in solitary confinement.
Therefore M. Sue also celebrates [in *The Mysteries of Paris*] the
system of solitary confinement.'[7] Such self-indulgences often
have sexual roots; and Marx's uncovering of such roots in his
comments on the blinding of the Schoolmaster anticipates
Freud's analyses of *Oedipus Tyrannos* and Hoffmann's 'The
Sandman': 'The Schoolmaster has misused his strength, and
Rudolph paralyses, lames, destroys it'. 'Human nature has to
be killed stone-dead so that its sickness can be healed.' 'The
punishment Rudolph inflicts on the Schoolmaster is that which
Origenes inflicted on himself. He *castrates* him; he robs him of
an organ of generation, the eye. "The eye is the light of the
body".'[8]

   At a third level of analysis Marx tries to hold the characters,
structures, incidents, and wording of *The Mysteries of Paris*, not
against the misunderstandings of an imperfect critic, not against
its author's own proclaimed or implied intentions, but against
the actualities of contemporary life whose 'mysteries' it professes
to reveal. It demonstrates the use Sue made of Jeremy Bentham's
ideas on judicial punishment and of the ideas, the very expressions, of Fourier—a use which Marx shows up as at once shallow
and perverse.[9] It demonstrates by contrast, how much social
truth may be hidden amidst the sensational incidents Sue has

        MEW II, 191–2, 197.   [8] *MEW* II, 188–9.
     [9] *MEW* II, 199, 205–6.

invented for his notary Jacques Ferrand: 'The stance maintained by the notary in Eugène Sue's novel is precisely that of
his official position. "Notaries are to the temporal life what
vicars are to the spiritual: they are the *depositories of our secrets.*
(Monteil, *Hist. des français et des div. états . . .*, t. ix, p. 37.)"'[10]
No wonder, Marx comments, that Parisian notaries saw in this
character a bitter libel on themselves and procured its excision
from the stage-version of *The Mysteries of Paris*. In other respects,
however, Sue was only too ready to make concessions to the
prejudices of his readers: Marx points particularly to the way
in which the sexual freedom of the Parisian *grisette* is lied away
in Sue's portrait of Rigolette: 'He had . . . to idealize the
grisette morally because of his devotion to the bourgeoisie and
his own over-exalted ideas. He had to remove the main point
from her situation in life and her character: the way the
grisette is ready to disregard the form of marriage, her naïve
relationship to the student and the workman. It is through this
very relationship that she presents a truly human contrast to
the hypocritical, narrow-minded, and selfish bourgeois wife
. . .'[11] Sue may not be reflecting the actualities of Parisian life
truly, any more than Dickens reflects those of London life when
he makes his prostitute characters, in *Oliver Twist* and *David
Copperfield*, so very genteel and self-abasing. What he does
convey truly, however, is something no less interesting to the
right reader: the prejudices of the social group for which his
work is written, and his own 'over-exalted ideas' which are also
socially directed and conditioned.

Such beliefs made Marx scrutinize the sayings as well as the
doings of Sue's characters with much greater scepticism than
Szeliga had done. The latter had greeted with enthusiasm the
'truth' revealed by an exclamation Sue had placed into the
mouth of the indigent workman Morel: 'If the rich only knew!
If the rich only knew! The misfortune is that they do not know
what poverty is.' Marx shows himself equally scornful of Sue
and of his Young-Hegelian interpreter:

What Mr Szeliga fails to appreciate is that Sue, in his desire to be
polite to the French bourgeoisie, here perpetrates an anachronism.
He modifies the motto of the French bourgeois in Louis XIV's
time—changing 'Ah! si le roi savait!' to 'Ah! si le riche savait!'—

---
[10] *MEW* II, 74.   [11] *MEW* II, 80.

and places it in the mouth of the workman Morel who lives in the time of Louis-Philippe's 'true charter' [*Charte vérité*]. In England and France at least such a *naïve* relationship between the rich and the poor no longer obtains. The scientific representatives of Wealth, the political economists, have made very detailed insights into the physical and moral miseries that attend on poverty widely accessible in these countries. To compensate for this they have proved that such miseries must stay as they are because the conditions which obtain today must stay as they are. In their careful calculations they have even reckoned out the *proportions* in which Poverty must decimate itself through death for the benefit of Wealth, and for its own benefit.[12]

Without some knowledge of historical facts, and of the various interpretations to which social relationships have been subjected, one cannot—in Marx's view—achieve the kind of insight which makes for good literary criticism.

A fourth level at which Marx's analysis proceeds need not detain us long. In the course of the novel Rodolphe is made to put into practice, and the implied narrator is made to expound, a number of Utopian social schemes—schemes which range from the establishment of a model farm to that of a bank for lending money to temporarily unemployed workers without charging interest. Marx has no difficulty in showing that such schemes are based on quite mistaken notions of how economic processes work or can be made to work. They depict operations on the body politic as absurdly impossible as the operation performed on the Schoolmaster's eyes would be on a living human body.

But—and this is the fifth and last level of discussion—Marx remained ever aware that *The Mysteries of Paris* must ultimately be judged as a novel, as a work of literature, and not as a piece of speculative philosophy, or a blue book, or a social tract. True, he does not use the guarded language of literary critics and speaks at times as though Sue were reporting facts from the lives of actually existing characters: as when he speculates on Rodolphe's way with his Gérolstein subjects, or when he tells us that Sue has 'preserved' (*aufbewahrt*) a remark the Schoolmaster made before his blinding, or when he calls a character Sue presents as honest and spiritually enlightened

[12] *MEW* II, 58–9.

a 'dissembling' priest. Peter Demetz has rightly taken him to task for this—here later writers must, clearly, tread more carefully than Marx did, and make important discriminations he has omitted to make.[13] His analysis of *The Mysteries of Paris* as a whole, however, leaves no doubt that Marx was fully aware of the distinction between fictional and real characters. One of the charges he brings against Sue is in fact precisely, as we have seen, that characters like Rigolette are not true to their real-life counterparts and that they are frequently motivated by laws that operate in the most trivial fictions.[14] Worst of all, Sue *talks* instead of *presenting*; motivation and action fall apart. His characters are said to have 'balloons' coming from their mouths, like old-fashioned cartoons, through which they explain to other characters and to the reader what the author is incapable of showing in action—they have to proclaim their author's literary intention, 'that which determines him to make them act in this way and no other', as if it were *their* reflection, the conscious motive of their action. The characters themselves, *post factum*, have to find the novelist's sensational procedures reasonable.[15]

'By locking me in a cellar,' [Sue makes the Schoolmaster say to La Chouette] 'by having me gnawed by rats, by making me suffer hunger and thirst, you have completed my regeneration. Solitude has purified me.' His animal howlings, mad rage, dreadful thirst for revenge, flagrantly contradict this moral phraseology.[16]

Such contradictions are not, Marx argues, the deliberate subtleties of an intelligent author. They are due rather to crude and clumsy literary techniques that match crudities of feeling and absurdities of thinking characteristic of the author as well as of the vast readership his thrillers found in nineteenth-century Europe. It should occasion no surprise, therefore, that (as Marx shows) of the two mentors Sue invents for his princely hero the intelligent one, Polidori, should be depicted as evil and corrupt, and the stupid one, Murph, as honest and virtuous.

With all its faults—which include the occasional failure, already diagnosed, to keep the characters invented by the novelist distinct from the characters of real life, as well as undue diffuseness coupled with somewhat elephantine playfulness—

---

[13] Demetz, *Marx, Engels und die Dichter*, p. 107.   [14] e.g. *MEW* II, 70.
[15] *MEW* II, 174, 193–4.   [16] *MEW* II, 194.

Marx's essay on *The Mysteries of Paris* remains one of the most instructive analyses of a best-seller that has ever been attempted. It makes one regret all the more that he never found time to put into execution any of the plans he formed to write an extended critique of greater works; plans which at one time included, if his son-in-law Paul Lafargue can be believed, a study of Balzac's *Human Comedy*.[17]

What gives Marx's discussion of *The Mysteries of Paris* its special interest and importance, however, is that it reveals more clearly than any other single text assumptions about the nature and the study of literature which Marx never had to gainsay in the course of his life. The first of these is that many different kinds of knowledge and insight must be co-ordinated if a work of literature is to be fully and fairly judged. Marx brings to bear his understanding of economic processes in modern society when he shows up the absurdity of schemes for social amelioration given authorial approval in *The Mysteries of Paris*; his experience of French society when he comments on the relative verisimilitude of various invented characters and actions; his reading of memoirs—notably those of François Vidocq—when he comes to speak of the role played by the police-spy *Bras rouge* in the mechanics of Sue's plot; his reading of French poetry (the *Poésies érotiques* of Évariste de Parny), as well as of travellers' tales, when he scrutinizes the *erotic* appeal of the *exotic* which Sue so skilfully exploits in the figure of Cécily; his reading of Sue's other works when he comments on his deliberate appeal to the reader's desire to be agreeably frightened and held in suspense; his wide acquaintance with other nineteenth-century novels when he shows up the literary conventions that Sue so readily adopts; and his knowledge of the great works of world literature when he uses allusions to *Faust, Don Quixote, Le Bourgeois Gentilhomme*, and *Georges Dandin* to 'place' Sue and his neo-Hegelian commentator, and to drive home his points. The reader who approaches a work of imaginative literature—as Szeliga seems to have approached *The Mysteries of Paris*—with little equipment save the experience of a German provincial and a head filled with cloudy neo-Hegelian notions, is likely to go badly astray. Marx pointedly compares Szeliga's reactions to Sue with those of a schoolboy reading

[17] *ÜKL* I, 21.

Schiller's *The Robbers*;[18] in both cases there are elements in the work which are particularly likely to call forth uncritical, over-emotional responses in the immature and unironic.

Among the equipment of a competent reader (so Marx's analysis suggests) common sense, a sense of proportion, and a sense of humour have an important place; and it is surely not without significance that in his discussion of *The Mysteries of Paris* Marx so naturally turns to folk-literature—chap-books, folk-songs, popular jingles—for an illustration of these qualities, for an exposure of stupidity, and for a deflation of pretentiousness or sentimentality. Szeliga and Sue's hero Rodolphe are mocked by a snatch of verse from the chap-book *The Seven Swabians* (*Die sieben Schwaben*):

> Hahnemann,
> Geh du voran,
> Du hast die großen Wasserstiefel an!

> Hahnemann,
> You go ahead,
> You are wearing your Wellingtons!;

the critic's unworldly innocence is likened to that of the nun in German folk-song:

> Ich gedenk' an keine Liebe,
> Ich gedenk' an keinen Mann,
> Ich gedenk' an Gott den Vater,
> Der mich erhalten kann.

> I do not think of love,
> I do not think of men,
> I think of God the Father
> Who can sustain me;

and the activities of 'critical criticism' under the leadership of Bruno and Edgar Bauer are summed up in a French jingle:

> Quand les bœufs vont deux à deux,
> Le *labourage* en va mieux!

> When the oxen walk two by two,
> Tilling the field goes all the better.

[18] *MEW* II, 214.

German chap-books—*Volksbücher*—are also drawn on for
symbols (like that of the inexhaustible purse in *Fortunatus*) and
types (like the hero of *Till Eulenspiegel*, with his characteristic
mixture of simplicity and cunning).[19] They thus perform much
the same function that *Don Quixote, Faust, Le Bourgeois Gentilhomme*, and *Georges Dandin* also perform in the chapters of *The
Holy Family* devoted to *The Mysteries of Paris*.[20] The literature
of the common people, and that of the educated and privileged,
may both enrich life and increase understanding; though there
are, as the case of Eugène Sue's novels is particularly well fitted to
show, some works of imaginative literature which are more apt
to obfuscate the unwary reader's understanding, and to pervert
his emotional life, than to enrich either.

In measuring imaginative literature against 'reality' Marx
is not crudely comparing a 'reflection' with some 'object out
there' which is reflected. Men's interpretations of reality
constitute an important part of the raw material of literature;
Sue's novel depicts and reveals such interpretations, and itself
constitutes a complex interpretation. This latter is not merely
personal but may be shown to be representative; its preconceptions are for the most part those of the readership which took
such delight in *The Mysteries of Paris*—the French (and the
European) bourgeoisie of the mid nineteenth century. Such
preconceptions shared by author and readers, such an appeal to
stock response, played an important part in the story of the
novel's reception and success.

Marx does not pay much attention to form and structure, but
all the more to the novelist's and dramatist's evocation of
character. In assessing fictional characters, he believes, the
critic must take into account not only descriptions of such
characters' *state of mind* and the *actions* they are made to perform, but also evocations of the *physical environment* in which they
have their being, and the *language* they are made to speak. The
discussion of Eugène Sue makes this quite explicit:

[19] *MEW* II, 172, 170, 223, 212, 213. Till Eulenspiegel had already served Marx
well in 1842, in a review of a book on Bruno Bauer; there Eulenspiegel had
appeared in close proximity to Sancho Panza.

[20] Marx introduces references to *Faust* and *Don Quixote* into his discussion of
Eugène Sue (*MEW* II, 65, 221). He also refers to Goethe's *Zahme Xenien* (*MEW*
II, 186), and Molière's *Le Bourgeois Gentilhomme* and *Georges Dandin* (*MEW* II,
57, 206). In addition we find parody of the Bible, and a quotation from the *Dies
irae* (*MEW* II, 222).

In the criminals' hiding-holes and their thieves' slang the criminal's character is mirrored [*spiegelt sich ab*]; they are part of his being, their depiction belongs to his depiction, just as the depiction of the *petite maison* belongs to the depiction of the *femme galante*.[21]

Above all: the critic must ask himself whether a given fictional character is at once individual and representative. Marx approves of Sue's portrait of Mme Pipelet, for instance, because she is a credible individual and also 'represents' her type, profession, and class: she is the essential Parisian *portière*. The verb Marx uses to express his approval, *repräsentieren*, has the two senses of 'depicting' and 'standing for'.[22] In the same way Sue's portrait of Jacques Ferrand is seen as representing, in important respects, the French notary.

Where an author fails to create convincing and 'representative' characters—as Sue frequently fails to do—two causes may operate, either singly or together. The author may be incompetent and careless—instead of creating lifelike characters he rests content with puppets who speak about themselves with the author's voice. The author may also, however, be serving the society whose paid entertainer he is, at the expense of his artistic integrity. He does this, consciously or unconsciously, by distorting reality, or the logic of his characters, in directions indicated by the self-interest of a dominant class, and by the morality which serves such self-interest. The sexual dishonesties of *The Mysteries of Paris*, and Sue's unsatisfactory presentation and development of many of his characters, Marx attributes to the second of these causes.

An author's intentions, in so far as they can be gathered from his own explicit utterances or deduced from the internal evidence provided by his works, are shown to be relevant to an analysis such as Marx attempts in *The Holy Family* and elsewhere:

Eugène Sue himself declares, that he . . . counts on his readers' *curiosité craintive*. In all his novels M. Sue counted on this fearful curiosity in his readers. One has only to recall Atar Gull, le Salamandre, Plick and Plock etc.[23]

[21] *MEW* II, 59.
[22] *MEW* II, 78 ('Bei Eugen Sue repräsentiert Anastasia Pipelet die *Pariser Portière*').
[23] *MEW* II, 59.

The reader should, however, always trust the tale more than its author. A work may reveal far more than its progenitor consciously intended. This may lead to several kinds of contradiction between implied intention and achievement. A work may throw an unexpected and unintended light on an author's most carefully hidden social attitudes, and those he presupposes in his audience. This is the case when Sue's hero Rodolphe, clearly meant to be (despite certain acknowledged faults) a dispenser of social justice, reveals to the probing eye a sadism and a predatory nature which come out with frightening clarity in his dealings with what would nowadays be called the underprivileged: he either maims them (in the person of the Schoolmaster) or pushes them into an unfruitful and unreproductive existence (in the person of Fleur-de-Marie) or reduces them to the status of a faithful dog (in the person of Le Chourineur). In his early pages on Fleur-de-Marie, on the other hand, Sue depicts reality—to Marx's approving eye—more fully and truly than his world-view would seem to allow. 'Eugène Sue has raised himself above the horizon of his own narrow *Weltanschauung*. He has delivered a slap in the face of bougeois prejudices.'[24] This is the kind of 'contradiction' which Engels and Lukács were later to praise so highly in the case of Balzac.

Marx's discussion of *The Mysteries of Paris* illustrates a further kind of interplay between surface and hidden meaning. Without knowing it himself, an author may speak of one thing to the conscious mind while whispering another to the subconscious. Marx was, as we have seen, particularly sensitive to the sexual overtones and undertones of Sue's novel. His comments on blinding as symbolic castration anticipate Freud; but they add an element of social criticism which was foreign to Freud's purpose. What ultimately matters about the blinding of the Schoolmaster in Sue's story is not simply that it provides an 'acceptable' substitute for castration. Marx presents it as an act of sadistic aggression perpetrated by one fictional individual against another in the guise of even-handed justice. Since such individuals are also 'representative', however, and are clearly represented as belonging to different social classes, it may ultimately be seen as a symbol of the relation between these classes: the dominant one tries to emasculate the other, to

[24] *MEW* II, 181.

drain away some of its strength in order to render it harmless or servile, while presenting the class-struggle as a simple battle between good and evil.

His disquisition on Sue's novel reveals something of the fundamental human values which Marx prizes. This is a point Stefan Morawski has made in commenting on Marx's treatment of Sue's Fleur-de-Marie. 'Fleur-de-Marie', Morawski tells us, 'is said by Marx to have a vitality that goes beyond her bourgeois context and forces its way through the clumsy moralizing imposed on the human subject-matter by Sue himself'.[25] The character, in other words, exhibits to the reader a force and a *joie de vivre* which seem to go well beyond Sue's conscious intention. Such force derives, of course, from the potential of the human type Sue has chosen to depict. And Morawski goes on to argue, with some justice, that the values embodied in Fleur-de-Marie have their equivalents in the values Marx finds in literature and the arts. 'The unfailing appreciation Marx shows for the expression in art of sturdy and robust sensuality . . ., indomitable will, resilient enthusiasm and passionate intellectual powers, is seen in his comments on the works of Aeschylus and Shakespeare.'[26]

Several other aspects of *The Holy Family* must be considered at least briefly in our context. One is the wide deployment of literary quotations, ranging from the rhymed motto of a revolutionary journal of 1789 (Loustalot's *Révolutions de Paris*) to a snatch from Marmontel's one-act comedy *Lucile*.[27] Bruno Bauer's somewhat bilious philosophy is reported in words taken from one of Mephistopheles' speeches in Goethe's *Faust* Part I, and—later—in words spoken by the protagonist of Heine's cycle *The North Sea*:

> Und ein Narr wartet auf Antwort

> And a fool waits for an answer.

In his analysis of contemporary German speculations about love Marx quotes, successively, from Shakespeare (Berowne's 'But love, first learned in a lady's eye / Lives not alone immured in the brain'—*Love's Labour's Lost*, iv. iii) and Schiller (four lines from *Das Mädchen aus der Fremde* ('The Maiden from

---

[25] *BM* 36.   [26] *BM* 36.   [27] *MEW* II, 87, 152.

Afar')).[28] The Shakespeare quotation, it will be noticed, is calculated to bring airy speculations down to earth; the Schiller
quotation, on the other hand, is used ironically to increase the
distance from reality. The juxtaposition of these two quotations
thus adumbrates that confrontation of a Shakespearian and
a Schillerian mode which will form so prominent a feature of
Marx's criticism of Lassalle's *Franz von Sickingen*. From now on
Marx will frequently quote Schiller in ironic contexts; he has
clearly come to feel that Schiller's work, however admirable it
may be in itself, is too easily annexed by German philistines.

The Holy Family, moreover, chastises the sins committed by
Bauer and his followers against the German language at least
as forcefully as their sins against life. 'Reichardt misuses foreign
words, which are quoted at length; Faucher creates German
words on English principles of word-formation; Edgar Bauer
mishandles Proudhon's French, which is, unlike German, "the
language of politics and of thoughtful observation"; Szeliga
mixes his metaphors; Bruno Bauer writes a hopeless jargon of
apology and qualification.'[29] Thus once again we see Marx, with
Engels's help this time, deploying the weapons of literary
criticism against his opponents; weapons which are sharpened,
more than once, by parody of his opponents' style.

In the course of *The Holy Family* Marx and Engels confront
what Edgar Bauer and others read into Proudhon with what
Proudhon really says; and in so doing they broach the problem,
which will become so prominent in Marx's later economic
works, of the differing 'intrinsic' and 'exchange' value of
literary works in a society given over to the accumulation of
wealth. They report Proudhon's belief that a man of talent is
not to be seen, in any simplistic or mechanistic way, as solely
a product of his society, and that the artist, the savant, and the
poet are best rewarded by being permitted to dedicate themselves without hindrance to their science and their art.[30]
No approval or disapproval of Proudhon's views is signalled
on this occasion; the authors of *The Holy Family* seek only to
report them more accurately than the 'critical critics' have
managed to do.

[28] *MEW* II, 150, 166, 22, 23. Marx slightly misquotes Heine's poem.
[29] S. E. Hyman, *The Tangled Bank. Darwin, Marx, Frazer and Freud as Imaginative Writers* (New York, 1966), p. 90.   [30] *MEW* II, 49–50.

The speculations of 'critical critics' are also devalued by the remark that in politics, in literature, and in theology they recognize only the highfalutin', grandiose, 'official' aspects of history (*die politischen, literarischen und theologischen Haupt- und Staatsaktionen der Geschichte*).[31] What no 'critical critic' seems able to appreciate, Marx and Engels declare, is the nobility shown by the 'lower' classes of their day: 'One must have experienced the urge to know, the moral energy, the restless drive to self-development, shown by the French and English workers, in order to gain some conception of the *human* nobility of this movement.'[32] Such human nobility is giving rise, Marx and Engels add, to a 'new literature in prose and poetry which emanates from the lower classes [*von den niedern Volksklassen*] in England and France'.[33] They provide no specimens of this 'new literature', and give their readers no hint of where to look—though one suspects that the frequent recourse to folk-literature already noted in *The Holy Family* (see above, p. 95) is not unconnected with their search for a noble and meaningful literature produced by the common people.

One last point made in *The Holy Family* cries out to be noticed. Marx and Engels here distance themselves, once and for all, from mystical-inspirational theories of literature and, at the same time, from any 'impersonal' theory which would divorce the work from the living human being who wrote it. 'In his critical naïvety', they say of Bruno Bauer, 'Herr Bruno divorces "the pen" from "the writing subject", and the writing subject as "abstract *scribe*" from the living, *historical human being* that did the writing. In this way he can enthuse over the *miracle-working* power of the pen . . .'[34] It cannot be part of my present purpose to elaborate—as Marx and Engels do not—on the suggestive connection which is here made between impersonal and inspirational theories of literature. What is significant is that Marx will have no truck with either. Just as the title *The Holy Family* is purely ironical, just as neither Marx nor Engels could find room in their system for any religious or mystical experience that claimed access to supernatural truth, so they will have nothing to do with a theory of literature which sees it as speaking in any way of a numinous or uncanny Beyond. Literature

[31] *MEW* II, 159. [32] *MEW* II, 89. [33] *MEW* II, 143.
[34] *MEW* II, 106.

speaks to man only of himself and the socio-historical world in which he lives and which he is helping to shape. The miracles of heightening and transmutation in literature—more 'true' than those of which religion tells, and more thrilling and profound than the meretricious mysteries that so fascinated the first readers of Eugène Sue—are worked, for Marx, by individual, historically and socially conditioned men. It is their voice he ever tries to hear.

5 · Praxis and Ideology

'The problem of descending from the world of
thoughts to the actual world turns into the problem
of descending from language to life.'

(*MEW* III, 432)

(i)

In 1845 Marx noted down those eleven points *ad Feuerbach*
which Engels was to publish after Marx's death, in a somewhat
altered form, under the title *Marx on Feuerbach*, and which have
since become rightly famous as the *Theses on Feuerbach*. The very
first of these has many implications for literary study:

The chief defect of all previous materialism (including that of Feuerbach) is that things, reality, the sensible world are conceived only in
the form of objects of observation, but not as human sense activity,
not as practical activity, not subjectively. Hence, in opposition to
materialism, the active side was developed abstractly by idealism,
which of course does not know real sense activity as such. Feuerbach
wants sensible objects that are really distinguished from the objects
of thought; but he does not understand human activity itself as
objective activity.[1]

Literature too, it might be thought, should be looked at, not as
an inertly faithful reflection of something outside, of a 'material'
reality, but as a union of the objective with the subjective, of
a world apprehended through the senses with a particular cast
of mind, temperament, and character. This applies to the
reception of literature as much as to its production.

Here we must keep ever in mind the clear distinction which
the third of these *Feuerbach Theses* seeks to make between Marx's
approach and that of 'mechanical materialists': 'The materialist
doctrine concerning the changing of circumstances and education

[1] *BR* 82; *MEW* III, 5.

forgets that circumstances are changed by men . . .' Those
who produce literature and those who read it are not passive
creatures of circumstance: they are engaged in activities that
can change the circumstances in which they find themselves.
And such activity is always, as the sixth and seventh theses tell
us, *social* activity. Writers and their successive readers belong
to particular ages, nations, and social groups:

The essence of man is not an abstraction inherent in each particular
individual. The real nature of man is the *ensemble* of social relations.

Feuerbach . . . does not see that . . . the abstract individual whom
he analyses belongs to a particular form of society.[2]

The discussion of *The Mysteries of Paris* will already have
shown what this implies in critical practice. There, as we have
seen, Marx tried constantly to discover the social component
in both the writing and the reading of literature. He tried to
demonstrate that Sue wrote for a definite public, with that
public's expectations in mind—a fact which had important
consequences for the nature of his work. He tried to show up
the ways in which Sue's modes of thinking and feeling had
been moulded by his social environment. He tried to demonstrate how readers ignorant of that environment, who approached Sue (as Szeliga did) with expectations very unlike
those of the public for which he wrote, would construct in their
minds a different novel from that constructed by Parisians. This
did not, however, as we have also seen, lead him to complete
critical relativism. He clearly believed his own reading of *The
Mysteries of Paris* to be fuller and truer than those of Szeliga
and the average subscriber to the *Journal des Débats*, and tried
to exhibit that superiority with close reference to the actual
text. Such critical activity was also a mode of *Praxis*;[3] in defining his interpretations against those of others, Marx could
gain greater clarity about his own ways of reading and the
grounds that might justify them. Through his criticism he not
only helped others to see more clearly; he also developed, and
in some sense remade, himself.

[2] *BR* 83; *MEW* III, 6, 7.
[3] Cf. the eighth Feuerbach thesis: 'All social life is essentially *practical*' (*BR* 84;
MEW III, 7). *Praxis* might well be regarded as the key concept of the *Feuerbach
Theses* as a whole.

'The standpoint of the old materialism', the tenth Feuerbach thesis reads, 'is "civil" society; the standpoint of the new is human society, or socialized humanity.'[4] That indicates the Utopian perspective, the prevision of a 'socialized humanity' of the future, which Marx has now begun to adopt. Literature too must be looked at in that perspective; its various historical manifestations can now be seen as contributing towards the advent of socialized humanity, or mirroring its progress towards that ideal, or revealing the forces impeding such progress, or anticipating, through its transcendence of mere exchange values, the values of the society that has yet to be born.

As for the final Feuerbach thesis: 'The philosophers have only *interpreted* the world in different ways; the point is to *change* it'[5]—we have already examined some of the ways, and will examine others, in which Marx enlists the help of literature in polemics designed to alter radically his readers' manner of thinking and through this their social action. In his appreciation of literature too *Praxis* is one of Marx's central categories; the end he has ever in view is not contemplation, not knowing or wisdom for its own sake, but doing and living well.[6]

(ii)

Among the jottings on the last two pages of the manuscript that contains the *Feuerbach Theses* we can find another important indication of the younger Marx's approach to the arts.

> Natural Science and History.
> There is no history of politics, of law, of science
> etc., of art, of religion.[7]

'There is no history ... of art.' Art—including literature— must be seen in a wider setting: as part of an all-embracing history, a history of all human endeavour and its natural foundations. This is one of the themes we will find treated at greater length in the next work on which Marx and Engels co-operated: *The German Ideology*.

Die deutsche Ideologie, a critique of Feuerbach, Bruno Bauer, Max Stirner, and other post-Hegelian German thinkers, was

---

[4] *MEW* III, 7. [5] *BR* 84; *MEW* III, 7.
[6] Cf. R. J. Bernstein, *Praxis and Action*, pp. x, 13 ff. [7] *MEW* III, 539.

written during the years 1845 and 1846. Only a few fragments of it, however, saw the light of print in the authors' lifetime; the manuscript, after being rejected by several publishers, was abandoned to what Marx called, characteristically, 'the gnawing critique of mice' (whose teeth have left a considerable imprint on the manuscript as we now have it and robbed posterity of many a winged word).

As its title suggests, the work is concerned with the cloud-cuckoo-land of post-Hegelian idealist philosophy, with a world in which *Geist* and *Idee* are the only ultimate realities. 'None of these philosophers', Marx and Engels complain, 'have thought of asking how German philosophy connects with the facts of German life or their own critique with their material surroundings.'[8]

In total contrast to German philosophy, which descends from heaven to earth, we here ascend from earth to heaven. That is to say, we do not set out from what men say, imagine, or conceive, nor from what has been said, thought, imagined, or conceived of men, in order to arrive at men in the flesh. We begin with real, active men, and from their real life-process show the development of the ideological reflexes and echoes of this life-process. The phantoms of the human brain also are necessary sublimates of men's material life-process, which can be empirically established and which is bound to material preconditions. Morality, religion, metaphysics, and other ideologies, and their corresponding forms of consciousness, no longer retain therefore their appearance of autonomous existence. They have no history, no development; it is men, who, in developing their material production and their material intercourse, change, along with this their real existence, their thinking and the products of their thinking. Life is not determined by consciousness, but consciousness by life. Those who adopt the first method of approach begin with consciousness, regarded as the living individual; those who adopt the second, which corresponds with real life, begin with the real living individuals themselves, and consider consciousness only as *their* consciousness.[9]

This is indeed Hegelianism turned upside down—or right side up, as Marx and Engels would claim. Literature and the arts receive no specific mention in this uncompromising passage; but it should not be difficult to see what dangerous consequences

[8] *MEW* III, 20.   [9] *BR* 90; *MEW* III, 26-7.

might flow from an unimaginative extension of such principles. Critics might all too easily be tempted into overlooking that literary forms do, to some degree at least, have a history and development of their own, and that material life is, in not inconsiderable ways, affected by human consciousness. Would there not be a danger that the baby of observation and good sense might find itself thrown out with the Hegelian bathwater? To obviate dangers of this kind, Marx and Engels stress, in a later passage of *The German Ideology*, that a complete view of the relationship between material life and consciousness must include the principle of *interaction*:

This conception of history therefore rests upon the development of the real process of production, taking its point of departure from the material production of immediate life, tracing the forms of social intercourse, bound up with, and produced by, this mode of production, and conceiving civil society in its various stages as the foundation of all history. It also describes civil society in its actions as state power, explains the origins and follows out the developing processes, of all its various theoretical creations and forms of consciousness, religion, philosophy, morality, etc. In this way, of course, this whole matter may be presented in its totality (*and therefore the reciprocal interaction of these various factors with one another*). [my italics][10]

'Totality' includes 'reciprocal interaction', *Wechselwirkung*. The notion of interaction significantly tempers that of one-sided dependence.

'Totality' is a key notion of *The German Ideology*, as it had been in the Paris Manuscripts; and Joachim Israel has usefully distinguished two of the ways in which Marx uses it. It may mean 'ideal totality' in the sense that man, as an ideal type, is 'endowed with all the characteristics which characterize the species and which can be increasingly manifested as society and its productive forces develop'. In this sense the term applies to 'society as thought and experienced'. In another sense, however, 'totality' may apply, not to mankind as a whole, but to individuals; and here its use is meant to raise questions about the chances given individuals or groups have of realizing their capacities and talents in a given social order. But, Israel rightly concludes, the two notions of 'totality' here distinguished are related. 'Total man as an ideal type, as the essence of the species' is 'approached by individual man in his historical process of development.' When he can 'appropriate his world' in the '"total" way' Marx thinks possible in the better society of the future, then the fully developed individual will approach, or coincide with, the ideal type.[11]

The concept of 'totality' stands in dialectical relation to another key notion of *The German Ideology*: division of labour. The division of labour characteristic of modern society is said to have opposed 'abstract' individuals to a 'totality' of productive forces which confront them in reified form; and this is said to imply a stunting of individual development that can only be overcome by the abolition of private property, by a remoulding of society in such a way that every man will be able to develop his full human potential and thus produce a new kind of 'totality'.[12] Marx and Engels concentrate particularly on one aspect of division of labour: the division between men busied with everyday material production, and men busy with the production of ideas. These latter, we are told, formulate or express for the most part the ideas, the ideology, of a dominant class. But, as the very existence of *The German Ideology* demonstrates, writers and thinkers can place themselves in opposition to dominant modes of thought. They are able to do this because there are already at work, at home or abroad, forces that contradict, forces that are destined to overthrow, the socio-economic system to which the ruling classes of a given society owe their superiority and hegemony.[13]

In the *Theses on Feuerbach* Marx had attacked 'mechanical materialists' for their one-sided stressing of human determination by external circumstances. What such materialists neglected, he believed, was the self-changing and liberating effect of *Praxis*. 'The coincidence of the changing of circumstances and of human activity or self-changing', the third Feuerbach thesis had proclaimed, 'can be conceived and rationally understood only as *revolutionary practice*'.[14] *The German Ideology* develops this theme. While stressing that 'men are the producers of their conceptions, ideas, etc.—real active men, as they are conditioned

---

[11] J. Israel, *Alienation. From Marx to Modern Sociology* (Boston, 1971), pp. 73–4.
[12] *MEW* III, 67–9.   [13] *MEW* III, 31–4.   [14] *BR* 83; *MEW* III, 6.

by a definite development of their productive forces and the intercourse corresponding to these', Marx and Engels also proclaim unequivocally that 'under favourable circumstances individuals can rid themselves of their local narrow-mindedness', and that thinkers born into the bourgeoisie need not be confined, for the rest of their lives, in the ideology of that class. What *The German Ideology* terms 'communist consciousness' depends on the existence of the proletariat, to whose sufferings and aspirations it corresponds; but such consciousness may well 'arise among the other classes too through the contemplation of the situation [of the proletariat]'. Marx and Engels thus find room for doctrines that, like their own, go counter to the interests of the class to which their proponents belong. All men, Marx believes, are products of circumstances; but he believes no less firmly that all men are potentially able to change their circumstances, and that in their striving for such change they acquire insights denied to those who passively acquiesce.[15]

Such qualifications and complexities must be kept in mind when we read the famous passage in which Marx and Engels attempt to describe the relationship of ideas to a 'dominant material force' and to 'dominant material relationships'. Read by itself the passage has an ominous reductional clarity ('The dominant ideas are nothing more than . . .') which its context in *The German Ideology* does something to counteract:

The ideas of the ruling class are, in every age, the ruling ideas: i.e. the class which is the dominant *material* force in society is at the same time its dominant *intellectual* force. The class which has the means of material production at its disposal, has control at the same time over the means of mental production, so that in consequence the ideas of those who lack the means of mental production are, in general, subject to it. The dominant ideas are nothing more than the ideal expression of the dominant material relationships, the dominant material relationships grasped as ideas, and thus of the relationships which make one class the ruling one; they are consequently the ideas of its dominance. The individuals composing the ruling class possess, among other things, consciousness, and therefore think. In so far, therefore, as they rule as a class and determine the whole extent of an epoch, it is self-evident that they do this in their whole range and thus, among other things, rule also as thinkers, as

[15] Cf. *GI* 22–3; *MEW* III, 6.

producers of ideas, and regulate the production and distribution of the ideas of their age. Consequently their ideas are the ruling ideas of their age. For instance, in an age and in a country where royal power, aristocracy, and the bourgeoisie are contending for domination and where, therefore, domination is shared, the doctrine of the separation of powers appears as the dominant idea and is enunciated as an 'eternal law'. The division of labour, which we saw earlier as one of the principal forces of history up to the present time, manifests itself also in the ruling class, as the division of mental and material labour, so that within this class one part appears as the thinkers of the class (its active conceptualizing ideologists, who make it their chief source of livelihood to develop and perfect the illusions of the class about itself), while the others have a more passive and receptive attitude to these ideas and illusions, because they are in reality the active members of this class and have less time to make up ideas and illusions about themselves.[16]

Later on *The German Ideology* experiments with other ways of describing the same relationship. In a passage on the philosophy of Kant, Marx and Engels try out various terms connected with 'mirroring' and 'correspondence':

The condition of Germany at the end of the last century is completely reflected [*spiegelt sich vollständig ab*] in Kant's *Critique of Pure Reason* . . . Kant's 'goodwill' wholly corresponds to [*entspricht vollständig*] the impotence, oppression, and wretchedness of the German bourgeoisie . . .[17]

The same passage goes on to call Kant a 'palliating spokesman' (*beschönigender Wortführer*) of the German bourgeoisie, berates his alleged ignorance of the way in which ideas are conditioned and determined (*bedingt, bestimmt*) by the nature of material production, and speaks of the 'idealistic expression [*Ausdruck*] of the real interests' (which latter are economic and determined by class).

Not surprisingly, *The German Ideology* deals not only with 'complete reflections of the kind just illustrated, but also with the distortions such reflections may introduce. Ideologies are described as 'diffused reflections' (*Reflexe*) and as 'echoes' of the 'real processes of living'. In ideologies, men and the conditions of their life 'appear upside down, as in a camera obscura'. Such distortions and inversions may be explained by reference

[16] *BR* 93-4; *MEW* III, 46.   [17] *MEW* III, 176-7.

to the historical processes within which men have their being (*aus ihrem historischen Lebensprozeß*).[18] It has been noted, however, that the images of 'mirroring' and 'reflecting' which play so important a part in later Marxist theory are not *directly* applied to literature in any work in which Marx himself had a dominant share.[19]

It is in *The German Ideology* too that Marx and Engels first unveil their famous model of 'base' and 'superstructure'. They speak of 'the social organization which develops directly out of production and social intercourse and which at all times forms the basis [*die Basis*] of the state and the rest of the idealist superstructure [*Superstruktur*]'; and they deplore the development of capitalism in so far as it converts everything into money relationships and thus destroys, for the worker, 'all natural and inherited family and political conditions, for instance, together with their whole ideological superstructure [*Überbau*]'.[20]

In his book on Marx's sociology Henri Lefebvre has admirably summarized the characteristics of 'ideologies' as Marx and Engels see them. Their starting-point is reality, but a fragmentary, partially apprehended reality; they refract (rather than reflect) reality via pre-existent representations selected by dominant groups and acceptable to them; they create false images of dominant classes and prove useful, for this and other reasons, in securing the assent of those who are dominated and exploited; they distort practical action by constructing abstract, unreal, fictitious theories, and fail to reflect—for the most part—on their own historical conditions and presuppositions, and on the consequences to which they are leading. Ideologies may, however, in the opinion of Marx and Engels, serve as instruments of progress: German idealist philosophy, for instance, 'transposed praxis to the realm of metaphysics' yet formulated that concept of dialectical change without which Marx's own theory, and the revolutionary action it was designed to foster, would be unthinkable.[21] And even where they distort truth,

---

[18] *MEW* III, 26–7.

[19] Cf. V. Karbusicky, *Widerspiegelungstheorie und Strukturalismus. Zur Entstehungsgeschichte und Kritik der marxistisch-leninistischen Ästhetik* (Munich, 1973).

[20] *MEW* III, 36, 356.

[21] Lefebvre, *The Sociology of Marx*, pp. 69–74; cf. Morawski's definition, *BM* 25: 'Ideology will here be considered as the statement or symptomatic expression of a pattern of social-class attitudes, interests, or habits of thought. When ideology

ideologies perform the important function of 'organizing values', consolidating belief in values essential for the functioning of a given group or class.[22]

In the Paris Manuscripts Marx had already turned his attention to 'the element of thought itself—the element of thought's living expression—*language*' and had insisted that this was of a 'sensuous' nature.[23] *The German Ideology* expands on this theme in an aside on the physical basis of language:

From the start the 'spirit' is afflicted with the curse of being 'burdened' with matter, which here makes its appearance in the form of agitated layers of air, sounds, in short, of language. Language is as old as consciousness—language *is* practical consciousness that exists also for other men, and for that reason alone it really exists for me personally as well; language, like consciousness, only arises from the need, the necessity, of intercourse with other men . . .[24]

This points to something constantly in evidence in Marx's response to literature: his sensitive awareness of its sound and movement (like his wife, and later his children, Marx loved to declaim and read aloud); and also his feeling that works of literature, linguistic artefacts, answered a specific human need, that in doing so they created new needs for which other works of art would provide new satisfactions.

Among the passages of *The German Ideology* dealing explicitly with literature and the arts there are some which are likely to be viewed with some scepticism by those for whom the writings of Marx and Engels are not canonical texts. Marx and Engels react sharply against Max Stirner's overstressing of the role individuals play in the production of art. They cite the example of Mozart, some of whose works were scored or completed by others, and that of Raphael, who left to his pupils the execution of many details in important paintings. This leads them to take a hopeful view of the part 'organization' might play in the

is exhibited directly, as symptomatic expression, the artist may or may not be aware of having adopted a position. Such patterns may be elucidated by the experienced, careful and knowledgeable critic.' The best non-Marxist account of ideology, including a history of the term, a sharp critique of the loose way in which it has been used, and an attempt at redefinition, is that of John Plamenatz in *Ideology. Key Concepts in Political Science*, ed. L. Shapiro (London, 1970).

[22] L. Kolakowski, 'Ideology and Theory', in *Karl Marx*, ed. T. B. Bottomore (New Jersey, 1973), pp. 119–22.

[23] *MEW EB* I, 544.

[24] *GI* 51; *MEW* III, 30.

production of not just more but *better* literature—a view they try to support by pointing to the popular stage in contemporary France, and by dubious analogies from historiography and the sciences:

The great demand for vaudevilles and novels in Paris has called forth an organization for the production of such articles which yet achieves better things than their 'unique' competitors in Germany. In astronomy men like Arago, Herschel, Encke, and Bessel have found it necessary to organize themselves to make their observations in common, and only after that did they reach some acceptable conclusion. In historical studies it is impossible for the single, 'unique' individual to achieve anything at all, and here too the French have outstripped all other nations, because they knew how to organize such work . . .[25]

'It goes without saying', Marx and Engels add, 'that all such organization based on modern division of labour leads to very limited results'; and they point forward to a future communist society in which the artist and poet as a specialist, a full-time expert, will be entirely superseded by the all-round man who is an artist amongst other things:

Exclusive concentration of artistic talent in single, unique individuals and (connected with this) suppression of such talent among the masses is a consequence of the division of labour. Even if, in certain social conditions, everyone were an excellent painter, this would not preclude his being also an *original* painter . . . A communist society will free the artist from local and national limitations which are solely due to division of labour. It will also free him from limitation to one particular art, from a state of affairs in which an individual must be exclusively a painter, a sculptor etc., where this very label expresses the bounds set to his commercial development and his dependence on division of labour. In a communist society there will be no painters; at most there will be men who—among other things—also paint.[26]

One doubts if Marx and Engels could have found many grounds, in the history of the fine arts up to their own time, for a belief that the future of painting lay with part-timers rather than professionals.[27] They are looking forward to an era from whose

---

[25] *MEW* III, 378.   [26] *MEW* III, 378–9.
[27] Cf. R. Wellek, *A History of Modern Criticism, 1750–1950*, vol. iii (London, 1966), p. 235.

vantage-point all previous history would appear as mere pre-history. It remains curious, nevertheless, as Charles Frankel has said, that Marx should propose the life of the dilettante as the model of the good life in the liberated society of the future—a life where men 'hunt in the morning, fish in the afternoon, rear cattle in the evening, just as they have a mind, without ever becoming hunter, fisherman, shepherd or critic'.[28]

Two principles enunciated in this book will, however, command more general assent. Neither was new; both, indeed, had been proclaimed, and brilliantly demonstrated, by Herder; but their restatement was none the less timely. 'Great nations like the French, the North Americans, and the English', Marx and Engels write, 'constantly compare one another, in practice and in theory';[29] and they call for an application of historically based comparative methods to the arts, both in an international and a national context. In such researches, they stress, the study of *Verkehr*—material and intellectual intercourse and interaction between individuals, social groups, and countries; international communications—will play an essential part:

If [Stirner] were to compare Raphael with Leonardo da Vinci and Titian he would see how strongly Raphael's work was conditioned by the flowering of Rome under Florentine influence, Leonardo's by Florentine circumstances, and that of Titian by the quite different development of Venice. Like any artist Raphael was conditioned by the technical advances made in art before his time, by the organization of society, by the division of labour in the locality in which he lived, and—finally—by the division of labour in all the countries with which that locality stood in communication.[30]

Comparison shows up the uniqueness, the individuality of an artist like Raphael; but it must also show to what extent the development of his talent was conditioned by time and place. Marx and Engels add that such development was conditioned by *demand* too, by the calls the artist's society makes on him, by the need it shows for his art—and that such demand 'depends, in its turn, on the division of labour and state of education [*Bildungsverhältnisse*] which results from it'.

[28] C. Frankel, 'Theory and Practice in Marx's Thought', in *Marx and Contemporary Scientific Thought*, Publications of the International Social Science Council, xiii (The Hague and Paris, 1969), p. 29.
[29] *MEW* III, 426.   [30] *MEW* III, 378.

What may be called the 'comparative' principle restated in *The German Ideology* is supplemented by renewed stress on the 'historical' principle: by an insistence that valid criticism of literature, no less than criticism of the visual arts, must be based on historical understanding. What a strange notion of 'uniqueness' and 'individuality' Max Stirner exhibited, Marx and Engels exclaim, when he complained of Klopstock's failure to take an 'original' view of the Christian religion!

Klopstock's attitude to religion, Stirner tells us, was not 'unique and individual', although it was a particular attitude to religion, namely that which made Klopstock what he was, which made Klopstock Klopstock. His attitude would, one supposes, have been 'unique and individual' only if he had adopted, not that of Klopstock, but that of a modern German philosopher![31]

The authors of *The German Ideology* make no secret of their personal distaste for Klopstock—'blessedly forgotten' they call him, *selig verschollen*. They insist, however, that he must be understood on his own terms and in his own setting; they insist that no literary critic is worth his salt if he lacks historical imagination.

The approach to literature characteristic of *The German Ideology* is resolutely historical in Hegel's sense: in the sense, that is, which sees recurring themes (the family, for instance, or the state, and the conflicts engendered by and within them) treated differently in each great epoch. There is a difference, however, that comes out clearly in the passage in which *The German Ideology* tries to trace the history of hedonism in modern Europe:

The philosophy of pleasure emerged in modern times with the decline of feudalism and the transformation of the feudal landed nobility into the lusty, pleasure-loving and extravagant court nobility of the absolute monarchy. Among this nobility it still takes the form, primarily, of *an immediate, naïve view of life which is given expression in memoirs, poems, novels* and so on [my italics]. It becomes a real philosophy only in the hands of several writers of the revolutionary bourgeoisie who participated, on the one hand, in the education and mode of life of the court nobility and who shared, on the other, the more general outlook upon affairs of the bourgeoisie—

[31] *MEW* III, 266.

an outlook based on the more general conditions of existence of the bourgeoisie. It was therefore accepted by both classes, although from quite different points of view. Among the nobility the language of pleasure was understood to be restricted to the confines of the first estate and its conditions of life; by the bourgeoisie it was generalized and applied to all individuals, without distinction; this meant abstracting from the actual conditions of life characteristic of such individuals, and the theory became transformed, therefore, into a stale and hypocritical moral doctrine. As the further course of development overthrew the nobility and brought the nobility into conflict with its opposite, the proletariat, the nobility became devoutly religious and the bourgeoisie solemnly moral and strict in its theories; although in practice the nobility did not in the least renounce pleasure while the bourgeoisie even made of pleasure an official economic category—*luxury*.[32]

Hegel would not have been surprised at this depiction of rococo or anacreontic literature as more 'immediate' and 'naïve' than the philosophy which grew up around it. What is specifically Marxian, however, in this passage from *The German Ideology*, is its stress (constant, from now on, in Marx's work) on the class-origins of both literature and philosophy and the class-conflicts of whose history their history is part.

The Paris Manuscripts had deplored German concentration on 'history in its abstract-general character—as politics, art, literature, etc.'[33] In *The German Ideology* Marx and Engels return to this charge. They pour scorn on the so-called 'true' socialists because of their absorption in books rather than life: 'The lack of any *real*, passionate, practical party conflict in Germany meant that even the social movement was at first a *merely* literary one. "True socialism" is a perfect example of a social literary movement that has come into being without any real party interests . . .';[34] and they constantly voice their suspicion of any culture that is merely belletristic. The creations of a novelist, Jean Paul Richter, are cited to illustrate the intermingling of 'petty huckstering and large illusions' in the mind of Germans who lived under Napoleonic occupation—and the authors add scornfully that this is evidence their butt Max Stirner will accept because belletristic sources are the only

---

[32] *MEW* III, 402–3; cf. S. Hook, *From Hegel to Marx, Studies in the Intellectual Development of Karl Marx* (Ann Arbor, 1962), p. 316.

[33] *MEW EB* I, 542.   [34] *GI* 120; *MEW* III, 443.

ones he knows.[35] The same charge recurs over and over again:
in one place Marx and Engels even compile a list of Stirner's
'sources' of historical information, which range from the Bible
to Lessing's *Emilia Galotti* and Willibald Alexis's novel *Cabanis*,[36]
and compose a mock-lament on the dilemma in which they are
helping to place their fellow Germans:

> Here Stirner provides a striking example of the sad position in
> which German theorizers have been placed by communism. They
> now have to take note of profane things like needle-factories etc., in
> face of which they behave like barbarians, like Ojibwa Indians and
> New Zealand Aborigines.[37]

To characterize Stirner and other theorizers and philosophers
in post-Hegelian Germany Marx and Engels constantly quote,
therefore, or allude to, contemporary writers like Willibald
Alexis, Friedrich Halm, Karl von Holtei, Nicolaus Becker,
Hoffmann von Fallersleben. Such allusions are clearly intended to convey the cultural ambience—stuffy and philistine,
in the opinion of Marx and Engels—in which German philosophers live and move and do their thinking. In such an
ambience, *The German Ideology* goes on to allege, the whole of
history begins to take on, for a thinker like Stirner, the guise
of the crudest contents of German lending libraries, while 'the
theatrum mundi shrinks to the Leipzig book-fair'.[38] The processes
of history appear as the plot of grandiloquent plays dealing
with kings and princes (*hochtönende Haupt- und Staatsaktionen*)
or even one of those Gothic tales of knights, robbers, and
ghosts—*eine Ritter- Räuber- und Gespenstergeschichte*—which had
been the favourite library-fodder of an earlier generation.[39]
To see life in the image of sub-literature: that is the nemesis of
those who fail to come to terms with modern politics, economics, and science. Their fate (a dreadful one in Marx's eyes!)
will be to be read by no one but *literati* just like themselves.
Germany's 'true socialists', *The German Ideology* prophesies,
'will concentrate more and more on a petty-bourgeois public
and on impotent and ragged *Literaten* as representatives of that
public'.[40]

Yet Marx and Engels clearly enjoy demonstrating, throughout *The German Ideology*, that they can cite literary sources with

[35] *MEW* III, 179.   [36] *MEW* III, 319.   [37] *MEW* III, 206.
[38] *MEW* III, 41, 429.   [39] *MEW* III, 36, 39–40.   [40] *MEW* III, 443.

the best of them. The Bible, as in *The Holy Family*, is ubiquitous, sometimes quoted 'straight', more often in riotous parody: 'Yes, consider the lilies of the field, how they are eaten by goats, transplated by man into his buttonhole, how they are crushed beneath the immodest embraces of the dairymaid and the donkey-driver!' Shakespeare's Timon is brought on once more, to show how much more clearly an Elizabethan dramatist could convey an essential function of money than a modern German philosopher:

How little money, the most generalized form of property, has to do with particular, personal qualities—how it is diametrically opposed to such qualities—Shakespeare knew better than a theorizing petty bourgeois:

> Thus much of this will make black, white; foul, fair;
> Wrong, right; base, noble; old, young; coward, valiant.[41]

The *Arabian Nights*, Homer, Lucian, Konrad von Würzburg, Rabelais, the *commedia dell' arte*, Goethe, Chamisso, the librettists of *The Magic Flute*, and *Der Freischütz* are raided for apt quotations, characterizations, and insight into the life and thought of past and present.[42] Literary parodies and parodies of opera-libretti enliven the argument.[43] Calderón's *The Bridge of Mantible* supplies a long list of compliments which are heaped on Max Stirner before he is contemptuously dismissed.[44] Snatches of folk-song are approvingly quoted, as usual:[45] but *The German Ideology* also cites a complete German folk-song, the *Jockellied*, to show how 'the common consciousness' (*das gemeine Bewußtsein*) can mock the kind of black and white, un-dialectical schemata of thought which Marx and Engels attribute to Max Stirner.[46] This folk-song, which has parallels in many lands, describes how a farm-servant fails to do his master's bidding until, successively, a dog has been sent out to bite him, a stick has been sent to beat the dog, a fire to burn the stick, water to quench the fire, an ox to drink the water, a butcher to kill the ox, and a hangman to hang the butcher. Whether such songs in fact 'mock' their own construction, as Marx and Engels claim, or whether they aim to reveal, in

[41] *MEW* III, 212.
[42] *MEW* III, 460, 353, 280, 171, 435, 175, 218; 43, 312, 313, 400, 420; 299, 475, 132 *et passim*.   [43] e.g. *MEW* III, 437.
[44] *MEW* III, 436.   [45] *MEW* III, 465.   [46] *MEW* III, 118-19.

humorous fashion, something true about the ways of the world, the reader must decide for himself.

As *The German Ideology* proceeds, we find the satiric poems of Heine being quoted, with increasing frequency, to characterize and knock down German opponents. Marx and Engels do not shrink, however, from treating these poems as *Gebrauchslyrik*, verse meant for use, verse whose original wording is not sacrosanct but may be altered and adapted to suit its new context.[47] Nor had Marx's reading in the 1840s been confined to Heine's satiric *poems*. In a letter which he wrote to Heine from Brussels in 1846, Marx expressed his appreciation of Heine's much-abused pamphlet *Ludwig Börne* and promised to defend it, in a German newspaper, against what he thought excessively stupid and uncomprehending attacks by German reviewers. Marx's review was never written; but it is evident that he and Engels now saw Börne through Heine's eyes. Their reference, in a circular of 11 May 1846, to 'catholicizing political fantasists like Lamennais and Börne'[48] recalls Heine's analysis of Börne's political position as well as his charge, in Book i of his pamphlet, that Börne fraternized with Lamennais and 'almost descended into Catholicism'.

The author who dominates *The German Ideology*, however, is not Heine but Cervantes. The whole work is shot through with allusions to, quotations from, and parodies of *Don Quixote*. In a representative passage, Max Stirner appears as Sancho Panza, with our old friend Szeliga as Don Quixote himself— but oh, how changed!

It is Sancho Panza this time, full of moral saws, maxims, and proverbs, who rides into battle against Sanctity, and Don Quixote who appears as his pious and faithful squire. Honest Sancho fights as bravely as the Knight of La Mancha did of yore, and like him, he does not fail to mistake, more than once, a flock of Mongolian sheep for a swarm of ghosts. Fat Maritornes meanwhile, 'through manifold changes and refractions in the course of time', has changed into a chaste Berlin seamstress succumbing to the green-sickness, which moves Saint Sancho to an elegy . . .[49]

Such allusions perform a patent structural function. They

---

[47] e.g. *MEW* III, 252, 316, 390, 450, 454, 457. Marx's adaptation of Heine's wording can be studied on p. 447.
[48] *MEW* IV, 4-7.   [49] *MEW* III, 174-5.

transform *The German Ideology* into a mock-epic, in which the
characters invented by Cervantes prefigure the German butts
of Marx and Engels. 'Supported by these sayings of Feuerbach,
Sancho begins a fight . . . already patterned out in the nineteenth chapter of Cervantes'; or again, in a passage which
characteristically merges Cervantes and the Bible: 'The battle
"for man" is the fulfilment of the word that stands chronicled
in Cervantes xix . . .'50 At the same time Cervantes provides
a standard: how much more heroic is the Knight of La Mancha,
we are meant to think, how much more sensible his squire,
than their later counterparts! And last but not least: Cervantes
provides, in this new context, occasion for a game of inversions,
of changing roles and sides, of permutations, which Marx was
always glad to play. Don Quixote and Sancho were in fact
made to exchange parts in the passage quoted at the beginning
of this paragraph—a process not unrelated to conspicuous
aspects of Marx's conception of history51 and to the chiastic
inversion which is so striking a feature of his style.

Similar use of the Bible, throughout *The German Ideology*,
serves similar purposes—with the additional advantage, from
the polemicist's point of view, that it might startle the pious
reader into attention and response through the still potent
shock of blasphemy. This purpose has also prompted Marx and
Engels to quote chapter and verse of *Don Quixote* in the manner,
and in the archaic style of vocabulary and syntax, in which pious
German writers and speakers were wont to quote their Bible.

A tiny example may serve to show that the authors of *The
German Ideology* do not introduce snatches of quotation into their
argument simply as disjointed gobbets. They expect, in many
cases, that the right reader will automatically supply the context from which the quotation has been lifted and the even wider
context in which the original functions. When summarizing
Max Stirner's exposition of the part that *idées fixes* play in his
thinking—ideas which cannot be shaken off however one twists
and turns—Marx and Engels interject, drily:

Der Zopf, der hängt ihm hinten.52

50 *MEW* III, 216–17, 220.
51 e.g. Marx's Hegelian notion that in the course of time 'tragedy' turns into
'comedy', and his belief that Germans had conceived a topsy-turvy picture of the
world which it was his task to turn right side up.   52 *MEW* III, 299.

These words, as most German readers of the time would have realized, form the refrain of a poem by Adalbert von Chamisso which Thackeray has transmogrified into English under the title 'A Tragic Story'.

> There lived a sage in days of yore
> And he a handsome pigtail wore;
> But wondered much and sorrowed more
>   Because it hung behind him.
>
> He mused upon this curious case,
> And swore he'd change the pigtail's place
> And have it hanging at his face,
>   Not dangling there behind him.
>
> Says he, 'The mystery I've found,—
> I'll turn me round',—he turned him round;
>   But still it hung behind him.
>
> Then round, and round, and out and in,
> All day the puzzled sage did spin;
> In vain—it mattered not a pin,—
>   The pigtail hung behind him.
>
> And right, and left, and round about,
> And up, and down, and in, and out,
> He turned; but still the pigtail stout
>   Hung steadily behind him.
>
> And though his efforts never slack,
> And though he twist, and twirl, and tack,
> Alas! still faithful to his back,
>   The pigtail hangs behind him.

But English readers who respond to Thackeray's adaptation are likely to miss another dimension of meaning which Marx and Engels clearly wished to indicate. The word *Zopf* has, in German, associations of antiquated formalism, pettifogging, pedantry, red tape, and the style of the old Prussian army which are necessarily diminished or cut out when the word is translated as 'pigtail'; associations on which Heine played, for instance, when he declared, in *Germany. A Winter's Tale*, that the long moustaches worn by the Prussian soldiers of his day were merely another phase of the 'pigtaildom', the *Zopftum*, of yore:

> Der Zopf, der früher hinten hing,
> Der hängt jetzt unter der Nase.

> The pigtail that once hung behind them
> is now hanging under their noses.

While all this is going on, *The German Ideology* continues the close scrutiny, begun in *The Holy Family*, of the way German writers use their language. Metaphors, grammatical constructions, even prose-rhythms are examined in an effort to demonstrate an opponent's incompetence, illogicality, or lack of imagination. If Bruno Bauer ever stopped to consider what the words he uses connote, could he then, Marx and Engels ask, talk as he does of 'a heaving undulating, wavy bodily structure' ('ein *wogender, wallender,* wellenförmiger Körper*bau*')?[53] Max Stirner, they maintain, betrays hidden assumptions by the way he introduces undefined essences, shadowy presences, by means of impersonal constructions—*The German Ideology* therefore analyses his use of the pronoun 'es'.[54] Rudolph Matthäi, we are given to understand, distracts attention from the vapidity of his argument through the hypnotic, lulling, pseudo-classical sing-song of his prose; *The German Ideology* therefore indicates his dactyls and trochees with the usual hooks and dashes:

> Die unendliche Mannigfaltigkeit aller Einzel-
> — ◡ ◡ — ◡ ◡ — ◡ ◡ — ◡ ◡ — ◡ ◡ — ◡
> Wesen als Einheit zusammengefaßt ist der Weltorganismus.[55]

Wherever they look, Marx and Engels find that German thinkers have allowed words and things to drift apart:

For the philosopher it is one of the most difficult tasks to descend from the world of thought to the real world. The immediate reality of thought is *language*. Just as the philosophers made thinking autonomous, so they had also to transform language into an autonomous realm. This is the secret of philosophic language in which thoughts, in the guise of words, have a content of their own. The problem of descending from the world of thought to the actual world turns into the problem of descending from language into life . . . The philosophers need only dissolve their language into the ordinary

---

[53] *MEW* III, 89.   [54] *MEW* III, 107-8.   [55] *MEW* III, 465.

language from which it is abstracted, to recognize it as the distorted language of the actual world and to realize that neither thought nor language constitutes . . . a separate realm—that they are only *manifestations* of actual life.[56]

Small wonder, then, that Marx and Engels should have come to see in language an immediate index of the health of thought, and that their early collaboration should have resulted in so much close textual analysis and criticism.

In the *Theses on Feuerbach* and *The German Ideology* the concepts of 'Praxis' and 'Ideology' first assume the important place they will ever afterwards retain in Marx's thinking. R. J. Bernstein has rightly said:

Praxis is the central concept in Marx's outlook—the key to understanding his early philosophical speculations and his detailed analysis of the structure of capitalism. It provides the perspective for grasping Marx's conception of man as 'the ensemble of social relationships' and his emphasis on production; it is the basis for comprehending what Marx meant by 'revolutionary practice'.[57]

This clearly affects Marx's approach to literature too—from the Paris Manuscripts onwards he sees all the arts as part of that universal creative activity through which man 'transforms and creates his world and himself'.[58] And though there is a good deal in *The German Ideology* which non-Marxists cannot easily accept, its central notion, that of 'ideology' itself, remains a useful one. It implies, as Karl Mannheim has notably demonstrated, that 'opinions, statements, propositions and systems of ideas are not taken at their face value but are interpreted in the light of the life-situation of the one who expresses them'.[59] It has made men more ready to look behind opinions, perceptions, and interpretations in order to discover life-situations with which they may be connected. It has made critics and theorists try to discover, with Louis Althusser and his disciples, the 'ideological field' into which an author is born, within which he has his formative intellectual experiences, and against which he has to define his own developing world-view. It has made them ask questions about the internal unity of given

---

[56] *MEW* III, 432–3; cf. *GI* 118.   [57] Bernstein, op. cit., p. 13.
[58] G. Petrović, *Marx in the Mid-Twentieth Century* (New York, 1967), pp. 78–9.
[59] K. Mannheim, *Ideology and Utopia. An Introduction to the Sociology of Knowledge* (London, 1960), p. 50.

systems of thinking and feeling, their special *problématique* marked by the absence of certain problems as much as by the presence of others. It has led to inquiries into the relation of particular works or particular systems to larger 'ideological fields' and, of course, into the relation of both to the economic, social, and political organization characteristic of given countries and periods.[60] To find such questions relevant and important we do not have to share Marx's, or Althusser's, political convictions; and we have cause to be grateful to Marxist critics for keeping them steadfastly before us. How sad that they so often interpose impenetrable barriers of Leftspeak between us and their answers.

[60] L. Althusser, *For Marx*, trans. B. Brewster (Harmondsworth, 1969), pp. 62 ff.

6 · From *Grobianus* to *Jean Ziska*

'Le combat ou la mort; la lutte sanguinaire ou le
néant. C'est ainsi que la question est invinciblement
posée.' (George Sand)
$$(MEGA\ I,\ 6,\ 228)$$

(i)

THE views on literature which underlie the Paris Manuscripts
and *The German Ideology* are significantly supplemented by an
article that appeared over Marx's signature in the journal
Mirror of Society (*Gesellschaftsspiegel*) edited by Moses Hess.
This took the form of a book review—a scrutiny of the memoirs
of one J. Peuchet—and was therefore entitled 'Peuchet on
Suicide' (*Peuchet: Vom Selbstmord*).

A strange collection of quotations could be compiled from famous
authors, and from poems written by men in despair who prepare
their own death with a certain amount of ceremony. In the moment
of wondrous cold-bloodedness which follows the decision to die an
infectious kind of enthusiasm arises in their soul and vents itself on
paper, even among those classes who are deprived of education. In
composing their minds before a sacrifice whose full implications
they fathom, they concentrate all their power and breathe their
last in some warm, characteristic expression.

A few of these poems, buried in official archives, are masterpieces.
A lumbering bourgeois who puts all his soul into his business and
makes his trade his God may find such a view very romantic and
may try to refute with a sneer agonies he cannot understand. His
disdain does not surprise us—what else can one expect from three-
percenters who have not so much as an inkling that day by day,
hour by hour, piece by piece, they are killing themselves, murder-
ing their human nature? But what is one to say of good people who
play at being devout and educated and who yet repeat the lumbering bourgeois' unsavoury sayings?[1]

[1] *Gesellschaftsspiegel. Organ zur Vertretung der besitzlosen Volksklassen und zur*

Here we have Marx's characteristic reiteration of Vico's, Hamann's, Herder's belief that poetry is the mother tongue of the human race; that under the stress of great emotion, in existentially significant situations, the springs of poetry will flow again, even in the modern world, and even among those who have been deprived of the mental development education can bring. A life dedicated to grasping and having leads inevitably to an atrophy of such creative powers and thus constitutes a kind of suicide: it murders what makes man truly human. Intellectuals who support the social order Marx deplored in the Europe of his time are therefore condemned for assisting at soul-murder, at the cultural suicide of humanity.

A year later, in October 1847, Marx contributed a series of articles to another paper, the *Brussels German Gazette* (*Deutsche-Brüsseler-Zeitung*), in which he deployed again the polemic techniques tried out in *The German Ideology*, including a multitude of literary prefigurations, parallels, allusions, and quotations. The target of these heavy guns was an obscure radical journalist, Karl Heinzen, who had dared to attack Engels in the same *émigré* journal in which Marx's counter-attack appeared. The attack on Heinzen is worth resurrecting, however, because it opens with the most elaborate characterization of a literary mode, or sub-genre, that Marx was ever to attempt. The mode in question is known as *grobianische Literatur*, or 'booby-literature':[2] it began with medieval disquisitions on table-manners, received fresh impetus from certain sections of Brant's *Ship of Fools* (1494), and culminated in *Grobianus*, a poem composed in Latin by Friedrich Dedekind (1549) and soon translated into German and other European languages.

Shortly before and during the Reformation there came into being in Germany a kind of literature whose very name is striking: *booby-literature*. Today we are moving towards a period of revolution analogous to that of the sixteenth century. No wonder that booby-literature should once again appear among the Germans. Interest

Beleuchtung der gesellschaftlichen Zustände der Gegenwart, Jg. II, Heft 7, 1846 (*MEGA* I, 3, 403).

[2] 'Boor-literature' might be a more accurate rendering; but the term 'booby' as equivalent of 'Grobianus' is well established in England since Roger Bull's translation of 1739: *Grobianus; or, the Compleat Booby. An Ironical Poem in Three Books. Done into English by Roger Bull, Esq.*

in this historical development will easily overcome the aesthetic distaste aroused by writings of this kind—a distaste already felt in the not very fastidious fifteenth and sixteenth centuries.

Shallow, boastful, swaggering, thrasonical, pretentious, and coarse when attacking, reacting hysterically to the coarsenesss of others; wielding the sword with enormous prodigality of effort, taking huge swipes only to let it fall on its flat side; constantly preaching good manners and constantly offending against good manners; comically mingling grandiloquence and vulgarity; concerned with just one subject, and constantly straying from that subject; presumptuously confronting popular understanding with petty-bourgeois half-educated 'learning', and scholarship and science with so-called 'healthy common sense'; gushing into formless breadth with a certain self-satisfied ease; giving philistine content a plebeian shape; wrestling with the written language in order to give it what might be called a purely 'physical' character; fond of pointing to the writer's own self in the background, itching to give proof of his strength, to show off his broad shoulders, to stretch his limbs in public; proclaiming a healthy mind in a healthy body; infected, without knowing it, by the wrangling and hair splitting of the sixteenth century as though by a physical fever; spellbound by narrow, dogmatic concepts but appealing, when confronted with real attempts to understand, to petty 'practice'; fulminating against reaction, yet itself reactionary in the face of progress; making up for the incapacity to ridicule an adversary through witty description by running, ridiculously, through a whole scale of abuse; Solomon and Marcolph, Don Quixote and Sancho Panza, enthusiast and suburban bourgeois at once; letting resentment take coarse and brutal forms; with an atmosphere of self-satisfied, self-consciously 'honest' philistinism wafting over everything—such was the 'booby-literature' of the sixteenth century. If our memory does not deceive us, German popular wit has erected a lyrical monument to it in the song of 'Heinecke, the mighty drudge'. Herr Heinzen has the merit of being one of the restorers of 'booby-literature' and thus one of the swallows which herald the coming spring-time of the nations. Heinzen's manifesto . . . provides a contemporary impetus for the study of a literary by-product whose historical interest for Germany we have indicated. Taking his manifesto as our basis, we shall portray the literary species Herr Heinzen represents in the same way as historians of literature characterize sixteenth-century writers—Thomas Murner, for instance—by examining the writings the sixteeenth century has left behind.[3]

[3] *MEW* IV, 331–2.

Marx's re-evocation of a vanished genre serves, it is clear, no merely antiquarian purpose. Similarity of social constellations, he suggests, will lead to similar literary phenomena. Since, therefore, Germany seemed to be entering a period of revolution which resembled, in some respects, that which preceded and accompanied the Reformation, the examination of fifteenth- and sixteenth-century literature might well turn out to be relevant to the present. It soon becomes clear, indeed, that we are to see the description of 'booby-literature' as a kind of inverted palimpsest—that we are to discern a characterization of a modern phenomenon, of Karl Heinzen and his like, in and through the characterization of a body of writings few Germans would otherwise be tempted to rescue from the oblivion to which time had consigned it. Literary antiquarianism can help us to understand the modern world, to combat its abuses, and thus—ultimately—to change it.

'Booby-literature', *grobianische Literatur*, represents one kind of temptation to which Germans of the nineteenth century, no less than those of the sixteenth, are subject: mistaking coarse stupidity for strength and insight. Marx's reference to the folk-song 'Heinecke the mighty drudge'[4] would seem to suggest that this was a temptation to which the middle classes succumbed more easily than the common people. But there was another kind of temptation—the polar opposite of the first—to which men are more subject in times of social upheaval; a temptation which Marx chose to illustrate, not from the literature of the Reformation, but from that of the eighteenth century. The focus, once again, is on German literature:

Thus in periods of noisy revolution, in a time of powerful denying and disowning like that of the eighteenth century, there appear honest, well-meaning men, well-educated decent satyrs like Salomon Gessner, who oppose to historical depravation a state not subject to development: the *idyll*. In praise of such idyllic poets it might, however, be said, that they weigh up scrupulously to whom they should award the palm of morality—the shepherd or the sheep.[5]

---

[4] This appears under the title *Hennecke Knecht* in Arnim and Brentano's collection of (adapted) folk-songs *Des Knaben Wunderhorn* (1805–8). Marx seems to have changed 'Hennecke' to 'Heinecke' in order to approximate the name to that of Karl Heinzen, the journalist he is attacking.

[5] *MEW* IV, 337.

The idyllic component of German literature continued to be anathema to Marx—he was to express his hearty dislike, for instance, of the hero of Goethe's epic idyll *Hermann und Dorothea*.[6]

What Marx tried to diagnose, in his remarks on 'booby-literature' and Gessnerian idylls, is various kinds of illusion, of 'false consciousness', to which he thought the German middle classes peculiarly subject in unquiet times. Were they not apt to stylize themselves as valiant giant-killers if they were radicals, as idyllic shepherds if they were not? Had not Karl Heinzen—the immediate occasion for these reflections—actually compared himself to a champion who expected to be felled by a communist Achilles and found himself attacked by a Thersites instead? 'Only a Hector', Marx comments, 'may divine that he will fall by the hand of Achilles', and he goes on to quote that scene in Shakespeare's *Love's Labour's Lost* in which the fantastic braggart Don Adriano de Armado is ridiculed for his inadequate assumption of the role of Hector. But what about that reference to Thersites? Could it be, Marx goes on to ask ironically, that Heinzen has derived his conception of the heroes of antiquity not from Homer, but from Schlegel's translation of Shakespeare's *Troilus and Cressida*? (The suggestion that Heinzen would not, of course, be able to read Shakespeare in the original will not have gone unnoticed.) In that case Heinzen's part is not that of Hector, but that of Ajax. And Marx goes on to assume the Thersites persona Heinzen had assigned to him by quoting, with obvious relish, from scenes in *Troilus and Cressida* in which the stupid, lumbering Ajax is baited by Thersites—the whole culminating in some words of Thersites which Marx adopts as his own: 'I had rather be a tick in a sheep than such a valiant ignorance.' He then proceeds to chronicle Heinzen's doughty deeds in mock-heroic style, ending with an extended quotation from *Reynard the Fox*, that European classic which Goethe had transformed, in the hexameter version from which Marx quotes, into a politically and socially instructive High German mock-epic.[7]

It is curious to remember that Marx had, in fact, adopted the perspective of Thersites before Heinzen ever thought of

---

[6] 'Der Goethesche Simpleton', letter to Engels, 6 Jan. 1859—*MEW* XXIX, 381.
[7] *MEW* IV, 332–5.

likening him to that character. In a letter to Arnold Ruge, written from Bonn on 27 April 1842, Marx had quoted Shakespeare's *Troilus and Cressida*: ' "Nothing but wars and lechery", says Thersites, and if one can't reproach the university here with waging wars, there is, at least, no lack of lechery.'[8] But then – the notion of 'Thersism', as a mean-spirited, envy-ridden perspective on life, was in the air in Young-Hegelian circles. Had not Hegel himself, in those lectures on the philosophy of history which Marx knew well, analysed the phenomenon in his own inimitable way?

Homer's Thersites, who reprimands kings, is a figure that recurs in all ages. It is true that he is not always beaten with a stout stick, as he is in Homer; but his envy, his stubborn wilfulness, is the thorn he has ever in his flesh, the immortal worm that gnaws at him. He is ever tortured by the knowledge that his intentions, even if excellent, and his cavillings, will remain wholly without success in the world. It is possible to take malicious pleasure in the fate of Thersism.[9]

For Marx it was natural to look from Homer's Thersites to Shakespeare's, and to recognize that adopting Thersites' perspective could be as conducive to a truthful view as adopting that of Mephistopheles. Here, as so often, he could stand Hegel on his head—he could believe that if Thersites spoke out clearly enough and often enough, the 'kings' he cavilled at might be seen for what they were. And that, in its turn, might be a step towards ridding the world of those who dominated it and the order they supported. 'Thersism' might not, in the end, prove as irrevocably doomed to failure as Hegel had believed.

What Marx found in the pageant-scene of *Love's Labour's Lost* and in *Reynard the Fox*, what he found above all in the figure of Thersites, was delight in pricking the bubbles of self-deception, illusion, false consciousness—a delight he had also found, of course, in Heine. The Latin phrase that Heine had hurled at the head of the pious painter Cornelius in *Germany. A Winter's Tale*, Marx now hurls at Heinzen: *cacatum non est pictum.*[10]

---

[8] *MEW* XXVII, 403.

[9] Hegel, *Vorlesungen über die Philosophie der Geschichte*, ed. T. Litt (Stuttgart, 1961), p. 78.

[10] *MEW* IV, 354; cf. Heine's *Deutschland. Ein Wintermärchen*, Caput XI.

(ii)

The attack on Heinzen in the *Deutsche-Brüsseler-Zeitung*, published in October and November 1847 under the title 'Moralizing Criticism or Criticizing Morality: A Contribution to German Cultural History', had been preceded, in June 1847, by an attack on a greater and more significant figure, a man whose condemnation of private property had played an important part in Marx's own intellectual evolution. This was Pierre Joseph Proudhon, whose philosophy of history Marx now found far too idealistic and Hegelian. 'This is old-fashioned Hegelianism, not history. It is not profane history, the history of men, but sacred history, the history of ideas. In his conception man is only an instrument, which the idea, or eternal reason, uses for its own development.'[11] Proudhon's *Philosophy of Poverty* (*Système des contradictions économiques ou Philosophie de la misère*) therefore elicited from Marx a counter-pamphlet, whose title once again displayed that chiastic inversion Marx found so well suited to his style of thought: *The Poverty of Philosophy* (*Misère de la philosophie. Réponse à la Philosophie de la misère de M. Proudhon*).

In attacking Proudhon, Marx sought to pillory the false abstraction and generalization of those who regarded economic laws as 'eternal' instead of applying only to one given moment of historic development; and he hoped, at the same time, to scourge all those who 'make a thing out of a word', who look at life as though it were literature. Proudhon, he tells us,

sees in the commodity 'labour', which is a terrible reality, nothing but a grammatical ellipsis. It follows from this that the whole of present-day society . . . is from now on founded on *a poetic licence, a figurative expression*. If society wants to 'extirpate all the ills' from which it suffers, let it change the language; all it has to do is to apply to the French Academy for a new edition of its dictionary. After all this we can easily understand why M. Proudhon has to insert long disquisitions on etymology and other grammatical matters into a book on political economy [my italics].[12]

Among the 'poetic licences' of Proudhon's book is his use of Marx's own favourite mythological hero: Prometheus.

[11] Letter to Annenkov, 28 Dec. 1846—*BR* 38; *MEW* XXVII, 451 ff.
[12] *MEW* IV, 88.

What now follows belongs to classical antiquity. It is a poetic narrative whose purpose is to allow the reader to recover from the effort involved in following the exact mathematical demonstrations which preceded it. M. Proudhon dubs his personified society 'Prometheus' and celebrates the deeds of that social Prometheus . . . He is a queer customer, that Prometheus of M. Proudhon's, as weak on logic as on political economy . . . Proudhon's way of explaining things has something of the Greek and the Hebrew at the same time; it is at once mystical and allegoric . . . What, then, is this Prometheus M. Proudhon has resuscitated? He is society, social relationships based on class-opposition. These relationships are not those of one individual to another, but those of worker to capitalist, tenant to landowner etc. If you delete these relationships, you dissolve the whole of society; your Prometheus is then no more than a phantom without arms and legs, i.e. without machines, without division of labour. In a word, he now lacks everything you originally gave him . . .[13]

Proudhon's personification of society in a mythical hero he first met in literature is more calculated to obfuscate truth than to reveal it. If you see the whole of human society in the guise of *one* character, you substitute a phantom for a divided and complex reality; you substitute words for things. Myth takes the place of theory and all truth is lost in an unholy combination of mysticism and allegory. In the wrong hands classical myths produce, and strengthen, harmful illusions.

What Proudhon has not understood, Marx goes on to claim, is that social relations are intimately connected with modes of production:

In acquiring new forces of production, men change their mode of production, their way of earning their living; they change all their social relations. The hand-mill will give you a society with the feudal lord, the steam-mill a society with the industrial capitalist.

The same men who establish social relations in conformity with their material power of production, also produce principles, laws, and categories, in conformity with their social relations. Thus, these ideas and categories are no more eternal than the relations which they express. They are *historical and transient products*.

There is a continuous movement of growth of the productive forces, of destruction of social relations, of formation of ideas; nothing is immutable but the abstract movement—*mors immortalis*.[14]

[13] *MEW* IV, 121–3.   [14] *BR* 108–9; *MEW* IV, 130.

I leave it to students of feudalism to determine how far Marx's statement about the hand-mill (meant, I suppose, symbolically rather than literally) may still be found acceptable. What matters in the present context is the place of literature in a scheme which sees ideas and categories as 'no more eternal than the relations they express', as 'historical and transient products'. That literary works are 'historical products' may be freely admitted—but how far are they 'transient'? The passage just quoted does not answer this question directly; but indirectly it does give a clear indication of Marx's sense of the trans-temporal, permanent value of great writings and the ideas expressed in them. It manages this by culminating, characteristically, in a reminder of one of the world's great poems, a poem whose power to delight, instruct, and stimulate many years after it was written Marx had often experienced. The phrase *mors immortalis* recalls that haunting line from Lucretius' *On the Nature of Things* which Marx had already quoted in his doctoral thesis:

> mortalem vitam mors cui immortalis ademit

> immortal death has stolen away his mortal life.[15]

Marx's relativizing theory is itself relativized by his practice of quotation.

The quotation from Lucretius is by no means the only instance of apposite literary reminiscence in *The Poverty of Philosophy*. Marx cites a line from Juvenal's eighth Satire to express his sense of the paradoxical nature of Proudhon's argument: *Et propter vitam vivendi perdere causas* ('and, for life's sake, lose that which makes life worth living').[16] This line of Juvenal's was destined to become one of Marx's favourite quotations; he came to see in it as clear a statement of the effects of economic laws in modern society as any he had found in Adam Smith and Ricardo.[17] Defoe's *Robinson Crusoe* makes a first fleeting

---

[15] Cf. *MEW EB* I, 294.   [16] *MEW* IV, 89.

[17] Marx was not the only nineteenth-century writer to feel the appositeness of this line from Juvenal. William Morris's lecture on 'Art and Socialism', delivered to the Secular Society of Leicester in 1884 and printed in *The Commonwealth* in the following year, includes an eloquent paragraph which culminates in an allusion to this same passage: 'Nor can it be pleaded for the system of modern civilization that the mere material or bodily gains of it balance the loss of pleasure which it has

appearance in *The Poverty of Philosophy,* to illustrate, conveniently, a situation in which the *social* element has been reduced to a minimum; left alone and untroubled by social considerations, Crusoe illustrates a hypothetical condition where every man is a hermit and produces only for himself.[18] Trotsky was later to adopt the same model and dub Proudhon (that revolutionary without party or class) 'the Robinson Crusoe of Socialism'.[19]

The Preface of *The Poverty of Philosophy* also brings distinct echoes of Heine's mock-respectful remarks on Victor Cousin in his book about German religion, philosophy, and literature (*De l'Allemagne*), and the opening of Marx's second chapter too is distinctly Heinesque; but Voltaire pervades the book more than Heine. Voltaire's analysis of money-value, in his remarks on Law's system in *The History of the Paris Parliament,* is quoted and praised,[20] and Voltaire's story *The Man with Forty Crowns* appears as evidence that Voltaire had a 'presentiment' of Proudhon and his system (' "L'homme aux quarante écus" a pressenti un Proudhon à venir'): ' "By your leave, Sir Creator —everyone is master in his own world; but you will never make me believe that the world in which we live is made of glass." '[21] Marx quotes these lines from Voltaire's story as a prophetic caricature of Proudhon, and as a suggestion of the sceptical, common-sense attitude we should adopt towards an account of the economic world which too many socialists were inclined, in Marx's day, to accept as gospel truth. As Marx explains,

M. Proudhon's work is not simply a treatise on political economy, a common or garden book—it is a Bible. 'Mysteries', 'secrets

brought upon the world; for as I hinted before those gains have been so unfairly divided that the contrast between rich and poor has been fearfully intensified, so that in all civilized countries, but most of all in England, the terrible spectacle is exhibited to two peoples living street by street and door by door, people of the same blood, the same tongue, and at least nominally living under the same laws, but yet one civilized and the other uncivilized. All this I say is the result of the system that has trampled down Art, and exalted Commerce into a sacred religion; and it would seem is ready, with the ghastly stupidity which is its principal characteristic, to mock the Roman satirist for his noble warning by taking it in inverse meaning, and now bids us all for the sake of life to destroy the reasons for living.' (*Political Writings of William Morris,* ed. A. L. Morton (London, 1973), p. 111.)

[18] *MEW* IV, 104.
[19] Cf. E. H. Carr, *Studies in Revolution* (London, 1950), p. 44.
[20] *MEW* IV, 109–10.   [21] *MEW* IV, 166.

snatched from God's bosom', 'revelations'—none of these are miss-
ing. But since nowadays prophets are discussed more conscientiously
than profane authors, the reader must be content to wander with
us through the arid and dark erudition of this *Genesis*, so that he may
later rise with M. Proudhon to the ethereal and fecund regions of
Super-socialism.[22]

The ironic passage just quoted occurs at the very beginning
of Marx's pamphlet—it is balanced, at the end, by a sentence
from George Sand's novel *Jean Ziska*, which was published in
Brussels in 1843, after gracing, in instalments, the columns of
the *Revue indépendante* of Paris:

Only in an order of things where there are no more classes and class-
antagonisms will *social evolution* cease to involve *political revolution*.
Until then the last word of social science, on the eve of every general
reconstruction of society will always be:

Battle or death; bloody struggle or annihilation—that is the
inexorable way in which the question is put.[23]

It must surely be deemed remarkable that Marx should look to
a contemporary *novel* for 'the last word of social science' in his
own time.

The Poverty of Philosophy also contains Marx's most direct
examination so far of the way in which our predilections, our
'personal' tastes, are directed and circumscribed by our position
in the socio-economic order:

The consumer is no freer than the producer. His opinion depends on
his means and his needs. Both are determined by his social position,
and this, in its turn, depends on the general organization of society.
True, the workman who buys potatoes and the kept mistress who
buys lace follow only their respective predilection; but the difference
in their predilections is explained by the different position they
occupy in the world; and that, in its turn, is a product of social
organization.[24]

Here Marx indicates the limits set to man's 'self-creation' in a
way which looks forward to his famous later analysis, in *Grundrisse*, of the social determination of private interests. 'It is', Marx
will there explain, 'the interest of a private individual; but its
content, its form, its means of realization are given by social

[22] *MEW* IV, 66.   [23] *MEW* IV, 182; *BR* 244.   [24] *MEW* IV, 75.

conditions.'[25] The relevance of this to the question of literary tastes, and the manipulations to which such tastes can be subjected, should be obvious without further demonstration.

(iii)

It was because of his anxiety that workmen's interests should not be confined to the buying of potatoes that Marx took time off from his reading and writing to found, and keep alive, a German Workers' Circle in Brussels. This *Brüsseler Deutscher Arbeiterverein*, which soon had some hundred members, met on Wednesday and Sunday evenings. Marx attended assiduously and introduced the tradition that while the Wednesday evenings were given over wholly to political and social discussions, the Sunday evenings should include literary and musical entertainments. From a report in the *Deutsche-Brüsseler-Zeitung* about New Year festivities in 1847–8 we learn that in the course of a dramatic entertainment at the Workers' Circle 'Frau Dr. Marx demonstrated her genius for recitation'.[26] The rationale for such entertainments might have been found in *The Poverty of Philosophy*; but Marx had in fact set it down more fully in the Paris Manuscripts of 1844:

When communist *artisans* associate with one another, theory, propaganda, etc., is their first end. But at the same time, as a result of this association, they acquire a new need—the need for togetherness—and what appears as a means becomes an end. In this practical process the most splendid results are to be observed whenever French socialist workers are seen assembled. Such things as smoking, drinking, eating, etc., are no longer required as means of contact or bringing together. Company, association, and conversation (which again has togetherness as its end) are enough for them; the brotherhood of man is no mere phrase with them, but a fact of their life, and the nobility of man shines upon us from their work-hardened bodies.[27]

To introduce 'work-hardened' artisans to political arguments designed to help them understand—and therefore change—existing social relationships was thus only one of the goals Marx

---

[25] *G* 74.
[26] Cf. H. Gemlow (and others), *Karl Marx. Eine Biographie*, p. 108; and H. Dornemann, *Jenny Marx. Der Lebensweg einer Sozialistin* (Berlin, 1969), pp. 96–7.
[27] *MEW EB* I, 553–4; *EPM* 154–5.

had before him when he helped to found and run the Workers' Circle. Another, clearly, was to arouse in its working-class members a need for cultural experiences which their position in society would not normally have allowed them to acquire or to satisfy.

While gladly making time for such socially useful activities, Marx continued to immerse himself in that 'sea of books' which constituted, in Ruge's memorable phrase, his natural element. He remained aware that the great contribution he now felt he could make to world history would necessitate an immense amount of critical reading and study—particularly of political economy. It is not surprising, therefore, to find him now turning, with increasing frequency, to English authors. The books he excerpted at Brussels include John Stuart Mill's *Essays on Some Unsettled Questions of Political Economy*—which seemed to Marx a most striking, if unwitting, demonstration of the maze of contradictions in which bourgeois theorists were losing their way; Defoe's *Giving Alms no Charity, and Employing the Poor* . . .; Carlyle's essay on Chartism; and William Cobbett's *Paper against Gold; or the History and Mystery of the Bank of England* . . ., which elicited several admiring comments and no unfavourable ones among his critical jottings.[28] With the writings of Defoe, Cobbett, and Carlyle he was to concern himself more than once in the years to come.

[28] *MEGA* I, 6, 603-9.

7 · World Literature and Class Conflict

> 'National one-sidedness and narrow-mindedness
> become more and more impossible, and from the
> numerous national and local literatures there
> arises a world literature.'
>
> (*MEW* IV, 466)

(i)

'THE combination of scientific analysis with moral judgment',
Bottomore and Rubel have said, 'is by no means uncommon in
the field of social studies. Marx is unusual, and his work is
exceptionally interesting, because, unlike any other major social
thinker, he was the recognized leader, and subsequently the
prophet, of an organized political movement.'[1] The document,
however, which was to do more than any other to ensure such
recognition, the *Manifesto of the Communist Party*,* went almost
unnoticed when it first appeared in London in February 1848.
Composed jointly by Marx and Engels at the invitation of the
Communist League, this manifesto is pervaded from the very
start by what may justifiably be called 'literary' imagery:
metaphors, images, from oral and written literature, from publishing, and from theatrical performance. 'A spectre is haunting
Europe', the famous opening words proclaim; and lest we mistake the fictional source of this image, Marx and Engels proceed
at once to speak of the need to confront 'this nursery-tale
[*Märchen*] of the spectre of Communism with a manifesto of the

---

* From now on this work will be called by its better-known title: *The Communist
Manifesto.*

---

[1] *BR* 40.

party itself'.[2] Many related images follow: 'spectacle' (*Schau-spiel*), 'song of lamentation' (*Klagelied*), 'lampoon' (*Pasquill*), 'pocket-edition (*Duodez-Ausgabe*) of the New Jerusalem'; and, more elaborate than these, a 'palimpsest' image which Marx and Engels may well have borrowed from Heine:

It is well-known how the monks write silly lines of Catholic saints *over* the manuscripts on which the classical works of ancient heathen-dom had been written. The German literati reversed this process with profane French literature. They wrote their philosophical nonsense beneath the French original. For instance, beneath the French criticism of the economic function of money, they wrote: alienation of humanity . . .[3]

German readers, in fact, will more than once feel that the Communist Manifesto is itself a palimpsest: that beneath the utter-ances of Marx and Engels they detect those of German poets. This may be just a matter of an image, or a phrase, that brings reminiscences of another context with it:

The aristocracy, in order to rally the people to them, waved the proletarian alms-bag in front for a banner. But the people, as often as it joined them, *saw on their hindquarters the old feudal coats of arms*, and deserted with loud and irreverent laughter [my italics].[4]

. . . *erblickte es auf ihrem Hintern die alten feudalen Wappen* . . . —no reader of Heine will fail to hear the echo of *Germany. A Winter's Tale*:

> Das mahnt an das Mittelalter so schön
> An Edelknechte und Knappen,
> Die in dem Herzen getragen die Treu
> Und auf dem Hintern ein Wappen.

> This is a beautiful reminder of the Middle Ages,
> Of noble servants and squires,
> Who bore loyalty in their heart
> And a coat of arms on their behind.[5]

---

[2] *SW* I, 108; *MEW* IV, 461.

[3] *SW* I, 131; *MEW* IV, 486. Heine used the palimpsest image in *Die Harzreise* and *Französische Maler*. The image is not, however, an uncommon one.

[4] *SW* I, 128; *MEW* IV, 483.

[5] Even the famous phrase which concludes *The Communist Manifesto* may be an echo of Heine. In his essay on Ludwig Marcus (*Ludwig Marcus. Denkworte*) Heine had spoken 'of that fraternal union of the workers of all lands [*Verbrüderung der Arbeiter in allen Ländern*], of that wild army of the proletariat [*von dem wilden Heer des Proletariats*], which is bent on doing away with all concern about nationality

Another and more complex kind of palimpsest effect is produced by the following passage:

Modern bourgeois society with its relation of production, of exchange, and of property, a society that has conjured up such gigantic means of production and of exchange, is like the sorcerer [*gleicht dem Hexenmeister*] who is no longer able to control the powers of the nether world that he has called up by his spells.[6]

In Goethe's poem 'The Sorcerer's Apprentice' (*Der Zauberlehrling*) it is the apprentice who calls up spirits he cannot, in the end, subdue, and it is the master, the *Hexenmeister*, who repairs the damage. In *The Communist Manifesto* the master-sorcerer himself has lost control: the magnitude of that disaster can be best felt if we perceive Goethe's contrasting text in and through that of the *Manifesto*.

The terms 'literature' and 'literary', *Literatur* and *literarisch*, occur frequently in *The Communist Manifesto*, and are used in three different ways. The first example is to be found only in the German version; it is absent from the familiar English translation:

Thus arose petty-bourgeois socialism. Sismondi was the head of this school, notably in France but also in England.

Es bildete sich so der kleinbürgerliche Sozialismus. Sismondi ist das Haupt dieser Literatur nicht nur für Frankreich sondern auch für England.[7]

Here the term *Literatur* denotes 'the body of technical books, pamphlets, etc., that treat of a given subject, and the writers who produce it'.

The sentence about Sismondi occurs in a section of *The Communist Manifesto* which is entitled *Socialist and Communist Literature* and opens as follows:

Owing to their historical position, it became the vocation of the aristocracies of France and England to write pamphlets against modern bourgeois society. In the French Revolution of July 1830, and in the English reform agitation, these aristocracies again

in order to pursue a common purpose in Europe, to call into being a true democracy'. Cf. Dolf Sternberger, *Heinrich Heine und die Abschaffung der Sünde* (Hamburg and Düsseldorf, 1972), p. 360.

[6] *SW* I, 113; *MEW* IV, 467.   [7] *SW* I, 130; *MEW* IV, 484.

succumbed to the hateful upstart. Thenceforth, a serious political struggle was altogether out of the question. A literary battle alone remained possible. But even in the domain of literature the old cries of the restoration period had become impossible.

In order to arouse sympathy the aristocracy was obliged to lose sight, apparently, of its own interests and to formulate its indictment against the bourgeoisie in the interest of the exploited working class alone. Thus the aristocracy prepared itself the vengeful satisfaction of singing scornful songs [*Schmählieder*] about their new master and whispering into his ear more or less sinister prophecies of coming catastrophe.[8]

Here 'literature', it would seem, denotes more than just the 'pamphlets' mentioned in the opening sentence. Poems, plays, and novels could qualify for inclusion if they had some sort of political slant or 'message'. We find one such novel, Étienne Cabet's *Journey to Icaria* (*Voyage en Icarie. Roman philosophique et social*, Paris, 1840 and 1842), mentioned a little later in this section.[9] This is, of course, the work to which 'communism' owes its very name; and it had already figured prominently in *The German Ideology* where it was used, through contrast and comparison, to show up the plagiarisms and misunderstandings which Marx and Engels ascribed to Karl Grün and other 'true socialists'.[10] Literature is not, for Marx, a separate, self-enclosed region. Poems like those of Heine and the song of the Silesian weavers, novels like those of Gustave Beaumont, Étienne Cabet, and George Sand, plays like Gustav Freytag's *The Journalists* (which Marx was to see much later in life), are clearly related to other, more utilitarian forms of writing, and may profitably be discussed alongside these.

The Communist Manifesto uses the term 'literary', however, in yet another sense—one which will not surprise readers of Marx's earlier works. In the section devoted to 'German or "true" Socialism', Marx and Engels discuss, once again, the introduction of French socialist and communist writings in eighteenth- and nineteenth-century Germany:

German philosophers, would-be philosophers, and *beaux esprits* eagerly seized on this literature, only forgetting that when these

[8] *SW* I, 127; *MEW* IV, 482–3.
[9] *SW* I, 136; *MEW* IV, 491. Marx had mentioned Cabet's Utopian novel before—in the letters to Ruge published in *Deutsch–Französische Jahrbücher* (*MEW* I, 344). [10] *MEW* III, 507 ff.

writings immigrated from France into Germany, French social conditions had not immigrated along with them. In contact with German social conditions, this French literature lost all its immediate practical significance, and assumed *a purely literary aspect* [*ein rein literarisches Aussehen*] . . . Thus, to the German philosophers of the eighteenth century, the demands of the first French Revolution were nothing more than the demands of 'Practical Reason' in general, and the utterance of the will of the revolutionary French bourgeoisie signified in their eyes the laws of pure Will, of Will as it was bound to be, of true human Will generally [my italics].[11]

Here 'purely literary' implies—as so often in Marx—a world of words floating loose, words cut off from things, cut off from social and political reality. The Manifesto goes on to describe this effect, in terms which carry suggestions of the sentimental, belletristic, and rhetorical, as a 'robe of speculative cobwebs, embroidered with flowers of rhetoric, steeped in the dew of sickly sentiment . . .', and to make the important point that such literature, however ethereally interpreted, is in nineteenth-century society itself an item of commercial transaction. Its writers and translators are concerned with the sale of their commodity (*Absatz ihrer Ware*) among the German public.

As such terms show, and as is not surprising in such a context, *The Communist Manifesto* bids us look at the way writers function in modern society, and concludes that romantic illusions can no longer hide the actualities of the market-place: 'The bourgeoisie has stripped of its halo every occupation hitherto honoured and looked up to with reverent awe. It has converted the physician, the lawyer, the priest, *the poet*, the man of science, into its paid wage labourers' [my italics].[12] Even poetry, then, is a commodity in the modern world and subject to its economic laws. Nor are poets exempt from that determination of men's thoughts which the *Manifesto* proclaims in uncompromising terms: 'Your very ideas are . . . outgrowths of the conditions of your bourgeois production and bourgeois property.'[13] And if writers are in this way a *product* of their society and the social groups for whom they write, those social groupings in their turn are affected by the writings they have indirectly produced and inspired: 'With very few exceptions, all the so-called socialist

[11] *SW* I, 130–1; *MEW* IV, 485–6.   [12] *SW* I, 111; *MEW* IV, 465.
[13] *SW* I, 123; *MEW* IV, 477.

and communist publications that now circulate in Germany belong to the domain of *this foul and enervating literature*' [my italics].[14] The nemesis of converting writers into paid hirelings is that their productions enervate their readers instead of enlivening and refreshing them with new ideas, new hopes, and new energies.

But if a nation's writings are the product of economic and social conditions, they will alter as those conditions alter—and *The Communist Manifesto* itself is clearly seen, by its authors, as a sign of the inevitability of change as well as a call to effect change:

Does it require deep intuition to comprehend that man's ideas, views, and conceptions, in one word, man's consciousness, changes with every change in the conditions of his material existence, in his social relations and in his social life? What else does the history of ideas prove, than that intellectual production changes its character in proportion as material production is changed? The ruling ideas of each age have ever been the ideas of its ruling class.[15]

The Communist Manifesto, we must infer, heralds the coming change by its resolute adoption and proclamation of ideas which, its authors think, will become those of the proletariat, the ruling class of a future in which 'the free development of each' will be 'the condition for the free development of all'.

The passage about the relation of consciousness to material existence which I have just quoted has often been attacked, by non-Marxists, as bleakly deterministic. Yet as René Wellek has rightly pointed out, Marx's wording seems designed to obviate this charge. Consciousness, he avers, changes *with* the conditions of material existence. 'If', René Wellek comments, 'one interprets the word "with" freely, no complete economic determinism is yet proclaimed; the intellectual life of man changes *with* the transformation of economic order. A parallelism, an analogy is taught—not one-sided dependence.'[16]

Marx and Engels proclaim, in particular, one great change in literature; a change that Goethe had foreseen in his old age, when he looked at the way increase in international exchange of material goods was bringing related increase in intellectual

---

[14] *SW* 132; *MEW* IV, 488.   [15] *SW* I, 125; *MEW* IV, 480.
[16] R. Wellek, *A History of Modern Criticism 1750–1950*, Vol. iii, p. 235.

and spiritual traffic and interchange. The old Goethe therefore spoke, more and more frequently, of 'world literature', *Weltliteratur*.[17] For Goethe, such 'world literature' did not imply an abandoning of national characteristics. On the contrary, each national literature would be valued by readers abroad for its distinctiveness and difference, for the special instrumental colour it added to the symphony of world literature. Through becoming conscious of the specific contributions of other nations and learning to value them, we would also learn to value our own. Our own literature, it is true, would to some extent change its character through such contacts; but this would be an enrichment, and the resulting symbioses, like Goethe's own *West–Eastern Divan* and *Chinese–German Seasons and Times of Day*, would continue to bear the imprint of the specific national culture within which the foreign works had been received, as well as that of their authors' genius and individual bent.

Such a conception was clearly congenial to Marx and Engels, who had described in *The German Ideology* how one generation after another learnt to develop further the material wealth, capital, and forces of production it had inherited:

In the course of this development, the circles which act upon one another expand—and the more they do this, the more the pristine isolation of individual nationalities is annihilated by perfected means of production, exchange and commerce [*Verkehr*] and a consequent division of labour between different nations, the more history becomes world history.[18]

The Communist Manifesto supplements this with speculations about the effect such developments will have on literature:

The bourgeoisie has through its exploitation of the world market given a cosmopolitan character to production and consumption in every country. To the great chagrin of reactionaries, it has drawn from under the feet of industry the national ground on which it stood. All old-fashioned national industries have been destroyed or are daily being destroyed. They are dislodged by new industries, whose introduction becomes a life and death question for all civilized nations, by industries that no longer work up indigenous raw material, but raw material drawn from the remotest zones; industries whose products are consumed, not only at home, but in

---

[17] Cf. F. Strich, *Goethe und die Weltliteratur* (Berne, 1946), pp. 13–103.
[18] *MEW* III, 45.

every quarter of the globe. In place of the old wants, satisfied by the production of the country, we find new wants, requiring for their satisfaction the products of distant lands and climes. In place of the old local and national seclusion and self-sufficiency, we have intercourse in every direction, universal interdependence of nations. And as in material, so also in intellectual production. The intellectual creations of individual nations become common property. National one-sidedness and narrow-mindedness become more and more impossible, and from the numerous national and local literatures there arises a world literature.[19]

What is chiefly remarkable about this passage, as about so many others in Marx's work, is the compliment it pays to the nineteenth-century bourgeoisie. Not for him the out-and-out anti-capitalism of the German Romantics, or of Thomas Carlyle— he never forgot the extent to which the order he wanted to overturn had in fact served the cause of progress. And what 'progress' meant in this context had once again been clearly spelt out in *The German Ideology*, where Marx and Engels had looked forward to a time when 'separate individuals will be liberated from the various national and local barriers, be brought into practical connection with the material and intellectual production of the whole world and be put into a position to acquire the capacity to enjoy this all-sided production of the whole earth (the creations of man)'.[20]

The Communist Manifesto goes on to consider the part a victorious working class would play in a process which affects literature along with all other spheres of life:

National differences and antagonisms between peoples are daily more and more vanishing, owing to the development of the bourgeoisie, to freedom of commerce, to the world market, to uniformity in the mode of production and in the condition of life corresponding thereto.

The supremacy of the proletariat will cause them to vanish still faster.[21]

It may well be thought that *The Communist Manifesto* does not, in this passage, make enough allowances for resistance to the trends it detected: national antagonisms and differences have not vanished as fast or as universally as the logic of production

[19] *SW* I, 112; *MEW* IV, 466.   [20] *GI* 55.
[21] *SW* I, 124–5; *MEW* IV, 479.

and commerce seemed to suggest. Marx came, in fact, to realize this and consistently distanced himself, in his later life, from would-be followers who underestimated the power of national feeling. In 1866 he ridiculed French delegates to a Council meeting of the First International for announcing 'that all nationalities and even nations were "antiquated prejudices"'. For these delegates, he added, 'negation of nationalities seemed to mean their absorption into the model French nation'. Later still he praised the Russian economist Flerovsky because he had 'a great feeling for national characteristics', and he took up the cause of the Irish as 'a national question'.[22]

The prophecy of *The Communist Manifesto* has not, however, gone wholly unfulfilled. We have seen, in this our twentieth century, a world-wide dissemination and mingling of 'national and local' literatures, through translations, paperbacks, theatre-tours, broadcasts, films, and television, which have transformed our cultural perspective in ways that would not have surprised Marx. 'World literature' has arrived with a vengeance—as a vast Imaginary Museum, as a great Library of Babel.

The Communist Manifesto is essentially a call to action. As such it commits itself, in the main, to what one might call a Dives and Lazarus view—or better, perhaps: a Master–Slave view—of modern society: the opposition of two classes, haves and have-nots, bourgeoisie and proletariat. But as a Polish scholar has pointed out,

if all political or religious struggles are to be interpreted as class struggles, if we are to correlate the various literary and artistic trends with underlying class relations, if we are to look for a reflection of class interests and class prejudices in moral norms, then we must make use of a greater number of classes than the two basic ones in *The Communist Manifesto*.[23]

This may help to explain why one can detect, in Marx's works, three-layered and other multi-layered models of class structure as well as the dichotomous one of the *Manifesto*; and also, per-

[22] Letters to Engels, 20 June 1866 and 12 Feb. 1870—*MEW* XXXI, 228–9 and XXXII, 443; to S. Meyer and A. Vogt, 9 Apr. 1870—*MEW* XXXII, 668.
[23] S. Ossowski, *Class Structure in the Socialist Consciousness*, trans. S. Patterson (London, 1963), p. 88. It is not irrelevant to recall that Disraeli's *Sybil; or The Two Nations* had been published in 1845, and that a character in Heine's *William Ratcliff* had as early as 1822 divided mankind into two warring nations: the well-fed and the hungry.

haps, why, when Marx at last addresses himself to a definition of 'class' in what was later to become volume III of *Capital*, his manuscript should so tantalizingly break off before the definition has properly begun.

What, then, of the intellectual, what of the artist, and his class-affiliations? Here we must remember what had been said about 'oppositional' writers and thinkers in *The German Ideology*. Such men, Marx and Engels had there suggested, can oppose dominant ideas because of the contradictions in society itself at any given moment. They can identify themselves with forces already at work in their society, or in similar societies beyond the frontiers of their own country; forces which are destined to change radically the socio-economic relations obtaining in a given society and hence, ultimately, to change intellectual and artistic life too. 'A portion of the bourgeoisie', we read, therefore, in *The Communist Manifesto*, 'goes over to the proletariat; in particular a portion of the bourgeois ideologists, who have raised themselves to the level of comprehending theoretically the historical movement as a whole.'[24] In this dynamic situation the bourgeois intellectual—whether as artist, as economist, or as historian—can free himself, through the exercise of his theoretical consciousness, from the shackles of the class to which he would seem to belong by birth and upbringing. *The Communist Manifesto* is clearly written from the point of view of men who think they have done just that; men who have constituted themselves champions of the proletariat and now address the bourgeoisie in that role:

You are horrified at our intending to do away with private property. But in your existing society, private property is already done away with for nine-tenths of the population, its existence for the few is solely due to its non-existence in the hands of those nine-tenths. You reproach us, therefore, with intending to do away with a form of property the necessary condition for whose existence is the non-existence of any property for the immense majority of society. In one word, you reproach us with intending to do away with your property. Precisely so; that is just what we intend.

The famous last sentence of the *Manifesto* is the more dramatic because here, for the first time, the authors directly address *the proletariat* instead of the bourgeoisie.

[24] *SW* I, 117; *MEW* IV, 471–2.

The Communist Manifesto was based on a 'catechism' drafted by Engels—but its final redaction belongs entirely to Marx. A single page of the manuscript, preserved by chance, shows how much trouble he took over the filing and refining of its formulations; and an outline plan for section III demonstrates the careful attention he paid to coherent and ordered presentation of his case. To him, therefore, must go the credit for the lucid over-all structure of the *Manifesto*, for its clear exposition, its subtle changes of tone and perspective, its indignation and humour, its powerful imagery, its skilful deployment of revolutionary slogans,[25] and its use of a multitude of rhetorical devices not for their own sake, but for the sake of the social message that was to be conveyed. David McLellan has listed some of the devices Marx constantly used in his works, though not always with the appositeness and the success characteristic of their use in the *Manifesto*: 'climax, anaphora, parallelism, antithesis and chiasmus'. To this should be added the distinctive rhythm and word-music of the *Manifesto* in its original German. The opening lines afford as good an example as any with their tolling word-repetitions, their linking alliterations and assonances (some of which I have underlined below), and their effective pairing of less and less well-matched partners, first monosyllabic titles (*der Papst und der Zar*), then polysyllabic names with two main stresses separated by four slacks (*Metternich und Guizot*), and finally the more intricate rhythms of the last deliberately ill-matched pair (*französische Radikale und deutsche Polizisten*).

Ein Gespenst geht um in Europa — das Gespenst des Kommunismus. Alle Mächte des alten Europa haben sich zu einer heiligen Hetzjagd gegen dieses Gespenst verbündet, der Papst und der Zar, Metternich und Guizot, französische Radikale und deutsche Polizisten.

---

[25] '*The Communist Manifesto* is almost an anthology of revolutionary rhetoric, and some of its most effective slogans are borrowed. Werner Sombart has shown that "The proletarians have nothing to lose but their chains" and "The workers have no country" are Marat's, and that "the exploitation of men by men" is from Bazard. The nexus of "cash payment" is Thomas Carlyle's, and had been quoted in Engels' *The Condition of the Working Class in England in 1844* . . .' (S. E. Hyman, *The Tangled Bank* (1966 edn.), p. 100.)

A spectre is haunting Europe—the spectre of Communism. All the powers of old Europe have entered into a holy alliance to track down and exorcise this spectre: Pope and Tsar, Metternich and Guizot, French radicals and German policemen.[26]

Marx did not always write with such distinction—but at his best he shows a command of didactic and polemical prose which assures his work a place in the history of German literature as well as in the history of ideas and political action.

(ii)

Not long after *The Communist Manifesto* appeared, revolution broke out in Paris, Marx's banishment from French soil was rescinded, and (hurried along by the Belgian police eager to be rid of his potentially dangerous presence) Marx returned to the French capital. Heine, whom he had been so sad to leave behind when he first moved to Brussels in 1845, was now mortally sick, and there does not seem to have been a great deal of personal contact between the two men. Their views were in any case beginning to diverge as Heine groped his way back to the God of his childhood while Marx became more and more interested in political economy. Heine himself recalled, some five years later, that Marx was among those who stood by him when it was revealed that he had received a pension from secret French state funds during the 1840s and when he was therefore accused, in Germany, of having allowed himself to be bribed into silence on important public issues:

I remember that several of my compatriots came to me at that time, including the most resolute and intelligent of them [*der entschiedenste und geistreichste*], Dr. Marx, to express their indignation at the slanderous article printed in the *Allgemeine Zeitung*, and to advise me not to answer it by a single word: they themselves, they assured me, had already inserted notices into the German papers to the effect that I might be supposed to have accepted the proffered pension

---

[26] *MEW* IV, 461. Cf. Pamela Hansford Johnson, 'The Literary Achievement of Marx', *The Modern Quarterly*, New Series, ii (1946–7), 240: 'This paragraph demonstrates two of his most notable stylistic traits. Firstly, the brief simple statement in the form of a metaphor, followed by a long and rolling sentence of qualification. Secondly, the use of bathos, the sharply descending curve of glory from the Pope to the German police spy. Examples of bathetic irony abound throughout his work . . .'

only in order to be able to take a more active part in supporting the poorer comrades in my party. This was said to me by the ex-editor of the *Neue Rheinische Zeitung* and by the friends that constituted his general staff . . .[27]

Marx's reaction to this passage in Heine's 'Retrospective Explanation' (*Retrospektive Aufklärung*) shows that not unaffectionate disrespect which seems to have been the attitude he adopted, in his later years and in private, towards Heine the man as distinct from Heine the poet. 'I now have Heine's three volumes at home', he writes to Engels on 17 January 1855;

amongst other things he retails the lie that I and others had come to comfort him when he was 'attacked' in the *Augsburger Allgemeine Zeitung* because he had received money from Louis-Philippe. Dear old Heine [*der gute Heine*] forgets on purpose that my intervention on his behalf occurred at the end of 1843, and could not therefore have had anything to do with facts that came to light *after* the February Revolution of 1848. But let it pass! In the fear inspired by his bad conscience (for the old dog has a monstrously good memory for all such muck) he seeks to cajole . . .[28]

Georg Weerth has another recollection of a visit Marx tried to pay the sick poet who had once been so close to him:

Heine had expressed the wish to make my acquaintance, and Marx took me to see him. We arrived, however, at a moment when the poor man was in such suffering that he could not receive us. It seems, therefore, that I am never to meet the one writer who interests me more than any other . . .[29]

The impression Marx, in his turn, left on Heine when they did meet again in 1849 may be gauged by the remark he is recorded to have made to Moritz Carrière when, in 1851, Marx's name came up in a conversation: 'When all is said and done, a man is very little if he is nothing but a razor.'[30] In his public utterances Heine showed greater respect, but Marx can hardly have been altogether delighted by Heine's description in the French version of his *Confessions* (*Geständnisse*) of 1854:

The more or less occult leaders of the German Communists are great logicians, the most powerful of which have come from the school of Hegel; and they are, without doubt, Germany's most

[27] *Gespräche*, 128.   [28] *Gespräche*, 129.   [29] *Gespräche*, 130.
[30] H. H. Houben (ed.), *Gespräche mit Heine*, p. 898 (1948 edition).

capable thinkers and most energetic characters. These revolutionary doctors and their pitilessly determined disciples are the only men in Germany who have any life; and it is to them, I fear, that the future belongs.[31]

(The book-edition of 1855 leaves out the words 'I fear'.) Marx will have relished even less the repetition, in these same *Confessions*, of mock advice Heine had given him publicly once before, in 1852, in a Preface he had added to the reissue of his account of *Religion and Philosophy in Germany*. 'The good Ruge and my even more obdurate friend Dr Marx', Heine had there told his readers, 'would do well to read the Book of Daniel and remember what happened to Nebuchadnezzar in his pride.' It is amusing to recall, in this connection, Franziska Kugelmann's later report about the way in which Marx coupled admiration of Heine's works with dislike of Heine's character. 'He blamed him in particular', Franziska Kugelmann recalls, 'for his ingratitude to friends who had been kind to him.'[32] In Marx's published works, however, Heine is never mentioned or quoted without unqualified approval; and in volume I of *Capital* (1867), Marx goes out of his way to call Heine his 'friend' and to commend his courage.[33]

More disappointing was renewed contact with another German poet, Georg Herwegh, that valued contributor to the *Rheinische Zeitung* whom Marx had warmly defended against philistine attacks on his extravagant life-style. Now he found him engaged in hare-brained revolutionary schemes which could do nothing but harm to the cause Marx had at heart; expostulation only drove him to hostility. 'Bornstedt and Herwegh', Marx reported sadly to Engels on 16 March 1848, 'are behaving like blackguards. They have formed a black-red-and-golden society against us here in Paris.'[34] Nor was this to be the last of Marx's disappointments. He always thought it important that poets whose voices were listened to in Germany should be made, or kept, sympathetic to the principles set out in *The Communist Manifesto*; but he always found them, in the end, unreliable and irritating allies. Not that Marx had a high

---

[31] D. Sternberger, *Heinrich Heine und die Abschaffung der Sünde*, p. 50.
[32] *ÜKL* I, 32. The testimony of Franziska Kugelmann, like that of Carrière (see note 30 above), must be treated with caution.
[33] *K* I—*MEW* XXIII, 637.   [34] *MEW* XXVII, 119.

opinion of Herwegh's poetry—among all the writers with whom he had personal contact in the course of his life, Heine remained the only one whose literary greatness he never ceased to acknowledge.

(iii)

Marx did not stay in Paris very long; in March the German revolutions achieved temporary victories in Vienna and Berlin, and in April Marx and Engels travelled to Cologne to start a new *Rhenish Gazette*, the *Neue Rheinische Zeitung*, devoted to the revolutionary cause. This brought Marx into close association with two German poets who, for a time, shared editorial responsibility with him: Georg Weerth, who was to be hailed by Engels as 'the first and most important poet of the German proletariat';[35] and Ferdinand Freiligrath, who had abandoned his apolitical stance in order to write rousing verse in support of liberal and radical causes. Marx had met Freiligrath in Brussels in 1845 and cultivated his friendship; now, in October 1848, he offered Freiligrath an editorial post on the *Neue Rheinische Zeitung*. Freiligrath accepted and, at the same time, joined the Communist League.[36]

The articles that Marx published in the *Neue Rheinische Zeitung* appeared—like all other articles in that journal—without their author's name. This was a matter of principle which Marx discussed, later, in *The Class-Struggles in France*:

As long as the newspaper Press was anonymous, it appeared as the organ of a numberless and nameless public opinion; it was the third power in the state. Through the signature of every article a newspaper became a mere collection of literary contributions by more or less known individuals. Every article sank to the status of an advertisement. Hitherto newspapers had circulated as the paper money of public opinion; now they dissolved into more or less bad solo bills, whose worth and circulation depended on the credit not only of the drawer, but also on that of the endorser.[37]

What mattered were the causes the journal fought for—the success of the German revolution, a war of liberation against Russia, self-determination for Italians, Hungarians, Poles, and

35 *ÜKL* II, 296–7.　　　　36 Demetz, *Marx, Engels und die Dichter*, pp. 92–6.
37 *SW* I, 292; *MEW* VII, 100–1.

the advance of the proletariat throughout the world;[38] it wanted to be a thorn in the flesh of reactionary authorities, not 'a mere collection of literary contributions'.

The very first article, however, which later research has traced unequivocally to Marx himself, demonstrates how important a part literary quotation, allusion, adaptation, and parody was once again destined to play in his polemics. Given over to a characterization of the new Prussian *Ministerpräsident* Ludolf Camphausen, it begins by speculating on the 'defects of the soul' covered by Camphausen's grave, insistent solemnity of manner—an allusion to the once famous definition of 'gravity' commended in Laurence Sterne's *Life and Opinions of Tristram Shandy*:

In the naked temper which a merry heart discovered, he would say, there was no danger,—but to itself:—whereas the very essence of gravity was design, and consequently deceit;—'twas a taught trick to gain credit of the world for more sense and knowledge than a man was worth; and that, with all its pretensions,—it was no better, but often worse, than what a *French* wit had long ago defined it,—*viz. A mysterious carriage of the body to cover the defects of the mind;*—which definition of gravity, *Yorick*, with great imprudence, would say, deserved to be wrote in letters of gold.[39]

Marx then calls Camphausen a 'thoughtful amateur of history', alluding to the title of a popular history textbook of the day, written by Karl von Rotteck;[40] and he goes on to invert the Hippocratic adage which Goethe had used to characterize Wagner in *Faust* Part I: 'Art—that is, revolution—is short, and life—the Camphausen ministry—is long.'[41] This in its turn leads to an adaptation and inversion of the best-known line from Shakespeare's *Richard III*: 'A kingdom for a doctrine! A doctrine for a kingdom!' is said to be Camphausen's motto.[42]

---

[38] W. Blumenberg, *Karl Marx in Selbstzeugnissen und Bilddokumenten* (Reinbek, 1962), pp. 87–90.

[39] *MEW* V, 25; Sterne, *The Life and Opinions of Tristram Shandy*, Book I, Ch. 11. Many years later Marx discovered that the 'French wit' to whom Sterne here refers was La Rochefoucauld.

[40] *MEW* V, 25; cf. *Allgemeine Geschichte vom Anfang der historischen Kenntniß bis auf unsere Zeiten. Für denkende Geschichtsfreunde bearbeitet von Karl von Rotteck* (Freiburg, 1834).

[41] 'Ach Gott! Die Kunst ist lang, / Und kurz is unser Leben . . .' (*Faust*, Part I, 'Nacht'.)

[42] Cf. *King Richard III*, v. iv.

From this the reader passes to a characterization of the now
defunct Prussian *Landtag* as 'this repulsive mixture of Gothic delusion and modern lies'; words which are clearly derived from
Heine's *Germany. A Winter's Tale*:

> Das Mittelalter, immerhin,
> Das wahre, wie es gewesen,
> Ich will es ertragen — erlöse uns nur
> Von jenem Zwitterwesen,
>
> Von jenem Kamaschenrittertum
> Das ekelhaft ein Gemisch ist
> Von gotischem Wahn und modernem Lug,
> Das weder Fleisch noch Fisch ist.
>
> All right, then—the true Middle Ages,
> As they really were,
> I will endure—only save us
> From this hybrid state,
>
> From these knights in gaiters
> Who are a repulsive mixture
> Of Gothic delusion and modern lie,
> Who are neither fish nor flesh.[43]

To show further how 'Gothic delusion' lives on under Camphausen, and to give his readers a sense at once of the ghostly,
the outmoded, and the ridiculous, Marx now revives the
trappings of the Gothic novel, the *Schauerroman*:

The responsible minister . . . seeks out the forgotten corpse and
conjures up the ghost of the dear, faithful, departed *Landtag*. This
duly appears; but it remains unhappily suspended in the air,
cutting the strangest capers, for it finds no ground under its feet . . .
The necromancer announces to the ghost that he has called it up to
liquidate its legacy and act as its loyal heir . . . The ghost, highly
flattered, wags its head like a Chinese nodding figure in response to
everything the necromancer tells it, and curtseys as it makes its
exit . . .[44]

After this 'Gothic' interlude Marx ends his article in a flurry
of classical allusion and parody:

Thus a goose turns into an egg and an egg into a goose. The people,
however, soon recognizes from the Capitol-saving cackling that the

---

[43] *Deutschland. Ein Wintermärchen*, Caput XVII.   [44] *MEW* V, 27.

golden Ledean eggs, which it laid in the course of the revolution, have been stolen from it. Even deputy Milde does not seem to be that son of Leda, far-shining Castor.[45]

Selbst der Abgeordnete Milde scheint nicht der Ledasohn zu sein, der fernhinleuchtende Kastor—hexameter cadence and Homeric phrase mockingly mark the distance between the 'heroes' of the Frankfurt parliament and those of the *Iliad*.

F. F. K. Hecker, one of the leaders of the abortive revolt in Baden, is ridiculed by Marx with methods similar to those used against K. A. Milde in the passage which has just been quoted. He exploits the coincidence that two men named Hecker were prominent during the events of 1848: one of them on the government side, the other a revolutionary:

Was Hecker the Solicitor for the Crown robbed of his sleep by Hecker the Republican? We do not know . . . Posterity will see the conflicts of the modern movement dramatically epitomized in these two gigantic figures. A future Goethe will unite them in a *Faust*. We will leave it up to him to decide which of these Heckers should be assigned the role of Faust and which should have that of Wagner.[46]

This is Marx's characteristic way of crying a plague on both houses. Goethe, we are given to understand, not only 'placed' both Heckers as Homer 'placed' Milde, by creating a figure of real stature (Faust) against which both Heckers shrink into insignificance; he also characterized both Heckers with equal appropriateness when he created his Wagner, that intellectually limited and blinkered—though not unsympathetic—pedant who makes such an effective foil to Faust in the early scenes of the play.

Heine's political poems—*Germany. A Winter's Tale* in particular—are ubiquitous in Marx's contributions to the *Neue Rheinische Zeitung*. Quotations from *Germany. A Winter's Tale* recall the hopes of May 1848:

> Damals stand alles im Blütenschmuck
> Und die Sonnenlichter lachten,
> Die Vögel sangen sehnsuchtvoll,
> Und die Menschen hofften und dachten —

[45] *MEW* V, 28.   [46] *MEW* V, 440.

> At that time all was clothed in blossoms,
> And the rays of the sun laughed down,
> The birds sang such a hopeful song,
> And men hoped and thought . . .;

sum up the programme of the extreme Left in the Frankfurt parliament:

> Bedenk ich die Sache ganz genau,
> So brauchen wir gar keinen Kaiser
>
> On reflection:
> We don't need an Emperor at all!;

or parody an unreasoning attachment to what is less than admirable in German life:

> Das ist ja meine Heimatluft!
> Die glühende Wange empfand es!
> Und dieser Landstraßenkot, er ist
> Der Dreck meines Vaterlandes!
>
> This is my native air!
> My glowing cheek felt it.
> And this mud of the streets is
> The muck of my fatherland.[47]

There are quotations also from Heine's 'Ritter Olaf', 'Der Tannhäuser', 'Our Navy' (*Unsere Marine*), 'Georg Herwegh', 'Anno 1829', 'The Changeling' (*Der Wechselbalg*), *Atta Troll*, and 'Kahldorf on the Nobility' (*Kahldorf über den Adel*).[48] Quotations from Bürger's 'Lenore' and from a play by Ferdinand Raimund appear in the *Neue Rheinische Zeitung* in contexts similar to those in which Heine had used them.[49] There are constant references to, and quotations from, the literature of the past: Homer, Virgil, the Bible, the Arabian Nights, Shakespeare, Molière, Beaumarchais, Goethe, and Schiller; minor works like Arnold Kortum's eighteenth-century mock epic *The Adventures of Hieronymus Jobs* (*Die Jobsiade*) are not neglected; and we find an allusion to Cooper's *The Last of the Mohicans*, a snatch from

---

[47] *MEW* VI, 200; V, 41; V, 278.

[48] *MEW* V, 101, 417; VI, 103, 219, 414; V, 421; VI, 477; V, 435; VI, 10.

[49] *MEW* V, 36 ('Die Toten reiten schnell'); V, 96 ('Scheint die Sonne noch so schön, / Einmal muß sie untergehn' — F. Raimund, *Das Mädchen aus der Feenwelt oder der Bauer als Millionär, II*, vi).

Matthias Claudius's 'Rheinweinlied', as well as repeated references to Freiligrath's translation of Robert Burns's 'For a' that and a' that'. Even the libretti of operas, from *The Marriage of Figaro* to Rossini's *Tancred*, are raided for quotations.[50] The narrative fiction of Cervantes proves its usefulness once again; but this time Marx takes telling illustrations of folly and knavery from the *Exemplary Tales* (*novelas exemplares*) and uses the figure of Don Quixote only in passing as a personification of out-of-date modes of thinking.[51]

Many of Marx's literary and mythological allusions are parodistic. Thus a Prussian state-solicitor appears as Aphrodite, the Prussian militia as Theseus, the *Neue Rheinische Zeitung* itself as Ariadne, Prince William of Prussia as Aeneas, the minister in charge of the Prussian police forces as 'the faithful Eckart of constitutional liberty', and so on. Biblical references in particular are often introduced into deliberately incongruous contexts—as when German patriots are ironically enjoined to behave, in face of antiquated and tyrannous customs, like Moses before the burning bush:

Put off thy shoes from off thy feet, o German patriot, for the place wheron thou standest is holy ground! These barbarities are the surviving fragments of Christian–Germanic glory, they are the last links of a chain that reaches through history and binds you to the effulgent dignity of your forefathers, right up to the Cheruscan forests.[52]

A somewhat garbled version of Goethe's 'Night-song' (*Wandrers Nachtlied*) is cited to describe a Prussian statesman's diplomatic desire for repose; an attack on the views expressed by the *New Prussian Gazette* (*Neue Preußische Zeitung*) is headed, like Book VI of *Wilhelm Meister's Apprenticeship*, 'Confessions of a

[50] *MEW* V, 57 (Homer, Virgil); V, 59, 96, 265, and VI, 11, 109, 139 (Shakespeare); VI, 69 (Milton's *Paradise Lost*—this article cannot be attributed to Marx with confidence, however); VI, 263 (Molière); VI, 190 (Beaumarchais); V, 24, 109, 163, 204, 218, and VI, 26, 105, 440 (Goethe); V, 10, 70, 148 (Schiller); VI 70, 102 (Kortum); V, 364 (Fenimore Cooper); VI, 62 (Claudius); V, 263, 303 (Freiligrath/Burns); V, 365 (Mozart/Da Ponte); VI, 71 (Rossini's *Tancred*).

[51] *MEW* V, 266, 270, and VI, 495–6; *MEW* V, 414, 423.

[52] *MEW* V, 278. Of the many other allusions to biblical passages, used in a sense deliberately different from that of the Bible, one deserves special mention: 'For whosoever hath, to him shall be given, and he shall have more abundance: but whosoever hath not, from him shall be taken away even that he hath.' (Matthew 13: 12.) That prophecy, the *NRZ* maintained on 26 July 1848, was being constantly fulfilled in the modern world (*MEW* V, 265).

Beautiful Soul'; and the loyal silences of the *National Gazette* (*National-Zeitung*) of Berlin are 'explained' by reference to the fate that seals the lips of Goethe's Mignon.[53] But not everything is parody. Again and again Marx finds that recourse to the poets can convey perfectly his own indignation, contempt, or amusement in face of German conditions. Falstaff's reactions to Justice Shallow describes what Marx feels about the contrast between the protestations of Prussian ministers and their actions: 'Lord, Lord, how subject we old men are to this vice of lying!'; Thersites's reactions to Ajax ('I had rather be a tick in a sheep than such a valiant ignorance') are patently the same as those of Marx to Count Wrangel; and Beaumarchais's 'Figaro, that's something you could not have invented!' is repeatedly found more adequate than any other form of words to convey Marx's astonishment at some particularly outrageous absurdity.[54] Sometimes Marx heightens or varies a well-known quotation, one which most of his readers would know sufficiently well to hold against his variation: as when he says, in face of the Prussian counter-revolution, that not 'something' but *everything* is rotten in this 'state of Denmark'.[55] It is striking to notice how frequently a quotation from one of the authors Marx most admired—Shakespeare, Goethe, Heine—will form the climax of one of those carefully constructed yet impassioned periods which are so characteristic a feature of his journalistic prose. He needed the words of great writers to confirm and sanction his own. In his article of 15 December 1848, on the bourgeoisie and the counter-revolution, an enormous but never unwieldy period thus leads inexorably towards an allusion to the second act of *As You Like It*. Marx is indicting the Prussian middle class:

. . . without belief in itself, without belief in the people, muttering upwards and trembling downwards, egoistic both ways and conscious of its egoism, revolutionary in face of conservatives, conservative in face of revolutionaries, mistrusting its own catch-phrases, with rhetoric instead of ideas, intimidated by the tempests of history yet making use of them, without energy in any direction, plagiaristic in all directions, coarse because unoriginal, original only in coarseness, horse-trading with its own desires, without initiative, without

[53] *MEW* VI, 218; VI, 24; VI, 204.
[54] *MEW* V, 422; VI, 11; V, 251, and VI, 190.   [55] *MEW* VI, 139.

faith in itself, without faith in the people, without world-historical calling, a cursed pantaloon who saw himself doomed to guide and deflect the youthful exuberance of a robust people in his own senile interest, *sans eyes, sans ears, sans teeth, sans everything*—that is how the Prussian bourgeoisie found itself at the helm of the state after the July revolution [my italics].[56]

The allusion to Jacques's speech on the Seven Ages of Man retrospectively colours the whole passage, with its terrifying portrait of a lean and slippered pantaloon in charge of historical destinies.

For those who know the speech on the Seven Ages of Man from which Marx here quotes an important nuance is added to his indictment of the Prussian bourgeoisie; but his indictment comes across powerfully even to those who cannot catch his allusion. This is an important point, for Marx now hopes to be understood, and heeded, by those who have not had his own educational advantages. His 'Wage-Labour and Capital' (*Lohnarbeit und Kapital*), which began life as a series of lectures to workmen in Brussels before appearing in the *Neue Rheinische Zeitung* in April 1849, makes this point at the very outset. 'We wish to be comprehensible to the workers', Marx tells his readers. But even when he is not consciously letting off literary fireworks, as he does in so many other journalistic articles, he cannot help alluding subliminally to the literary works he knows and loves. The following passage from 'Wage-Labour and Capital' affords a characteristic example:

But the exercise of labour power, labour, is the worker's own life-activity, his own expression of life. And this *life-activity* he sells to another person in order to secure the necessary *means of subsistence*. Thus his life-activity is for him only a means to enable him to exist. He works in order to live. He does not even reckon labour as part of his life, it is rather a sacrifice of his life. It is a commodity which he has made over to another. Hence, also, the product of his activity is not the object of his activity. What he produces for himself is not the silk that he weaves, not the gold that he draws from the mine, not the palace that he builds. What he produces for himself are *wages*; and silk, gold, palace, resolve themselves for him into a definite quantity of the means of subsistence, perhaps into a cotton jacket, copper coins and a basement dwelling. And the worker who for twelve hours weaves, spins, drills, turns, builds, shovels,

[56] *MEW* VI, 109.

breaks stones, carries, etc.—does he consider this twelve hours'
weaving, spinning, drilling, turning, building, shovelling, stone-
breaking as an expression of his life, as life? On the contrary, life
begins for him where this activity ceases, at table, in the public
house, in bed. The twelve hours' labour, on the other hand, has no
meaning for him as weaving, spinning, drilling, etc., but as *earning*,
which brings him to the table, to the public house, into bed. If the
silk worm were to spin, in order to continue its existence as a cater-
pillar, it would be a complete wage worker.[57]

That image of the silk-worm brings, to the educated German
reader, a reminiscence which lends additional force to Marx's
argument: the description, by the eponymous hero of Goethe's
Torquato Tasso, of the true poet's mode of existence, the ways
of a man who does not work merely in order to sustain life:

Ich halte diesen Drang vergebens auf,
Der Tag und Nacht in meinem Busen wechselt.
Wenn ich nicht sinnen oder dichten soll
So ist das Leben mir kein Leben mehr.
Verbiete du dem Seidenwurm zu spinnen,
Wenn er sich schon dem Tode näher spinnt.
Das köstliche Geweb' entwickelt er
Aus seinem Innersten, und läßt nicht ab,
Bis er in seinen Sarg sich eingeschlossen.
O geb' ein guter Gott uns auch dereinst
Das Schicksal des beneidenswerten Wurms,
Im neuen Sonnental die Flügel rasch
Und freudig zu entfalten!

I try in vain to resist the urge
That drives me on, in changing fashion, by day and night.
If I am not to think and write
Then life is no longer life to me.
Try to forbid the silk-worm to spin
Even though he is spinning himself towards death.
He draws the precious web
From his own depths, and does not desist
Until he has enclosed himself in his coffin.
O that a kind God would grant us too, in times to come,
The fate of that enviable worm,
To unfold its wings rapidly and joyously,
In a new sun-lit valley.[58]

[57] *SW* I, 153. [58] Goethe, *Torquato Tasso*, v. ii.

Those who recall that passage from *Torquato Tasso* will find another dimension—a counter-image—added to Marx's description of alienated labour: of the way work has ceased to be that act of self-discovery and self-creation which great poetry can at once exemplify and symbolize.

'Wage-Labour and Capital', it should be noted in passing, is only part of a longer, unpublished analysis of the way the market economy seemed to Marx to be working in the nineteenth century:

Firstly: everything patriarchal has . . . fallen away, and only huckstering, buying and selling, have remained; money-transactions are now the only remaining relationship between employer and worker. *Secondly*: the halo has dropped off all the relations pertaining in the old society; these have dissolved into money-relations.

In the same way all so-called 'higher' forms of labour—intellectual, artistic etc.—have been changed into commodities and have thereby lost their old sanctity. What great progress it was to have the whole regiment of parsons, physicians, lawyers, etc. (i.e. religion, jurisprudence etc.) defined solely in terms of its commercial value![59]

That artists and art have been similarly reduced might prove, in Marx's context, another cause for rejoicing—such reduction or deformation may convince men that present conditions are dehumanizing and intolerable, and may thus become the agent of change.

Marx's contributions to the *Neue Rheinische Zeitung* are for the most part very well written and make effective, unexaggerated use of rhetorical devices, images, gradations of rhythm, and literary allusion. At least one of his articles, that of 29 June 1848, is as powerful a piece of German prose as *The Communist Manifesto* itself.[60] This lends force and conviction to the stylistic critiques in which the *Neue Rheinische Zeitung* constantly indulges under Marx's editorship: critiques of verbal confusions and mistranslations;[61] of grammatical ineptitudes;[62] of unwieldy, clumsily constructed sentences;[63] of grandiloquent phrases and clichés, and the nonsense talked by men intoxicated by their own verbosity;[64] of the involuntary verse-rhythms into which editorial-writers of rival newspapers tended to fall when

[59] *MEW* VI, 555–6.   [60] *MEW* V, 133–7.   [61] *MEW* VI, 229, 227.
[62] *MEW* VI, 153.   [63] *MEW* VI, 199, 201.   [64] *MEW* VI, 262.

composing their over-solemn prose.[65] It lends force also to a charge the *Neue Rheinische Zeitung* levelled from the first against the orators to be heard in the Frankfurt parliament: 'It bores the German people instead of sweeping it along or being swept away by it . . . Far from being the central organ of the revolutionary movement, it has hitherto not even shown itself as its echo.'[66] The interest Marx here shows in political rhetoric—an interest in the art of giving effective utterance, and direction, to popular thought and sentiment—is to remain with him for the rest of his life.

While making constant use of literary analysis in its political polemics, the *Neue Rheinische Zeitung* also applied the vocabulary of literary theory and criticism to the political scene. Metaphors from drama and stage-shows are frequent.[67] Camphausen is said to have composed an 'epic' and to deliver himself of 'dithyrambs'; the political reporters of the *Kölnische Zeitung* write in the elegiac genre and in the lyrical sublime; while social conditions in Belgium and Switzerland present to Marx's eyes 'tragicomic genre-pictures akin to caricature in the great historical tableau'.[68] The last example shows clearly how literary-critical classification may merge with the vocabulary of art-criticism.

Finally: the *Neue Rheinische Zeitung* seizes the opportunity afforded by the political career of Alphonse de Lamartine to scrutinize the role played by a Romantic author in the political life of his country. The result is not inspiring. As early as December 1847 Marx had charged Lamartine with naïvely confused views of historical development. He had written in the *Deutsche-Brüsseler-Zeitung*.

M. Lamartine believes that he has proved bourgeois property eternal by suggesting that property in general marks the transition from a state of savagery to one of civilization, and by suggesting that the process of breathing and the engendering of children presuppose property-rights no less than the existence of private property.

M. Lamartine sees no difference between the period of transition betwixt savagery and civilization, and the period in which we

---

[65] *MEW* VI, 262.   [66] *MEW* V, 41.
[67] e.g. *MEW* V, 97, 419, 457; VI, 74, 112, 257, 493.
[68] *MEW* V, 58; VI, 261; VI, 398.

ourselves are living, nor does he see any difference between 'appropriating' the air we breathe and 'appropriating' social products; both, after all, are 'appropriations', just as both periods are periods of 'transition'.

In the 'more copious' polemic against communism which he has promised M. Lamartine will no doubt find an opportunity to draw from the general phrases which spring from his 'feelings' a 'logical' sequence of even more general phrases.—Perhaps we shall then also find an opportunity to throw 'more copious' light on such phrases.[69]

Now, in the *Neue Rheinische Zeitung*, Marx looks at what happened after Lamartine's brief, eloquent, but inglorious membership of the provisional government of 1848. 'The last official remnant of the February Revolution, the Executive Commission, has melted away, like a misty wraith, before the seriousness of events. The fireworks of Lamartine have become the incendiary rockets of Cavaignac'.[70] A few months later, on 22 October 1848, Marx returns to the subject of Lamartine and sees him now as the embodiment of a bourgeois dream on which nothing but disillusion could follow:

Lamartine was the bourgeois republic's imaginative vision of itself, the extravagant, fantastic, enthusiastic self-image it created, its dream of its own glory. What cannot be performed in imagination! As Aeolus unleashed all the winds out of his bag, so Lamartine let loose all the aerial spirits, all the windy phrases of the bourgeois republic, and blew them to the east and to the west; airy words about the brotherhood of all peoples, about the emancipation all peoples might expect from France, about France's self-sacrifice on behalf of all nations.

He did—nothing.

The deed that went with his phrases was performed by Cavaignac and his executive tool Bastide.[71]

In this sense the 'will-o'-the-wisp' Lamartine was 'the true man of the hour', *der wahre Mann der Situation*.[72] Again and again, in the *Neue Rheinische Zeitung*, Marx looks back on the euphoric period of the 1848 Revolution; and to characterize, for his German readers, the hopes which had swept Lamartine into

---

[69] *MEW* IV, 422 (26 Dec. 1847).   [70] *MEW* V, 133-4.
[71] *MEW* V, 436.   [72] *MEW* V, 449.

office, Marx quotes lines from Schiller's 'Ode to Joy' which Beethoven's music had carried all over Europe:

Never was a revolutionary movement opened with an overture as edifying as that of 1848. The Pope gave it the blessings of the Church; the Aeolian harp of Lamartine quivered under dulcet philanthropic airs whose text was *fraternité*, the brotherhood of all members of society and all nations.

> 'Seid umschlungen, Millionen,
> Diesen Kuß der ganzen Welt!'

At this moment the Pope, driven from Rome, is residing at Gaëta, under the protection of the tigerish idiot Ferdinand, the *iniziatore* of Italy, intriguing against Italy with its hereditary enemy Austria which he had threatened, in his happier period, with an interdict. The last presidential elections in France have provided statistical tables to document the unpopularity of the traitor Lamartine. Nothing could be more generally benevolent, more humane, and more weak than the revolutions of February and March; nothing could be more brutal than the necessary consequences of such *humanity of weakness*. Witness Italy, Poland, Germany, witness, above all, those who were conquered in June.[73]

The dream of Schiller, the dream of Beethoven, the dream of 'the traitor Lamartine', are alike confounded by the realities of power. 'No more *Pio nono* in Italy,' the *Neue Rheinische Zeitung* concluded, 'no more Lamartine in France. The period of airy enthusiasm, of goodwill, and of flowery oratory has been worthily brought to an end with bombs, large-scale butchery, and deportations. Notes from Austria, notes from Prussia, notes from Russia were the most fitting answers to Lamartine's proclamations.'[74]

In the year of Revolution, then, Marx had continued to use the writers he admired as weapons in what he now saw as a *class*-struggle—through allusions, quotations, and subliminal reminiscences. He had especially come to find Heine, the Heine of the early forties, an invaluable source of pithy, witty, pugnacious, and disrespectful formulations. His admiration was tempered by growing doubt about Heine's personal integrity, though this in its turn was held in check by his pity for Heine's failing health. Another poet had disappointed him more

[73] *MEW* VI, 148.   [74] *MEW* VI, 308.

gravely: his early ally Georg Herwegh clearly showed weaknesses of character that reflected themselves in his political
activities. But new alliances had been forged: with Georg
Weerth and with Ferdinand Freiligrath, whose sympathies
with the growing proletariat seemed to match Marx's own.
Against these stood Lamartine, the embodiment, in Marx's
eyes, of Romantic-bourgeois illusions; his personality and work
together served Marx as a textbook example of the political
nature of European Romanticism, which (as Marx saw it) hid
material interests, egoism, and all the prosaic or brutal concomi-
tants of class-struggle under a cloud of beautiful words. The
function of such words was to lull men into inactivity; to secure
assent to oppression and exploitation from those who might
otherwise work towards their removal. But the logic of the
times, Marx believed, was against the Lamartines; oppression,
it appeared to him, had shown its face too nakedly, the bourgeoisie had gone too far in tearing the halo from poets and
poetry by dragging them into the market-place. Contempt for
literature can therefore become, as Mikhail Lifshits has put it,
a 'mighty revolutionary factor'; the decline of art Marx detects
in modern society may be seen as 'progressive even from the
standpoint of art itself'.[75]

Above all: the economic development with which, in Marx's
view, the fate of literature was inevitably bound up, was working towards the creation of *world* literature. On the evidence
of Marx's literary allusions in *The Communist Manifesto* and the
Neue Rheinische Zeitung one might say that in one important
sense the era of world literature had already arrived. It already
existed in Marx's mind, that store-house of literary experiences
and reminiscences from many centuries and many lands.

[75] M. Lifshits, *The Philosophy of Art of Karl Marx* (1933), pp. 100, 101.

8 · The Reign of Pecksniff, Crevel, and Crapülinski

'The leading talents of the bourgeoisie are in decline.'

(*MEW* VII, 255)

(i)

IT was not to be expected that the Prussian authorities, once they had brought the revolution under control, would allow the activities of the *Neue Rheinische Zeitung* to go unchecked. In May 1849 the paper was suppressed—its last issue, which opened with a defiant poem from the pen of Ferdinand Freiligrath, was printed entirely in red—and Marx found himself expelled from Prussia. He went first to Paris; but when he learnt that the French authorities were only prepared to let him settle away from the capital, in an insalubrious part of Britanny, he decided to move to London instead. In August 1849, therefore, Marx left for England, and was followed by his family in September. From then until the end of his life London was to remain his home.

His first care, in the year of poverty and deprivation that followed, was to carry on the work which the Prussian government had interrupted. He sought contact with English and *émigré* members of the Communist League and founded a monthly which would, he hoped, perpetuate and carry on the policies of the *Neue Rheinische Zeitung*. He even gave it the same name, adding only the words: *Political-Economic Review* (*Neue Rheinische Zeitung. Politisch-ökonomische Revue*). Since it could not be effectively distributed in Germany, the *Revue* lasted less than a year: but in that time it published such important essays as Engels's study of the German Peasant Wars and Marx's first hard look, from his London vantage-point, at that political scene in France from which he was to draw, in the course of his life, lessons which later revolutionaries have found instructive and helpful: The Class-Struggles in France (*Die Klassenkämpfe in Frankreich*).

The image which dominates this work, published in the *Revue* during January, February, and March 1850,[1] is that of the theatre or stage; a *topos* on which Marx rings innumerable changes:

> On the most prominent stages of bourgeois society, the same scenes were publicly enacted which led the *Lumpenproletariat* to brothels, workhouses, and lunatic asylums, before the magistrate, to prison, and to the scaffold.

> The official scene was transformed in a trice: scenery, costumes, language, actors, supers, dummies, prompters, the themes of the play, the content of the conflict, the whole situation.

Some actors 'vanish from the stage', like Armand Marrast; others, like Louis Napoleon, 'expose themselves to the eyes of the gallery'. There are sudden *coups de théâtre*, like that which deprived the provisional government of 1848 of its ready cash. Actors assume different parts: Louis-Philippe *on* the throne plays Robert Macaire (a shady character created by Benjamin Antier and Frédéric Lemaître in their play *Robert et Bertrand*, 1834); *off* the throne he plays, no less successfully, 'the role of a *pauvre honteux*'. Louis Napoleon himself assumes the most un-dignified part of all: 'a filthy figure', 'a marionette', *punchinello* (Hanswurst); and he is said to need a troupe of paid *claqueurs* to avoid being hissed off the stage. As for the French peasants—'for a moment active heroes of the revolutionary drama, they could no longer be forced back into the inactive, will-less role of chorus'. Parts change so rapidly, the confusion is so great, that even the audience becomes involved in the play: 'all classes of French society were suddenly . . . forced to leave the boxes, the stalls, the gallery, and to act in person on the revolutionary stage'.

Nor are we long left in doubt of the nature of the plays that are being performed on the political stage described in *The*

---

[1] *R* 23–38, 73–93, 127–48; *MEW* VII, 11–107.

Class-Struggles in France. Occasionally, as when the peasants abandon the role of chorus, the play has some dignity; for the most part, however, it approaches 'tragicomedy' at its best, and at its worst 'vile farce', a third-rate conjuring show, or a mindless melodrama of ghosts and vampires. The great playwrights of the past are constantly called upon to suggest the atmosphere of these political and social entertainments. Louis Blanc's ill-fated national workshops recall at once Shakespeare's *Comedy of Errors* and a Spanish 'comedy of servants'. When the 'party of order' gains the upper hand, Marx reminds his readers of the 'lamentable comedy . . . of Pyramus and Thisbe' performed by Bottom and his friends: 'June 1849 was not a bloody tragedy in which the antagonists were wage-labour and capital, but the prison-filling and lamentable play of debtor and creditor.' The behaviour of French Republicans brings memories of Molière ('this comedy of the *républicains malgré eux*'), while Odilon Barrot presents 'points worthy of a Beaumarchais'.

The literary form that comes most forcibly to mind, however, as Marx contemplates the French scene, is that of *parody*. 'Louis Napoleon, with his emperor's hat and eagle, parodied the original Napoleon no more miserably than the *montagne* [of the new parliament], with its phrases borrowed from 1793 and its demogogic poses, parodied the original *montagne*.'[2] Heine too, we remember, had frequently experienced this feeling of watching a theatrical parody: nowhere more forcibly than in the Barbarossa chapters of *Germany. A Winter's Tale*:

> Jag fort das Komödiantenpack,
> Und schließe die Schauspielhäuser,
> Wo man die Vorzeit parodiert —
> Komme du bald, o Kaiser!

> Chase away that rabble of comedians,
> Close down those theatres
> In which earlier times are parodied—
> Come soon, O my Emperor![3]

When Marx and Engels, in the *Revue*, look across at Germany, they see not just parody, but parody of parody:

---

[2] *R* 80; *MEW* VII, 45–6.
[3] *Deutschland. Ein Wintermärchen*, Caput XVII, last stanza.

Old E. M. Arndt's question 'What is the German's fatherland' is answered by Frederick William IV: 'Erfurt'. It was not so difficult to travesty the *Iliad* in the *Batrachomyomachia*, but no one has yet dared to contemplate a parody of the *Batrachomyomachia*. The Erfurt-plan succeeds in this: it parodies that war of frogs and mice which was the Frankfurt parliament.[4]

No wonder that Marx, in *The Class-Struggles in France*, not only speaks of parody, but constantly falls into writing it: 'Saul Cavaignac slew a million votes, but David Napoleon slew six million'.[5]

In *The Class-Struggles in France* Marx raises, at the very beginning, the question of the relationship in which French intellectuals stood to the bourgeoisie and other classes and sub-groups he sought to distinguish. He speaks of *Capacitäten*, leading talents or authorities, among 'savants, jurists, physicians, etc.', and describes these as 'the ideological representatives and spokesmen' of various classes discontented with the amount of political influence they were able to exercise in the France of Louis-Philippe.[6] He later returns, not unnaturally, to the subject of Lamartine and his involvement in the events of 1848. Marx reproduces verbatim the attack on Lamartine which had appeared in the *Neue Rheinische Zeitung*,[7] but he tries this time to formulate more precisely how he sees Lamartine's relation to the social classes of mid-nineteenth-century France:

Lamartine, finally, as a member of the provisional government: that meant, in the first instance, no real interest, no definite class—that was the February Revolution itself, the common uprising with its illusions, its poetry, its conception of its own import, and its fine phrases. For the rest this spokesman of the February Revolution belonged, by his position as by his views, to the bourgeoisie.[8]

The role Lamartine played in the establishment of the Second French Republic was therefore an ominous one: it fell to him, Marx believed, to spread illusions about the non-existence of a class-war which would lull the destined victims of that war into a false security.

To the Luxembourg commission, this creation of the Paris workers, remains the merit of having disclosed from the European

---

[4] *R* 115–16; *MEW* VII, 214.   [5] *R* 79; *MEW* VII, 44.
[6] *R* 24; *MEW* VII, 13.   [7] *R* 37; *MEW* VII, 31.
[8] *R* 26; *MEW* VII, 17.

tribune the secret of the revolution of the nineteenth century: the *emancipation of the proletariat.* The *Moniteur* raged when it had to propagate officially the 'wild ravings' which up to that time lay buried in the apocryphal writings of the Socialists and only reached the ears of the bourgeoisie from time to time as remote, half terrifying, half ludicrous legends. Europe awoke astonished from its bourgeois doze. In the ideas of the proletarians, therefore, who confused the finance aristocracy with the bourgeoisie in general; in the imagination of good old republicans, who denied the very existence of classes or, at most, admitted them as a result of the constitutional monarchy; in the hypocritical phrases of the section of the bourgeoisie up to now excluded from power, the *rule of the bourgeoisie* was abolished with the introduction of the republic. All the royalists were transformed into republicans and all the millionaires of Paris into workers. The phrase which corresponded to this imagined liquidation of class relations was *fraternité*, universal fraternisation and brotherhood. This pleasant abstraction from class antagonisms, this sentimental equalisation of contradictory class interests, this fantastic elevation above the class struggle, *fraternité*, this was the special catchword of the February Revolution. The classes were divided by a mere *misunderstanding* and Lamartine baptised the Provisional Government on February 24 as 'un gouvernement qui suspende ce malentendu terrible qui existe entre les différentes classes' ['a government which removes the terrible misunderstanding that exists between the different classes']. The Parisian proletariat revelled in this generous intoxication of fraternity.[9]

Nor was the role that other French men of letters played in the events of 1848 and 1849 at all calculated to increase Marx's respect for their political understanding and the ideological function he believed them to perform. Victor Hugo, whose vehement opposition to Napoleon III lay still in the future, is dismissed with an *allons donc!*,[10] and the very appearance of Eugène Sue on the political stage is seen as a satire on the progress of the revolution:

The revolutionary meaning of 10 March, the rehabilitation of the June insurrection, was finally completely doused by the candidature of Eugène Sue, that sentimental petty-bourgeois weaver of social fantasies, which the proletariat could accept, at best, as a joke to please the shop-girls.[11]

[9] *R* 29–30; *MEW* VII, 21.   [10] *R* 134–5; *MEW* VII, 75.
[11] *R* 322; *MEW* VII, 98.

That the French government later introduced a press-law which imposed a stamp-duty on those *romans feuilleton* to which Sue owed his fame and fortune seemed to Marx a suitably ironic answer to his parliamentary candidature and election.

His cool look at the part played by poets and novelists in the mid-century revolution in France made Marx anxious not to be lumped too readily, by his readers and admirers, with German men of letters who seemed, to a superficial eye, to be on his side. This helps to explain the article entitled 'Gottfried Kinkel', published in the April number of the *Revue*, in which Marx and Engels distance themselves from the sentimental, declamatory poet named in the title; a poet whose physical courage during the abortive German revolution Engels had commended in a letter to Jenny Marx dated 25 July 1849. Marx and Engels now declare:

We know in advance that we shall provoke general indignation among sentimental frauds and democratic orators . . . But this is of no concern to us at all. Our task is criticism, without fear or favour; and in maintaining this position, we are glad to renounce any claims to cheap democratic popularity.[12]

Here Marx and Engels are taking the first step on the road which two years later was to lead to their attack on Kinkel and his crew in *The Great Men in Exile*.

Writers not ranged on the revolutionary side are also, of course, subjected to criticism. Thus Marx and Engels (whose respective contribution to the *Revue* cannot be neatly disentangled) characterize the poet, scholar, and translator Friedrich Daumer by analysing the kind of literature he admires, the kind of authorities he quotes, the kind of prose he writes; they produce, in this way, a satirical portrait of what Nietzsche was later to call the *Bildungsphilister*, the educated German philistine.[13] The term Marx uses, here and elsewhere, is *Spieß-bürger*, which holds additional suggestions of the petty-bourgeois and the obsolete. A creature of this kind will close his eyes, Marx tells us, to modern scientific knowledge that might force him to face the world as it is, and construct himself a literary peasant-idyll. Here Marx finds his cue for railing against the backwardness of rural Bavaria ('the soil in which priests and

---

[12] *R* 218; *MEW* VII, 299.   [13] *R* 105–8; *MEW* VII, 198–9.

Daumers grow equally well') and casting a scornful glance at a literary genre whose popularity was steadily increasing. This was the *Dorfgeschichte* or village story, whose most widely read (and least astringent) representative turned out to be that friend of Moses Hess whom we have met in an earlier chapter, the German–Jewish writer Berthold Auerbach. Marx jeers at Daumer's 'fear of a renewal of [political] battles which might, once again, prove an unpleasant distraction from his preoccupation with Hafiz, Mohammed, and Berthold Auerbach . . . In face of the historical tragedy by which he feels threatened Herr Daumer takes refuge in a blear-eyed peasant-idyll that would pass for nature.'[14] Marx was never to show much patience with literary attempts to portray an idyllic country-life. Meeting Bruno Bauer again in London he professed himself amazed, in a letter to Engels, at hearing Bauer romanticize the German farmer—how curious, he reflects, to hear this 'critical critic' admit by implication that 'critical criticism' boiled down to Berthold Auerbach in the end.[15]

The creation of deceptive idylls seems to be the best that men of Daumer's stamp are capable of; Marx can see no *tragedy* in the decline of their kind:

Whereas the decline of former classes—that of the knights, for instance—could furnish material for magnificent tragic works of art, the *Spießbürger* fittingly provide nothing but impotent manifestations of fanatical malice and a collection of Sancho-Panzean sayings and maxims.[16]

There is a sad contrast, then, between the nineteenth-century bourgeoisie under threat, and the tragic decline of knighthood. But even if one compares Daumer with an earlier German *Spießbürger*, like that shoemaker-poet Hans Sachs whom Marx was never to see through Wagner's admiring eyes—even then the comparison is not to Daumer's advantage: 'Herr Daumer is a continuation of Hans Sachs, but dry and bare of all humour.'[17]

It will not have escaped notice that in his efforts to characterize Daumer's brand of philistinism Marx had recourse once again to the figure of Sancho Panza in Cervantes's masterpiece.

---

[14] *R* 107; *MEW* VII, 201–2.
[15] Cf. Marx's letters to Engels: 14 Dec. 1855, 18 Jan. 1856, and 12 Feb. 1856— *MEW* XXVIII, 466, XXIX, 6 and 15.
[16] *MEW* VII, 203.   [17] *MEW* VII, 203.

Having thus discussed a recent German publication as a document of bourgeois intellectual life in Germany, Marx and
Engels looked around for similarly representative works in
France and England. They came up with a pamphlet by
François Pierre Guillaume Guizot, which gave them a comfortable sense that not only kings but also the leading talents of the
bourgeoisie were on their way out—'In der Tat, nicht nur les
rois s'en vont, sondern auch les capacités de la bourgeoisie s'en
vont';[18] and they followed their discussion of Guizot with a
piece on Carlyle's *Latter-Day Pamphlets*. Carlyle held a threefold
interest for them. Engels had learnt a great deal from him in
earlier years—particularly, of course, from *Past and Present*—and
had inspired Marx to read (and make notes on) his work;
Carlyle was much read and discussed when Marx first settled
in England; and he presented himself, as the *Revue* stresses, as
'the one English writer on whom German literature has exerted
a direct and very important influence'.[19] After reading the first
two of the *Latter-Day Pamphlets*, Marx and Engels found the
diagnosis of their Guizot essay fully confirmed: 'the leading
talents of the bourgeoisie', they repeat, 'are in decline'.[20] They
now try to see traces of this decline in Carlyle's earlier and
better work, and find them in his romanticism, his *backward-
looking* opposition to capitalist developments.[21] They pour
scorn on his belief in 'eternal' laws of nature, which blinds him,
in their view, to the realities of the class-struggle and predisposes
him to see the life of his times in terms of the simple moralities
of *The Magic Flute*.[22] They deride his hero-worship which makes
him see injustice and oppression as signs of genius.[23] They accuse
him of ignorance and bad faith: 'what looks like nobility
becomes caddish and stupid when looked at in practice'; 'the
lofty protestations of nobility transform themselves into down-
right baseness as soon as he descends from the heaven of high-
flown and sententious phrases to the world of actually existing
conditions'; 'In his expiatory wrath, this affirmative genius
justifies and exaggerates fantastically the infamies of the
bourgeois.'[24]

The decline Marx and Engels see in Carlyle's morality and

[18] *MEW* VII, 212.   [19] *MEW* VII, 255.   [20] *MEW* VII, 255.
[21] *MEW* VII, 255–6.   [22] *MEW* VII, 261.   [23] *MEW* VI, 256.
[24] *MEW* VII, 263–4.

logic—a decline hindsight may deem inevitable—is matched, in their eyes, by a falling-off in his style:

Carlyle's style is like his ideas. It is the same direct, forcible reaction against the modern bourgeois English Pecksniff-style whose stilted limpness, careful prolixity, and sentimentally moral, desultory tediousness passed from its original inventors, the educated cockneys, to the whole of English literature. Old turns of speech and words are dug up and new ones are invented, in the German fashion—more particularly the fashion of Jean Paul. Carlyle's new style was often heaven-storming and tasteless, but it was frequently brilliant and always original. In this too the *Latter-Day Pamphlets* show a remarkable retrogression.

It is significant, we should say in passing, that in the whole of German literature Carlyle should have been influenced most, not by Hegel, but by the literary apothecary Jean Paul.[25]

Four features of this passage are remarkable. First, the way the creations of a great novelist, Dickens, are used as a kind of characterizing shorthand: the term *Pecksniff-Stil* relieves Marx and Engels of the necessity to describe the language and life-style of a social type. 'Read your Boz', they would seem to say to their readers, 'and you will understand'. Second, the way the character of one writer is defined by reference to that of another whom he admires and imitates: Jean Paul Friedrich Richter helps to 'place' Carlyle. Third, the resolute endeavour, made here and elsewhere in the *Revue*, to see writers as representative figures: as individuals who, even while asserting themselves against their class and their time, represent that class and that time. What Carlyle consciously *says* in his work must be seen together with what he unconsciously *reveals*. Lastly: 'literature' is not simply a matter of novels, plays, and poems: Hegel is no less part of *Literatur* than Jean Paul, the philosopher no less than the purveyor of fictions. In fact, the *Revue* had earlier poured scorn on those who think their education complete when they have assimilated their country's belles-lettres: 'the application of the Hegelian dialectic is . . . somewhat more difficult than quoting little verses by Schiller'.[26]

It should be remembered, however, that what Marx thought of as Carlyle's 'decline' did not, in his eyes, devalue Carlyle's insights. As late as 1870 he looked at 'Handsome William' of

[25] *R* 187–8; *MEW* VII, 256.   [26] *R* 109; *MEW* VII, 204.

Prussia, who was soon to rule a newly unified Germany as Kaiser Wilhelm I, with a quip of Carlyle's sardonically in mind: 'When God wants to do something especially great, says old Carlyle, he always chooses the stupidest people.' Six years later we find him reading Carlyle again (this time it is *Oliver Cromwell's Letters and Speeches* which arouses his interest); and Pamela Hansford Johnson may well be right in feeling that Marx's own style has not remained wholly unaffected by his continued study of an author to whom Engels had first directed his attention in the 1840s.[27]

One other book review published in the short-lived London continuation of the *Neue Rheinische Zeitung* affords valuable insight into Marx's views on literature and the arts. This is a discussion of the memoirs of two French police-spies, Adolphe Chenu and Lucien de la Hodde, which opens with a notable contrast between a 'Rembrandtian' and a 'Raphaelesque' mode of character-drawing:

Nothing could be more desirable than that men who headed the party of change, either in secret societies or in the Press before the revolution or in official positions afterwards, should be depicted in robust Rembrandtian colouration, in their full vitality. The representations we have had hitherto never depict such personalities in their true shape—they depict them only in official poses with buskins on their feet and haloes round their heads. In these glorified Raphaelesque pictures all truth of representation is lost.[28]

The contrast here suggested between two modes of painting (in which the palm is clearly awarded to the Rembrandtian mode) anticipates Marx's later confrontation, in his critique of Lassalle's play *Franz von Sickingen*, of a Shakespearian and a Schillerian mode of character-drawing (in which the Shakespearian mode is explicitly preferred). A robust and vital realism is contrasted with idealizations that glorify (*verhimmeln*) human truth out of existence.

The memoirs of de la Hodde also provide an occasion, in this same review, to demonstrate how works of literature may

---

[27] Letter to Engels, 8 Aug. 1870—*MEW* XXXIII, 32; M. Rubel and M. Manale, *Marx without Myth. A Chronological Study of his Life and Work* (Oxford, 1975) p. 301; P. H. Johnson, 'The Literary Achievement of Marx', *The Modern Quarterly*, New Series, ii (1946–7), 243–4.

[28] *R* 194; *MEW* VII, 266.

be used to project a false self-image. The work so used is James Fenimore Cooper's novel *The Spy*:

> M. de la Hodde seeks to depict himself, in his brochure, as the 'Spy' of Cooper's novel. He has, he maintains, deserved well of society because he paralysed the secret societies for eight years. But the road from Cooper's *The Spy* to M. de la Hodde is a very long one . . .[29]

In the rest of the review Marx and Engels then analyse the falseness of de la Hodde's literary self-image, and 'place' it by comparing de la Hodde's memoirs with those of Adolphe Chenu. Here once again a literary work supplies the essential, characterizing touch:

> The masses of paint and patchouli under which prostitutes try to smother the less attractive aspects of their existence have their literary counterpart in the *bel esprit* with which de la Hodde perfumes his pamphlet. The literary character of Chenu's book, on the other hand, frequently recalls in its naïveté and vividness of presentation, that of *Gil Blas*. Just as Gil Blas in his most varied adventures always remains a lackey and judges everything from that perspective, so Chenu remains, from the uprising of 1832 to his removal from the Prefecture of Police, the same subordinate conspirator . . .[30]

Gil Blas here provides, for Marx and Engels, a point of reference they share with their educated readers. It is a known standard against which Chenu's book can be held and measured even as that book is itself the standard that helps us to judge the memoirs of de la Hodde.

(ii)

Marx's first years in London were years of poverty, growing ill health, and disappointment. Serious differences of opinion developed in the Communist League, which were exacerbated by squabbles with the London *émigré* community and which led to Marx's increasing isolation. The defeat of a workers' insurrection in Paris had convinced Marx by 1850 that the time was not ripe for revolution, and that he ought to sink himself in studies which could further the task of constructing a powerful revolutionary theory. Such studies, he now believed, must concentrate on political economy:

[29] *R* 195; *MEW* VII, 266–7.   [30] *R* 198; *MEW* VII, 270–1.

The enormous material for the history of political economy which is accumulated in the British Museum, the favourable vantage point afforded by London for the observation of bourgeois society, and finally the new stage of development into which the latter appeared to have entered with the discovery of gold in Australia and California, determined me to begin afresh from the very beginning and to work through the new material critically. These studies led partly of themselves into apparently quite remote subjects on which I had to dwell for a shorter or longer period.[31]

This work could not, however, go on without interruption. The trial of members of the Communist League in Cologne, supported by evidence which had in part been forged, involved Marx in the immense labour of exposing forgeries and rebutting charges without access to court-documents or means to travel; and the necessity of providing a more or less regular income for himself and his family—apart from the subventions of the ever-faithful Engels—made him accept an invitation from Charles A. Dana to become a regular contributor to the radical *New-York Daily Tribune*. His direct political activity, however, grew less after the dissolution of the Communist League in 1852.

The first articles sent to the *New-York Daily Tribune* in Marx's name were in fact the work of Engels, even though Marx collected payment for them and though they were ascribed to him when they were later issued as a separate pamphlet under the title *Germany: Revolution and Counter-Revolution*. It was Engels, too, who translated Marx's German articles into English until Marx felt sure enough of English idiom to write in that language himself. This left Marx more time and energy for his work on economics. It also allowed him to turn his attention to the French scene again, where Louis Napoleon had staged his *coup d'état* in 1851 and proclaimed himself Emperor in 1852. He analysed the social and economic implications in a series of articles entitled (with an allusion to the *coup d'état* of Napoleon I) *The Eighteenth Brumaire of Louis Bonaparte*. These first appeared, not in the *New-York Daily Tribune*, but in a short-lived New York monthly called *The Revolution* (*Die Revolution*). Though composed in great haste, and amid constant financial worries, *The Eighteenth Brumaire* will always count among Marx's best-written and most incisive works; the silence with which it

[31] *SW* I, 505; *MEW* VIII, 10–11.

was received at the time, and a similar lack of response to his work on the Cologne Communist trial, occasioned him bitter disappointment.

The Eighteenth Brumaire opens with an allusion to a passage in Hegel's *Philosophy of History* to which Engels had drawn his attention in a letter of 3 December 1851:

Hegel remarks somewhere that all great, world-historical facts and personages occur, as it were, twice. He has forgotten to add: the first time as tragedy, the second as farce. Caussidière for Danton, Louis Blanc for Robespierre, the *Montagne* of 1848 to 1851 for the *Montagne* of 1793 to 1795, the Nephew for the Uncle. And the same caricature may be discerned in the circumstances in which the second edition of the Eighteenth Brumaire is coming out.[32]

The dramatic analogy of the opening sentence merges with an analogy from publishing in the second, and is extended, in the paragraph that follows, to theatrical performance:

. . . they anxiously conjure up the spirits of the past, take them into their service, and borrow from them names, battle-slogans, and costumes in order to perform the new scene of world history [*die neue Weltgeschichtsszene aufzuführen*] in this time-honoured disguise and this borrowed language. Thus Luther donned the mask of the Apostle Paul, the Revolution of 1789 to 1814 dressed itself up now as the Roman Republic, now as the Roman Empire . . .

That, in its turn, leads to yet another analogy with literary associations: with the activity of *translating*:

In the same way the beginner who has learnt a new language always translates it back into his mother tongue; but he has assimilated the spirit of the new language and can produce freely in it only when he moves in it without remembering the old . . .

As in *The Class-Struggles in France* metaphors from the theatre, from popular entertainments, and from literary parody act as leitmotivs that hold the work together. 'Theatrical costumes', 'dramatic effects', 'upstage' and 'downstage', 'the boards', 'scenery', 'theatre-tickets', 'overture', 'curtain', 'mask', 'hollow declamations', 'ghosts' appearing 'in the later acts' of a play,

[32] *SW* I, 398; *MEW* VIII, 115. Marx alludes here to Part III of Hegel's *Lectures on the Philosophy of History*; he had made a similar point about historical tragedy recurring at a later period as comedy in his Critique of Hegel's *Philosophy of Right* of 1843-4 (*MEW* I, 381-2).

'chorus', 'solo-performers', 'comedies of intrigue', 'court comedies', *Haupt- und Staatsaktionen*—these are but some of the theatrical metaphors Marx uses in his efforts to discredit Napoleon III and his entourage. They are incompetent performers parodying a better play. Louis Napoleon, Marx tells us,

interprets the historical life of the nations and their *Haupt- und Staatsaktionen* as comedy in the most vulgar sense, as a masquerade in which grand costumes, words, and postures serve only as masks for the pettiest knavery . . . In his Society of 10 December he assembled ten thousand rascally fellows, who must play the part of the people, as Nick Bottom plays that of the lion. At a moment when the French bourgeoisie itself acted out the most complete comedy, but in the most serious manner in the world, without infringing any of the pedantic conditions of French dramatic etiquette, and was itself half deceived, half convinced by the solemnity of its own *Haupt- und Staatsaktionen*—at such a moment the adventurer who took the comedy as plain comedy was bound to win. Only when he has eliminated his solemn opponent, when he himself now takes his imperial role seriously and with the Napoleonic mask thinks to play the part of the real Napoleon, does he become the victim of his own conception of the world, the serious *Hanswurst*, who no longer takes world history for a comedy, but his comedy for world history . . . Bonaparte in public before the citizens, with the official phrases of order, religion, family, property, and with the secret society of the Schufterles and Spiegelbergs, the society of disorder, prostitution, and theft, behind him—this is Bonaparte as original author, and the history of the Society of 10 December is his own history.[33]

What is translated as 'history' in that last sentence—the word *Geschichte*—can also mean 'story' or 'plot'. Napoleon III is not only performer, but also author, of a risible piece. And behind him Marx conjures up memories of other 'authors' in whose work Louis Napoleon and his crew may be seen prefigured: the popular playwrights who created *Hanswurst*, the German Mr. Punch; the writers of *Haupt- und Staatsaktionen*; Shakespeare, who in *A Midsummer Night's Dream* extracted high comedy from the spectacle of men trying to play parts for which they were fitted neither by nature nor by training; and the young Schiller, who had presented, in the Schufterle and Spiegelberg of his early play *The Robbers*, types of knavery whose

[33] *SW* I, 442–3; *MEW* VIII, 161–2.

real-life counterparts were not confined to Germany or to the eighteenth century.

The images of *parody* which we have seen recurring so often in Marx's savage portrait of Louis Napoleon and his times gain much of their force from being seen against the background of another, worthier kind of imitation and stylization. The revolutionaries who had performed their world-historical task of securing power for the middle classes had known better when to draw on their reading of the Roman and Hebrew classics:

Unheroic as bourgeois society is, it yet had need of heroism, of sacrifice, of terror, of civil war and of national battles to bring it into being. And in the classically austere traditions of the Roman Republic its gladiators found the ideals and the art forms, the self-deceptions, which they needed in order to conceal from themselves the bourgeois limitations of the content of their struggles and to keep their passion at the height of the great historical tragedy. Similarly, at another stage of development, a century earlier, Cromwell and the English people had borrowed speech, passions and illusions from the Old Testament for their bourgeois revolution. When the real aim had been achieved, when the bourgeois transformation of English society had been accomplished, Locke supplanted Habakkuk.

The awakening of the dead in those revolutions therefore served the purpose of glorifying the new struggles, not of parodying the old; of magnifying the given tasks in imagination, not of taking flight from their solution in reality; of finding once more the spirit of revolution, not of making its ghost walk again.[34]

But now, Marx believed, the time for stylization had passed. There had been too much caricature, too much false consciousness, too much illusion. The present age must no longer look to the past for its 'poetry'; it must do away with the 'superstition' that today's battles can only be won in the costumes of yesteryear:

The social revolution of the nineteenth century can only draw its poetry from the future, not from the past. It cannot begin with itself before it has stripped off all superstition in regard to the past. Earlier revolutions required world-historical recollections in order to drug themselves concerning their own content. In order to arrive at its own content, the revolution of the nineteenth century must let the dead bury their dead. There the phrase went beyond the content; here the content goes beyond the phrase.[35]

[34] *SW* I, 399; *MEW* VIII, 116.   [35] *SW* I, 400; *MEW* VIII, 117.

Significantly, Marx here supports his call for a poetry drawn
from the future with a reference to the New Testament (Matthew 8: 22). Drawing your inspiration from a vision of an unalienated society yet to be created never implies, in Marx's
work, that the literary and cultural traditions of the past should
be denied or forgotten. Constantly, therefore, readers of *The
Eighteenth Brumaire* find themselves reminded of their Bible: of
the 'flesh-pots of Egypt', of Samuel, of Saul, of King David.

For help in exposing the shams of the present, Marx looks,
in *The Eighteenth Brumaire*, to two contemporary writers. It is
Heine who supplies the name he will never cease to apply, from
this time on, to Louis Napoleon himself: the name 'Crapülinski' which Heine had coined in a cruel poem about Polish
exiles in Paris entitled 'Two Knights'.[36] And it is a contemporary
French novelist who helps Marx characterize, at the very end
of *The Eighteenth Brumaire*, the moral climate of the new France:
'One can visualize these upper strata of the Society of 10 December clearly if one reflects that *Véron-Crevel* is its moralist and
Granier de Cassagnac its thinker.'[37] The compound *Véron-Crevel*
brings together a real-life original (Louis Véron, editor of *Le
Constitutionnel*) with the unforgettable literary character he
helped, unknowingly, to suggest: Crevel in Balzac's *La Cousine
Bette*. This is the first time we see Marx looking to Balzac for the
succinct presentation, in a recognizably individual character, of
typical modes of thinking and feeling in nineteenth-century
France. 'He considered Balzac', Paul Lafargue was later to
recall, 'not only as the historian of his time, but also as the
prophetic creator of characters which were still in embryo in
the days of Louis-Philippe and did not fully develop until after
his death, under Napoleon III.'[38]

The Eighteenth Brumaire is, once again, full of subliminal quotations and recollected snatches from great works of literature;
it is also full of Marx's characteristic inversions, as when Chamisso's Peter Schlemihl, who had a body but no shadow, is
countered by the inverted Schlemihls (*umgekehrte Schlemihle*) of
today, 'shadows that have lost their body'.[39] Above all: Marx

[36] *SW* I, 406; *MEW* VII, 123. Heine's poem *Zwei Ritter* appears in Book I
of *Romanzero*.
[37] *SW* I, 487; *MEW* VIII, 206–7.   [38] *ÜKL* I, 21.
[39] *SW* I, 419; *MEW* VIII, 136.

here inquires, more fully than in any previous work, into the relation of authors to those social classes whose conflicting interests had moved into the forefront of Marx's attention. He sees 'literary men', *Literaten*, as representatives of bourgeois interests which are often slighted in the pursuit of other interests:

Still more unequivocally than over the falling-out with its *parliamentary representatives* the bourgeoisie displayed its wrath against its own literary representatives, against its own Press . . . The *extraparliamentary mass of the bourgeoisie*, by its servility towards the President, by its vilification of Parliament, by the brutal maltreatment of its own Press, invited Bonaparte to suppress and annihilate its speaking and writing section, its politicians and its *Literaten*, its platform and its Press, in order that it might then be able to pursue its private affairs with full confidence in the protection of a strong and unrestricted government.[40]

This passage had been preceded by another in which Marx had questioned the term 'representative' he used in this context. One must not imagine, he had said of literary men whose writing seemed to him to reek of the petty-bourgeoisie, that

the democratic representatives are all shopkeepers or enthusiastic champions of shopkeepers. According to their education and their individual position they may be separated from them as widely as heaven from earth. What makes them representatives of the petty-bourgeoisie is the fact that in their minds they cannot transcend the limits which the latter cannot transcend in life, that they are therefore driven theoretically to the same tasks and the same solutions to which material interest and social position drive the latter in practice.[41]

'In general', Marx adds, in an aside that has made this passage one of the most frequently quoted in Marxist disquisitions on the place of writers in the class-structure, 'that is the relationship of *political* and *literary representatives* to the class they represent.'

[40] *SW* I, 465–6; *MEW* VIII, 184–5.
[41] *SW* I, 424; *MEW* VIII, 142. Ian Birchall has applied Goldmann's notion of 'structural homology' to this passage: 'This is not a deterministic formulation. Rather it points to a structural homology between the world-view of a social class and the work of a writer who—for whatever individual or social reason— does not go beyond the limits of this world-view.' ('The Total Marx and the Marxist Theory of Literature' in *Situating Marx*, ed. Walton and Hall, p. 134.)

This is not to say, however, that in Marx's view all literary men of bourgeois origin must 'represent' their class in this way. He thinks, rather, that their peculiar social position offers such men a choice that city proletarians or agricultural workers do not have; they may speak for the bourgeoisie, or they may throw in their lot with that of other social classes. For intellectuals, as Shlomo Avineri has argued, there is in Marx's scheme 'no *a priori* determination, as in the case of the capitalist or the worker. Choice is the very embodiment of the intellectual's determined "social being".'[42]

Two further passages in *The Eighteenth Brumaire* demand to be pondered in connection with this important point. The first of these is Marx's justly famous mediation between freedom and determinism in all human history: 'Men make their own history, but they do not make it just as they please; they do not make it under circumstances chosen by themselves, but under circumstances directly encountered, given, and transmitted from the past.'[43] The second of these passages goes back to the term 'superstructure' (*Überbau*), which had been used in *The Communist Manifesto* to describe social stratification[44] but which in *The Eighteenth Brumaire* takes on a meaning nearer to that it had borne in *The German Ideology*. It now suggests political institutions together with the beliefs, the modes of thought, feeling, and looking, characteristic of a given class at a given time:

The Legitimate Monarchy was merely the political expression of the hereditary rule of the lords of the soil, as the July Monarchy was only the political expression of the usurping rule of the bourgeois *parvenus*. What kept the two sections apart, therefore, was not any so-called principles, it was their material conditions of existence, two different kinds of property, it was the old contrast of town and country, the rivalry between capital and landed property. That at the same time old memories, personal enmities, fears and hopes, prejudices and illusions, sympathies and antipathies, convictions, articles of faith and principles bound them to one or the other royal house, who is there that denies this? Upon the different forms of

[42] S. Avineri, 'Marx and the Intellectuals', *Journal of the History of Ideas*, xxviii (1967), 277.

[43] *SW* I, 398; *MEW* VIII, 115.

[44] 'The proletariat, the lowest stratum of present-day society, cannot stir, cannot raise itself, without blowing sky-high the whole superstructure [*Überbau*] of strata that constitute official society.' (*MEW* IV, 473.)

property, upon the social conditions of existence rises an entire *superstructure* [my italics, S.S.P.] of distinct and characteristically formed sentiments, illusions, modes of thought and views of life. The entire class creates and forms them out of its material foundations and out of the corresponding social relations. The single individual who derives them through tradition and education may imagine that they form the real motives and the starting point of his activity. If Orleanists and Legitimists, if each section sought to make itself and the other believe that loyalty to their two royal houses separated them, it later proved to be the case that it was rather their divided interests which forbade the uniting of the two royal houses. And as in private life one distinguishes between what a man thinks and says of himself and what he really is and does, still more in historical struggles must one distinguish the phrases and fancies of the parties from their real organism and their real interests, their conception of themselves from their reality.[45]

Marx himself, it is clear, believes that he has been able to look beyond the ideological superstructure of contemporary bourgeois society. He now sees himself as speaking, not for the bourgeoisie, but for proletarian forces which will, he thinks, destroy the capitalist order and substitute a juster one.

On the road to that new and better order, however, Marx sees many obstacles and enemies. These include workers who are not class-conscious, who look nostalgically to the past rather than to a future that must be attained through revolution—men whom Marx dismisses, in his correspondence and conversations, as *Knoten* and *Straubinger*; they include also the 'rabble' of great cities like that which in Paris (Marx tells us) showed itself so ready to support Napoleon III. *The Eighteenth Brumaire* contains a spirited description of the composition of that 'rabble', now designated *Lumpenproletariat*, which affords yet another glimpse of literary men:

On the pretext of founding a benevolent society, the *Lumpenproletariat* of Paris had been organized into secret sections, each section being led by Bonapartist agents, with a Bonapartist general at the head of the whole. Alongside decayed *roués* with doubtful means of subsistence and of doubtful origin, alongside ruined offshoots of the bourgeoisie eager for adventures, were vagabonds, discharged soldiers, discharged jail-birds, escaped galley-slaves, swindlers, mountebanks, *lazzaroni*, pickpockets, tricksters, gamblers,

[45] *SW* I, 421; *MEW* VIII, 139.

procurers, brothel-keepers, porters, *Literaten*, organ-grinders, rag-pickers, knife-grinders, tinkers, beggars, in short the whole indefinite, disintegrated mass thrown hither and thither, which the French term *la bohème* . . .[46]

Wedged between porters and organ-grinders, the *literati* of this eloquent passage have lost all dignity. They are at once part of the *Lumpenproletariat* and part of a *bohème* which held no Murgerian charms for Marx. He was no bohemian intellectual—in his writings as in his personal life he regarded bohemian attitudes and behaviour with a disapproval as absolute as that shown by more conventional representatives of the Victorian middle class.

(iii)

The letters that Marx wrote to Engels during his first years in London are full of literary quotations, most of them playful:

> Dear Engels,
> iterum Crispinus!

Marx will begin, with an allusion to Juvenal's first Satire; or else:

> Dear Engels,
> I come late, but I do come . . .—

which alludes to the opening of Schiller's *The Piccolomini*. He will roguishly combine the Greek and the Hebrew heritage of Europe, which Heine so often opposed to each other, by speaking of Homeric laughter by the waters of Babylon; or, in more serious vein, explain the revolutionary ardours of a contemporary whom all men had thought quiet and peace-loving by 'emending' Juvenal's *facit indignatio versum* to *indignatio facit poetam*.[47] Most interesting of all, in these letters, is the way Marx brings literature into his life by bestowing literary nicknames on public men that engage his attention and on private acquaintances he encounters in his daily life. Napoleon III thus appears as Heine's vulgar and cowardly adventurer Crapülinski, and Gladstone as a combination of Butler's Hudibras, Hudibras's squire Ralph, and Sue's Rodolphe de Gérolstein: 'Hudibrasiac Rodolpho Gladstone'.[48] Arnold Ruge takes on

[46] *SW* I, 442; *MEW* VIII, 160-1.
[47] *MEW* XXVII, 543, 184; XXVIII, 81; XXVII, 324.
[48] *MEW* XXVII, 384; XXVIII 254.

the guise of Atta Troll, the clumsy dancing bear invented by Heine to caricature untalented German liberals; Ferdinand Freiligrath that of his own negro-prince, the *Mohrenfürst*, which had inspired some of Heine's best jokes at Freiligrath's expense; and Wilhelm Pieper appears, invariably, as Tupman—a clear allusion to the *Pickwick Papers*.[49]

Not unnaturally Marx also reflects, in these letters to Engels, on the task of the historian as he envisaged it in these early years in London, and as he found others practising it;[50] and as he does so, he finds himself, inevitably, drawing parallels between the activities of the historian and those of the novelist. Louis Blanc, for instance, whose book on the July revolution (*Histoire de dix ans, 1830–1840* (Paris, 1841–4)) Marx had recently been reading, is said to write his historical works as the elder Dumas writes his feuilleton-novels: he always gathers just enough material for his next chapter. This, Marx adds, has the advantage of a certain freshness, for what he has to tell is as new to him as it is to his readers; but such an advantage hardly suffices to compensate for the unavoidable weakness of the whole work.[51] That Marx read the elder Dumas's novels for entertainment and relaxation during his London years is also attested by Paul Lafargue.[52]

The letters that passed between Marx and Engels in the early 1850s show a growing exasperation with the activities of German *émigrés* in England; they detested in particular that same Gottfried Kinkel whose activities in Germany they had so severely criticized in the *Politisch-ökonomische Revue* (see above, p. 171). Kinkel's posing and self-advertising seemed so intolerable to Marx that he yielded easily to the persuasion of the shady Colonel Johann Bangya to expose Kinkel and his entourage in forthright and undiplomatic terms. The resulting pamphlet, *The Great Men in Exile* (*Die großen Männer des Exils*),

[49] *MEW* XXVII, 165, 596, 244 *et passim*.

[50] Marx read many historical works throughout his life; in these early years in London his reading included (as his notebooks attest) several German studies of the history of culture and civilization such as J. G. Eichhorn's *Allgemeine Geschichte der Cultur und Litteratur des neueren Europa* (Göttingen, 1769); W. Drumann, *Grundriß der Culturgeschichte* (Königsberg, 1847); Gustav Klein, *Allgemeine Culturgeschichte der Menschheit* (Leipzig, 1847–9); and W. Wachsmuth, *Allgemeine Culturgeschichte* (Leipzig, 1850). Cf. M. Rubel, *Marx Critique du Marxisme. Essais* (Paris, 1974), pp. 319 and 327.

[51] *MEW* XXVII, 194.   [52] *ÜKL* I, 20.

remained unpublished in Marx's lifetime, and now that Kinkel and his crew have sunk into deserved oblivion, it has lost a good deal of its interest; but in our context it does deserve some attention if only because it is the longest, hardest look Marx ever took at the life and work of a German man of letters.

Where the central metaphor of *The Eighteenth Brumaire* had been the drama and the theatre, that of *The Great Men in Exile* is the epic. It opens with a deliberately anticlimactic adaptation of Klopstock's Christian epic *The Messiah* (*Der Messias*)— 'Sing, immortal soul, the salvation of sinful mankind, through Gottfried Kinkel', and continues with a plethora of direct quotations and parodies of other epic poems, notably Wolfram von Eschenbach's *Parzival*, Ariosto's *Raging Roland* (*Orlando furioso*), and (most prominent of all) Matteo Boiardo's *Roland in Love* (*Orlando inamorato*). There are occasional 'dramatic' sections too —the sixth, for instance, is divided into six 'scenes' (*Auftritte*) and an 'intermezzo'; but on the whole the mock-epic tone is so steadily sustained that this work might well have borne the title *The Kinkeliad*.

This *Kinkeliad* adds new strokes to that portrait of the educated German philistine, the *Bildungsphilister*, which had been begun in the Daumer review of the *Politisch-ökonomische Revue*. It shows how Gottfried Kinkel, who is presented (not altogether unfairly) as a stupid and vain writer of no literary merit, stylizes his life after the works he reads but manages only to parody these works: the poems of the Göttingen group, Schiller's *Intrigue and Love*, Goethe's poems and plays, Novalis's *Heinrich von Ofterdingen* are all used, and degraded, in this way. It is therefore fitting that Marx should draw on the whole range of literature, from Miller's sentimental novel *Siegwart* at one end of the scale to Goethe and Diderot on the other, to characterize Gottfried Kinkel and his friends:

Gottfried is the hero of the democratic *Siegwart*-period, which has produced in Germany such endless patriotic melancholy and tearful lamentation. His debut was that of an ordinary lyrical Siegwart . . .

. . . dreaming of future immortality, [Kinkel] performs Old Testament histories and modern lending-library fantasies à la Spieß, Clauren, and Cramer and thus relishes himself, in his own imagination, as a romantic hero . . .

Here Gottfried reveals the whole Romantic lie in which he dressed himself; the carnival-urge to disguise himself as someone else is his true 'inner essence'. As earlier he called himself Gottfried von Straßburg so he now treads the stage as Heinrich von Ofterdingen. What he seeks is not the 'blue flower', but a woman who will appreciate him as Heinrich von Ofterdingen . . .

Herr Rudolph Schramm, a brawling, gossiping, extremely confused little man, who has chosen, as his life's motto, that saying of *Rameau's Nephew*: 'I would rather be an impertinent gossip than not be at all.'

Meyen, this little hedgehog who—through some mistake—came into the world without quills, has already, in earlier days, been described by Goethe under the name *Poinsinet* . . .[53]

In thus exhibiting the mental furnishings of a group of minor scribblers, and drawing on greater authors for a characterization of their essential selves, Marx hoped to throw light also on the tastes, the thoughts, and the social ambience of Kinkel's admirers in post-revolutionary Germany:

The German philistine, a 'beautiful soul' by nature . . . found his sweetest illusions cruelly disappointed by the hard knocks of 1849. None of his hopes had come to fruition . . . A melancholy weariness softened all hearts, and men felt the need of a democratic Christ, a real or imagined martyr who would bear, through his sufferings, the sins of the philistine world with the courage of a lamb . . . To meet this universally felt need the May-Bug Society [*Maikäferverein*], led by Johanna Mockel, got under way. And who, after all, was better fitted to perform this great Passion-Comedy than Kinkel, that imprisoned passion-flower at the spinning-wheel, that inexhaustible, tearful sponge of deeply felt emotion, who united in one person the preacher, the professor of fine arts, the parliamentary deputy, the political huckster, the musketeer, the newly discovered poet, and the old-established theatre-director? Kinkel was the man of the hour; and as such he was immediately accepted by German philistia.[54]

This representative role played by an untalented writer—a role which alone makes him worthy of notice—had its commercial implications too; Marx tries to show how Kinkel and his unhappy wife Johanna Mockel exploited his sudden fame and converted it into hard cash:

[53] *MEW* VIII, 235, 243 (*bis*), 269, 313.   [54] *MEW* VIII, 262.

With ripened experience Mockel learnt how to gain a practical advantage from the public's tender-heartedness, and without delay she organized a most active industry. She had new editions of all Gottfried's published and unpublished works brought out . . . and pushed them in public; she found purchasers . . . for her own records of life among the insects—*The Story of a Glow-Worm*, for instance; she had Gottfried's most secret feelings (communicated to his diary) prostituted to the public by the may-bug Adolph Strodtmann for a sizeable sum; she organized collections of all kinds and incontestably exhibited industrial skill and endurance which transformed the feelings of the educated world into hard cash.[55]

Here Marx touches a number of important themes: the *industry* of literature; the way corrupted taste and corrupted feelings can be played on by skilful manipulators; the commercial exploitation of political fame or notoriety; the cult of personality in the literary field. A later passage describes in detail how Kinkel acted as the agent of his own fame in London, inducing Dickens to celebrate him in *Household Words*, manœuvring his portrait into the *Illustrated London News*, sending out droves of free tickets for his lectures:

No running about, no puff, no charlatan tricks, no importunities towards the public were left untried; and not surprisingly, his efforts were successful. Complacently Gottfried now mirrored himself in his own fame and in the gigantic glass of the world's crystal palace . . .[56]

The poetaster's manipulation of his fame is thus linked with new methods of commercial advertising and with the huge puff for British industry and ingenuity represented by the Crystal Palace and the Great Exhibition of 1851. In his annoyance with Kinkel, Marx seems, however, to have overestimated the degree of Kinkel's success and influence, and to have exaggerated the financial rewards he received for his exertions.

A point especially important for Marx's argument is made by the juxtaposition of Kinkel's life and career, revealingly exposed by himself in his own autobiographical writings, with those of an earlier expatriate who had literary leanings and ambitions: Harro Harring. E. J. Hobsbawm has spoken of

[55] *MEW* VIII, 263.   [56] *MEW* VIII, 265.

Harring's activities as those of 'a fairly typical expatriate libera-
tor of peoples':

Harro Harring of (as he claimed) Denmark, successively fought for
Greece (in 1821), for Poland (in 1830–1), as a member of Mazzini's
Young Germany, *Young Italy*, and the somewhat more shadowy
Young Scandinavia, across the oceans in the struggle for a projected
United States of Latin America and in New York, before returning
for the 1848 Revolution; meanwhile publishing works with such
titles as 'The Peoples', 'Drops of Blood', 'Words of a Man', and
'Poetry of a Scandinavian'.[57]

Marx ironically likens Harring's own account of this tempes-
tuous career to Julius Caesar's descriptions of his campaigns,
and goes on to describe it with that mixture of sarcasm and
invective which characterizes the manner of *The Great Men
in Exile*. His ridicule of Harring's autobiographical, poetic,
dramatic, and political writings is designed to put Kinkel in
perspective—to show the *émigrés* of the 1840s re-enacting the
follies of earlier *émigrés* whose importance was magnified, in
their own eyes and in those of their contemporaries, by political
proscription. In the context of *The Great Men in Exile* Harring's
significance is that of a primal archetype, an *Urbild*, 'which all
our great men in exile, the Ruges, Struves, and Kinkels, strive
to emulate more or less consciously and with varying degrees of
success; an *Urbild* they may, perhaps, attain if no untoward
circumstances prevent them, but one which they will hardly be
able to surpass'.[58]

As the last-quoted sentence shows, Kinkel is joined in *The
Great Men in Exile* by other German exiles with whom Marx
felt he had scores to settle. These include his old associate Arnold
Ruge, who is compared to the eighteenth-century publisher,
bookseller, and critic Friedrich Nicolai:

Ruge played, in the *Halle Yearbooks*, the same part that the dear
departed bookseller Nicolai played in the old *Berlin Monthly Review*.
Like Nicolai he sought merit and profit mainly in printing the
works of others and deriving from them financial advantage and
literary material for his own effusions. But Ruge knew how to raise

    [57] E. J. Hobsbawm, *The Age of Revolution, 1789–1848*, Mentor edn. (New York and
Toronto, 1962), p. 161.
    [58] *MEW* VIII, 292.

this rewriting of his collaborators' articles, this literary digestive process, to a much higher potential than his model . . .[59]

Marx then puts the finishing touches to this unflattering portrait of Ruge by saying that his anti-Romanticism came to the fore only after Hegel and Heine had done an efficient demolition-job, but that, unlike Hegel, Ruge thought himself justified, by his opposition to Romanticism, 'in setting up a vulgar philistinism, and (above all) his own philistine character, as a perfected ideal'.

This passage is of particular importance because it contains one of the few explicit mentions of Hegel's *Aesthetics* in Marx's work: 'Like Nicolai', he writes, '[Ruge] fought bravely against Romanticism just because Hegel had already demolished it critically in his *Aesthetics* and Heine had demolished it in literary form in his *Romantic School*.'[60]

In his analysis of the appeal Kinkel made to the German philistine, Marx suggests that Kinkel acted out philistine dreams in his life and that he tapped philistine wish-fulfilment fantasies in his writings. These writings, however, appealed at a deeper than conscious level. Marx quotes an apparently innocuous passage from Kinkel's memoirs and underlines those features of it which seemed to him to carry a hidden sexual message: '"This heavenly flower, which has hardly opened its first leaves, already smells so sweet. As though . . . the summer ray of manly power were unfolding the inner leaves of its calyx!"'[61] It is not irrelevant to recall, at this point, that Marx himself occasionally made political points through sexual imagery—in *The Eighteenth Brumaire*, for instance, Louis Bonaparte's coup is depicted as an act of seduction and rape; and that he showed some interest, at various periods of his life, in the way sexual matters could be presented in literature. Kinkel's *sub rosa* suggestions contrast with an extract from the writings of Pietro Aretino which he sent to Engels on 3 July 1852 and which Engels found rather too strong an antidote.

In the service of its polemic against another littérateur *The Great Men in Exile* enlists the help of the Grimms' fairy-tales— with an allusion to the story entitled *The Wishing Table* Karl Heinzen's style is called 'an eternal "Cudgel, out of the bag!"'.

The same writer is deprived of his Christian name and constantly called 'Rodomonte Heinzen'; a reminder of Ariosto which is elaborated in the following characteristic passage:

In the Italian epics of chivalry powerful, broad-shouldered giants appear at every moment; they are armed with enormous clubs, but although they thresh about them barbarously and make a great deal of noise, their blows strike the surrounding trees rather than their opponents. Mr. Heinzen is an Ariostonian giant of this kind. Endowed by nature with a ruffian-like figure and enormous masses of flesh, he saw in this endowment a call to become a great man. His ponderous corporality dominates his literary demeanour, which is corporeal through and through. His opponents are always seen as little men, as dwarves which hardly reach his ankle and which he overlooks with his knee-caps. When actual physical intervention is called for, however, this 'uomo membruto' takes refuge in literature or the law-courts.[62]

Images from French and German Arthurian epics join those from Ariosto as Marx seeks to characterize his opponents with varying degrees of irony; he makes Kinkel set sail to America in search of party funds in the guise of Parzival seeking the Holy Grail. To ridicule an Austrian democrat, Karl Tausenau, Marx bids us remember Cicero's *De Divinatione*, in which two soothsayers could not look at one another without laughing; Tausenau, he declares, has only to look into the mirror to achieve the same effect. Shakespeare's history-plays provide a nickname for Léon Faucher, who becomes 'the Ancient Pistol of the Free-Trade party'. Don Quixote and Sancho Panza ride again, as usual. Rudolf Schramm, as we have seen, brings to mind Diderot's *Rameau's Nephew*. Goethe's distinction between 'literary manner' and 'literary style', *Manier* and *Stil*, is used to devalue the writings of Gustav Struve. The title of Clemens Brentano's *Tale of Gockel, Hinkel and Gackeleia* provides an oblique means of comparing Kinkel and his wife to barnyard fowls (Marx always had a penchant for comparing his opponents to animals or giving them animal names; his letters contain a choice bestiary of dogs and asses, pigs and oxen, monkeys, bugs and lice). The minor writers impressed to make various satirical

[62] *MEW* VIII, 284, 283. 'The romances of knighthood with their great swashbuckling heroes stand in vivid contrast to the achievements of the "heroes" of the Exile, while the pretensions of the latter yield in nothing to those of the Middle Ages.' (R. S. Livingstone, Introduction to his translation of *The Communist Trial in Cologne* and *Heroes of the Exile*, London 1970, p. 32.)

points in *The Great Men in Exile* range from the seventeenth-century preacher Abraham a Santa Clara to Kotzebue, Arnold Kortum, J. T. Hermes, and Paul de Kock.[63] As always in Marx's satiric-polemical writings, the presence of Heine makes itself constantly felt. When he relates an author's physical appearance and domestic circumstances to his public life and his writings, Marx falls into the manner of Heine's *Ludwig Börne*; he adopts word-coinages and phrases from Heine (*Menschenkehricht, Konfusius*); and in his portrait of Arnold Ruge he cites Heine's opinion of Ruge's character and quotes some famous lines from *Atta Troll*.

What welds together all these disparate materials is Marx's indignation with conceited littérateurs who play at politics; men who offer what he sarcastically describes as 'aesthetic lectures on the economic basis of world-historical cosmogony from a geological standpoint with musical accompaniment';[64] men who debase poetry and politics alike by their self-important coquetting with any public that will listen to them. But if the observer is keen-eyed enough, he can discern the truth through all the clouds of self-admiring phrases. 'In practice', *The Great Men of Exile* says of Kinkel, 'he cannot help exhibiting the ugly side, for his flights of fancy turn directly into lies, his forced enthusiasm into vulgarity.'[65] And Ruge's constant invocation of 'humanism', the pamphlet tells us, casts doubt on others who have sought to champion *Humanismus*. 'A hollow term', Marx calls it, 'which has served all the confused minds of Germany, from Reuchlin to Herder, as a cloak for their perplexity.'[66] In his invocation of this term which ought to mean so much and which in practice means so little, *le père* Ruge once again performs what Marx sees as his essential function: 'he represents . . . the understanding, or rather the lack of understanding, of the petty-bourgeois philistine'.[67]

(iv)

Some of the material of *The Great Men in Exile* did see the light of print in an essay against August Willich, a Communist in exile who opposed Marx's views. This slight work bore the

[63] *MEW* VIII, 334, 325, 314, 269, 270, 249, 325, 291, 282, 277.
[64] *MEW* VIII, 307.   [65] *MEW* VIII, 311.   [66] *MEW* VIII, 278.
[67] *MEW* VIII, 281. For Kinkel's debased Romanticism, and its relation to philistine life-styles, see R. S. Livingstone, op. cit., pp. 31–3.

title 'The Knight of the Magnanimous Consciousness' (*Der Ritter vom edelmütigen Bewußtsein*) and appeared in 1854. Here we find again the mock-heroic tone and the allusions to Boiardo's *Orlando inamorato* familiar from *The Great Men in Exile*; but as the title serves to suggest, the central point of reference is *Don Quixote*. The essay comes to rest, appropriately enough, on the title of a romance of adventure which would have gladdened Don Quixote's heart; and that is followed, immediately, by a quotation from *King Lear* II. ii, deflating pretensions of honesty:

This is the end of the sweet-sounding, wondrous, high-stepping, true and adventurous tale of the world-famous Knight of the Magnanimous Consciousness.

> An honest man and plain, he must speak truth;
> An they will take it, so; if not, he's plain.
> These kind of knaves I know.[68]

Here, once again, Marx does not hesitate to wrest from one of Shakespeare's most loathsome characters, Cornwall in *King Lear*, lines with whose sentiments he clearly identifies himself and with which he asks the reader to agree.

After all these attacks one can well imagine how galling it must have been for Marx to find a letter probably written by August Willich (and bearing, to make the cup really overflow, distinct traces of Kinkel's influence) attributed to himself, to Karl Marx, in the course of a trial of members of the Communist League! He writes, indignantly, in his *Revelations about the Trial of Communists at Cologne* (*Enthüllungen über den Kommunistenprozeß zu Köln, 1853*),

No one who has ever read a single line by Marx could possibly saddle him with the authorship of that melodramatic accompanying letter. The midsummer night's dream hour of 5 June, the crudely obtrusive procedure of pushing something 'red' under the front-doors of revolutionary philistines—that might point to the mind of a Kinkel, perhaps . . .[69]

The close stylistic examination which follows brings together the legal and literary interests of his youth, as Marx defines his own style against that of contemporary nonentities and mocks the distortions that great literature, even Shakespeare's *A Midsummer Night's Dream*, may suffer in the minds of little readers.

---

[68] *MEW* IX, 489 ff.   [69] *MEW* VIII, 456–7.

In *Revelations about the Trial of Communists at Cologne* Marx
again speaks, when occasion serves, in the very words of
Goethe's Mephistopheles;[70] and he also pays, once more, both
direct and indirect tribute to Heine. The tribute is direct when
he quotes the eighth poem of Heine's early cycle *Dream-Pictures*
(*Traumbilder*) as an apt characterization of the mentality of the
witnesses for the prosecution called by the Prussian authorities;[71]
it is indirect when he adopts as his own what readers of Heine
will recognize as the views Heine had put forward in the essays
on German religion, philosophy, and literature written during
the 1830s:

Have the first Christians ever been accused of aiming at the overthrow of some obscure and insignificant Roman prefect? The
Prussian state-philosophers from Leibniz to Hegel worked towards
the dethronement of God, and if I dethrone God, I do the same
for the king who rules by the grace of God. But have these philosophers been persecuted because of an attempt against the house of
Hohenzollern?[72]

Such summaries and reminiscences are supplemented, in Marx's
pamphlet about the Cologne trials, by parody—parody, above
all, of sub-literature, from sentimental domestic novels to Sue's
The Mysteries of Paris, from 'police- and servant-comedy'
(*widrige Polizei- und Bedientenkomödie*) to melodrama and opera-
libretti.[73] With their lies and intrigues, Marx would seem to be
saying, the Prussian authorities have distorted life until it looks
like bad literature; but these *Revelations* will help readers to see
events in their true form and colour, and estimate their significance more justly than the Cologne jury was able to do.

In his first four years in London, then, Marx had found the
terminology of theatrical and literary criticism more adequate
than ever for discussing political conditions; 'parody' was now
the key concept, and parody (especially of the Renaissance
epic) had also provided the leitmotivs and structural under-
pinning of his polemical pamphlets. Life itself, it seemed at
times, was taking on the guise of bad literature. He had sought
to show in greater detail than ever before how writers of all
camps and countries—from Lamartine and Carlyle to Gottfried

---

[70] *MEW* VIII, 468.   [71] *MEW* VIII, 430.   [72] *MEW* VIII, 415.
[73] *MEW* VIII, 444, 453, 433 *et passim*.

Kinkel—might be seen as 'ideological representatives' of economic and social interests, as well as the way in which their
literary works tapped fantasies characteristic of their class and
time, and the way in which they clouded or revealed political
realities. He had voiced his suspicion of a newly popular genre,
Auerbach's village stories, as a pernicious form of deceptive
idyll, and had opposed to stylization based on the poetry of
the past his notion of a 'poetry drawn from the future'. But
even in characterizing such poetry as that, he had found his
aptest phrases in the writings of the past; just as even now,
while he was more and more absorbed in economic studies, he
could best describe his own age by reference to Sancho Panza,
Gil Blas, or Schufterle and Spiegelberg. And when he looked
around at the characters that peopled and ruled his world,
he discovered that nineteenth-century novelists and poets had
named them more aptly than he could do himself; that the
style of representative writers was the style of Dickens's Pecksniff,
that the ethos of contemporary moralists was the ethos of
Balzac's Crevel, and that the monarch who seemed destined to
shape the immediate future of Europe most decisively was a
French version of Heine's Crapülinski.

9 · Historical Tragedy

'You would then have found yourself compelled
to *Shakespearize* more, while now I see *Schillerizing*
. . . as your gravest fault.'

(*MEW* XXIX, 591)

(i)

THE letters Marx wrote to Engels after the composition of *The
Great Men of Exile* reveal continuing, and growing, impatience
with such German men of letters as crossed his path. Abuse of
Kinkel and the unfortunate Johanna Mockel is constant, and
recalls, even in its phrasing, Heine's comments on Börne's
entourage in his pamphlet *Ludwig Börne*.[1] For a poem of Herwegh's, which found its way into a publication with which he
was himself associated, he could find no better term than 'that
pig of a poem' (*Das Saugedicht*).[2] With Freiligrath he tried to
find some accommodation; he hoped to keep him as a useful
ally; but the letters to Engels reveal how difficult he found it to
remain civil. The story of Marx's relations with Freiligrath is,
however, so instructive that it deserves a fuller account.

Freiligrath's poetry had acquired a new life during his association with Marx in the days of the *Neue Rheinische Zeitung*;
poems like 'In Spite of All' (*Trotz Alledem*) and 'The Dead to
the Living' (*Die Toten an die Lebenden*) owe much of their
vigour and conviction to Freiligrath's enthusiastic espousal of
the cause Marx also had at heart. It was Freiligrath, therefore,
who had been entrusted with a defiant 'Word of Farewell'
(*Abschiedswort der Neuen Rheinischen Zeitung*) in the centre of the

---

[1] Marx had promised Heine to review this work, but never found time to do so.
When he refers to Johanna Kinkel's 'bitter flesh' (*bitteres Fleisch*) (letter to Engels,
14 Feb. 1861—*MEW* XXX, 158) he merely repeats a phrase Heine had used in a
similar sexual context in *Ludwig Börne*.

[2] To Engels, 1 Aug. 1859—*MEW* XXIX, 466.

front page of the famous 'red issue' with which the paper bowed itself out. When he and Marx found themselves together in England after the failure of the 1848 Revolution, Freiligrath for a long time acknowledged that both of them belonged to the same 'party' (or 'synagogue', as he jocularly called it)—even though no kind of political party-organization existed after the dissolution of the Communist League.

Marx was aware that he had, in Freiligrath, a most valuable ally—not a great poet like Heine, perhaps, but an effective one, whose voice would be heard in Germany more readily than his own. He therefore tried to mould Freiligrath's poetic talent in the way he had earlier (according to Ruge's testimony) tried to influence Heine's: by counselling him to try his hand at *satiric* verse. Freiligrath, for his part, readily accepted Marx's advice; he wrote two satiric epistles for Joseph Weydemeyer, who published them in the same short-lived journal (*Die Revolution. Eine Zeitschrift in zwanglosen Heften*) which also brought out Marx's *Eighteenth Brumaire*. Nor did Freiligrath only accept Marx's advice on the *kind* of poem he was to write; he submitted a section of one of these poems to Marx for approval, asking him whether the facts satirized (Gottfried Kinkel's manœuvres to get his portrait into the English papers) were adequately presented. Marx replied:

The stanza you sent me is very fine and expresses the *corpus delicti* in an artistic fashion; but I think it harms the over-all impression made by the whole poem. For, first of all: *can* Kinkel be called a German poet? I and a great many other *bons gens* have some modest doubts about this. And then: is not the important contrast between the 'German poet' and the 'commercial Babylon' [= London] diminished by the additional contrast between the 'free' poet and the 'servile' one? All the more because in the figure of [H. C.] Andersen you have exhaustively portrayed the relation in which the conceited *Literat* stands to the world that confronts the poet. Since, in my opinion, there is no inner necessity for dragging in Kinkel at this point, opponents would have an excuse for attacking the poem as the expression of personal irritation or rivalry. Since the stanza is very successful, however, and should not be lost, you would, I am sure—if you agree with my view of the matter—find an opportunity for including it in a different context, perhaps in a later poetic epistle. For your portrait is most charming.[3]

[3] *Freiligraths Briefwechsel mit Marx und Engels*, ed. M. Häckel (Berlin, 1968), i. 37.

Freiligrath accepted Marx's reasoned and diplomatically expressed advice, and did not include the Kinkel stanza in his poem.

During the time of their common exile in London Freiligrath found many opportunities to be of service to Marx—opportunities he took in a selfless, undemonstrative, and gentlemanly way. And Marx, though amused by that need for flattery and applause which Freiligrath shared with the other poets he had known, felt grateful to Freiligrath and able to respect him. 'Write a friendly letter to Freiligrath', he told Joseph Weydemeyer on 16 January 1852.

Don't be afraid to compliment him, for all poets, even the best of them, are plus ou moins des courtisanes, et il faut les cajoler pour les faire chanter. Our F. is the kindest, most unassuming man in private life, who conceals un esprit très fin et très railleur beneath his genuine simplicity, and whose pathos is 'genuine' without making him 'uncritical' and superstitious. He is a real revolutionary and an honest man through and through—praise that I would not mete out to many. Nevertheless, a poet—no matter what he may be as a man—requires applause, admiration. It lies in the very nature of the species.[4]

This friendly and fundamentally respectful attitude did not last, however. In the course of the 1850s, Freiligrath moved closer to other emigrant groups, including the coterie of that same Gottfried Kinkel who had formed the subject of the satiric stanza about which Freiligrath had asked Marx's advice. Matters came to a head during preparations for the centenary celebrations of Schiller's birth in 1859, with which Freiligrath and Kinkel were both publicly associated. 'Ad vocem Freiligrath', Marx writes to Engels on 7 June 1859; 'Between ourselves: he is a turd. The devil take this whole guild of songbirds.' 'The fat philistine . . . has composed a cantata in the metre of Schiller's *Dithyramb*; he has read the stuff to me—it's all hollow pomposity.' 'This fellow finds it natural to hear cries of "Hurrah" when he has broken wind.'[5] Marx's resentment was increased by Freiligrath's refusal to take his part unequivocally in his quarrel with Karl

[4] *BM* 120–1; *MEW* XXVIII, 471–2.
[5] *MEW* XXIX, 448–9 (7 June 1859); 397–8 (15 Feb. 1859); 500 (3 Nov. 1859); 513 (19 Nov. 1859).

Vogt. In the course of a correspondence sparked off by this quarrel Freiligrath expressed, in dignified and eloquent terms, his desire to be free of the 'party-cage' in which Marx wanted to imprison him. In his answer Marx pointed out, correctly, that since the dissolution of the Communist League he belonged to no organized 'party' (. . . *von* 'Partei' *im Sinne Deines Briefs weiß ich* nichts *seit 1852*); no 'party', that is, except one which 'naturally grows, everywhere, from the soil of modern life'.[6] Not until 1866–9, the heyday of the First International, was Marx able to feel that the ideas of *The Communist Manifesto* had once again the backing of a political organization. Towards this, however, Freiligrath had not worked with him. How far the poet had in fact failed to keep pace with the evolution of his ideas was startlingly revealed to Marx by the friendly letter Freiligrath (a gentleman to the last) wrote to him after receiving volume I of *Capital*. In this Bible of the Communist movement, this 'terrible missile aimed at the heads of the ruling classes', Freiligrath could see nothing but a useful manual for 'young merchants and factory-owners' and a convenient 'source-book' for later scholars.[7]

In face of Freiligrath's failure to remain on the revolutionary path, and Herwegh's later desertion of the Marxian way for that of Lassalle, Marx tried more than once to encourage minor writers to cultivate such talent as they possessed and use it in the cause proclaimed by *The Communist Manifesto*. The first candidate for this vacant post is one Karl Siebel: 'Could not your relative S.', Marx writes to Engels on 13 August 1859, 'although I don't think much of his poetry, compose some little rhymed piece for *Das Volk*? Only nothing serious and grandiloquent [*Aber nur nichts Pathetisches*]. To annoy Freiligrath we must bring forward some kind of poet, even if we have to write his verses for him ourselves.' Siebel would not do, of course, and we soon find Marx looking elsewhere. He writes to one Johann Philipp Becker in order to praise two satirical poems he had recently written, and to suggest ways of getting them published; but he is soon forced to acknowledge that even when compared

---

[6] *ÜKL* II, 277 (29 Feb. 1860).

[7] *Freiligraths Briefwechsel mit Marx und Engels*, i. 182. For further light on the relations between Marx and Freiligrath see the Introduction to this edition of the correspondence, and F. J. Raddatz, *Karl Marx. Eine politische Biographie* (Hamburg, 1975), pp. 160–83.

to Herwegh and Freiligrath, Becker is very small beer.[8] It is
not surprising, therefore, that Marx's thoughts should turn
again and again to the one great poet who had ever supported
his cause: to Heine, whom he is proud, whenever he can, to
call his friend. When he refers to Heine directly in these years,
in letters not intended for publication, he shows some amused
disrespect for Heine the man, horrified amazement at his professed 'return' to God, unjustified contempt for Heine's wife
(about whom he is ready to believe the vilest slanders); but he
never voices such sentiments in public. His admiration for
Heine's literary achievements remains undiminished, and he
has nothing but scorn for those who denigrate them.[9] Indirectly
he continues his homage to Heine by echoing his phrases and
seeing public figures (as well as private acquaintances) through
Heine's eyes. While Napoleon III continues to appear as
Crapülinski, a group of *émigré* Poles in London are dignified
with the name Heine had invented for the second of his 'Two
Knights': 'These stupid *Waschlapskis* understood nothing of the
matter of course.'[10] The Rhenish patriot Jacob Venedey assumes the guise of a carnival figure with which Heine had first
endowed him (*Kobes I*), and Ruge is dignified with an appellation Heine had invented for Schelling: *Konfusius*.[11] Even the
term *Lumpenproletariat*, which had been used in *The Communist
Manifesto* and which now becomes an established part of
Marx's stock of descriptive abuse, would seem to owe something
to Heine. In a passage of *French Conditions* (*Französische Zustände*)
dated 19 April 1832, Heine had spoken of the community of
interests that showed itself, during a cholera epidemic in Paris,
between Parisian rag-pickers (*Lumpensammler*) and the aristocratic Carlists:

These latter had at last found their natural allies, rag-pickers and
old clo' women, who now staked their claims according to the same
principles, as champions of customary rights, of traditional, inherited
rights to trash, of every kind of rottenness [*Verfaultheiten jeder Art*].

[8] *MEW* XXIX, 475; XXX, 527 (to J. P. Becker, 9 Apr. 1860); XXXI, 30
(to Engels, 24 Nov. 1864).
[9] *ÜKL* II, 235–7.
[10] To Engels, 2 Dec. 1853—*MEW* XXVIII, 312. The name means 'milksop'
or 'ninny'.
[11] To Engels, 2 Dec. 1854, and to J. Weydemeyer, 23 Jan. 1852—*MEW* XXVIII,
418, 478.

It is precisely this alliance between an aristocracy and what *The Communist Manifesto* calls 'social scum, that passively rotting mass [*diese passive Verfaulung*] thrown off by the lowest layers of the old society'—it is precisely this alliance which Marx seeks to scourge whenever he speaks of the *Lumpenproletariat*. Like Heine, he is helped by the fact that the term *Lumpen* denotes not only rags, but also rogues and rascals.

Heine's early, non-political poems also come frequently to Marx's mind and pen; quotations like 'Leise zieht durch mein Gemüt / Liebliches Geläute' and 'Es ist eine alte Geschichte / Doch bleibt sie ewig neu' attest his fond memory of the *Book of Songs* (*Buch der Lieder*).[12]

Heine, however, is only one of many admired authors on whose work Marx draws in his endeavour to characterize and caricature his contemporaries. In the course of a single letter Marx's fellow *émigré* Wilhelm Pieper, for instance, is seen as Malvolio ('he does smile his face into more lines than is in the new map with the augmentation of the Indies'), as a German Romantic hero ('Wunderhold, son of Wunderhorn'—the 'horn' suggestions here cast strange light on Pieper's parentage!), as Shakespeare's Benedick and—in his own estimation—as a cross between Leibniz and Byron; a later letter ridicules Pieper's amorous adventures by turning him first into Fridolin, the loyal hero of one of Schiller's ballads, and then into King Visvamitra, who—according to Heine's poem—must have been an ox because he suffered so much for a cow.[13] A German *émigré* in Paris, Ludwig Simon, twice appears as the gentle Cunégonde of Voltaire's *Candide*.[14] Shakespeare plays as dominant a part as ever in this literary game—where Pieper recalls Malvolio and Benedick, Eduard Schläger (a German *émigré* in New England who had ventured to criticize Marx's style) recalls Costard inadequately cast as Pompey in the pageant-scene of *Love's Labour's Lost*, while Julius Faucher is said to combine the qualities of Münchhausen with those of Ancient Pistol.[15] Marx sends Engels Diderot's *Rameau's Nephew* and *Jacques the Fatalist* to read, and recalls Friedrich Nicolai's

---

[12] To Lassalle, 1 June 1854; to Engels, 22 July 1854—*MEW* XXVIII, 607, 377.
[13] To Engels, 22 Apr. 1854 and 13 Feb. 1856—*MEW* XXVIII, 348, and XXIX, 18.   [14] To Engels, 19 and 26 Dec. 1860—*MEW* XXX, 131, 133.
[15] To Adolf Cluss, June 1853—*MEW* XXVIII, 590; to Engels, 23 Apr. 1857—*MEW* XXIX, 131.

Sebaldus Nothanker when he mockingly bestows the name of
its eponymous hero on a contemporary nonentity.[16] Among
English authors, Dickens increasingly joins Shakespeare in this
task of transforming, illuminating, and caricaturing Marx's
world. Richard Cobden is found 'umble' like Uriah Heep,
while Friedrich Zabel, the editor of the Berlin *National-Zeitung*,
turns up as Wackford Squeers.[17] Goethe too continues to
supply prefigurations, archetypes, and standards. When Bruno
Bauer speculates in landed property to finance his researches,
Marx comments: 'He may have been a little influenced by remembering that Faust becomes a landed squire in Part II [of
Goethe's play]. What he forgets is that the money for this
transformation came from the devil.' Marx himself assumes the
guise of that devil, when he parodies a line spoken by Mephistopheles: 'If only I knew how to start a business! My worthy
friend, gray are all theories, and business alone is green';[18]
while another letter presents his maladroit self as Chamisso's
Peter Schlemihl.[19] The Bible and many of the authors of
ancient Greece and Rome are also frequently quoted with
similar purpose and effect. In particular Marx finds in the
works of Horace useful material for self-characterization. He
writes to Lassalle, for instance, that in respect of Karl Vogt's
accusations against him he feels himself 'integer vitae scelerisque
purus'; he tells Kugelmann that unlike 'the local demagogic
refugees' who attack despots from a safe distance he finds charm
in such attacks only when they occur 'vultu instantis tyranni';
and in 1863 we find him proudly declaring to Engels: 'I have
brought to light voluminous works in diverse and formidable
regions of scientific knowledge; I have not shunned exertion or
spared the midnight oil in my endeavour to widen the limits of
such knowledge; and I may, perhaps, say with Horace: "mili-
tavi non sine gloria".'[20]

[16] To Engels, 20 July 1852 and 13 Feb. 1856—*MEW* XXVIII, 92; XXIX, 16.
[17] To Engels, 25 Jan. 1854 and 9 Feb. 1860—*MEW* XXVIII, 322, and XXX, 31–2.
[18] To Engels, 10 Jan. 1857 and 20 Aug. 1862—*MEW* XXIX, 94, and XXX, 280. Cf. *Faust* Part I, 'Studierzimmer', where Mephistopheles says to the Student: 'Grau, teurer Freund, ist alle Theorie, / Und grün des Lebens goldner Baum' ('My worthy friend, all theory is grey, The golden tree of life alone is green.')
[19] To Engels, 3 June 1854—*MEW* XXVIII, 363.
[20] Letters dated 3 Mar. 1860, 29 Nov. 1869, and 28 Jan. 1863—*MEW* XXX, 499; XXXII, 637; XXX, 323.

Marx also begins at this time, in his letters to Engels, to use authors' names as a sort of shorthand for methods of polemic or publication. When he tells Engels, for instance, that Lassalle has seen fit to adopt 'a sort of Lessing manner', he has no need to describe any further a polemical technique that seeks to defend a particular interpretation by cut-and-thrust attacks on those who hold different opinions, attacks which refute different opponents' points one by one.[21] Or when, several years later, he tells Engels that 'the Jacob Grimm method' is 'in general more suited to works not dialectically constructed', he does not need to explain to his correspondent that he is referring to Grimm's habit of sending portions of his work to the printer before the whole had been completed—a habit to which Grimm specifically refers in the Preface of his *History of the German Language*.[22] Marx frequently consulted that *History*, and many an etymological excursus in his economic works as well as his letters rests on Jacob Grimm's authority.

Whatever literary experience Marx has is at once assimilated into his life and merges with other experiences. He reads Machiavelli's play *Mandragola* in 1852, and immediately applies an exchange between two of its characters, Nicia and Ligurio, to a cuckold in whose affairs he and Engels took an interest.[23] During a brief visit to Berlin in 1861 he is taken to the theatre to see a play by Gustav Freytag and also attends a session of the Prussian parliament where he hears the liberal deputy G. E. F. Vincke make a speech.

In a bad comedy by Gustav Freytag which I saw in Berlin (it was called *The Journalists* [*Die Journalisten*]) there appears a fat Hamburg philistine, a wine-merchant named Piepenbrink. Vincke is the spit image of this Piepenbrink. Revolting Hamburg-Westphalian patois, a few words quickly chewed through one after the other, not a single sentence correctly constructed or brought to a proper conclusion. And this is the Mirabeau of the *Hasenheide*! The only characters that at least look decent in this pigmean stable are Waldeck on the one side, and on the other Wagener and Don Quixote von Blanckenburg.[24]

[21] To Engels, 1 Feb. 1858—*MEW* XXIX, 274.
[22] To Engels, 31 July 1865—*MEW* XXXI, 132.
[23] To Engels, 3 July 1852—*MEW* XXVIII, 82.
[24] To Engels, 10 May 1861—*L* 295 (*MEW* XXX, 168).

This revealing passage begins with an allusion to a play written in 1852; it goes on to parody a poem by Heine ('To a former Disciple of Goethe', 1832) which contains the lines:

> In der Fern hör ich mit Freude
> Wie man voll von deinem Lob ist,
> Und wie du der Mirabeau bist
> Von der Lüneburger Heide!

> From far afield I hear with joy
> That men are full of praise for you,
> And that you are the Mirabeau
> Of the Lüneburg Heath!

and it ends by likening a Conservative politician to Don Quixote. In its marriage of the political and the literary, the contemporary and the classics of the past, the dramatic, the lyric-satirical, and the epic, the narrowly German and the European, this passage is wholly characteristic of the Marx–Engels correspondence.

That correspondence affords in addition a good deal of evidence about Marx's literary tastes between 1852 and 1862. Though he found that Georg Weerth had become too bourgeois (*verdammt verbürgert*) in his later years, he continues to respect him as a man, sympathizes with his politics, and is 'deeply affected' by his death; there is nothing to suggest, however, that he allowed these sympathies to persuade him to share Engels's high estimate of Weerth's literary works. But if political *sympathies* did not affect Marx's judgement, there is evidence that political *antipathies* could and did affect it. An aristocratic-conservative writer like Chateaubriand draws down the full vials of his wrath:

This adept of 'fine writing' . . . combines in the most revolting way the aristocratic scepticism and Voltairianism of the eighteenth century with the aristocratic sentimentalism and romanticism of the nineteenth. This combination was bound to inaugurate a new epoch in France, although for all its artistic tricks even his style is often patently false. As for his *political* side: that he has himself fully exposed in his *Congress of Verona*, and the only question which remains is whether Tsar Alexander paid him in ringing coin or only in those flatteries to which the vain coxcomb is so unusually susceptible . . . The *vanitas* of M. le Vicomte peeps out at every pore, despite his coquettish, half-Mephistophelian, half Christian, play with the notion of *vanitas vanitatum*.[25]

This is a development and sharpening of views Heine had expressed in 1844–5, the time of Marx's closest association with him. In the fragmentary *Letters on Germany* (*Briefe über Deutschland*) found among Heine's papers after his death, Heine had assigned to Chateaubriand the role of remoulding France in the image demanded by the Holy Alliance, turning the French into 'Christians and Romantics and *burgraves*'. 'Chateaubriand', Heine had said, 'came along with an enormous bottle of Jordanwater, rebaptising a France that had become pagan.'[26] It is worthy of notice, however, that Marx's attack on Chateaubriand is not only directed against his political actions and convictions, but also against his style. The falsity of an alleged combination of scepticism, sentimentality, and Romanticism, of Mephistophelian cunning and Christianity, is seen as having its counterpart in the alleged falsity of Chateaubriand's style. This concern with style and form as well as with ideological import gives Marx's remarks on Chateaubriand a significance that transcends their immediate subject and occasion.

The Marx–Engels correspondence also reveals how alive Marx always was to the distinction between literature and other modes of cognition. He had nothing but scorn for men who equated the insights afforded by literature with those afforded by philosophy and therefore demanded philosophical 'systems' of their favourite poets. 'The blockhead Ruge has proved . . . that "Shakespeare was not a dramatic poet" because "he had no philosophical system", but that Schiller, since he was a Kantian, was a truly "dramatic poet" . . .'[27] As the year 1859 approached, and with it the centenary celebrations of Schiller's birth, Marx found himself more and more exasperated by the antics of Schiller's admirers; and this had a part, no doubt, in his growing dislike of *das Schillern*, by which he meant following in Schiller's path rather than Shakespeare's.

The letter about Ruge which has just been quoted demonstrates clearly that Marx (unlike some of his later disciples)

    [25] To Engels, 26 Oct. 1854—*MEW* XXVIII, 404.
    [26] Heine, *Werke und Briefe*, ed. H. Kaufmann, vol. vii, p. 303 (*Briefe über Deutschland*).
    [27] To Engels, 24 Nov. 1858—*MEW* XXIX, 370.

was never in danger of confusing philosophic understanding and coherence with literary excellence—even where he approved of the philosophy. And here it is important to remember how aware he always was of literature as a sound–look system, as something which appealed not only to the intellect, to the moral sense, and to an abstract sense of form, but also to human ears and eyes. We know from many reminiscences—notably those of his daughters and of Wilhelm Liebknecht—that the Marx household in London was full of the sound of poetry being declaimed, or novels and plays being read aloud; and that Marx himself loved the sonorities of *Faust* so much that he tended to overdo his declamations. We can also, in his correspondence, catch occasional glimpses of his response to the appearance of literature on the printed page. 'Have the poem printed carefully', he writes to Weydemeyer in January 1852, 'the stanzas separated at adequate intervals, and the whole thing set without an eye to saving space. Poetry loses much when the verses are printed all crowded together.'[4]

Above all: Marx's letters show at every turn his concern for, and his sensitivity to, literary style. He is saddened by his own inability to approach his stylistic ideal; a sick liver, he complains, condemned him to a 'blunt, wooden manner of writing'.[28] By contrast he finds himself delighted with the 'brilliant', 'plastic', 'striking' style of François Bernier's memoirs and discovers a 'masterpiece' in Machiavelli's *History of Florence*.[29] He castigates a letter sent to the British Press by three Frenchmen: 'no style, no ideas, not even decent French . . .' and deplores German journalism in the early sixties: 'A fine mob! What a style, and what nonsense!' 'Vico', he adds in another letter, 'says in his *New Science* that Germany is the only country in Europe in which a "heroic language" is still spoken. If he had ever had the pleasure of getting to know the Vienna *Presse* and the Berlin *National-Zeitung*, the old Neapolitan would soon have unlearnt that prejudice.'[30]

Karl Liebknecht, who spent a good deal of time with the Marx family in the 1850s and early 1860s, has left an amusing

[28] To Lassalle, 12 Nov. 1858—*MEW* XXIX, 566–7.
[29] To Engels, 2 June 1853 and 25 Sept. 1857—*MEW* XXVIII, 252, and XXIX, 193.
[30] To Engels, 2 Mar. 1858, 10 Jan. 1861, and 28 Apr. 1862—*MEW* XXIX, 291; XXX, 143 and 228.

account of the way Marx's German patriotism would break out *quand même*: how he once startled a gathering of Oddfellows in a London pub by an impromptu speech on the greatness of German culture, and the superiority of German music over that of England.[31] Liebknecht also testifies emphatically to Marx's interest in stylistic questions, and the connection of that interest with his love of literature:

Marx attached extreme importance to pure and correct expression. And he chose himself the highest masters in Goethe, Lessing, Shakespeare, Dante, and Cervantes, in whose works he read almost every day. He was most conscientious and scrupulous in everything that concerned purity and correctness of language. I remember that he once, at the beginning of my stay in London, gave me a dressing-down for using the expression *stattgehabte Versammlung* in an article. I pleaded usage as an excuse, but Marx broke out: 'Those wretched German secondary schools, at which no one learns any German, those wretched German universities . . .' and so on. I defended myself as well as I could and even cited examples from the classics; but I never did speak of a *stattgehabte* or *stattgefundene* event again and have weaned many others of the habit.[32]

Marx was convinced that great literature offered the surest way to a mastery of foreign languages if one could not actually go and live in the foreign countries concerned. Liebknecht recalls:

How he scolded me one day because I did not know . . . Spanish! He snatched up *Don Quixote* out of a pile of books and gave me a lesson immediately . . . And what a patient teacher he was, he who was in other respects so fiery and impatient! The lesson was cut short only by the entrance of a visitor. Every day I was examined and had to translate a passage from *Don Quixote* or some other Spanish book until he judged me capable enough.[33]

Liebknecht's later descriptions of Sunday outings with the Marx family confirm, as we have just seen, that Marx loved the sound of great literature as well as its sense: he would declaim long passages from the *Divine Comedy*, the works of Shakespeare, and Goethe's *Faust*.

We have a good deal of evidence, too, from Marx's own letters as well as the reminiscences of Liebknecht and Sir Mountstuart E. Grant Duff,[34] of his life-long fascination with

[31] *Gespräche*, 256.   [32] *Gespräche*, 213; *METEC* 58.
[33] *ÜKL* I, 23–4; *METEC* 52.   [34] *Gespräche*, 245, 505.

questions of comparative philology, and his veneration for the work of Jacob Grimm. He disliked dialect, however; Lieb-knecht recalls how intent he was on ironing out the Hessian peculiarities of Liebknecht's speech and transforming it into the High German spoken by the educated.[35]

In his letters of these years we occasionally glimpse Marx practising what he preached to others. Most of his days—and a good many of his nights—were spent in reading, excerpting, and pondering works on economics and politics, or government Blue Books; but he did make time for other reading too:

At odd hours I am learning Spanish now. I started with Calderón, from whose *Magico prodigioso*—the Catholic Faust—Goethe has taken not only a few isolated gobbets, but the structure of whole scenes, when composing his own *Faust*. Then—horribile dictu!— I read in Spanish what I could never have read in French, *Atala* and *René* by Chateaubriand and some stuff by Bernardin de St. Pierre. Now I am in the middle of *Don Quixote* . . .[36]

At a time of great mental stress and physical discomfort we find Marx giving up reading newspapers:

In exchange I now read, for recreation in the evenings, Appian's account of the Roman civil wars in the original Greek. A very valuable book . . . Spartacus appears as the most capital fellow to be found in the whole of ancient history. A great general (*not* a Gari-baldi!), a noble character, a true representative of the ancient proletariat. Pompey is nothing but a turd . . . Shakespeare, in *Love's Labour's Lost*, seems to have had some inkling of what Pompey really was.[37]

Marx's family, it soon becomes obvious from these letters, lived in a perpetual flurry of allusions to English literature. 'Little Jenny', he reports to Engels, 'called [Pieper] "Benedick the married man", but little Laura said: Benedick was a wit, he is but "a clown" and "a cheap clown" too. The children are con-stantly reading their Shakespeare.'[38] That confirms a literary orientation—and, in particular, a cult of Shakespeare—which few visitors to the Marx household in London failed to remark on. The handful of letters from Marx to his family which has been preserved also bears constant witness to this.

[35] *Gespräche*, 214.   [36] To Engels, 3 May 1854—*MEW* XXVIII, 356.
[37] To Engels, 27 Feb. 1861—*MEW* XXX, 160.
[38] To Engels, 10 Apr. 1856—*MEW* XXIX, 40.

Chief among these family letters is the charmingly playful epistle Marx sent to his wife (who was away in Germany for a brief visit) on 21 June 1856. A poem from Heine's *Homecoming* (*Die Heimkehr*, 25) which ends with the words 'Madame, ich liebe Sie', *Othello*, and Hamlet's 'Look here, upon this picture, and on this' III. iv) are drawn into the game of love that Marx here plays with his absent wife:

I see you bodily before me, I take you in my arms, I kiss you from head to foot, and I fall on my knees before you, groaning 'Madame, I love you.' And I do love you, more than the Moor of Venice ever loved . . . Who among my many detractors and serpent-tongued enemies has ever reproached me with being called on to play the part of first lover in a second-rate theatre? And yet it is true. If the rascals had any wit, they would have painted on one side 'the conditions of production and commerce', and on the other me, lying at your feet. 'Look to this picture and to that!'—that's what they should have written underneath. But they are stupid rascals, and they will remain stupid in seculum seculorum.

What makes him a complete human being, Marx avers in this same letter, is not 'Feuerbach's idea of man, or the metabolism of Moleschott, or the proletariat, but love'—and to express his sense of deprivation while the woman he loves is far away, he looks to Ovid:

You will smile, dear heart, and ask how I come by such rhetoric all of a sudden. If I could press your sweet white heart against mine I would be silent . . . But since I cannot kiss with my lips I must kiss with my tongue, with words. I could even compose verses and imitate Ovid's books of lamentation, *libri tristium*. He was only exiled from the Emperor Augustus—but I am exiled from you, and that is something Ovid would not understand.[39]

Here literature is enrolled in a game that at once speaks and veils the language of the heart. Elsewhere in Marx's family letters the graceful play is less obviously shot through with warmth of feeling, though there too a fundamental seriousness lurks constantly beneath the fun. This is true, for instance, of a letter to his cousin Antoinette Philips, in which Marx defends his decision to stay in England rather than return to Germany. In the course of this defence he alludes successively to the story

[39] *MEW* XXIX, 532–5.

of Circe in the *Odyssey*, the legend of Theseus, Schiller's *Wilhelm Tell*, and the Irish song 'The Girl I left Behind Me'.[40]

(ii)

From a literary point of view the most important correspondence of the 1850s and early 1860s is undoubtedly that with Ferdinand Lassalle. The word 'literary' has once again the widest application here—as when Marx speaks, in letters to Lassalle, of an illness that has left him unable to write not only 'in a literary but in the literal sense of the term'; of ' "official" literature' in the field of economics; and of 'the whole literature of mathematics'.[41] He came, in fact, to dislike Lassalle more and more, to think of him as a playboy and a dangerous influence on German socialism; in his letters to Engels he continually alludes, in unfriendly and unflattering fashion, to Lassalle's Jewishness. He calls him 'Ikey' (*Itzig*) and parodies German folk-songs to denigrate him:

'O Itzig, o Itzig, was hast Du gedenkt,
Daß Du Dich an den Herwegh und den Moses Heß gehenkt?'

'O Ikey, o Ikey, what were you thinking of
When you hooked on to Herwegh and to Moses Hess?'[42]

Nothing hurt Marx more, in later years, than to find his old associate Georg Herwegh writing the Marseillaise of the Lassallean party ('Bundeslied für den Allgemeinen Deutschen Arbeiterverein'); a betrayal which led to many a bitter jest about Herwegh's 'platonic love for labour and practical love for beautiful Muses'.[43] But in his letters to Lassalle himself Marx could discuss Epicurus, the stoics, and the sceptics; voice his admiration for the ancient historians, whose works remained, in his eyes, ever new ('diese Alten', he writes after rereading Thucydides, 'bleiben wenigstens immer neu'); air his views on

---

[40] To Antoinette Philips, 13 Apr. 1861—*MEW* XXX, 594–5.
[41] 31 May 1858, 16 June 1862—*MEW* XXIX, 560; XXX, 628.
[42] To Engels, 15 Aug. 1863—*MEW* XXX, 369. In the original folk-song, the lines read: 'Ach Tochter, liebe Tochter, was hast du gedenkt, / Daß du dich an die Landkutscher und die Fuhrleut' hast gehenkt?'
[43] e.g. letter to Engels, 7 Sept. 1864—*MEW* XXX, 433.

The Origin of Species: 'Darwin's book is very important and suits me well as giving a scientific basis to the historical class-struggle. One has to accept, of course, the crude English way in which the theme is developed'; and convey his impression of literary critics like Julian Schmidt in whom he saw the quintessence of educated philistinism: 'Although I have read very little of Schmidt—one can't call it "reading" at all, I just leafed through his volumes—I have always loathed him deeply as a quintessence of middle class 'snobism' [*sic!*] which I find as revolting in literature as everywhere else.'⁴⁴ To Lassalle he confesses how little he has in fact kept up with recent German writings—a state of affairs the latter tried to remedy, when Marx visited him in Berlin, by dragging him to the theatre to see what Marx later described as 'a Berlin comedy full of Prussian self-glorification. All in all, a revolting affair.'⁴⁵ He could say 'post tot discrimina rerum' and be sure Lassalle would recognize the *Aeneid*; Marx might even chuckle quietly at the thought that in his letters to Engels he was in the habit of accompanying his critical accounts of Lassalle's sayings and doings with an ironic exclamation culled from this same book of the *Aeneid*: 'Macte puer virtute.' If he talked of 'dogs in little journals', he knew that Lassalle would reconstruct a stanza from Heine's *Germany. A Winter's Tale* around this phrase. In letters to Lassalle Marx could playfully allude, with the certainty of being understood, to the *Satire Menippée* of the sixteenth century, Beaumarchais's *Marriage of Figaro*, Schiller's *Wallenstein*, or a poem in Heine's *Book of Songs*.⁴⁶ In more serious vein he could remind his correspondent, when reporting the death of a child, of the consolations Bacon had offered, in *The Advancement of Learning*, to men of well-stocked mind, and declare Bacon's consolation inadequate in his own case.⁴⁷ In these letters Marx could hold a contemporary economist, W. G. F. Roscher, against the pedant Wagner in Goethe's *Faust*, stressing contrasts as much as resemblances:

⁴⁴ 21 Dec. 1857, 16 Jan. 1861, 29 May 1861, 16 June 1862—*MEW* XXIX, 547; XXX, 578, 606, 626.
⁴⁵ To Lassalle, 16 Jan. 1861—*MEW* XXX, 578; to Antoinette Philips, 24 Mar. 1861—*MEW* XXX, 590.
⁴⁶ 8 May 1861, 6 Nov. 1859, 8 Nov. 1855, 2 Oct. 1859, 1 June 1854—*MEW* XXX, 602; XXIX, 621; XXVIII, 624; XXIX, 612; XXVIII, 607.
⁴⁷ 28 July 1855—*MEW* XXVIII, 617.

What a self-satisfied, self-important, medium-sly, eclectic dog [this Roscher is]! If such a professorial disciple, whose nature just allows him to absorb instruction and teach others what he has learnt, who has never acquired the art of self-instruction, if such a Wagner as this were at least honest and conscientious, he might be of some use to his pupils . . .[48]

To Lassalle Marx could speak, with wistful sadness, of the stylistic shortcomings of his own works.[49] Above all: it was Lassalle who tempted him, on two occasions, to make important excursions into literary theory.

The first of these was prompted by a grandiloquent tragedy, clumsily constructed, cliché-ridden, lacking subtlety of character-drawing and versification alike,[50] with which Lassalle hoped to conquer the German stage. It was entitled *Franz von Sickingen*, and was set in that period of Reformation and Peasant Wars which proved of such overwhelming interest to all who hoped for a revolution in nineteenth-century Germany, and of which Engels had written a classic study. Lassalle sent the play to Marx, whose comments were to become (together with those of Engels) key documents in the development of Marxist literary theory and criticism. Marx's letter, dated 19 April 1859, is so important for the determination of his approach to literature, and so inaccessible in English, that despite its length it deserves quotation in full.

Dear Lassalle,

I have not acknowledged the receipt of £14. 10s. from you on 14 January because your letter was registered. I would, however, have written sooner, had I not been visited by a damned 'Cousin from Holland' who arrogated to himself, IN THE MOST CRUEL MANNER*, my surplus working-time.

HE IS NOW GONE, and I can breathe again.

Friedländer has written to me. The conditions he offers are not as favourable as those he originally communicated to you, but they are

---

* Words in small capitals appear in English in the original.

[48] 16 June 1862—*MEW* XXX, 628.   [49] 12 Nov. 1858—*MEW* XXIX, 567.

[50] 'Lassalle's very means of presentation . . . the whole bundle of trite "fire"-metaphors, the religiose enthusiasm, the rockets of verbal clichés originating in the . . . 1780s . . . tempt one to ask the question Georg Lukács pointedly put in 1931: could not regressive tendencies be discerned in Lassalle's very style?' (Walter Hinderer, 'Der ritterliche Adam und die Bauernrevolte', *Germanisch-romanische Monatsschrift*, NF xxiii (1973), pp. 179–80.)

still 'RESPECTABLE'. Once a few minor points have been cleared up between us—and that, I hope, will happen in the course of this week—I will write to him.

Here in England the class-struggle is making the most gratifying progress. Unfortunately no Chartist journal is being published any more at the moment, so that for two years now I have had to give up my literary collaboration with this movement.

I now come to 'Franz von Sickingen'. D'abord I must praise its composition and action—and that is more than can be said for any modern German drama. IN THE SECOND INSTANCE, leaving aside all purely critical relation to this work, I found that it greatly excited me at a first reading; it will therefore produce this effect even more strongly in readers in whom the emotional faculties [*das Gemüt*] are more dominant. And this is a second, very important aspect. Now to THE OTHER SIDE OF THE MEDAL. *First*—this concerns the purely formal side—since you decided to write in verse, you might have wrought your iambics somewhat more artistically. But, much as *professional poets* will be shocked by such negligence, I regard it on the whole as an advantage, since our brood of poetic epigones has nothing to show but formal smoothness. *Secondly*: the collision you intended to portray is not only tragic—it is the very collision which has rightly caused the downfall of the revolutionary party of 1848-9. I therefore approve wholeheartedly the decision to make it the axis on which a modern tragedy turns. But then I ask myself whether the theme you have chosen to treat was suitable for the depiction of this collision. Balthasar, it is true, can think that Sickingen would have won if only he had raised his banner against the emperor, and waged open war against the princes, instead of hiding his revolt under the guise of a knightly feud. But can we share that illusion? It was not guile that caused Sickingen's downfall (and—more or less—that of Hutten too). He succumbed because he rebelled against existing conditions, or rather against their new form, as a *knight*, as the *representative of a class in decline*. If one strips Sickingen of everything that pertains to the individual with a particular education, formation, natural endowment, etc. then what remains is—Götz von Berlichingen. That miserable fellow showed the tragic antagonism between knighthood on the one hand and emperor and princes on the other in an adequate form, and Goethe has therefore acted rightly in making him the hero of his play. Inasmuch as Sickingen— and Hutten too, to a certain extent, though in his case as in that of all ideologists of a social class such judgments have to be modified in important respects—fights against the princes (he turns against the emperor only because that potentate changes from an emperor of the knights into an emperor of the princes), he is nothing but a Don Quixote, even if a historically justified one. That he begins his revolt as a knightly feud signifies only that he begins it as a knight would. If he had wanted to begin it in any other way, he would have had to appeal directly, right from the outset, to the cities and the peasants—to the very classes, that is, whose development implies the negation of knighthood.

If, therefore, you did not want to reduce the collision simply to that already depicted in *Götz von Berlichingen*—and that was not what you planned—then Hutten and Sickingen had to go under because they imagined themselves revolutionaries (which cannot be said of Götz) and because, just like the *educated* Polish nobility of 1830, they made themselves spokesmen of revolutionary ideas while representing, at the same time, reactionary class-interests. The *aristocratic* representatives of the revolution—behind whose talk of unity and liberty still lurk the old dreams of imperial power and the right of the stronger—should not, then, have been allowed to engross interest as entirely as they do in your play; the representatives of the peasants (these especially!) and of revolutionary elements in the towns would have had to be shown, significantly active, in the background. Then you would have been able, to a much greater extent, to allow the most modern ideas to speak in their purest form, while now, in effect, besides *religious* freedom, it is civil unity [*bürgerliche Einheit*] which constitutes the central idea. You would then have found yourself compelled to *Shakespearize* more, while now I see *Schillerizing*, the transformation of individuals into mere mouthpieces for the spirit of the time as your gravest fault. Did you not, in a sense, commit—like your own Franz von Sickingen—the diplomatic error of setting the Lutheran-knightly opposition above the plebeian-Münzerian one?

I miss, moreover, the 'characteristic' element in your characters. I except your Charles V, Balthasar, and Richard of Trier. Was there ever a time in which character was more robust and pronounced than in the sixteenth century? I find your Hutten too much the mere representative of 'enthusiasm', and that is boring. Was he not also clever and devilishly witty, and has he not, therefore, suffered a great injustice at your hands?

How greatly even your Sickingen—who, by the by, is also drawn far too abstractly—suffers from a conflict that is quite independent of his personal calculations, comes out in the way in which he has to preach friendship with the towns etc. to his knights, while taking pleasure, at the same time, in exercising the law of the stronger [*faustrechtliche Justiz*] against the towns.

To get down to details: I must find fault, here and there, with the way your characters over-indulge in reflection about themselves—and this again stems from your predilection for Schiller. On p. 121, for instance, when Hutten tells Marie the story of his life, it would have been most natural to have made Marie say:

'The whole gamut of feelings . . .' etc. down to:

'And it weighs more heavily than mere years could do.' The verses which precede this passage, from 'They say' to 'has aged', could follow on, but the reflection 'In a single night the virgin ripens into a woman' (although it shows that Marie knows more of love than its mere abstraction) was wholly unnecessary; least of all, however, should Marie have been allowed to begin with reflections about her own 'ageing'. After recounting all she experienced in that one, single hour, she could have expressed her feelings in a general way with her observation on growing old. Furthermore: in the lines that follow I am shocked by the words 'I thought it (i.e. happiness) a *right*'. Why give the lie to the naïvety of outlook with which Marie has so far credited herself by transforming it into a legalistic doctrine? Perhaps I shall explain my meaning more fully another time.

The scene between Sickingen and Charles V seems to me particularly successful, though on both sides the dialogue turns a little too much into a presentation of the case for the defence; also the scenes in Trier. Hutten's *sententiae* about the sword are very fine. And now enough for this time.

In my wife your play has found a special partisan. Only Marie does not satisfy her. Greetings!

Your K. M.

By the way: in Engels's 'Po and Rhine' there are some nasty misprints; I am adding a list of these on the last side of this letter.[51]

This document must be seen in a fourfold context: (*a*) as a response to *Franz von Sickingen* and to the theoretical essay on his idea of tragedy with which Lassalle had accompanied his play when he submitted it to Marx and Engels for their approval; (*b*) as an incident in Marx's uneasy relations with Lassalle, whom he detested but in whom he saw a potentially useful ally; (*c*) as a restatement of a view of German history that had found its classic expression in a series of essays which Engels had contributed to the *Revue* in the summer of 1850, and which

---

[51] *ÜKL* I, 179–82 (*MEW* XXIX, 590–3). My translation assumes that in his comments on Marie's speech towards the end of the letter Marx wrote *erzählt* (= told) in error for *erlebt* (= experienced).

was later issued as a separate pamphlet under the title *The German Peasant War*; (*d*) as a stage in Marx's ever-renewed attempt to integrate literature into his total 'science of man'—an attempt which resulted in the late 1850s in such memorable texts as the *Introduction* that forms part of a complex of manuscripts now known as *Grundrisse*, and the *Preface* Marx composed for a work published in the very year that saw his letter to Lassalle: *Towards a Critique of Political Economy*.

The letter begins (after the acknowledgement of a small financial transaction) with an amusing demonstration of the way in which Marx stylized his own life in the image of literature. A relative from the Dutch branch of his family has been on a visit and claimed more of his time than Marx thought he could spare; and his sense of the comic aspect of this annoyance manifests itself in the simple device of enclosing the words 'Cousin from Holland' (*Vetter aus Holland*) in inverted commas, as though it were—like 'Franz von Sickingen' a little further down—the title of a play. An incident from his own daily life thus becomes analogous to a whole series of plays which held the German stage after F. L. Schröder's *The Cousin from Lisbon* (*Der Vetter aus Lissabon*, 1786) and Theodor Körner's *The Cousin from Bremen* (*Der Vetter aus Bremen*, 1815).[52] The opening paragraphs also demonstrate the way in which Marx, in his London years, had to feel his way back into German out of the English he now so frequently spoke and wrote. At first English phrases constantly intrude into his German text, but gradually these disappear until he moves again, with ease, in the German language.

The paragraphs that follow throw some light on the need for diplomacy in Marx's relations with Lassalle. He had lost what little journalistic outlet he had ever had in England, and needed all the help he could muster to gain access to German-language journals which would not only print his views with as little distortion as censorship and prudence permitted, but would also pay him for his contributions and thus help alleviate the financial straits in which he so often found himself. In such

[52] The relative in question was probably J. C. Juta, the husband of Marx's sister Louise. He is therefore Marx's brother-in-law (*Schwager*) rather than cousin (*Vetter*)—but Marx needed *Vetter* for his literary joke. Cf. W. Hinderer, *Sickingen-Debatte. Ein Beitrag zur materialistischen Literaturtheorie* (Darmstadt and Neuwied, 1974), p. 412.

matters Lassalle was an invaluable go-between.[53] He had just been mediating, as the letter shows, between Marx and Max Friedländer, who was Lassalle's cousin and who edited the journal *Die Presse* in Vienna. In the early 1860s Marx did, in fact, contribute a number of articles to *Die Presse*. 'Here in England the class-struggle is making the most gratifying progress'—if he was to further this struggle in Germany in an equally 'gratifying' way, Marx would need all the allies he could find. Lassalle, who had contacts with German Social Democrats which Marx himself, in his London exile, could no longer hope to have, and who had again protested his deep friendship for Marx in the letter with which he accompanied *Franz von Sickingen*, was not an ally to be lightly spurned. Marx could not therefore say directly, as an unprejudiced modern reader would perhaps like to do in face of the inert rhythms, hackneyed imagery, rhetorical exaggerations, and shallow character-drawing of Lassalle's still-born play: 'This will never do as literature, and as political propaganda it is misconceived.' He does, in fact, suggest precisely this judgement; but he is clearly trying, with all his might, to find something he could, with a good conscience, praise, and in the process he reveals, with unwonted clarity, some of the grounds on which his literary opinions rested.

He begins by lauding the over-all structure of *Franz von Sickingen* and its choice of subject—and here it is worth noting how much importance he attaches to the *Gestalt*, the composition and plot of a play. When, however, he elevates Lassalle's work above other modern German dramas in this respect, one has to note that Marx was not at all well placed to speak judiciously of German dramatic literature after Goethe. In London he had no opportunity to see German plays staged, and there is no evidence that his voracious reading ever included a single work by Grillparzer,* or Hebbel, or Otto Ludwig (to say nothing of Georg

---

* There is a snatch from Grillparzer's *Die Ahnfrau* in *Herr Vogt* (*MEW* XIV, 477); but since Marx misattributes this to Müllner, it is doubtful whether he ever read or heard it in its proper context.

---

[53] Only a few months before, on 1 Feb. 1859, Marx had acknowledged to Weydemeyer that Lassalle's 'extraordinary zeal and power of persuasion' had induced the publisher Franz Duncker to accept Marx's *Towards a Critique of Political Economy* for publication (*MEW* XXIX, 572).

Büchner, whose works were, in the 1850s, as inaccessible in Germany as they were in England). Marx's praise is therefore hollow; he does not dwell on it, but passes at once to one of his rare acknowledgements of the visceral excitement to be derived from literature. 'Leaving aside all purely critical relation to this work'—this is an ominous aside, one might well think, from a man whose constant watchword was *Kritik*, who included the word *Kritik* in the title or sub-title of many of his most important writings. Nevertheless, Marx tells Lassalle, he did derive excitement from his first reading of *Franz von Sickingen*; and since *Gemüt*, the emotional faculties, are so little dominant in his own psychic make-up, the effect on readers differently organized is likely to be even more powerful. Marx does not say what feature of Lassalle's play caused this excitement; we may hazard a guess that it is precisely the *Aktion*, the plot or subject, he had praised earlier in the same paragraph. Here was a play about that German 'revolution' in which Engels, with Marx's approval, had discerned important analogies with, and important lessons for, the revolutions of the nineteenth century.[54] An attempt, made by an author with avowed revolutionary sympathies, to capture the essence of that earlier uprising in a literary work, might well be cause for excitement. In a larger context it is interesting and important to notice Marx's recognition that there is such a thing as a pre-critical response, an immediate emotional response, to literature, and that this must be deemed 'a very important aspect'.

Marx now turns to the blank verse in which *Franz von Sickingen* is written. However diplomatically he puts his criticism, it is clear that he thinks Lassalle's handling of his iambic metre incompetent. Few modern readers would disagree with Marx on this point—and it is worth remembering that Marx on other occasions could deal very scathingly with German authors who could not even scan.[55] Yet there was one thing Marx by now hated even more than halting verse; and that, of course, was *Belletrismus*, epigonism, highly competent, polished writing which had nothing to say. This enables him to soften

[54] Cf. Marx's macaronic letter to Engels, dated 16 Apr. 1856: 'The whole thing in Germany wird abhängen von der Möglichkeit, to back the proletarian revolution by some second edition of the Peasants' War. Dann wird die Sache vorzüglich.' (*MEW* XXIX, 47.)

[55] e.g. *MEW* XIII, 652–3.

the blow he is administering to Lassalle, and even assume an amateur stance (he is not, after all, a 'professional poet') from which halting verses may appear as a positive advantage. Lassalle later professed himself amused by this device, but he clearly understood Marx's criticism as the serious objection which in reality it was.[56]

In the lines that follow, Marx considers Lassalle's *intentions* in writing his play—intentions the author had clarified for him in the essay on tragedy with which he had accompanied *Franz von Sickingen*. He does not, therefore, have to rely on the play itself for a revelation of the tragic conflict its author intended to portray; he has Lasselle's theoretical disquisition to guide him. Lassalle had there explained that his interest in the German Peasant Wars had been kindled and fostered by his experiences during the Revolutions of 1848–9; that in *Franz von Sickingen* he had tried to depict what he now regarded as a conflict common to all revolutionary periods. The mass of the people needs leaders highly conscious of their own purposes; but in these leaders such heightened consciousness may sap the force of 'enthusiasm' (*Begeisterung*), may undermine the will and the power to act decisively.

Indeed, difficult though it is for our understanding to admit this, it does almost seem as though there were an unresolvable contradiction between the speculative Idea which constitutes the power and justification of a revolution, and the finite Understanding with its cleverness. Most of the revolutions that failed did so—as everyone who really knows his history will have to admit—because of such cleverness; or at least all those revolutions failed which put their trust in cleverness of this kind. The great French Revolution of 1792, which won through in the most difficult circumstances, did so only because it knew how to shoulder the Understanding aside.

This is also the secret of the strength we find, during revolutions, in the most extreme parties; and this is the secret, finally, which as a rule, makes the instinct of the masses so much more trustworthy during revolutions than the insights of the educated.

Und was kein Verstand der Verständigen sieht, das übet usw.

And what the understanding of reasonable people fails to see,
A childlike spirit will practise in its simplicity.

[56] *ÜKL* I, 189.

It is precisely the *lack of education* [Mangel an Bildung] characterizing the masses which saves them from the reefs of cleverly deliberate proceedings.[57]

Marx readily agrees that the German intellectuals who had led the revolution in 1848–9 had not shown enough revolutionary energy, had not trusted the people enough, and had thus become an easy prey to counter-revolutionary forces. 'The collision you intended to portray is not only tragic—it is the very collision which caused the downfall of the revolutionary party of 1848–9. I therefore approve wholeheartedly the decision to make it the axis on which a modern tragedy turns.'[58] What he cannot agree with, however, is Lassalle's generalization about *all* revolutions. There is a profound difference, Marx insists, between 1848 and 1525, and it is unhistorical to project the nineteenth-century problem into the sixteenth as simplistically as Lassalle has done. Sickingen and Hutten belonged to a class that had had its day; and whatever they themselves or their followers may have thought, their interests could not have harmonized, in the long run, with those of the townsfolk and those of the peasants. They were not, in fact, 'revolutionaries' in the sense Lassalle intended—they were, on the contrary, fighting a rearguard action *against* the forces of progress. The intended analogy with the events of 1848–9 therefore broke down. If a contemporary analogy for the struggles of Sickingen and Hutten had to be found, then (as Engels had pointed out in *The German Peasant War*) it was with the Polish nobility of 1830 rather than the revolutionaries of 1848.

In the course of conducting this argument, Marx makes three important points about literature. The first of these has often been misunderstood. He is *not* saying that the only fit subject for tragedy is that of the representative of an oppressed class whose assertion of its rights is crushed. On the contrary: he specifically recognizes that Goethe was right in making Götz von Berlichingen the hero of a tragedy. He may judge the historical Götz to have been a 'miserable fellow' (an examination of the part

---

[57] Ferdinand Lassalle, *Gesammelte Reden und Schriften*, ed. E. Bernstein, i. 139 (*ÜKL* I, 171–2).

[58] Lifshits reports that among Marx's jottings on his reading of F. Th. Vischer's *Aesthetik* occurs the remark: 'Revolutions are the proper theme for a tragedy' ('Das rechte Thema für eine Tragödie sind die Revolutionen'). (*Karl Marx und die Ästhetik*, 2nd edn. (Dresden, 1967), p. 152.)

he plays in Engels's account of the Peasant Wars makes this judgement understandable); nevertheless, his story embodies what Marx recognizes as readily as Hegel or Hebbel as a tragic conflict: that of the representative of an older order who goes under fighting the new.

Georg Lukács is quite right, therefore, when he says that Marx does not decry the sort of tragic conflict to which Hegel had devoted so much attention: the struggle of a man who succumbs while defending a world-order that is being superseded. For Marx as for Hegel, the type and exemplar of this kind of protagonist is Goethe's Götz von Berlichingen. Marx adds to this, however, a second kind of hero: the revolutionary who has come too early, for whom the time is not yet ripe. Modern German dramatists, he believed, had the ideal protagonist for this kind of drama at hand: Thomas Münzer, as he is described in Engels's *The German Peasant War*. There can be no doubt that Marx sees both kinds of tragedy as episodes in the struggle between different classes; and for this reason too he thinks the knightly Franz von Sickingen an unsuitable choice for the kind of 'hero come too early', the 1848-revolutionary *avant la lettre*, whom Lassalle had in mind.[59]

The second general point which emerges from Marx's argument is that writers may be seen as 'ideologists'; as men who present in their works views and sentiments peculiar to the class from which they sprang or whose cause they have espoused. This fact must be taken into account when considering their writings and sayings; the words and deeds of Hutten, a culture-hero to nineteenth-century liberals from Heine to D. F. Strauss, can only be fully understood in such a context.

The last general point is made in passing, when Sickingen is called 'nothing but a Don Quixote, even if a historically justified one'. A great writer like Cervantes can create individual figures who are at the same time eternally recognizable, and eternally recurrent, types; historical trappings and circumstances vary, historical justifications vary, but 'a Don Quixote' may be found in a sixteenth- or a nineteenth-century setting, in Spain or in Germany.

In his letter to Lassalle, Marx more than once picks up the

[59] Lukács's essay is reprinted, along with a great deal of other relevant material, in Walter Hinderer's *Sickingen-Debatte*, pp. 159–206.

actual wording of the essay on tragedy with which Lassalle
had accompanied his play. 'The *educated* Polish nobility of
1830' (*der* gebildete *polnische Adel von 1830*), for instance, recalls
Lassalle's sentence, already quoted: 'It is precisely the lack of
education [*Mangel an Bildung*] characterizing the masses which
saves them from the reefs of cleverly deliberate proceedings.'
A little after this Lassalle made another point: 'An object', he
writes, referring his readers to Aristotle and Hegel for confirmation of what seems a very dubious argument, 'can only be attained by a given means if those means are themselves wholly
suffused with the peculiar nature of the object. Therefore an
object can be attained only by something which corresponds
to its inner nature, and therefore *revolutionary objects* can not be
attained by *diplomatic means*.' But, a reader is likely to ask, is
not Lassalle himself, with his tragedy, pursuing revolutionary
ends with diplomatic means? The conclusion of his essay on
tragedy points explicitly, once again, to the perspectives on
contemporary history he wanted his *Franz von Sickingen* to open:

On the one hand [Lassalle explains] consciousness of the present-day
world brings an element of reconciliation *into the tragedy*, for the fact
that the battle has been resumed constitutes the greatest triumph of
the hero and his purposes. On the other hand such consciousness, in
the midst of the painful struggles of our present time, can draw
from the tragedy consolation and confidence *for itself*: for in this
resumption of battle after three hundred years, and the eternal
nature of its purposes which such resumption demonstrates, lies the
most potent proof of the *necessity of its victory*.[60]

But if this was indeed the purpose of the tragedy, Marx coun-
ters, then Lassalle has mistaken his diplomacy: for he has
engaged his audience's sympathies far more with the representatives of an aristocracy, with knightly rebels against progress, than with that 'plebeian-Münzerian opposition' on which
Engels had focused his analysis in *The German Peasant War*.
Whatever else it was, *Franz von Sickingen* was *not* good propaganda
for a nineteenth-century revolution.

But neither, we now come to recognize more and more, could
Marx regard it as good literature in the way he could so regard
Goethe's *Götz von Berlichingen*, which treats the same period

[60] Lassalle, ed. cit., i. 148 (*ÜKL* I, 178).

and cannot by any stretch of the imagination be regarded as revolutionary propaganda. Here we see another of the constants of his literary criticism: the application of touchstones, the measuring of one work against another, comparative criticism in the true sense. And this is not just a matter of measuring individual works against each other—it involves also the recognition of different strands, different kinds, of literary tradition. Without having read Georg Büchner or Otto Ludwig (who had reached strikingly similar conclusions from their observations of contemporary life and letters and their own attempts to write meaningful plays in nineteenth-century Germany), Marx contrasts a Schillerian and a Shakespearian tradition and exalts the latter at the expense of the former. He does not, it should be noted, denigrate Schiller's own work. What he deplores is the activity of a 'brood of poetic epigones' already castigated earlier in the letter to Lassalle; he deprecates 'Schillerizing' (*das Schillern*—an untranslatable pun), iridescent imitation of Schiller by those who lacked his genius. Following Schiller's way, we are to think, does more harm—in a mid-nineteenth-century context—than following the way of Shakespeare; it is certainly responsible for what Marx now castigates as the most heinous fault of *Franz von Sickingen*: 'the transformation of individuals into mere mouth-pieces for the spirit of the time'.

Here we are at the heart of Marx's conception of literature; here we see him as one of the great mediators between the classical aesthetics of the eighteenth century and the realist aesthetics of the nineteenth. From this position he levels three charges against Lassalle, and illustrates them from his play. (*a*) Lassalle has not created individual characters who, in and through their very individuality, represent something greater than themselves. His characters are hollow, mouthpieces of what their author thinks the 'spirit of the time'—whether we take that spirit to be the *Zeitgeist* of the sixteenth century, in which the action is set, or that of the nineteenth, in which the author is writing. (*b*) He has not only made his characters mouthpieces of the *Zeitgeist*, but he has also made them into mere representatives of abstract qualities. Hutten, for instance, is not a true individual at all: he represents enthusiasm, *Begeisterung*, and everything he says and does in the play is conditioned by that function. Such lack of 'characteristic', individual qualities (*das Charakteristische in den Charakteren*) appears the more unpardonable because, in Marx's eyes, the age of Luther and Münzer, unlike the nineteenth century, was one in which character could still flourish and exhibit itself in all its quirky individuality. 'Was there ever', he asks, 'a time in which character was more robust and pronounced than in the sixteenth century?' In presenting the wearisome enthusiast who gushes his way through *Franz von Sickingen* under the name of 'Hutten', Lassalle is doing a grave injustice to the real, the historical Hutten, who was a much more interesting, intelligent, and witty fellow than his counterpart in the play. (*c*) Lassalle has violated the consistency of his dramatis personae by putting into their mouths his own interpretation of their character. Such balloons may be justified on occasions; but Lassalle overdoes them, and is therefore censured for 'the way in which your characters over-indulge in reflection about themselves'. This is a charge we know from Marx's analysis of Eugène Sue's way with the figures he has created; but he now connects it up with the baneful influence of Schiller. Once again, however, Schiller's own practice is *not* censured. It is his lesser followers, among whom Lassalle must be reckoned, that are to blame. The example Marx quotes is Marie, Sickingen's daughter in Lassalle's play, in whose naïve innocence we are asked to believe while seeing it constantly contradicted by her self-conscious moralizing and legalistic arguments.

Marx brings one further charge against *Franz von Sickingen* before he tries to make up for the blows he has been administering by praising a few individual passages. 'How greatly even your Sickingen—who, by the by, is also drawn far too abstractly —suffers from a conflict that is quite independent of his personal calculations, comes out in the way he has to preach friendship with the towns etc, to his knights, while taking pleasure, at the same time, in exercising the law of the stronger against the towns.' By means already analysed, Lassalle has made his personal views and sympathies all too clear—yet the events he depicts run counter to these views and sympathies, show Sickingen as much less admirable than his creator would have us believe. The logic of history is not to be denied; it asserts itself even against deliberate or ignorant distortions. Lassalle's objections, in a later letter, that Marx wanted him to write a *Thomas Münzer* rather than a *Franz von Sickingen*, and that all Marx's objections applied to the historical Sickingen but not to the figure of that name in Lassalle's nineteenth-century play, will not serve his turn. It is precisely Lassalle's Sickingen who is censured here, for 'abstraction' (i.e. lack of individuality) and for internal contradictions; while Goethe's *Götz von Berlichingen*, which is obviously far from being the sort of play a *Thomas Münzer* might have been, is praised for its true tragic spirit and for a form wholly consonant with its content.

The appreciation of certain features of Lassalle's play at the end of Marx's letter is notable for its persistent qualifications; but one passage, 'Hutten's *sententiae* about the sword', is singled out for unqualified praise—unless, that is, we take the view that *sententiae* (*Sentenzen*) have no place in drama at all. Here are the lines which Marx calls 'very fine' (*sehr schön*):

> Denkt besser von dem Schwert!
> Ein Schwert, geschwungen für die Freiheit, ist
> Das fleischgewordne Wort, von dem Ihr predigt,
> Der *Gott*, der in die *Wirklichkeit* geboren.
> Das Christentum, es ward durchs *Schwert* verbreitet,
> Durchs *Schwert* hat Deutschland jener Karl getauft,
> Den wir noch heut' den Großen staunend nennen.
> Es ward durchs Schwert das Heidentum gestürzt,
> Durchs Schwert befreit des Welterlösers Grab!
> Durchs Schwert aus Rom Tarquinius vertrieben,
> Durchs Schwert von Hellas Xerxes heimgepeitscht
> Und Wissenschaft und Künste uns geboren.
> Durchs Schwert schlug David, Simson, Gideon!
> So vor- wie seitdem ward durchs *Schwert* vollendet
> Das Herrliche, das die Geschichte sah,
> Und alles Große, was sich jemals *wird* vollbringen,
> Dem *Schwert* zuletzt verdankt es sein Gelingen!

> Think better of the sword!
> A sword, brandished in the cause of freedom, is
> That Word made flesh of which you preach,
> The God born into earthly reality.
> Christianity was propagated by the sword,
> Germany was baptised by the sword wielded by that Charles
> Whom even now, admiringly, you term 'the Great'.

Heathendom was conquered by the sword,
The Holy Sepulchre was liberated by the sword!
The sword drove Tarquin from Rome,
The sword whipped Xerxes home out of Hellas,
And the sciences and arts were born to us.
David, Sampson, Gideon vanquished with the sword!
By the sword was completed, before and since,
All that is glorious in history;
And every great achievement that will ever come about
Will, in the end, owe its success to the sword.[61]

Can this have been the kind of passage which caused the visceral excitement of which Marx spoke early in his letter? It certainly proclaims rousingly enough something Marx himself firmly believed: that necessary change would not come, in Germany, through gradual evolution, but would require violence for its effective accomplishment. It was a point over which he and Lassalle were to disagree; indeed, Marx's break with Lassalle's followers among the German Social Democrats came precisely over this disagreement, over Marx's refusal to believe that compromise with an existing state—state-socialism in the way the Social Democrats envisaged it in Bismarck's Prussia—would do anything but decorate the slaughter-house with geraniums. And when, some six years after his comments on *Franz von Sickingen*, Marx put this disagreement into words in a letter to Ludwig Kugelmann, he did so by drawing on the works of that very Schiller whom Lassalle had admired and, ineptly, imitated: 'Lassalle has betrayed the party. He has formally concluded an alliance with Bismarck . . . Lassalle wanted to play the Marquis Posa of the proletariat before Philipp II of the Uckermark . . .'[62] King William I of Prussia as King Philipp in Schiller's *Don Carlos*, confronted by Lassalle as Marquis Posa—the Schiller-parody Lassalle had perpetrated in literature suddenly has a counterpart in the Schiller-parody of his life. The reference, however, to the Uckermark—the northern part of the province of Brandenburg—leaves no doubt that not only Schiller but Heine too is, once again, in Marx's mind. He is thinking of Heine's poem 'Georg Herwegh', whose

[61] Lassalle, ed. cit., i. 224.
[62] *SW* II, 414; *MEW* XXXI, 452. There are related passages in letters to Engels dated 4 Nov. and 10 Dec. 1864—in the last-named Marx again calls Lassalle 'Marquis Posa des uckermärkischen Philipp II' (*MEW* XXXI, 10, 38).

eponymous hero is made to see himself in the guise of Schiller's
Posa, and Frederick William IV of Prussia in that of Schiller's
King Philipp:

>,,Aranjuez, in deinem Sand,
>Wie schnell die schönen Tage schwanden,
>Wo ich vor König Philipp stand
>Und seinen uckermärk'schen Granden."

>'O Aranjuez, how quickly in your sand
>There vanished away those beautiful days
>In which I stood before King Philipp
>And his Uckermarkian grandees.'

Like Heine, Marx recognizes that in *Don Carlos* Schiller has
created types which may help us to understand men of a later
time. Such understanding can refer itself directly to Schiller's
play, where the conflict between Posa's sentiments and his
actions, his good intentions and the devious means he uses to
further them, suggest interesting parallels with later enthusiasts;
it can also refer, however, to men's understanding of themselves,
their conscious or unconscious role-playing, their frequently
absurd self-identification with Posa. These games of parallelism
and contrast are possible because the Schiller of *Don Carlos*
had done what Cervantes had been able to do in *Don Quixote*,
and Goethe in *Götz von Berlichingen*: call into being individual
characters that are at the same time types, characters clearly
created at a definite moment in time, yet capable of illuminating figures of a later age. Lassalle's own life and writings demonstrate this, and thus bear unconscious witness to a strength of
the Schillerian mode which *Franz von Sickingen* had signally
failed to emulate.

Marx's letter of 19 April 1859 has a postscript, drawing attention to a work by Engels which had recently been sent to Lassalle. This is the first overt mention of Engels in the whole letter
—yet indirectly he had been present throughout. One of the
chief sources for *Franz von Sickingen* had been D. F. Strauss's
biography of Ulrich von Hutten; Lassalle gives no sign, either
in the play itself or in the accompanying treatise, that he had
also read Engels's *The German Peasant War*. Marx's letter, on the
other hand, takes its stand throughout on a view of sixteenth-
century German history most forcefully expressed in Engels's

work. Had Lassalle read and marked this, we are allowed to infer, he might not, in Marx's eyes, have become a better writer—but he might have become a better historian and a more effective propagandist.

Marx's letter, supplemented by one from Engels who also exhorted Lassalle not to forget Shakespeare over his Schiller, elicited a long reply from Lassalle. Nothing he could say would save his play, which was still-born and doomed to failure on the stage and in the closet; but two points in his rejoinder are worth noting.

The first of Lassalle's objections is this: For all his concern with the characteristic and individual, Marx is too obsessed with a Hegelian view of history, and therefore inclined to neglect the individual's part in *making* history:

This critical-philosophical conception of history, in which one iron necessity links on to the next, and which overrides and extinguishes the need for *individual* decisions and actions, is not a suitable basis either for practical revolutionary action or for an imagined and depicted dramatic action.

The ineluctable basis for both of these is, rather, a belief in the ability of *individual* decisions and actions to achieve transformations. Without this neither a stirring and interesting drama nor a bold action are possible.[63]

This leads on to another, related charge we have already noted: that Marx had not drawn a clear distinction between the hero of Lassalle's play and the historical figure on whom he was based:

Most of your objections concern the historical Sickingen, not mine. *My* Sickingen could not perish by reason of 'reactionary purposes' because I never attributed such purposes to him: I gave him only some reactionary limitation, a nature which had not made a revolutionary breakthrough, which was determined by his class-position.[64]

What riled Lassalle especially, however, was Marx's question whether he had not fallen into the 'diplomatic error' of his own Franz von Sickingen by setting the knightly-Lutheran

---

[63] *ÜKL* I, 191. Lassalle's objection has been emphatically endorsed by Peter Demetz in *Marx, Engels und die Dichter*, p. 115.
[64] *ÜKL* I, 202.

opposition above the plebeian one of Münzer and his followers. Lassalle clearly thought that in charging him with a 'diplomatic error' Marx was suggesting that in his eagerness to get *Franz von Sickingen* performed in Germany he had made 'diplomatic' concessions to theatre-managers and political censors. But this interpretation of Marx's phrase misses the mark. Marx was charging Lassalle not with too much diplomacy, but with too little. It would have been more 'diplomatic' of Lassalle to have stressed the plebeian opposition: for that is where his own interest lay, that is where his contemporaries could find a spur to the sort of action that Lassalle, like Marx, wanted them to take. Marx was suggesting a subtly propagandist view of literature rather than charging Lassalle with accommodation to ruling ideas.

When Lassalle's answer arrived, however, Marx felt that he had more important things to do and think about than an abortive historical drama and its offended author. In a letter to Engels dated 10 July 1859, he describes Lassalle's rejoinder as 'a whole forest of closely written pages', a 'grotesque' document, and comments: 'I find it incomprehensible how a man, in this season and these world-historical conditions, not only finds time to draw such stuff out of himself but also expects us to find time to read it.'[65] Literary theory and criticism, after all, could only claim a limited amount of Marx's attention, though when he gave himself to it he did so with his whole being and entire seriousness.

In 1861 correspondence with Lassalle once again prompted Marx to formulate his views on an important literary issue. The occasion, this time, was a discussion of the Roman law of inheritance and its relation to later, especially German, law: a question in which Marx's early legal studies predisposed him to be interested. He agrees with Lassalle that German jurists had misunderstood the Roman law on wills and testaments, and that therefore German developments of that law may be said to rest on a misunderstanding. He continues:

But it by no means follows from this that the testament in its modern [German] form . . . is the Roman testament misunderstood. Otherwise it might be said that every achievement of an earlier period

65 *MEW* XXIX, 450.

that has been appropriated by a later one is something old which has been misunderstood. It is certain, for instance, that the theory of the three unities worked out by French dramatists under Louis XIV rests on a misunderstanding of Greek drama. It is equally certain, however, that they understood the Greeks in a way which corresponded exactly to their own artistic needs, and that they therefore held on to this so-called 'classical' drama long after Dacier and others had explained to them what Aristotle really said. In the same way, modern constitutions rest, for the most part, on a misunderstanding of the English constitution, which accepts as essential precisely those features that appear as a degeneration of the English constitution—a so-called 'responsible cabinet', for instance. The misunderstood form is precisely the one generally accessible—the one which can be generally used at a certain stage in the development of society.[66]

Shuddering briefly at a state of mind which can see in a 'responsible cabinet' a sign of constitutional degeneration (*Verfall*), we pass on to note two implications of this passage. First, that Marx tries to see literature together with law and government; what is true of one is true of the other, developments in one can illustrate developments in another. This holist view is characteristic of a man who was ever seeking fundamental and generally applicable laws. Second, it is significant that for Marx a literary theory, or a work of literature, is not something static, something given, something there once and for all. Literary theories, literary works, have their history, a history affected by the artistic needs, the *Kunstbedürfnis*, of a specific period. 'Every age', Heine had said, 'when it acquires new ideas, also acquires new eyes, and sees much that is new in the old works of the spirit.'[67] Marx agrees with this and adds the rider that it is wrong to regard these new interpretations as 'false', as impermissible deviations from an unchanging norm established when the theory was first formulated or the work first written. If a Corneille, or a Lessing, 'misinterpreted' Aristotle or Sophocles, they did so in ways well calculated to fructify their own creative work and that of their contemporaries. No mere antiquarian, however scholarly and well informed, could have achieved such a result.

[66] To Lassalle, 22 July 1861—*MEW* XXX, 614–15.
[67] In the section of *Reisebilder* which is entitled 'Die Nordsee. Dritte Abteilung'.

10 · Orators and Culture-heroes

'The view which he *pretended* to represent, and which he presented in the *imagination* of a crowd without power of judgement, lies outside the bounds of my criticism. I discuss the view he *really* represented.'

(*MEW* XIV, 387)

(i)

IN the summer of 1848 Charles A. Dana and Albert Brisbane had visited Cologne and met Marx, whose personality and journalistic flair impressed them greatly. Dana was editor, and Brisbane foreign correspondent, of the radical *New-York Daily Tribune*, and their visit to Germany bore fruit some three years later when they invited Marx to become one of their regular European correspondents. Desperately in need of money, Marx agreed; and though he often persuaded Engels to write his contributions for him, though he grumbled at having to waste on such 'blotting-paper' time he would rather expend on his economic studies, he did produce between 1852 and 1862 a large number of articles for the readers of the *New-York Daily Tribune* and other papers. These are no longer narrowly focused on German affairs, as in the *Rheinische Zeitung* days, or on French affairs, as in the *Revue*: they take in English politics, Russia and Turkey, colonial policy in Ireland, India, and China, crises and wars all over the globe. Marx's contributions to the *New-York Daily Tribune*, the *People's Paper*, and the *Free Press* were at first written in German and translated into English by Engels; but he could soon dispense with this aid and learnt to handle the English language with only occasional awkwardness. His writing is lively and vigorous, and though Marx never devoted an article to a specifically literary theme, he constantly used the literary works he admired to reinforce his political points and give emotional colour to his arguments.

Many of Marx's articles are given over to pen-portraits of prominent English parliamentarians and critiques of their policy: it is not surprising, therefore, that the now familiar metaphors from drama and the stage should constantly recur. The very first article devoted to Lord Palmerston offers a characteristic example:

Ruggiero is again and again fascinated by the false charms of Alcine, which he knows to disguise an old witch—Sans teeth, sans eyes, sans taste, sans everything, and the knight-errant cannot withstand falling in love with her anew whom he knows to have transmuted all her former adorers into asses and other beasts. The English public is another Ruggiero, and Palmerston is another Alcine. Although a septuagenarian, and since 1807 occupying the public stage almost without interruption, he contrives to remain a novelty, and to evoke all the hopes that used to centre on an untried and promising youth. With one foot in the grave, he is supposed not yet to have begun his true career. If he were to die tomorrow, all England would be surprised at learning that he has been a Secretary of State half this century.

If not a good statesman of all work, he is at least a good actor of all work. He succeeds in the comic as in the heroic—in pathos as in familiarity—in the tragedy as in the farce: although the latter may be more congenial to his feelings. He is no first-class orator, but he is an accomplished debater. Possessed of a wonderful memory, of great experience, of a consummate tact, of a never-failing *présence d'esprit*, of a gentlemanlike versatility, of the most minute knowledge of Parliamentary tricks, intrigues, parties, and men, he handles difficult cases in an admirable manner and with a pleasant volubility, sticking to the prejudices and susceptibilities of his public, secured from any surprise by his cynic impudence, from any self-confession by his selfish dexterity, from running into a passion by his profound frivolity, his perfect indifference, and his aristocratic contempt . . . He manages international conflicts like an artist, driving matters to a certain point, retreating when they threaten to become serious, but having got, at all events, the dramatic excitement he wants. In his eyes, the movement of history itself is but a pastime, expressly invented for the private satisfaction of the noble Viscount Palmerston of Palmerston.[1]

[1] *NYDT* 19 Oct. 1853—*OB* 204, 205–6.

That shows, clearly, the range and nature of literary quotations
and allusions in these articles. The very opening sentence weds
Ariosto's *Orlando furioso*, which depicts Ruggiero's fascination
with the Circean wiles of Alcina, to Shakespeare's *As You Like It*
(the last of the Seven Ages of Man). The passage shows no less
clearly, as it proceeds, how the old uses of the stage- and drama-
metaphors are now supplemented by a new one: they show the
aristocratic politician, himself removed—by financial and social
advantages—from many of the strains and stresses of life, treating the world as a stage on which he can do what a dramatist,
or a theatrical producer, does on the stage of an actual theatre.
In another, later passage Palmerston appears as a marionetteer
controlling the wires that set in motion the spectacle of public
life.[2] Marx depicts him, throughout, as a statesman who tries to
emulate the *artist* by manipulating world history as a writer
manipulates words. But this manipulation involves words in yet
another way, for words may be used to hide realities:

Yielding to foreign influence in facts, he opposes it in words . . . He
knows how to conciliate a democratic phraseology with oligarchic
views, how to cover the peace-mongering policy of the middle-
classes with the haughty language of England's aristocratic past . . .
how to utter brave words in the act of running away . . . If the art of
diplomacy does not shine in the actual results of his foreign negotia-
tions, it shines the more brilliantly in the construction he induced
the English people to lay upon them, by accepting phrases for facts,
phantasies for realities and high sounding pretexts for shabby
motives.[3]

The cadences and structure as well as the content of such statements explain the interest Marx shows, in this and other articles,
in an art which joins literature and politics, an art that had
fascinated him ever since his journalistic debut in the *Rheinische
Zeitung*: the art of political oratory.

Many of the most scathing pages of his journalistic writings in English are therefore devoted to different modes of
parliamentary address. In his portrait of Lord John Russell,
for instance, he repeats the analogy between aristocratic politicians and literary men which had already been used in the

[2] *NYDT* 4 Aug. 1858—*MEW* XII, 528.
[3] *NYDT* 19 Oct. 1853—*OB* 206-7.

Palmerston articles, and then goes on to describe Lord John's literary as well as his parliamentary performances:

So honest was his belief in the sufficiency of false pretences that he considered it quite feasible to become, on false pretences, not only a British statesman but also a poet, thinker and historian. Only this can account for the existence of such stuff and nonsense as his tragedy *Don Carlos, or Persecution,* or his *Essay on the History of the English Government and Constitution, from the Reign of Henry VII to the Present Time,* or his *Memoirs of the Affairs of Europe from the Peace of Utrecht.* To the egoistic narrowness of his mind every object is nothing but a *tabula rasa* on which he is at liberty to write his own name. His opinions never depended upon the realities of the case; on the contrary, as far as he was concerned the facts depended on the order in which he arranged them into locutions. As a speaker he has bequeathed to posterity not a single noteworthy idea, not a single profound maxim, not a single penetrating observation, no vivid description, no beautiful thought, no poignant allusion, no humorous depiction, no true emotion. A *sheer mediocrity,* as Roebuck admits in this history of the Reform Ministry, he never surprised his audience, not even when he performed the greatest deed of his public life: when he introduced his so-called Reform Bill in the House of Commons. He has a peculiar way of combining his dry, drawling, monotonous, auctioneerlike delivery with schoolboy illustrations from history and a certain solemn gibberish on 'the beauty of the Constitution', the 'universal liberties of the country', 'civilisation', and 'progress'. He gets really heated only when personally provoked or goaded by his opponents into abandoning his pretended attitude of arrogance and self-complaisance and into betraying all the symptoms of impassioned feebleness.[4]

In another article of this same period, published in German in the *Neue Oder-Zeitung,* Marx works out a whole aesthetics of oratory by chronicling the qualities Lord Russell's speeches *fail* to show. The passage allows us to gather that Marx's ideal orator would delight his hearers with unusual ideas, profound maxims, solid observation, powerful descriptions, fine thoughts, lively allusions, humorous word-painting, and—of course— truth of feeling.[5] Disraeli, it would seem, occasionally approaches

[4] Written 25 July 1855—*OB* 246–7.
[5] 'Als Redner hat er nicht einen erwähnenswerten Einfall hinterlassen, nicht eine tiefe Maxime, keine solide Beobachtung, keine gewaltige Beschreibung, keinen schönen Gedanken, keine lebendige Anspielung, kein humoristisches Gemälde, keine wahre Empfindung . . .' (*NOZ* 28 July 1855—*MEW* XI, 384).

that ideal; but often he too falls far short of it, as when he tries to 'explain' the Indian Mutiny in the House of Commons:

The three hours' speech delivered last night in 'the Dead House', by Mr. Disraeli, will gain rather than lose by being read instead of being listened to. For some time, Mr. Disraeli affects an awful solemnity of speech, an elaborate slowness of utterance and a passionless method of formality, which, however consistent they may be with his peculiar notions of the dignity becoming a Minister in expectance, are really distressing to his tortured audience. Once he succeeded in giving even commonplaces the pointed appearance of epigrams. Now he contrives to bury even epigrams in the conventional dullness of respectability. An orator who, like Mr. Disraeli, excels in handling the dagger rather than wielding the sword, should have been the last to forget Voltaire's warning that '*Tous les genres sont bons excepté le genre ennuyeux*'.

Besides these technical peculiarities which characterize Mr. Disraeli's present manner of eloquence, he, since Palmerston's accession to power, has taken good care to deprive his parliamentary exhibitions of every possible interest of actuality. His speeches are not intended to carry his motions, but his motions are intended to prepare for his speeches. They might be called self-denying motions, since they are so constructed as neither to harm the adversary, if carried, nor to damage the proposer, if lost. They mean, in fact, to be neither carried nor lost, but simply to be dropped. They belong neither to the acids nor to the alkalis, but are born neutrals. The speech is not the vehicle of action, but the hypocrisy of action affords the opportunity for a speech. Such, indeed, may be the classical and final form of parliamentary eloquence; but then, at all events, the final form of parliamentary eloquence must not demur to sharing the fate of all final forms of parliamentarism—that of being ranged under the category of nuisances. Action, as Aristotle said, is the ruling law of the drama. So it is of political oratory. Mr. Disraeli's speech on the Indian revolt might be published in the tracts of the Society for the Propagation of Useful Knowledge, or it might be delivered to a mechanics' institution, or tendered as a prize essay to the Academy of Berlin. This curious impartiality of his speech as to the place where and the time when and the occasion on which it was delivered, goes far to prove that it filled neither place, time, nor occasion. A chapter on the decline of the Roman Empire which might read exceedingly well in Montesquieu or Gibbon would prove an enormous blunder if put into the mouth of a Roman senator, whose peculiar business it was to stop that very decline.[6]

[6] *NYDT* 14 Aug. 1857—*CM* 199–200.

The feeling is, once again, that dreary words—deliberately dreary words in the case of the witty Disraeli—are meant to lull asleep, to hide a *praxis* that goes on in darkness or behind the scenes, to conceal actions and motives never avowed in public.

But if English politicians fail to speak the truth, English novelists do not. Could one not go to the nineteenth-century novel for truths obfuscated by politicians, publicists, and moralists? An essay on 'The English Middle Class', published in the *New-York Daily Tribune* on 1 August 1854, suggests that one could and should:

> The present splendid brotherhood of fiction-writers in England, whose graphic and eloquent pages have issued to the world more political and social truths than have been uttered by all the professional politicians, publicists and moralists put together, have described every section of the middle class from the 'highly genteel' annuitant and Fundholder who looks upon all sorts of business as vulgar, to the little shopkeeper and lawyer's clerk. And how have Dickens and Thackeray, Miss Brontë and Mrs. Gaskell painted them? As full of presumption, affectation, petty tyranny and ignorance; and the civilised world have confirmed their verdict with the damning epigram that it has fixed to this class that 'they are servile to those above, and tyrannical to those beneath them'.[7]

That, it must be said, is an entirely inadequate characterization of the novelists mentioned, whose portraits of middle-class characters are far more subtle and differentiated than is here suggested. There are some characters, particularly in Dickens, to whom this description applies; but there are many more to whom it does not, for Dickens's novels teem with sympathetic annuitants and fund-holders, shopkeepers and clerks, from Mr. Pickwick and Mr. Brownlow to Traddles and Dick Swiveller. It is even more inadequate for Mrs. Gaskell, whether she is describing the country-world of *Cranford* invaded by the new railways, or the factory-world of Mr. Thornton in *North and South*. There must be some doubt, however, whether this passage represents accurately what Marx had written. The editors of the *MEW* adduce grounds for believing that parts of the manuscript of this article were radically revised by the editors of the *New-York Daily Tribune* before being published as a leading article in that journal.[8]

[7] *OB* 218.　　[8] *MEW* X, 693 (note 297).

Many of the literary references, characters, and comparisons which enliven the pages of Marx's journalistic writings between 1852 and 1862—articles in English for the *New-York Daily Tribune* and the *People's Paper*, articles in German for the *New Oder Gazette* (*Neue Oder-Zeitung*) and the *People* (*Das Volk*)—come from much further afield than the nineteenth-century novel for which the *NYDT* of 1 August 1854 found such equivocal words of praise. The *Arabian Nights*, which we know Marx to have read aloud to his children, contribute images of oriental tyranny to hold against the tyranny of contemporary Indian nabobs and rajahs: images of sudden surprise—Londoners in the midst of a cabmen's strike contemplate their cabless streets with the astonishment of the sultan in *Aladdin* who wakes one morning to find only an empty space where a splendid palace had stood the night before; and the image of an incubus that cannot be shaken off. Palmerston, the readers of the *Neue Oder-Zeitung* are told, 'resembles that cursed old man of the sea whom Sindbad the Sailor found it impossible to shake off once he had allowed him to mount on his shoulders'.[9] There are also, however, many references to children's favourites from nearer home: to Old Mother Goose, to the land of Cocaigne, and to the legend of the Seven League Boots, which Marx sees as a dream-like symbol of the German people's capacity to make more rapid progress than others once it has made up its mind to do so.[10]

Not surprisingly, the classics of Greece and Rome once again provide much grist for Marx's journalistic mill. Homer and his later parodist, for instance, are made to act as a generalized standard of reference: the reign of Napoleon III, Marx tells us, bears to that of Napoleon I the same relation as the *Batrachomyomachia* bears to the *Iliad*.[11] Just as, in the context of modern politics, the *Iliad* appears in association with its parody, so reminiscences of Greek tragedy are summoned up only to degenerate into parody and melodrama:

When a member of the Coalition Cabinet, he [=Lord John Russell] amused the House with a Reform Bill which he knew would prove another Iphigenia, to be sacrificed by himself, another Agamemnon,

---

[9] *NYDT* 25 July 1853 and 12 Aug. 1853—*MEW* IX, 201, 228; *NOZ* 14 July 1855—*MEW* XI, 353.   [10] *MEW* VIII, 360; X, 523; XII, 683.
[11] *PP* 5 Apr. 1856—*MEW* XI, 597.

or the benefit of another Trojan War. He performed the sacrifice indeed in true melodramatic style, his eyes filled with tears . . .[12]

A German version of the same article, published in the *Neue Oder-Zeitung* early in August 1855, explains that the 'melodramatic style' was that of Metastasio.[13] Classical myths are made to prove, once again, their perennial power and timeless application: when *The Times* appears on Marx's stage as the sleeping Epimenides; when all Westminster cannot furnish an Oedipus to solve the riddle posed by the Indian empire; when dying soldiers in the Crimea suffer the pains of Tantalus without his guilt, unable to reach provisions that were available; when General Pélissier fails to emulate the power, once attributed to Achilles, of healing the wounds he had himself inflicted.[14] Pindar appears as the type and exemplar of a rhapsodist (Palmerston is called 'that Pindar of the "glories of the constitutional system"') and the great Latin poets are constantly drawn on for incisive formulations whose employment gives a sense of shared education and experience: *Arcades ambo* and *quantum mutatus ab illo* from Virgil, *et propter vitam vivendi perdere causas* and *hoc volo, sic iubeo* from Juvenal, and many more.[15] Dante appears in his own person, to assert the pains and indignities of exile against a snide leader in *The Times*:

In the 'heaven of Mars' Dante meets with his ancestor, Cacciaguida de Elisei, who predicts to him his approaching exile from Florence in these words:

Tu proverai si come sa di sale
lo pane altrui, e com' è duro calle
lo scendere e il salir per l'altrui scale.

Thou shalt prove how salt the savour is
Of others' bread, how hard the passage
To descend and climb by others' stairs.

Happy Dante, another being of that wretched class called 'political refugees', whom his enemies could not threaten with the misery of a *Times* leader! Happier *Times* that escaped a 'reserved seat' in his 'Inferno'![16]

---

[12] *NYDT* 28 Aug. 1855—*OB* 254.   [13] *MEW* XI, 391.
[14] *MEW* IX, 161; IX, 180; XI, 162; XII, 418.
[15] Examples of such common tags will be found in *MEW* XI, 284; XIII, 171; XV, 431, and passim.   [16] *NYDT* 4 Apr. 1853—*L* 174-5.

(Heine, it must be remembered, had alluded to the same passage from Dante on more than one occasion; he had also
threatened his exalted enemies with a place in a Dantean
inferno at the end of *Germany. A Winter's Tale.*) The *Inferno*
comes to mind again during a languid session of the House of
Commons: Marx likens the boredom M.P.s must have felt to
the mud which Dante, in Canto 3 of the *Inferno*, made the
eternal dwelling of the indolent.[17] And looking at Garibaldi,
Marx thinks he detects in him a kind of intellectual penetration
which he had learnt to admire as typically Italian from his
reading of Dante and Machiavelli.[18]

Don Quixote, as always, is ubiquitous: whenever Marx sees
men defend, gallantly, an outmoded or outworn cause, Cervantes's hero springs to mind.

Thus Lord Eglinton, the Don Quixote who wanted to resuscitate the
tournaments of chivalry in money-mongering England, was to be
enthroned Lord Lieutenant at Dublin Castle, and Lord Naas,
notorious as a reckless partisan of Irish landlordism, was to be made
his First Minister. The worthy couple, *arcades ambo*, on leaving
London, were, of course, seriously enjoined by their superiors to
have done with their crotchets . . .[19]

When applied to wilier politicians than Lord Eglinton, the
sobriquet 'Don Quixote' takes on a more ironic tinge: thus
Palmerston, 'a permanent and eminent member of the Tory
administration', is termed 'that Don Quixote of "free institutions"'. It may also be deliberately counterpointed against
Cervantes's original in other ways—as when the guerrillas who
won their fight against Napoleon in the Peninsular War are
compared to Don Quixote sallying out with his lance to face a
world that had learnt to use gunpowder, or when Don Carlos
of Spain is called the 'Don Quixote of the Auto-da-fé'; but more
often the parallel is straight. Thus we are told, for instance, that
Espartera resembles Don Quixote in having a fixed idea (the
Constitution) and a Dulcinea de Toboso (Queen Isabella).[20]

[17] *NOZ* 21 July 1855—*MEW* XI, 365.
[18] *NYDT* 15 Oct. 1860—*MEW* XV, 185.
[19] *NYDT* 11 Jan. 1858—Karl Marx and Friedrich Engels, *Ireland and the Irish
Question* (Moscow, 1871), p. 87.
[20] *NYDT* 19 Oct. 1853, 30 Oct. 1854, 21 Nov. 1854, 19 Aug. 1854—*OB*, 207;
MEW X, 460, 634, 386.

The *novelas ejemplares* provide, once again, a striking image for a type of folly: the financial proposals of Dr. Richard Price's *Observations on Reversionary Payments* put Marx in mind of a character in Cervantes's story of Cipión and Berganza who proposed solving Spain's budgetary problems by making the whole nation go without food once a month.[21] Other Spanish writings are alluded to with less sympathy and reverence than the work of Cervantes: proclamations issued by Spanish revolutionary juntas remind Marx unpleasantly of an element of bombast and exaggeration in Spanish literature which he regards, with Sismondi, as 'Oriental'; the heroes of Calderón are also berated for what Marx regards as boastfulness.[22]

References to Shakespeare abound in these newspaper articles. His mingling of the sublime and the low, the terrible and the ridiculous, which so shocked Voltaire, Marx finds ever true to life—yet Shakespeare's sure literary tact saved him from impairing his tragic, heroic effects in the way sudden intrusions of farce so often impair what would otherwise seem tragic or heroic in modern affairs:

A singularity of English tragedy, so repulsive to French feeling that Voltaire used to call Shakespeare a drunken savage, is its peculiar mixture of the sublime and the base, the terrible and the ridiculous, the heroic and the burlesque. But nowhere does Shakespeare devolve upon the clown the task of speaking the prologue of a heroic drama. This invention was reserved for the Coalition Ministry. My Lord Aberdeen has performed, if not the English clown, at least the Italian pantaloon. All great historical movements appear, to the superficial observer, finally to subside into farce, or at least the commonplace. But to commence with this, is a feature peculiar alone to the tragedy entitled *War with Russia*, the prologue of which was recited on Friday evening in both Houses of Parliament . . .[23]

Paul Lafargue has testified that after 1848, when Marx wanted to perfect his command of English, 'he sought out . . . all the peculiar expressions used by Shakespeare'[24] as well as those used by Cobbett. No wonder, then, that in composing his political reports he should constantly find Shakespeare's phrases

---

[21] *NYDT* 7 May 1858—*MEW* XII, 448.
[22] 'Das revolutionäre Spanien', Sept.–Oct. 1854—*MEW* X, 447, 452.
[23] *NYDT* 17 Apr. 1854—*The Eastern Question. A Reprint of Letters written 1853–1856 dealing with the Events of the Crimean War by Karl Marx*, ed. E. Marx-Aveling and E. Aveling (London, 1897). [24] *ÜKL* I, 20.

coming to his pen, ranging from the hackneyed 'milk of human
kindness' to a little-known line from *King Henry VIII* which
helps him describe the glitter of empty pageantry: 'all clinquant,
all in gold, like heathen gods'.[25]

Who is better suited than Shakespeare, Marx seems constantly to be asking his readers, to supply elegant or witty
insults to throw at one's opponents? You 'minimus, of hind'ring
knot-grass made!', he calls out to Lord Russell, in imitation of
Shakespeare's Lysander; Monckton Milnes is contemptuously
dismissed with the words of Shakespeare's Mark Antony:

> Do not talk of him
> But as a property;

a *Times* editorial is ironically greeted with Demetrius's encouragement to Snug: 'Well roar'd, lion!'; and when popular indignation at attempts to forbid the sale of liquor on Sundays vents
itself in witticisms directed against the pious proponents of this
Draconian measure, Marx notes with satisfaction that Shakespearian prototypes, *die Shakespeareschen Vorbilder*, still flourish in
the second half of the nineteenth century.[26]

It is not surprising, therefore, that Marx should find Shakespeare's inventions ideally suited to convey to his readers his
own impressions of modern life and affairs. 'The noble lord', we
are told of Palmerston, 'is as uncertain of the day the Porte
implored his aid, as Falstaff was of the number of rogues in
buckram suits who came at his back in Kendal green.' This
comes from the fourth instalment of the sustained critique of
Palmerston's ministry which Marx published in the *New-York
Daily Tribune*; the fifth directly refers back to it by taunting
Palmerston with a quotation from *Henry IV* Part I: 'What
tricks, what devices, what starting-hole, canst thou now find to
hide thee from this open and apparent shame? Come, let's
hear, Jack—what trick hast thou now?'; while the sixth carries
on the Falstaff parallels by beginning with a disquisition on the
illusory nature of honour.[27] The Ministry of Lord Aberdeen, we
are told, is at one with Falstaff in thinking discretion the better
part of valour, and Gladstone's parliamentary tactics also

[25] *PP* 5 Apr. 1856—*MEW* XI, 594.
[26] *PP* 26 Apr. 1856; *NYDT* 2 Sept. 1853; *NOZ* 6 Jan. 1855; *NOZ* 22 Jan.
1855—*MEW* XII, 5; IX, 281; X, 594; X, 623.
[27] *SDH* 196, 208, 209.

remind Marx of Falstaff's way with the men in Kendal green. Yet while he thinks Falstaff a fitting image for men like Palmerston, Gladstone, and Aberdeen, who have a certain style and panache, he puts behind him the temptation to dub John Bright's portly adversary Sir John Potter 'Sir John Falstaff of Manchester'. Potter, he tells us, is disqualified from such a title not only by his fat purse but also by his lean understanding. Lesser opponents, however, can be seen through the eyes of Falstaff himself: 'it is not necessary', Marx writes in the *Neue Oder-Zeitung* of 16 August 1855, 'to describe Mr. Tite more exactly. Shakespeare has done this already when he invented the immortal Justice Shallow, whom Falstaff compares to a man made after supper of a cheese-paring.'[28]

Nor is it only *modern* politics that may be illuminated by Shakespeare. Marx projects his characters back into history too, as when he terms the Prince Regent, later George IV, a 'royal Caliban'.[29]

Other characters and scenes from Shakespeare's history-plays come to Marx's mind as he contemplates the political scene. He recalls Buckingham's advice to Richard III to 'stand between two churchmen' when trying to fool the people of London, but adds that Palmerston has chosen to stand between a churchman on one side and an opium-smuggler on the other. What such smugglers purvey can also be described by phrases from Shakespeare's history-plays—culled this time from the Bastard's speeches in *King John* I. i and ii):

Palmerston does not exactly comply with the advice tendered by Buckingham to Richard III. He stands between the churchman on

[28] *NOZ* 13 Feb. 1855; *NYDT* 17 Apr. 1857; *NOZ* 16 Aug. 1855—*MEW* XI, 59; XII, 170; XI, 489. This point is of some importance because it shows how much more sensitively Marx responded to literature than those of his self-styled followers who tell us that he saw in Falstaff a purely negative figure, 'a clearcut type of the era of primitive accumulation.' 'Falstaff for Marx', writes M. Nechkina, 'was a kind of "personified capital" of the epoch of the dawn of capitalism, which gave birth to the bourgeois of the epoch of primitive accumulation . . . Shakespeare, regretfully watching the downfall of the feudal world, showed his rejection of the coming bourgeois world in the comic character of Falstaff.' ('Shakespeare in Karl Marx's "Capital" ', *International Literature*, No. 3 (1935), 75.) What remains true is that Marx nowhere stresses the *pathos* of Falstaff, who figures in his writings primarily as a combination of liar, coward and bon-vivant. This nexus of qualities makes him, for Marx, the primal type, the *Urtyp*, of the fat politician and academic whom he pillories in *Herr Vogt*.

[29] *PP* 26 Apr. 1856—*MEW* XII, 14.

the one side, and the opium-smuggler on the other. While the Low
Church bishops, whom the veteran impostor allowed the Earl of
Shaftesbury, his kinsman, to nominate, vouch his 'righteousness',
the opium-smugglers, the dealers in 'sweet poison for the age's
tooth', vouch his faithful service to 'commodity, the bias of the
world' . . . While Pindar commenced his hymn on the Olympian
victors with the celebrated 'Water is the best thing (*Ariston men
hudor*), a modern Liverpool Pindar might, therefore, be fairly
expected to open his hymn on the Downing Street prize-fighters
with the more ingenious exordium 'Opium is the best thing'.

Along with the holy bishops and the unholy opium-smugglers,
there go the large tea-dealers . . .[30]

Inevitably, when discussing political ambitions, Marx finds
himself quoting King Henry's 'Uneasy lies the head that wears
a crown' and Macbeth's 'I am in blood / Stepp'd in so far that,
should I wade no more, / Returning were as tedious as go o'er.'[31]
But, Marx goes on to suggest, the heroes and villains of Shakespeare's tragedies and history-plays are on too grand a scale for
the politicians of the Victorian age; fitter images for them are
to be found in Shakespeare's comedies, in Snug the Joiner
playing the lion, or Costard playing Pompey in *Love's Labour's
Lost*, in Christopher Sly the tinker being made to think he is
a lord, or in Dogberry being helped by the Sexton to examine
a malefactor in Act IV of *Much Ado about Nothing*.[32] In face of
a political scene dominated by Lord Lyndhurst, Lord Derby,
and Lord Grey, Marx finds himself impelled to quote the words
Isabella hurls at Angelo in *Measure for Measure*:

> But man, proud man,
> Drest in a little brief authority,
> Most ignorant of what he's most assured,
> This glassy essence, like an angry ape,
> Plays such fantastic tricks before high heaven
> As makes the angels weep.

In face of a political scene dominated by what Marx sees as
Shallows, Snugs, Costards, and Slys, Marx himself sympathizes,
more than once, with the point of view of Shakespeare's

[30] *NYDT* 31 Mar. 1857; Karl Marx and Friedrich Engels, *On Colonialism*
(Moscow and London, 1960), pp. 98–9.
[31] *NYDT* 26 Mar. 1859, 31 Mar. 1859—*MEW* XIII, 272, 286.
[32] *Das Volk*, 20 Aug. 1859; *NOZ* 7 Aug. 1855, *NYDT* 18 Oct. 1859—*MEW*
XIII, 466; XI, 392; *CM* 391.

Thersites. After describing Russian and Turkish manœuvres in the field of diplomacy Marx quotes, with evident approval, from Act v, scene iv, of *Troilus and Cressida*:

The policy of those crafty, swearing rascals—that stale old mouse-eaten dry cheese, Nestor, and that same dog-fox, Ulysses, is not proved worth a blackberry—they set me up in policy, that mongrel-cur, Ajax, against that dog of as bad a kind, Achilles: and now is the cur Ajax prouder than the cur Achilles, and will not arm to-day; whereupon the Grecians begin to proclaim barbarism, and policy grows into an ill opinion.

Yet just as in the case of Falstaff Marx remained conscious of the wit, perverted dignity, and stature of the character Shakespeare invented, so in that of Thersites he never forgets, at this stage of his life, that even when the fellow is right, he is still despicable. J. A. Roebuck, who tried out filibuster-techniques in the House of Commons, is presented as 'the small, Thersites-like but cunning advocate, perfectly skilled in parliamentary tactics'; the party whips who make use of his services are likened to Ulysses, with one significant difference: 'As far as we know, Thersites was never employed by Ulysses; but Roebuck *is* employed by the whips, who are, in their own way, as cunning as Ulysses was.'[33]

Finally: Shakespeare supplies a composite image for revolutionaries undermining the established order in Europe. In a speech delivered on 14 April 1856, when the Chartist *People's Paper*, to which Marx occasionally contributed, celebrated its anniversary, Marx enthralled his audience with as powerful a picture as he had ever painted of the contradictions inherent in their society—where, as he put it, 'the victories of art seem bought by the loss of character'.

There is one great fact, characteristic of this, our nineteenth century, a fact which no party dares deny. On the one hand, there have started into life industrial and scientific forces, which no epoch of the former human history had ever suspected. On the other hand, there exist symptoms of decay, far surpassing the horrors recorded of

---

[33] *NYDT* 3 Aug. 1854; *NOZ* 27 Jan. 1855—*MEW* X, 343; XI, 5. In the course of an attack on Lord Clarendon's attitudes to Turkey (*PP* 26 Apr. 1856—*MEW* XI, 635) Marx plays a characteristic variation on his Thersites-theme by making Thersites a pedant who criticizes the Danaides.

the latter times of the Roman empire. In our days everything seems
pregnant with its contrary; machinery gifted with the wonderful
power of shortening and fructifying human labour, we behold
starving and overworking it. The new-fangled sources of wealth,
by some strange weird spell, are turned into sources of want. The
victories of art seem bought by the loss of character. At the same pace
that mankind masters nature, man seems to become enslaved to other
men or to his own infamy. Even the pure light of science seems
unable to shine but on the dark background of ignorance. All our
invention and progress seem to result in endowing material forces
with intellectual life, and in stultifying human life into a material
force. This antagonism between modern industry and science on the
one hand, modern misery and dissolution on the other hand; this
antagonism between the productive powers, and the social relations
of our epoch is a fact, palpable, overwhelming, and not to be
controverted. Some parties may wail over it; others may wish to get
rid of modern arts in order to get rid of modern conflicts. Or they
may imagine that so signal a progress in industry wants to be completed by as signal a regress in politics.

But, Marx went on, he and his audience were not likely to
'mistake the shape of the shrewd spirit that continues to mark
all these contradictions'.

We know that to work well the new-fangled forces of society, they
only want to be mastered by new-fangled men—and such are the
working men. They are as much the invention of modern times as
machinery itself. In the signs that bewilder the middle class, the
aristocracy and the poor prophets of regression, we do recognize our
brave friend, Robin Goodfellow, the old mole that can work in the
earth so fast, that worthy pioneer—the Revolution.

The references to Act ii, scene i, of *A Midsummer Night's Dream*
and Act i, scene iv, of *Hamlet* are unmistakable. Old Hamlet's
ghost working in the cellarage is fused with the shrewd and
knavish sprite Puck to convey a humorous yet threatening
image of the coming revolution.[34]

The only figure from Molière which is impressed into the
service of Marx's political polemics in his newspaper articles is,

---

[34] *OB* 262–3. Marx had used the 'old mole' image to characterize the revolutionary forces at work in Europe in *The Eighteenth Brumaire* (*MEW* VIII, 196); and
Hegel had used it before him to describe the Spirit working within history (*Vorlesungen über die Geschichte der Philosophie*, in *Hegel, Sämtliche Werke*, ed. H. Glockner
(Stuttgart, 1927 ff.), xix. 691).

not surprisingly, Tartuffe. The whips are called 'Grand Masters of Corruption, hypocrites of religion, Tartuffes of politics', while the London *Times*, fulminating against the Indian mutineers, appears as a 'Tartuffe of Revenge'.[35] If perverted logic rather than hypocrisy is to be pilloried, the figure of Samuel Butler's Hudibras immediately springs to mind.[36] The creations of Goethe, too, are frequently summoned—though they are not, of course, as constantly invoked in the English as in the German writings. In *Faust* Part II Marx finds a telling image for political creations that are not viable in their present form, that are bound to dash themselves against the rocks of hard political circumstances: 'The world owes [Palmerston], indeed, the invention of the "constitutional" kingdoms of Portugal, Spain and Greece—three political phantoms, only to be compared with the *homunculus* of Wagner in "Faust".'[37] Attempts to transform Prussia into an honest broker, a mediator between warring nations, bring to mind another 'mediator'—the professional busybody Mittler in Goethe's *Elective Affinities* whose interventions in the affairs at the centre of the novel prove less than helpful.[38] And Goethe, finally, supplies, in lines from the *West–Eastern Divan*, the perfect formulation of the 'cunning' of world-historical reason as Marx now sees it: a painful process kept in motion by greed, causing suffering to many, which is yet necessary if the world is to progress, if the sum of human happiness is ultimately to be increased. He is talking about the British rule in India:[39]

England, it is true, in causing a social revolution in Hindustan, was actuated only by the vilest interests, and was stupid in her manner of enforcing them. But that is not the question. The question is, can mankind fulfil its destiny without a fundamental revolution in the social state of Asia? If not, whatever may have been the crime of England she was the unconscious tool of history in bringing about that revolution.

Then, whatever bitterness the spectacle of the crumbling of an ancient world may have for our personal feelings, we have the right, in point of history, to exclaim with Goethe:

[35] *NYDT* 21 Aug. 1852, 16 Sept. 1857—*OB* 114; *CM* 227.
[36] *NYDT* 9 Feb. 1853—*MEW* VIII, 499.   [37] *SDH* 193.
[38] *Das Volk*, 6 Aug. 1859—*MEW* XIII, 456.
[39] *NYDT* 25 June 1853—*CM* 95.

„Sollte diese Qual uns quälen
Da sie unsre Lust vermehrt,
Hat nicht Myriaden Seelen
Timurs Herrschaft aufgezehrt?"

Should this torture then torment us
Since it brings us greater pleasure?
Were not through the rule of Timur
Souls devoured without measure?

In his doctoral thesis, it should be recalled, Marx had used a classical example to suggest another facet of such 'Cunning-of-Reason'-arguments:

Plutarch, in his biography of Marius, provides us with an appalling historical example of the way in which this type of morality destroys all theoretical and practical unselfishness. After describing the terrible downfall of the Cimbri, he relates that the numbers of corpses was so great that the Massilians were able to manure their orchards with them. Then it rained and that year was the best for wine and fruit. Now, what kind of reflections occur to our noble historian in connection with the tragic ruin of those people? Plutarch considers it a moral act of God, that he allowed a whole great, noble people to perish and rot away in order to provide the philistines of Massilia with a bumper fruit harvest. Thus even the transformation of a people into a heap of manure offers a desirable occasion for a happy revelling in morality![40]

It all depends on what is to be justified, and by whom. To show this dual face of the argument Marx places the very lines from Goethe's *West–Eastern Divan* which he had quoted (with apparent approval) in his essay on the British role in India, into the mouth of an imaginary spokesman for the Manchester School of economists. If the activities of English manufacturers were allowed to go unchecked and uncontrolled, he tells readers of the *Neue Oder-Zeitung* on 20 January 1855, then very soon 'a whole generation of workmen would have lost fifty per cent of its physical strength, mental development, and ability to live'; yet the Manchester School, which bewails the sacrifice of English lives in the Crimean War, 'will answer, when we object to this: "Should this torture then torment us, / Since it brings us greater pleasure?"'.[41]

[40] *MECW* I, 84.   [41] *MEW* X, 607.

In many cases Marx adapts his quotations quite ruthlessly. To bring home to readers of the *Neue Oder-Zeitung* the gist of what a British politician said of the British soldier in a speech made in the House of Commons he introduces a German couplet into his report:

> Zuschlagen, da sind sie respektabel,
> Denken gelingt ihnen miserabel.

> When they strike out, they are worthy of respect;
> In thinking their success is miserable.[42]

What Goethe in fact wrote, in the section headed 'Proverbial' (*Sprichwörtlich*) of his *Collected Poems*, reads as follows:

> Was ich mir gefallen lasse?
> Zuschlagen muß die Masse,
> Dann ist sie respektabel;
> Denken gelingt ihr miserabel.

> What I will accept?
> The masses must strike out,
> Then they are worthy of respect;
> In thinking their success is miserable.

Once again, then, we notice that a great author's words are not sacrosanct to Marx; that—like Hegel before him—he will mould them to his immediate purpose without philological scruples.

Several other eighteenth-century writers make their appearance in Marx's journalistic articles. There are some passing allusions to Voltaire; Goldsmith's Tony Lumpkin is brought in to characterize Peel: 'Tony Lumpkin and Beau Brummel rolled into one—that would give you some idea of the incongruity which appears in the person, dress and manner of Sir Robert Peel';[43] and on one occasion Marx even tries his hand—not very successfully—at parodying Dr. Johnson.[44] Like A. W. Schlegel and Heine before him, Marx showed no understanding of the insight, critical acumen, humanity, and wit of Samuel Johnson. He was more in sympathy with Jonathan Swift, whom he

---

[42] *NOZ* 1 Feb. 1855—*MEW* XI, 19.
[43] *NOZ* 16 Aug. 1855—*MEW* XI, 488.
[44] *NYDT* 1 Feb. 1859—*MEW* XII, 683.

quotes, ironically, in his discussion of Irish affairs for the *New-York Daily Tribune*: 'And this is the same country [Marx writes, after citing statistics about the prevalence of lunacy in nineteenth-century Ireland] in which the celebrated Swift, the founder of the first Lunatic Asylum in Ireland, doubted whether 90 madmen could be found.'[45] Despite several allusions to Gulliver among the Lilliputians, however, Marx's knowledge of Swift's work does not appear to be wide or deep; he was to acquire such knowledge much later in life, after he had bought a fourteen-volume edition of Swift's works in 1870.[46] Swift interests Marx mainly as a writer on Irish affairs, just as Robert Southey enters his world as the author of a *History of the Peninsular War* and not as a poet on the fringes of the Lake School, and Captain Mayne Reid as 'an American filibuster' and not as a writer of adventure-novels.[47]

In Schiller, however, Marx continued to see the writer of tragedies and lyric poems rather than the historian of the Revolt of the Netherlands and the Thirty Years War. Again and again Schiller's nobler characters and exalted diction are adduced as contrasts to nineteenth-century realities. 'Fould . . . as Marquis Posa!', he exclaims with pretended incredulity, bringing together a French financier-politician and a character from Schiller's *Don Carlos*; '*Applaudite, amici!*' The hero of Schiller's *The Robbers* supplies a no less ironic counter-image: 'If the death of a hero, as Schiller says, resembles the setting of the sun, the exit of the East India Company bears more likeness to the compromise effected by a bankrupt with his creditors.'[48] Above all, Schiller serves to characterize the taste of Marx's German contemporaries. The Berlin philistine, he writes,

is a man imbued with the notion that Berlin is the first town of this world; that there is to be found no 'Geist' (an idea not to be translated, although ghost is etymologically the same word; the French esprit is quite another thing) save at Berlin; and that *Weißbier*, a disgusting beverage for every outside barbarian, is the identical

---

[45] *NYDT* 12 Aug. 1853—Karl Marx and Friedrich Engels, *Ireland and the Irish Question*, p. 66.
[46] B. Kaiser and I. Werchan, *Ex Libris Karl Marx und Friedrich Engels. Schicksal und Verzeichnis einer Bibliothek* (Berlin, 1967): cf. *MEW* XXXII, 504.
[47] *NYDT* 25 Sept. 1854—*MEW* X, 444. Mayne Reid is mentioned in Marx's letter to Engels dated 23 Feb. 1853 (*MEW* XXVIII, 214).
[48] *Die Presse* 19 Nov. 1861; *NYDT* 24 July 1858—*MEW* XV, 376; *CM* 337.

drink quoted in the *Iliad* under the name of nectar, and in the *Edda* under the name of meth. Beside these harmless prejudices, your average Berlin luminary is an incorrigible wiseacre, indiscreet, fond of talk, indulging a certain low humour, known in Germany as *Berliner Witz*, which plays more with words than with ideas, a curious compound of a little irony, a little scepticism and much vulgarity—altogether no very high specimen of mankind, nor a very amusing one, but still a typical character. Well, my Berlin friend answered my question by quoting, in the true Berlin tone of mockery, the following strophe from Schiller's *Glocke*. I may remark, *en passant*, that your average Berliner praises nobody but Goethe, yet quotes nobody but Schiller!

> O zarte Sehnsucht, süßes Hoffen,
> Der ersten Liebe goldne Zeit!
> Das Auge sieht den Himmel offen,
> Es schwelgt das Herz in Seligkeit.
> O daß sie ewig grünen bliebe,
> Die schöne Zeit der jungen Liebe!

> O tender longings, sweet hopes,
> Golden time of first love!
> The eye sees heaven open,
> The heart luxuriates in bliss.
> O, that it could bloom for ever,
> That fair time of young love![49]

Marx recalls Wieland too, whose novel *The Men of Abdera* (*Die Abderiten*) is said to prefigure the battles between the 'cheerers' of the city and the 'groaners' of the House of Commons.[50] Of a later generation Marx quotes Friedrich Schlegel, whose famous characterization of the historian as a prophet turned backwards (*ein rückwärts gekehrter Prophet*) does duty in a description of David Urquhart; Herwegh, whose lines about the 'winging of a free soul' are ironically applied to Palmerston; and—as usual —Heine. 'How right Heine is', a characteristic sentence runs, 'when he says that "true craziness is as rare as true wisdom"!'[51] From Béranger Marx borrows the phrase 'myrmidons of mediocrity'; and he uses the figure of Robert Macaire to deflate the

---

[49] 'The New Ministry', *L* 255–6.
[50] *NOZ* 10 May 1855—*MEW* XI, 201.
[51] *NOZ* 8 June 1855—*MEW* XI, 269 (Fr. Schlegel); *NOZ* 12 June 1855— *MEW* XI, 283 (Herwegh); *MEW* XII, 41 and XIII, 416 (Heine).

doings and sayings of politicians. Only a French ear, he declares, can fully savour such phrases as occur in Napoleon III's letters to Palmerston: 'Entendons nous loyalement comme d'honnêtes gens, que nous sommes, et non comme des larrons, qui veulent se duper mutuellement.' Here, Marx maintains, politics imitates art; Napoleon's very style has been anticipated by Antier and Lemaître in their famous play.[52]

Above all, however, Marx impressed into the service of his journalism the 'splendid brotherhood' of nineteenth-century writers of fiction. Not all of these, of course, were English. In the *People's Paper* he likens Sir James Simpson, whom he regards as one of Palmerston's 'creatures', to a *golem*, a clump of earth roughly shaped into human form and animated by sorcery, explaining to his English readers that the German poet Achim von Armin had recently introduced that folklore figure into German literature. Frederick William IV of Prussia puts him in mind, he tells the readers of the *New-York Daily Tribune*, of *The Young Englishman* (*Der junge Engländer*), a story by Wilhelm Hauff in which a provincial German city is fooled into accepting a dressed-up monkey as an elegant if eccentric British lord. A court-case in Ireland recalls the atmosphere and incidents of one of Balzac's more sensational novels: murder, adultery, attempts to wangle an inheritance, fraud. Napoleon III, on the other hand, brings to mind (through a natural association of ideas) *The Hunchback of Notre-Dame* by his enemy Victor Hugo: he can therefore be called 'the Quasimodo of the French Revolution',[53] though Marx is careful to point out elsewhere that Napoleon III sought to be a *terrifying* Quasimodo rather than the pathetic grotesque Hugo had invented. Dickens supplies Wackford Squeers as an image of cruelty towards the defenceless,[54] and the Artful Dodger as one of programmatic unscrupulousness which ultimately defeats itself. 'Artful as the dodging was', we read in the fifth instalment of Marx's Palmerston series of 1853, 'it would not do'. There are also, inevitably, references to the 'Pickwickian sense' in which politicians use their words.[55] From Thackeray Marx borrows Yellowplush, the

---

[52] *NYDT* 7 Apr. 1853—*MEW* IX, 6; *NYDT* 22 Aug. 1860—*MEW* XV, 118.

[53] *PP* 26 Apr. 1856; *NYDT* 23 Oct. 1858; *NOZ* 24 Feb. 1855; *NYDT* 30 June 1860; *NYDT* 31 Mar. 1859—*MEW* XI 631; XII, 594; XI, 74; XV, 67; XIII, 278.

[54] *NYDT* 3 Aug. 1854—*MEW* X, 347.   [55] *SDH* 204, 182.

West-End footman with a lackey's outlook on life: an article on
'English Public Opinion', which appeared in the *New-York
Daily Tribune* in February 1862, speaks of '*The Times,* the *Post*
and other Yellowplushes of the London Press'. This is supplemented by a figure from *Punch,* a vulgar lick-spittle of the
aristocracy called Jenkins, who retails the 'witticisms', and
praises the dresses and parties of the rich:

The *Morning Post* is in part Palmerston's private property. Another
part of this singular institution is sold to the French embassy. The
rest belongs to high society and supplies the most exact reports for
court-toadies and ladies' tailors. Among the English people the
Morning Post is accordingly notorious as the Jenkins of the Press.

Marx feels, however, that Jenkins alone does not convey his full
sense of what the *Morning Post* really is. In order to describe
what he believed to be that paper's mixture of arrogance and
servility he has to add a character from Ariosto's *Orlando
furioso* and call the *Morning Post* a strange amalgam 'of Jenkins
and Rodomonte'.[56] Marx also quotes, with approval, from a
letter by 'the well-known humorist' Douglas Jerrold; and Fenimore Cooper's *The Spy* turns up once more to characterize, as
before, the mistaken self-image of police-informers.[57]

Marx never, alas, refers to Disraeli's *Sybil*—it would have
been good to know what he thought of its 'two nations'; but
when he finds himself able to praise the simplicity, perspicuity,
and lightness of touch which mark one of Disraeli's speeches, he
compares it, favourably, to *The Young Duke*. In later years, in a
letter to Engels dated 27 July 1866, he will identify Disraeli with
the hero of his first novel, *Vivian Grey*.[58] In more waspish mood
he tries, in the *Neue Oder-Zeitung* of 9 June 1855, to relate the
fiction of Edward Bulwer Lytton to his performances in Parliament. 'Bulwer', he writes of one of his orations, 'hovered
between the heroic mood of his king-maker [a reference, pre-
sumably, to the figure of Warwick in *The Last of the Barons*] and
the contemplative mood of his *Eugene Aram*. In the former he

[56] *NYDT* 11 Jan. 1862; *Die Presse,* 31 Dec. 1861; *NYDT* 25 Dec. 1861—*OB*
328, 321; *MEW* XV, 418.
[57] *NOZ* 22 Jan. 1855—*MEW* X, 623; 'Hirschs Selbstbekenntnisse', 1853—
MEW IX, 39.
[58] *NYDT* 7 May 1858—*MEW* XII, 445; *MEW* XXXI, 243.

threw down the gauntlet to Russia, in the latter he crowned the brow of Metternich with a wreath of myrtles.'[59] That ridicules the man and the writer at once; in later discussions of Lord Lytton Marx will ignore the writer and concentrate on the weaknesses of the man, whose involvement in a family scandal he chronicles in some detail. Elsewhere, however, he repeatedly demonstrates his belief that just as the printed version of a politician's speech helps one to see more clearly the truth behind his clouds of rhetoric, so a statesman's literary and philological activities offer important clues to the human qualities by which his policies are directed. That is why he spends a good deal of time ridiculing Lord John Russell's tragedy *Don Carlos*, his history of the British constitution, and his political memoirs. Such 'trifles', Marx would have his readers believe, show Russell's egotism, show that he sees in every subject nothing but a *tabula rasa* on which to inscribe his own name.[60]

The writer who emerges as the real hero of these journalistic essays is William Cobbett. Marx shows himself perfectly aware of 'backward-looking' elements in Cobbett's political philosophy, and points out more than once his inability to penetrate to the root-causes of economic misery; but this in no way impairs his affection and respect. Cobbett, he tells the readers of the *New-York Daily Tribune* in July 1853, was a true John Bull, yet he anticipated the Chartists; he was at once the purest incarnation of Old England and the boldest pioneer of Young England; he was at once the most conservative and the most destructive of Britons—and as a writer he remains unsurpassed.[61] From 1853 onwards Marx's works and letters are peppered with references to 'Old Cobbett' and quotations from the *Political Register*— quotations used with the kind of admiration and approval which had earlier been reserved for quotations from Heine's satirical works. Indirectly, Marx pays Cobbett the greatest compliment of all; for the style, manner, and tone of his newspaper articles show clearly that Cobbett had now joined the Heine of the polemical prose-works (especially *Ludwig Börne*) as a model and an influence.

In a series of articles dealing with parliamentary debates and high politics, it is not surprising to find a constant recurrence of

[59] *NOZ* 9 June 1855—*MEW* XI, 272.
[60] *NOZ* 28 July 1855—*MEW* XI, 384.   [61] *MEW* IX, 191–3.

those images from tragedy, comedy, farce, public performances (including gladiatorial shows), and stage-machinery which have been examined in other works. Marx now assumes, more than once, the persona of a literary connoisseur and theatre-critic in order to ridicule the political scene before him:

Connoisseurs in the field of high comedy will find a source of purest pleasure in the French *Moniteur* of 17 November. As in the old classical drama, Fate, invisible and powerful, enmeshes the heroes— Fate in the shape of a deficit of a thousand million francs. As in the drama of antiquity, the dialogue takes place between two characters, Oedipus-Bonaparte and Teiresias-Fould. Tragedy turns into comedy, however, because Teiresias says only what has previously been whispered to him by Oedipus. One of the most characteristic devices of the bonapartist comedy is that of reintroducing its stale old personae dramatis again and again in the guise of brand-new heroes . . . Fould puts in another appearance as Turgot, as Marquis Posa! *Applaudite, amici!*[62]

When he turns from the French to the English scene, Marx often finds himself reminded of vaudeville and comic opera; and in connection with this he speaks of his weird sense that English statesmen derive their idea of foreigners, and their manner of dealing with them, from evenings spent at vaudeville performances or curled up with one of those novels of Paul de Kock with which Marx himself frequently beguiled his leisure hours. Sir John Seymour, we are told, begins by treating the Sultan as the *Grand Turc* of vaudeville and ends by referring to him, in the manner of Paul de Kock, as 'ce monsieur'.[63] Lord John Russell's attempts to speak French reminded Marx irresistibly of the figure of 'Mylord' in *Fra Diavolo*, while the same statesman's advice to the Northern States involved in the American Civil War can be summed up in a quotation from *Don Giovanni*: 'Let him go—he's not worth your anger.'[64] As for the reaction of the London *Times* to the Indian mutiny: Marx can convey that, and his feelings about it, only by a profusion of literary references

[62] *Die Presse*, 19 Nov. 1861—*MEW* XV, 374-6.

[63] *NYDT* 11 Apr. 1854—*MEW* X, 160. Cf. Paul Lafargue's reminiscences of Marx: 'From time to time he would lie down on the sofa and read a novel; he sometimes read two or three at a time, alternating one with another . . . The more modern novelists whom he found most interesting were Paul de Kock, Charles Lever, Alexandre Dumas père, and Walter Scott . . .'—*METEC* 26.

[64] *NYDT* 27 Apr. 1855; *Die Presse*, 7 Nov. 1861—*MEW* XI, 178; XV, 339.

which begin with Cobbett, end with the Bible, and pivot around the figure of Osmin in Mozart's *Abduction from the Seraglio*:

The frantic roars of the 'bloody old *Times*', as Cobbet used to call it —its playing the part of a furious character in one of Mozart's operas, who indulges in most melodious strains in the idea of first hanging his enemy, then roasting him, then quartering him, then spitting him, and then flaying him alive—its tearing the passion of revenge to tatters and to rags—all this would appear but silly if under the pathos of tragedy there were not distinctly perceptible the tricks of comedy. The London *Times* overdoes its part, not only from panic. It supplies comedy with a subject even missed by Molière, the Tartuffe of Revenge. What it simply wants is to write up the funds and to screen the Government. As Delhi has not, like the walls of Jericho, fallen before mere puffs of wind, John Bull is to be steeped in cries for revenge up to his very ears, to make him forget that his Government is responsible for the mischief hatched and the colossal dimensions it had been allowed to assume.[65]

Such persistent 'stage'-imagery gains additional point if we remember how Marx viewed his own activities after the International had been founded:

The demonstrations by London workmen, marvellous when compared with what we have seen in England since 1849, are wholly the work of the International . . . Here may be seen the difference between working behind the scenes [*hinter den Kulissen*] unseen by the public and the way of the democrats who give themselves an air of importance in public while doing nothing.[66]

Effective activity away from the glare of the footlights is explicitly contrasted, in this letter to Engels of 7 July 1866, with the strutting deceptiveness of the public stage.

Though few of Marx's newspaper articles deal with literary questions directly, much light is thrown on his literary tastes and beliefs by such incidental references as have so far been examined. His dislike of anything bombastic has already appeared clearly; his dislike of anything simply dashed off, relying on 'inspiration' and eschewing hard work, is no less obvious. 'Has one ever heard of great improvisators being also great poets? They are the same in politics as in poetry. Revolutions are never made to order. After the terrible experience of '48 and '49, it

[65] *NYDT* 16 Sept. 1857—*CM* 227. [66] *MEGA* III, 3, 343.

needs something more than paper summonses from distant leaders to evoke national revolutions.'[67] The articles also demonstrate clearly Marx's fine appreciation of linguistic nuances, as when, in the *Neue Oder-Zeitung* of 28 February 1855, he explains to German readers the aura of meaning around the English word 'clever'.[68] He even finds an opportunity, in the course of renewed polemics against Gottfried Kinkel, for a disquisition on German hexameters. Kinkel, it seems, had been rash enough to publish, in his journal *Hermann*, an epic poem on the battle of Solferino:

> The metre in which the battle is celebrated is that of the heroic epic, the hexameter. Kleist, as is well-known, extended the hexameter [in German] by a short one-syllable anacrusis. Our generous bard [Kinkel] outdoes Kleist by not worrying about a few syllables more or less, either at the beginning of the line or at its end. On the other hand it is also true that hexameters which have just emerged from a battle cannot be blamed for lacking a foot here and there, or for having a few dislocated limbs.[69]

Marx concludes his onslaught by actually scanning a few verses from this epic to show their deviation from any acceptable standard.

What primarily engages Marx's interest, in his journalistic writings, is the relation of literature to politics. What light does a statesman's literary work throw on the nature of his policies? The case of Lord John Russell, of Disraeli, of Bulwer Lytton, and—later on—of Gladstone as an editor of Homer, may supply an answer. What happens when a man of letters joins the politicians in government? Chateaubriand and Lamartine had provided a horrid warning; Manuel José Quintana (1772–1857) sets a less discouraging example. The Spanish junta which had the good taste to employ Quintana to draft its manifestos, Marx tells his readers, ensured thereby that the power of its proclamations far exceeded the efficacy of its administration.[70] And beyond that Marx tries to see how far it is possible to detect a 'national style' which unites a nation's writings and its politics. Again and again we find him relating an element of

[67] *NYDT* 8 Mar. 1853—*MEW* VIII, 527.
[68] *NOZ* 3 Mar. 1855—*MEW* XI, 92.
[69] *Das Volk*, 16 July 1859—*MEW* XIII, 652–3.
[70] *NYDT* 20 Oct. 1854—*MEW* X, 452; *NYDT* 30 Oct. 1854—*MEW* X, 459.

exaggeration, even of bombast, in the political proclamations of revolutionary Spain to the style of Calderón, or trying to explain the nature of Garibaldi's public persona by means of a reference to Dante and Machiavelli. National styles can, however, be modified; Mazzini, Marx believed, had made a decisive break with older Italian modes, and might thus be said to have founded a new school of Italian letters.[71]

In his constatation of such 'national styles', Marx shows himself mindful of the audience whose tastes the writer must take into account. When he has occasion to quote, in the *New-York Daily Tribune*, a fable by some 'anonymous Tyrtaeus' in Russia, he is careful to point out that the simplicity of its language and structure has been geared to the demands of the popular, largely uneducated audience the poet wishes to reach.[72]

In his journalistic work as elsewhere Marx thus demonstrates, again and again, his refusal to see literature apart from its context in life and history, and his concern to 'place' works and periods by means of judicious collocation. 'To understand a limited historical epoch', he wrote in the third of his articles on 'The Secret Diplomatic History of the Eighteenth Century', published in the *Free Press* in 1856, 'we must step beyond its limits, and compare it with other historical epochs'.[73] That is a maxim he applied to the history of literature no less than that of society and politics. In the modern world literary forms may be abused and abased—in the poetry of Kinkel, for instance, or that of Liverpudlian merchants who are said to 'enrich' English poetry with odes in praise of the slave-trade[74]—but the essential value of literature is never in question. When Marx refers to Plato's exclusion of poets from his Republic, he leaves us in no doubt of the absurdity of such an action, and of his own disapproval of it:

Now I share neither in the opinion of Ricardo, who regards 'Net Revenue' as the Moloch to whom entire populations must be sacrificed, without even so much as complaint, nor in the opinion of Sismondi, who, in his hypochondriacal philanthropy, would forcibly retain the superannuated methods of agriculture and proscribe science from industry, as Plato expelled poets from his Republic.[75]

[71] *MEW* X, 447, 452; XV, 185; XII, 420.
[72] *NYDT* 14 June 1854—*MEW* X, 264.   [73] *SDH* 85.
[74] *Die Presse*, 4 Feb. 1862—*MEW* XV, 458 (*OB* 337).
[75] *NYDT* 22 Mar. 1853—*OB* 164.

With its opening reference to Hebrew and its closing reference
to Greek writings, with its concern for poets in the midst of
concern for social justice and right economic action, this passage
is wholly characteristic of Marx's journalistic writings between
1852 and 1862.

(ii)

His work for C. A. Dana and the *New-York Daily Tribune* led
Marx, indirectly, to some concentrated thinking on aesthetic
questions. In 1857 Dana asked him to contribute an article on
'Aesthetics' to an encyclopedia he was then editing; and though
in his letters to Engels Marx ridiculed this proposition (how
could one treat Aesthetics in a single page?) he was stimulated
to read, and to excerpt, F. Th. Vischer's *Ästhetik* and the article
on Aesthetics in a leading German encyclopedia. The notes he
made have been described and analysed by Georg Lukács in an
illuminating essay.[76] Lukács there points to three significant
features of Marx's notes. The first of these is the interest Marx
shows in the structure, the over-all arrangement of Vischer's
four-volume work: not only was he interested in the range of
topics covered, but (as his letter to Lassalle of 22 February 1858
makes clear) he saw in Vischer's instalment method of publishing a possible model for bringing his own work on economics
before the public piecemeal yet in orderly progression. The
second point Lukács makes had already been made by Mikhail
Lifshits. Marx (Lukács and Lifshits demonstrate) dwelt particularly on those parts of Vischer's system in which art most
nearly touched life, on 'boundary-subjects' like the interplay of
the subjective and objective, 'moments of beauty', the comic
and the ugly. This made him reflect on the relation between the
nature of things and their aesthetic significance. He collected from
Vischer several of Kant's observations on such themes and thus
used Vischer's *Ästhetik* as a gateway to the *Critique of Judgment*.
Lukács's last point is the most important of all. Marx's most
copious extracts, he tells us, come from that part of Vischer's
Ästhetik which deals with myth—which follows Hegel in seeing
myth as the expression of a particular, now vanished, world-
historical epoch, and contrasts the 'free worldly imagination of

---

[76] Georg Lukács, 'Karl Marx und Friedrich Theodor Vischer', in *Beiträge zur
Geschichte der Ästhetik* (Berlin, 1954), pp. 217–85.

modern times' with the 'religiously determined imagination' of
earlier ages. Such ideas are clearly in Marx's mind when he
comes to sketch out, in 1857, the General Introduction which
preludes his *Foundations [Grundrisse] of Political Economy* (see
below, Chapter 11).

Even this by no means exhausts the interest and significance
of Marx's excerpts from Vischer's *summa* of eighteenth- and
nineteenth-century aesthetics. Lifshits has noted that this work
brought Marx closer not only to Kant but also to Schiller, from
whose works Vischer had quoted an excerpt Marx copied out
for himself with evident approval: 'Beauty is simultaneously an
object and a subjective state. It is at once form, when we judge
it, and life, when we feel it. It is at once our state of being and
our creation'; that it reminded him of the aesthetics of Hegel
which he had absorbed in earlier days; that it stimulated his
interest in sublimity and a concept of 'measure' or 'proportion'
which is dialectically related to it.[77] 'Measure' and 'measureless-
ness', Lifshits shows, are concepts as important in Marx's
economic as in his aesthetic thinking. His aesthetic studies of
1857–8 therefore bore fruit not only in the letter on Lassalle's
Franz von Sickingen which has already been analysed; they related
also to the economic studies which issued in *Towards a Critique
of Political Economy* and *Capital*.

(iii)

The techniques he had practised in his articles for American,
English, and German journals stood Marx in good stead when
he felt compelled to compose, in 1859, a detailed rebuttal of
attacks that were being made on him in German-speaking
countries. He was attacked, and libelled, with especial vehemence by Karl Vogt, an academic scientist who had once been
a prominent left-wing member of the Frankfurt parliament but
who had later made himself, or been induced to make himself,
into the spokesman of those who saw Napoleon III as the white
hope of Europe. Marx's *Eighteenth Brumaire* was an obstacle to
such a view; Vogt therefore tried to discredit its author by
showing him as the head of a subversive secret organization
whose funds were derived from blackmail and from denouncing

[77] M. Lifshits, *The Philosophy of Art of Karl Marx*, pp. 95–7.

its own less valued members to the police authorities. These charges were taken up by the newspapers, and when Marx tried to bring an action against his calumniators in the Prussian courts he was not allowed to do so. To clear his name, therefore, and to remain useful to the cause to which he was devoting his life, Marx wrote and published *Herr Vogt* (1860). Necessarily this work had to concern itself, for much of the time, with minor personages now long forgotten, and with issues which are no longer pressing to most readers. This means that *Herr Vogt* has nothing like the permanent interest of *The Eighteenth Brumaire* or the later *Civil Wars in France*; but it does contain individual passages of great historical importance (Marx's own account, for instance, of the history of the *Communist League*, in rebuttal of Vogt's gross libels) and may also be studied, in our context, as an anthology of all the ways in which Marx had learnt to incorporate literary allusions and quotations into his polemics.

No other work, in fact, in the whole corpus of Marx's writings, shows his absorption in world literature as fully and plainly as *Herr Vogt*. The ancients are represented mainly by quotations from Cicero, tags from Virgil and Persius, and a brief quotation —in the original—from the Greek epigrammatists; Luther's translation of the Bible mainly by passing references to biblical characters and by phrases that had passed into common usage. There is a dazzling display, however, with often esoteric quotations and allusions, of Marx's knowledge of older German literature—Hartmann, Gottfried, Wolfram, Walther, the *Nibelungenlied, Der Weinschwelg*, Fischart's adaptation of Rabelais . . .; of Goethe and Schiller, Heine of course, Ludwig Uhland, and lesser authors like F. W. Hackländer. Shakespeare is prominent, as always; he is here joined, however, by the older Samuel Butler (the author of *Hudibras*), by Pope (particularly *The Dunciad*), 'Peter Pindar', the Sterne of *Tristram Shandy*, Byron (with a scabrous *Epitaph* on Castlereagh), and the Dickens of *Oliver Twist* and *Martin Chuzzlewit*. In sometimes startling contexts we encounter Dante, Calderón, Cervantes, Rabelais, Voltaire, Victor Hugo, Balzac, and many others. A preliminary notice which Marx had inserted in the Berlin *Volkszeitung* in February 1860 had called *Herr Vogt* a 'literary' answer (*eine literarische Antwort*) to his German calumniators, as opposed to the 'juridical' answer the Prussian courts would not allow him to give; the multitudinous uses to which he here puts the works of the world's great writers make it 'literary' in another, more specialized sense than the one he intended.

In *Herr Vogt* Marx uses again, to good effect, the literary leitmotiv technique he had worked out with Engels in *The German Ideology*. Since Karl Vogt was a fat man and had told palpable lies, allusions to Falstaff's exploits run right through Marx's pamphlet: 'These lies are as the father that begets them — / Gross as a mountain, open, palpable.' How other identifications may follow from this use of *King Henry IV* Part I, can be seen in Marx's tribute to a recently deceased co-editor of the *Neue Rheinische Zeitung*:

Schramm's impetuous, bold, active, and fiery nature, which was never to be bound by common considerations, was suffused with critical understanding, power to think for himself, ironic humour, and naïve joviality. He was the Percy Hotspur of our party.[78]

Constantly, in this work, Marx uses literary characters as short-hand notations of a cluster of qualities and defects: Napoleon III is 'the imperial Pecksniff' at one point, 'Quasimodo' at another.[79] Once again very different literary characters are fused to give a more accurate portrait of a complicated contemporary. The respect which unadulterated 'Falstaff' comparisons might lead us to conceive for Vogt is tempered by comparisons with Gargantua in Rabelais and Fischart, with stage-clowns, with the arch-liar Münchhausen, and with the tyrannical governor (*Vogt, Landvogt*) in Schiller's *Wilhelm Tell*. The last-named is clearly there because of a punning relationship to Vogt's name—and *Herr Vogt* is indeed distinguished from other of Marx's works by the constant and consistent use it makes of such verbal hooks. Quotations from the medieval German *Song of Louis* (*Ludwigslied*), for instance, are frequent because Vogt is said to be singing a new 'song of Louis': singing a tune called by *Louis* Napoleon, now emperor of the French. The epigraph from Calderón which heads the very first chapter owes its presence to another such verbal hook: it speaks of sulphur (*azufre*), and Marx had been accused by Vogt of heading a secret society called 'The Sulphur Gang' (*Die Schwefelbande*).[80] Great writers are enlisted to suggest

---

[78] *MEW* XIV, 445.   [79] *MEW* XIV, 531, 566, 577.
[80] *MEW* XIV, 389. The quotation comes from Calderón's *El mágico prodigioso*.

a contrast with the little writers whom Marx felt compelled to honour with his attention—Vogt is called a 'Tacitus of the Antichamber', for instance; or to provide a ludicrous commentary on their admirers—as when Schiller's *Don Carlos* is constantly cited, either 'straight' or with deliberate deformations, in an inappropriately 'low' context; to conjure up, before the readers' eyes, a whole world of corruption—as when Marx breaks off his characterization of contemporary journalism by referring his readers to 'a certain novel by Balzac' (*Lost Illusions* is clearly meant); or to suggest, in words taken from Dante's *Inferno*, Marx's growing sense of having to wade through a sea of ordure:

> tristo sacco
> Che merda fa di quel che si trangugia

> that wretched sack
> Which makes filth of what it swallows;

or again:

> Vidi un col capo sì di merda lordo,
> Che non parea s'era laico o cherco,
> Quei mi sgridò: Perchè se' tu sì ingordo
> Di riguardar più me che gli altri brutti?

> I beheld one with a head so smeared with filth
> That it did not appear whether he was layman or cleric,
> He cried to me: 'why are you so eager
> To look at me rather than the others in their nastiness?

Literature is also enlisted to supply a battery of more or less elegant insult. The *Inferno* supplies a description of the Devil which Marx uses to characterize Vogt himself ('egli è bugiardo e padre di menzogna'—'he is a liar and the father of lies') as well as a list of some denizens of hell that can be made to describe Vogt's associates:

> onde nel cerchio secondo s'annida

> ipocrisia, lusinghe e chi affatura,
> falsità, ladroneccio e simonia,
> ruffian, baratti, e simile lordura.[81]

[81] *MEW* XIV, 513, 425, 545, 613, 620, 435, 459, 565.

Hence in the second circle nests

Hypocrisy, flattery, and sorcerers,
Cheating, theft and simony,
Pandars, grafters and other filth of this kind.[82]

As might be expected, Pope's *Dunciad*,[83] and Heine's 'Kobes I', *Germany. A Winter's Tale* and *Ludwig Börne*,[84] yield a particularly rich harvest of insults and characterizations.

In *Herr Vogt* Marx seems unable to look at any political or social phenomenon without feeling himself reminded of some situation in world literature. Take the Frankfurt parliament, for instance:

In Spanish drama one can count two buffoons to each hero. Calderón even endows Saint Cyprian, the Spanish Faust, with a Moscón and a Clarín. In the same way the reactionary general von Radowitz had two comic adjutants in the Frankfurt parliament: his harlequin Lichnowski and his clown Vincke.[85]

The literary allusion compounds the insult to Radowitz, Lichnowski, and Vincke. They are not even original grotesques, they have been anticipated, long ago, by writers with an understanding of human foibles and follies. The Frankfurt Parliament of 1848 is thus made to appear an unworthy parody and pastiche of foreign literature as well as of foreign politics.

The 'Falstaff' allusions to which reference has already been made concentrate on one particular play and one particular scene: *King Henry IV*, Part I, Act II, scene iv. Here Falstaff is led on by Prince Hal to ever wilder inventions and self-contradictions. Through his persistent allusions to this scene, in which Falstaff's attackers constantly grow in number, and the illumination changes with the colour and texture of the attackers' garments, Marx tries to make his readers see the mechanism of deception in Vogt's writings; tries to show up the perverted logic by which a harmless expatriate's club like *Die Schwefelbande* had to grow, in Vogt's account, into a dangerous secret society that threatened the peace of Europe. In this sense Marx calls

[82] *MEW* XIV, 410, 565.
[83] *MEW* XIV, 593, 603 (quotations from Pope's *Dunciad*). In his abuse of F. Zabel and others Marx makes a good deal of play with the English term 'dunce'.
[84] *MEW* XIV, 430, 467, 468, 634.   [85] *MEW* XIV, 606.

Falstaff the 'primal archetype', the *Urtyp*, of Karl Vogt, and would have us see in the portly zoologist a 'zoological rebirth' of Shakespeare's character. By paralleling Vogt's story of the *Sulphur Gang*'s dangerous conspiracy with Falstaff's account of the men in buckram who attacked him, Marx thus pays tribute to Shakespeare's insights into the springs and wheels of human behaviour, and his ability to construct models which exhibit the way they work. He shows his readers yet another (and very important) reason for the homage he so constantly pays to Shakespeare and to the 'immortal' character—*dem* unster-blichen *Sir John Falstaff*—he had created.[86]

The presence of great literature throughout *Herr Vogt* also sets up stylistic standards. The great writers provide an antidote, a positive counter-image, to the stylistic offences with which Marx's opponents are charged: the absurdity of their imagery, the clumsy, ungrammatical, illogical nature of their writing, which Marx reveals through detailed stylistic analyses and annotations.[87] Such presence of great literature also acts as a spur to Marx himself to consider his local and his over-all effects with particular care. He was conscious, he tells the readers of *Herr Vogt*, of having to compose his pamphlet carefully and husband his effects 'because I have to treat my "pleasant" subject with at least some degree of artistry'.[88]

The 'artistry' with which Marx tried to treat his 'pleasant subject' entailed much heart-searching about the title his work was to bear. He had read in the Press that bonapartist pamphlets circulating in Algeria had been rendered into Arabic by a translator known as 'Dâ-Dâ'; and for a long time he clung to the belief that his own pamphlet should bear the title 'Dâ-Dâ Vogt'. His family and friends objected to this as too obscure, and in the end Marx gave way. He did so reluctantly, for (as he had written to Engels): 'Dâ-Dâ puzzles the philistine and is comical', and again: 'The fact that Dâ-Dâ will puzzle the philistine pleases me and fits well into my system of mockery and contempt.'[89] More than half a century later a group of expatriate artists in Zurich came to exactly the same conclusion when they found the word 'dada' in a French dictionary.

---

[86] *MEW* XIV, 390.   [87] *MEW* XIV, 406, 432, 435, 466.
[88] *MEW* XIV, 403.
[89] To Engels, 25 Sept. and 2 Oct. 1860—*MEW* XXX, 97, 101–2.

Marx's account of the activities of Dâ-Dâ and of Vogt is calculated to create the impression that both of them speak with the voice of Napoleon III rather than their own. This leads him to add yet another item to the list of undignified theatrical entertainers with whom (as we have seen) he so constantly compares the creator of the Second French Empire. 'Vogt', Marx declares in a characteristic passage, 'was only one of the innumerable mouthpieces through which *the grotesque ventriloquist* of the Tuileries projected his voice in alien tongues'[90] [my italics].

It must be admitted, however, that Marx overstrains the technique of literary quotation and allusion in *Herr Vogt*. His dragging-in of the most diverse literary works at every opportunity seems frenzied and forced; it tends to weary the reader and dissipate the intended effect. There had been earlier signs of this danger—few readers of *The German Ideology* will respond as delightedly to the twentieth reference to 'Saint Max' or Sancho Panza as to the first; but it had never appeared so clearly. Marx himself grew aware, in later years, that there was something amiss with his assimilation of other people's books, and conveyed his sense of unease in a letter written (in English) to his daughter Laura on 11 April 1868:

You'll certainly fancy, my dear child, that I am very fond of books, because I trouble you with them at so unseasonable a time. But you would be quite mistaken. I am a machine, condemned to devour them and then throw them, in a changed form, on the dunghill of history.[91]

The man who could see his own weaknesses so clearly, and describe them so wittily and ingeniously, was well on the way to mitigating their worst effects and even turning them into strengths. A prolonged study of Marx's works will lead most readers to agree with Bakunin, who had little cause to love Marx and may therefore be seen as an impartial witness: 'Very few men have read so much and, it may be added, have read so intelligently, as M. Marx.'[92]

---

90 *MEW* XIV, 516.
91 *KMP* 121.
92 Quoted in Isaiah Berlin, *Karl Marx. His Life and Environment*, 3rd edn. (Oxford, 1963), p. 110.

(iv)

Marx's last journalistic venture was a series of articles contributed to the Viennese journal *Die Presse* towards the end of 1861
and during the year 1862. Here once again we find him drawing
on classical antiquity for illustrations and striking phrases. His
account of the construction of the Thames Embankment in
London is an interesting case in point. The traffic-congestion
the Embankment was designed to relieve reminds Marx of a
satire in which Juvenal depicts himself as making his will before
venturing out into the Roman streets where he might well be
run over. The British aristocracy, Marx tells his readers, have
on the whole welcomed the new embankment, since it will add
to the amenities of their Thames-side mansions at public expense; they have, however, one serious reservation:

The line of the projected construction is to be *interrupted* at intervals,
and there the public highway would be built directly alongside
their own property. This means that they would be brought into
direct contact with the 'misera contribuens plebs'. The olympian
detachment of those who are 'fruges consumere nati' is not to be
disturbed by the sight or the sound or the breath of the vulgar
world of everyday business. The Duke of Buccleuch is at the head of
these aristocratic sybarites . . .[93]

Here phrases from Horace and Juvenal clearly characterize, not
only the disdainful attitudes British noblemen may be thought
to share with Roman patricians, but also the classical education
which was such an essential part of the privileges enjoyed by the
British aristocracy of Marx's day.

Writing for a German-speaking audience, Marx once again
turns to Heine for telling images. Ironically he likens the British
Press in the era of Palmerston to the knight who appears in the
prologue of Heine's *New Spring*; a knight who would fain ride
out into battle but is prevented from doing so by *amoretti* that
rob him of his sword and bind him with garlands of flowers. The
British Press, Marx's readers are to understand, is prevented
from fighting its battles not by tyrannous compulsion, as in
absolutist states, but by more charming and flattering obstacles
(*holde Hindernisse*) which the wily Palmerston insidiously puts in
its way. The 'indecent gesture' Goethe's Mephistopheles is made

[93] *Die Presse*, 11 July 1862—*MEW* XV, 517–18.

to perform by a stage-direction in *Faust* Part I enlivens Marx's account of an incident in the American Civil War; da Ponte's libretto for Mozart's *Don Giovanni* ironically counterpoints the advice Lord John Russell felt called upon to give the Northern States in that war; and Macaulay's description of the Earl of Essex is used to characterize General McClellan, a candidate for the American presidency in 1862.[94] In Marx's most serious vein, Dante's *Inferno* is called upon to yield the nearest possible parallel to the sufferings of the poor, illustrated by a heart-breaking case of deprivation reported from the West Riding of Yorkshire: 'The tragedy played out by Ugolino and his sons repeated itself, though without its cannibalism, in that Padmon-den cottage.'[95] Like Heine in *Shakespeare's Girls and Women* Marx looks to Shakespeare's plays for the image of an England that once existed but now has vanished from all but literature; he then uses that image as a means of criticizing the England of his own day and the 'phantoms' of England that persist in the heads of those who do not know her present condition at first hand.

On the continent of Europe it is thought that John Bull on his island is characterized by 'originality' and 'individuality'. This, by and large, confuses the Englishman of the past with the Englishman of the present. The emergence of sharp class divisions, extraordinarily complete division of labour, and a so-called 'public opinion' which is manipulated by the Brahmins of the Press have, on the contrary, brought into being a monotonous sameness of character that would make Shakespeare, for instance, fail to recognize his compatriots. Differences no longer pertain to individuals; they pertain, rather, to 'professions' and classes. Outside his profession, in his day-to-day relationships, one 'respectable' Englishman so much resembles the other that even Leibniz would find it hard to discover a *differentia specifica* between them.[96]

Marx adds, however, in mitigation of his harsh judgement, that English individualism may still be observed in private life and occasionally, therefore, in courts of law, where private caprices are dragged before the public. He illustrates this contention with an amusing account of the law-case brought by a London tailor against the painter Sir Edwin Landseer.

---

[94] *MEW* XV, 409, 509, 339, 479.
[95] *MEW* XV, 546; cf. Dante, *Inferno*, Canto XXXIII.
[96] *MEW* XV, 464.

Other literary references and parallels which Marx introduced into his articles for *Die Presse* range from the 'Junius'
letters to Cooper's *Pathfinder*;[97] but by far the most interesting of
these occur in the course of his character-portrait of Abraham
Lincoln on 12 October 1862. He detects in Lincoln

no urge to take the initiative, no forceful idealistic fervour, no
buskin, no historical drapery. He constantly performs important
and significant actions in the most insignificant form possible . . .
Hesitatingly, reluctantly, unwillingly he sings the bravoura aria
his role prescribes for him, as though he begged forgiveness that
circumstances forced him to 'come hither as a lion' . . . Nothing is
easier than to point out what is aesthetically displeasing, logically
inadequate, formally burlesque, and politically contradictory in
Lincoln's dramatic acts of state [*Haupt- und Staatsaktionen*]: and this
the English Pindars of slavery, *The Times*, the *Saturday Review*, and
the rest, never fail to do. Yet in the history of the United States and
that of mankind Lincoln will have a place immediately behind
Washington. Is it not worthy of notice that today, when on this
side of the Atlantic the insignificant struts and frets melodramatically about the stage, the significant goes about its business in the
new world wearing everyday clothes?
   Lincoln is not the product of a popular revolution. The ordinary
play of universal suffrage, unconscious of the great destinies it had
to decide, brought to the top a plebeian who had worked his way
up from navvy to Illinois senator; a man without intellectual
sparkle, without outstanding greatness of character, without
extraordinary importance—an average man of good will. The new
world never won a greater victory than when it proved that in the
context of its political and social organization it needs only average
men of good will to perform deeds it would take heroes to perform
in the old world.
   Hegel has already noted that comedy surpasses tragedy, the humour of reason its pathos. If Lincoln does not command the *pathos* of
historical action, he does—as a popular, average figure—command
its *humour* . . .[98]

The imagery from various kinds of stage-entertainment—Greek
tragedy with its buskins, the *Haupt- und Staatsaktionen* of seventeenth-century Germany, opera with its bravoura arias—is as
impossible to miss here as in *The Eighteenth Brumaire*. But now it
is only negatively present, as it were: it is only there to tell us

[97] *MEW* XV, 406, 383.   [98] *MEW* XV, 552–3.

what Lincoln is *not*, what he does *not* do. Lincoln, the imagery
tells us directly, provides a counter-image to Napoleon III,
whom Marx always saw as a strutting caricaturist of heroism.
This brings in its train another theatrical reminiscence: Shakespeare's hard-handed Athenian, Snug the Joiner, apologizing
for being forced, by the exigencies of amateur dramatics, to play
the lion. Snug appears the more sympathetic because of Lincoln; Lincoln is understood better because of Snug. Touching
on Pindar by the way, in an ironic juxtaposition of that rhap-
sodic poet with *The Times* and the *Saturday Review*, the passage
comes to rest on an application to world history of Hegel's
aesthetics: of that strange valuation of comedy first suggested in
the *Phenomenology of the Spirit* and elaborated in the *Aesthetics*.[99]
The career of Lincoln, and its contrast with the careers of
European statesmen, at once illustrates and justifies Hegel's
aesthetic contention in a world-historical context.

(v)

Marx planned, in the early 1860s, one other work that would
take a close look at the orators and culture-heroes of his time—
a work on the Polish Question which was sparked off by the
Polish insurrection of January 1863, but of which we have
nothing beyond a few excerpts from books and pamphlets
accompanied by fragmentary notes. These notes focus not so
much on Poland itself as on the policies of Prussia and France.
Here Marx again sees statesmen as 'comedians' and 'punchi-
nellos', and speaks of Frederick the Great's alliance with Russia
as a 'sad *epigram* on his whole career';[100] here he again draws on
Heine for terms of abuse (Frederick the Great is constantly
dignified, as in Heine's poem 'The Changeling' [*Der Wechselbalg*], with the appellation 'der alte Sodomiter').[101] Here he
states unequivocally his belief that the Chateaubriand who
wrote *The Congress of Verona* and conducted French foreign
affairs for a time was a 'tool of [Tsar] Alexander' and a Russian
agent;[102] and here he inserts, into a chronicle of French policies

---

[99] Hegel, *Phenomenology of the Spirit*, CC, vii, B, c; *Lectures on Aesthetics*, Book III,
Section A.
[100] *Manuskripte*, 97, 98, 99, 101, 119. Italics are mine.
[101] *Manuskripte*, 119, 140; cf. letter to Engels, 24 Mar. 1863—*MEW* XXX, 335.
[102] *Manuskripte*, 188, 189.

towards Russia, a reflection on the representative function of great writers:

Apart from the facts enumerated, showing how much the acts and the professions, or if you like, the acts and the intentions of that government were discrepant, we ought not to forget that the government, official or secret, of Louis XV was not France. Voltaire and Diderot represented France much more then the duc de Broglie and the count of Vergennes. Voltaire blew the trompet [*sic*] for Frederick II, as Diderot did for Catherine II. The French encyclopaedists of the eighteenth century laboured as hard in the service of Czarina Catherine II as their romantic antagonist Chateaubriand did in the service of Czar Alexander.[103]

To understand the political forces at work in eighteenth-century France we must heed the words of Voltaire, Diderot, and the Encyclopaedists as much as, or even more than, the policies of kings and ministers. Nothing could be more misleading, however, than to approach these eighteenth-century writers with expectations derived from nineteenth-century liberalism. Without abating his admiration of *Candide* and *Rameau's Nephew* or becoming one jot more inclined to see good in the works of Chateaubriand, Marx bids us recognize that Voltaire and Diderot were as devoted to absolute monarchs outside their own country as some nineteenth-century Romantics were to the Holy Alliance and its chief begetter. Culture-heroes can be fully understood only in the context of their time.

[103] *Manuskripte*, 176. This passage was written (in English) in Dec. 1864.

11 · Models and Metaphors

'Ideas do not exist apart from language.'
(G 80)

(i)

'I SHALL, therefore, publish my critique of law, morals, politics etc. in a number of independent brochures; and finally I shall endeavour, in a separate work, to present the interconnected whole, to show the relationship between the parts, and to provide a critique of the speculative treatment of this material.'[1] Such was the plan Marx had formed in the early 1840s, when he first became interested in political economy and its relation to the state, law, morality, and all aspects of man's intellectual and spiritual life. In 1850 and 1851 he had high hopes of being able to complete the first of these 'brochures', devoted to a critique of political economy; but working in the British Museum from nine in the morning to seven at night, filling notebook after notebook with excerpts whose significance he tried to think through during the nights, he came to see more and more complications and ramifications in his subject. Other factors combined to make him put off actually writing his book: not least among these was the refusal of an eminent publisher, F. A. Brockhaus, to consider his proposal to bring out a critique of modern English writings on political economy. In 1857, an economic crisis he had foreseen and foretold made Marx renew his resolve to publish his own reflections. A letter to Engels shows him 'working madly through the nights on a synthesis of my economic studies'.[2] In August 1857 he sketched out a General Introduction (*Einleitung*) surveying the field, and

---

[1] Sketch of a preface for Paris Manuscripts of 1844, *MEW EB* I, 467; cf. Introduction to *Karl Marx: Early Writings*, ed. T. B. Bottomore (London, 1963), p. 63.
[2] Dec. 1857—*MEW* XXIX, 225 (cf. *GM* 18).

in the six months that followed he filled seven notebooks with manuscript jottings in which he tried to think through, in the light of his reading of Smith and Ricardo, Malthus and Carey, Bastian and many others, the problems he had first raised for himself in the Paris notebooks of 1844. This manuscript, which was to constitute the quarry of Marx's later important publications, remained unpublished until 1939. It is now known as *Grundrisse*, an abbreviation of the title chosen by its first editors: *Foundations of a Critique of Political Economy* (*Rough Draft*) (*Grundrisse der Kritik der politischen Ökonomie* (*Rohentwurf*)).[3]

The General Introduction of 1857 begins with a survey of 'material production', and insists that all such production is *social*:

The individual and isolated hunter and fisherman with whom Smith and Ricardo begin belongs to the unimaginative conceits of eighteenth-century Robinson-Crusoe-stories [*Robinsonaden*]. These do not express, as cultural historians imagine, simply a reaction against over-refinement and a return to the misunderstood natural life. They are no more based on such naturalism than Rousseau's *contrat social*, which brings naturally independent subjects into relation and association by means of a contract. This is the semblance, and nothing but the aesthetic semblance, of Robinson-Crusoe-stories great and small. What we are here faced with, rather, is the anticipation of 'bourgeois society', in preparation since the sixteenth century and making giant strides towards its maturity in the eighteenth. In this society of free competition the individual appears free from natural bonds etc. which made him, in earlier epochs, part of a definite, limited human conglomerate. Smith and Ricardo still stand with both feet on the shoulders of the eighteenth-century prophets, to whom this eighteenth-century individual— the product, on the one hand, of a dissolution of feudal forms of society, on the other of the new forces of production which had developed since the sixteenth century—appears as an ideal which, they believe, had existence in the past. Not as a result of history, but as its starting-point.[4]

Robinsonaden, stories in the wake of Defoe's *Robinson Crusoe*, describe the life of men isolated, for a time, from human society

---

[3] For a full account of the history and content of this work, see *GN* 7–80 and *GM* 13–25. My own translations draw heavily on those of Nicolaus and McLellan.

[4] *G* 5 (*GM* 26–7; *GN* 83). The conjunction of *Robinson Crusoe* and Rousseau is not fortuitous; Book III of *Émile* had provided the spectacles through which many eighteenth- and nineteenth-century readers saw Defoe's novel.

and civilization.[5] Marx pronounces them misleading—misleading by their 'aesthetic semblance' (*aesthetischer Schein*), a term which Schiller had tried so hard, in his theory of art, to divest of all taint of deception.[6] He points to the danger of a dichotomy between 'aesthetic semblance' and truth, and calls works which exhibit that dichotomy and thereby mislead their readers 'unimaginative conceits' (*phantasielose Einbildungen*). This attack on *Robinsonaden*, 'Robinson-Crusoe-stories great and small', does not, it should be remembered, touch their fount and origin, *The Strange and Surprising Adventures of Robinson Crusoe*. Defoe's novel (unlike J. H. Campe's adaptation of it for German readers) by no means shows, or sets out to show, that material production begins with isolated individuals or that its eponymous hero is ever in a pure 'state of nature'. Crusoe himself may entertain such illusions at one stage (in chapter 3, when he begins to plant corn without proper implements, and thinks himself 'reduced to a mere state of nature'); but Defoe is ever aware, and makes his hero aware, of how much Crusoe owes to the implements, materials, and skills he has salvaged from the highly developed social world of eighteenth-century England. What Marx really attacks, therefore, in this passage, is not *Robinson Crusoe* itself but the illusions fostered in certain readers by lesser imitations, or by unperceptive and prejudiced reading, or by wishful thinking. He is attacking the *myth* of *Robinson Crusoe*, not the book itself.[7]

Marx in fact goes on to make something like this point a little further down in his General Introduction:

Man is in the most literal sense a *zoon politicon*; not only a gregarious animal, but one which can individuate itself only in society. Production by an individual thrown back upon himself outside society—a rare exception which can occur when a civilized man in whom the social forces are already dynamically present is cast into the wilderness by accident—is as much of an absurdity as the development of language without individuals living *together* and talking to one another. There is no need to dwell on this any longer. It would not

---

[5] Cf. H. Ullrich, *Robinson und die Robinsonaden. Bibliographie, Geschichte, Kritik*, Part I (Weimar, 1898); H. Ullrich, *Defoes Robinson Crusoe. Geschichte eines Weltbuches* (Leipzig, 1924); and H. Brunner, *Die poetische Insel. Inseln und Inselvorstellungen in der deutschen Literatur* (Stuttgart, 1967).

[6] Cf. Schiller, *On the Aesthetic Education of Man. In a Series of Letters*, ed. E. M. Wilkinson and L. A. Willoughby, pp. 327–9.

[7] Cf. Ian Watt, 'Robinson Crusoe as Myth', in *Essays in Criticism* (1951), 95–119.

be necessary to touch on this point at all had not this twaddle, which had sense and reason in the eighteenth century, been dragged back in all seriousness, by Bastiat, Carey, Proudhon etc., into the centre of the most modern economics. For Proudhon and others it is, of course, very convenient to be able to give an historico-philosophic account of the source of an economic relation, whose historic origins he does not know, by inventing the myth that Adam or Prometheus stumbled on the idea ready-made, and then it was adopted etc. Nothing is more tedious and dry than the fantasies of a commonplace mind.[8]

It is in commonplace minds, then, a category in which Marx would include most nineteenth-century economists, that cast-away stories, or stories of Adam and Prometheus, set crude and misleading fantasies in motion. He is thinking particularly of H. C. Carey's *Principles of Political Economy*, where the activities that lead Crusoe, on his island, to acquire 'various species of property, to which he attaches the idea of *value*' are described without any reference to the implements and skills he has sal-vaged from the civilized world; and of works like John Gray's *The Social System. A Treatise on the Principles of Exchange*, which had drawn a grossly simplified contrast between 'man in society' seeking to *exchange* and Robinson Crusoe seeking to *produce*.[9] Terrell Carver has rightly stressed that for Marx the attitudes and behaviour of Defoe's hero must be seen in the light of 'specific socio-economic changes, viz. "the dissolution of feudal forms of society" and "the powers of production newly developed since the sixteenth century"'.[10] Indeed, Marx had himself shown, in *The Poverty of Philosophy*, and was to show again, in *Capital*, what meaningful use might be made of the Robinson Crusoe model in economic contexts. Here, in *Grundrisse*, he suggests a particularly interesting perspective. *Robinsonaden* are now seen, not as the image of some primitive social organization, but as so clear a view of tendencies inherent in English society of the eighteenth century that they can serve as a symbolic adumbration of that society's future. On closer examination the

[8] *G* 6 (*GM* 27-8; *GN* 84-5).
[9] Carey (Philadelphia, 1837), vol. i, p. 7; Gray (Edinburgh, 1831), p. 21. Terrell Carver, in *Karl Marx: Texts on Method* (Oxford, 1975), quotes relevant extracts from Carey and shows that Frédéric Bastiat's view of *Robinson Crusoe* is closer to that of Marx than the latter's dismissive reference would lead us to expect.
[10] Carver, op. cit., p. 91.

loneliness of Robinson Crusoe becomes a symbol for social alienation in the 'civil society' of the nineteenth century. Literature may thus be 'prophetic', even if in most cases the prophecy could be clearly recognized only by hindsight.

In recent years an appreciation has gained ground that the way in which the General Introduction recognizes and dismisses 'bad generalizations' is immediately relevant to literary criticism. 'There are', Marx writes, 'certain conditions [*Bestimmungen*] which all stages of production have in common, and which thought fixes as general ones; but the so-called "general conditions" of all production are nothing more than abstract moments which do not make up any real historical stage of production.' Marx therefore warns us against allowing our recognition of continuity and sameness to blind us to those essential differences which alone enable us to understand development. 'Even though the most developed languages have laws and conditions in common with the least developed, what is characteristic of their development is precisely that in which they differ from the general and common.'[11]

A later section of this Introduction pours scorn, in a way now familiar to us, on socialist writers whose work belongs more to the history of belles-lettres than to that of economics and sociology; and in the analysis of the relationship between production and consumption that follows this attack, Marx elaborates thoughts about the relation of art to human needs which he had already begun to formulate in the Paris Manuscripts of 1844:

Production not only supplies a material for the need, but it also supplies a need for this material . . . The need the consumer feels for the object is created by his perception of it. The *objet d'art*—like every other product—creates a public that appreciates art and that is capable of enjoying beauty. Production thus not only creates an object for the subject, but also a subject for the object.[12]

This is as concise a statement as we will find anywhere of the truth that art creates, to an important extent, the very taste by which it is enjoyed. What must not be forgotten, however, is that Marx now stresses the importance of scrutinizing not only the means of material production within the society which

[11] *G* 10, 7 (*GM* 32, 28; *GN* 88, 85); cf. H. Gallas, *Marxistische Literaturtheorie* (Neuwied and Berlin, 1971), p. 173.
[12] *G* 13–14 (*GM* 36; *GN* 92).

produces works of art and delights in them, but also the class-structure of that society:

'Population' is an abstraction if I leave out, for example, the classes of which it consists. These classes, in their turn, are but an empty word if I do not know the elements on which they rest, such as wage-labour, capital etc. These latter presuppose exchange, division of labour, prices etc. Capital, for instance, is nothing without wage-labour, value, money, price etc. If, therefore, I were to start out with 'population', we would have only a chaotic conception of the whole, and by means of further determination I would move, analytically, to ever simpler concepts, from the imagined concrete towards ever thinner abstractions, until I had reached the simplest determinations. From there the return-journey would have to be made until I finally came back to population, but this time not as a chaotic conception of an integral whole, but as a rich totality of many determinations and relations.[13]

What is said of population in general applies of course, in particular, to those who produce and those who 'receive' works of literature.

At the same time Marx recognizes, in this General Introduction, what Ian Birchall has rightly (if inelegantly) called 'the specificity of artistic representations of reality'. In the section which describes the method of political economy as Marx now conceives it, he declares: 'The whole, as it appears in the head as a thought-aggregate, is the product of a thinking head which assimilates the world in the only way open to it, *a way which differs from an artistic*, religious or practically-minded *assimilation*' [my italics].[14] The speculative philosopher, then, or the political economist, 'assimilates' the world (*eignet sich die Welt an*) in a way which differs from that of the artist. But, Marx continues, that recognition must not lead us to confuse reality thus assimilated with reality *tout court*:

The concrete subject continues to lead an independent existence, as it did before, outside the head—so long as the head contemplates it only speculatively, theoretically. Even when we employ the theoretical method, therefore, the subject, society, must always be kept in mind as the premiss from which to start.

---

[13] *G* 21 (*GM* 44–5; *GN* 100).
[14] Ian Birchall, 'The Total Marx and the Marxist Theory of Literature', in *Situating Marx*, ed. Walton and Hall, p. 135. *G* 22 (*GM* 46).

Marx is in no doubt—as Herder, Goethe, Hegel were in no doubt—that literature and social developments are inter-connected. But how? Was there not a patent 'inequality' of development which complicated the relationship between the 'ideal' production of literature and the 'material' production of the economic life? These questions agitate the fragmentary notes with which Marx's sketch of a General Introduction ends—notes which mark his break, once and for all, with crude notions of steady and uniform progress; his break, above all, with positivistic notions about a direct relation between advance in social organization and advance in aesthetic merit.

6. *The uneven relation between the development of material production and that of art, for instance.* Altogether the concept of progress is not to be conceived in the usual abstractness. Modern art etc. This dispropor-tion is not as important or as difficult to grasp as within practical social relations themselves. E.g. those of education. Relations of the United States to Europe. The really difficult point, however, which is to be discussed here is how the relations of production develop unevenly as legal relations. Thus for example the relation of Roman private law (this is less the case with criminal and public law) to modern production.

7. *This conception appears as a necessary development.* But legitimation of chance. How. (Also Freedom and other topics.) (Influence of means of communication. World history has not always existed; history as world history a result.)

8. *The point of departure, naturally, from determination by nature*; subject-ively and objectively. Tribes, races etc.

In the case of the arts it is well-known that certain periods in which they flowered are out of all proportion to the general development of society, hence also to its material basis, the skeletal structure, as it were, of its organization. The Greeks, for instance, compared with the moderns or also Shakespeare. It is even recognized that certain forms of art, the epic, for instance, cannot be produced in their world-epoch-making, classical form once the production of art as such begins; that therefore certain significant formations within the domain of art itself are possible only at a low stage of development. If this is true of the relation of different kinds of art within the domain of art itself, it is already less surprising that the same should be true of the relation in which the whole domain of art stands to the general development of society. The difficulty lies only in the general formulation of these contradictions. As soon as they have been specified they are already explained.

Let us take, for instance, the relation of Greek art, and then that of Shakespeare, to the present time. It is well-known that Greek mythology is not only the arsenal of Greek art but also its foundation. Is the view of nature and of social relations which underlies the Greek imagination and also, therefore, Greek [mythology], possible with self-acting machines, railways, locomotives, and telegraphs? What chance has Vulcan against Roberts & Co., Jupiter against the lightning-conductor, and Hermes against the *crédit mobilier*? All mythology overcomes and dominates and shapes the forces of nature in the imagination and by the imagination: it therefore disappears when these have been truly mastered. What becomes of Fama alongside Printing House Square? Greek art presupposes Greek mythology, i.e. nature and the social forms themselves already reworked by the popular imagination in an unconsciously artistic way. That is its material. Not any mythology whatever, i.e. not any arbitrarily selected unconscious artistic reworking of nature (here including everything objective, hence including society). Egyptian mythology could never have been the foundation or the womb of Greek art. But certainly *a* mythology. Hence, in no way a development of society which excludes all mythological relations to nature and all mythologizing relations to her; which therefore demands of the artist an imagination independent of mythology.

Looked at from another side: is Achilles possible with powder and lead? Or the *Iliad* with the printing-press, to say nothing of the printing-machine? Do not song and saga [*das Singen und Sagen*] and the Muse necessarily come to an end with the printer's bar, do not therefore the necessary conditions of epic poetry vanish?

But the difficulty lies not in understanding that Greek art and the Greek epic are bound up with certain forms of social development. The difficulty is that they still afford us artistic pleasure and that in a certain respect they still count as a norm and as unattainable models.

A man cannot become a child again, or he becomes childish. But does he not find joy in the child's naïvety, and must he not himself strive to reproduce its truth at a higher stage? Does not the specific character of each epoch come alive, in its true nature, in the nature of the child? Why should not the historic childhood of humanity, its most beautiful unfolding, exert an eternal attraction as a stage that

will never return? There are ill-bred children and precocious
children. Many of the peoples of antiquity belong in this category.
The Greeks were normal children. The attraction their art has
for us does not stand in contradiction to the undeveloped stage of
society on which it grew. It is, rather, its result; it is inextricably
bound up, rather, with the fact that the immature social conditions
under which it arose, and under which alone it could arise, can
never return.[15]

When he comes to think about the now famous 'lags', the
'uneven development' of art and material production, Marx
finds this by no means the most difficult problem he has to face.
He is exercised by even more vexatious problems of social and
legal analysis, by the difficulty of defining progress, by the
relation between necessity, freedom, and chance, by the complexity of historical study in an age in which more rapid and
efficient communications have transformed all history into *world*
history. All these must be taken into account when facing, as
Marx now tries to do, the history of art. Like everything else,
this too must start (as Herder had insisted long before) with
determination by nature—Marx mentions tribe and race in
particular. And the world of nature enters into his very vocabulary as he now turns to the history of art itself. Like the German
Romantics, he likens the development of art to the seasonal life
of plants by speaking of *Blütezeiten*, seasons of flowering. But as
everything that went before in the Introduction had already
suggested, it is not enough, for Marx, to look at art's internal
development; art must be brought into relation with the over-all
development of society, *zur allgemeinen Entwicklung der Gesellschaft.*
That, in its turn, means looking at the material foundation
(*materielle Grundlage*) of society. But does not the very term
'foundation', *Grundlage*, denote something too architectural, too
rigid, to serve as sole metaphor? Marx seems to have felt this,
and immediately supplements it with another term: economic
conditions, organizations of production, are now seen as the
'bone-structure' (*Knochenbau*) of the body politic. Unlike a
'foundation', a 'bone structure' can grow and change according
to innate laws, though it changes less and endures longer than
the rest of the body.

[15] *G* 29–31 (*GM* 54–7; *GN* 109–11).

All this, however, is still too abstract; Marx therefore passes immediately to two actual examples taken from the history of literature. The examples he chooses had been dear to the hearts of the German Romantics too, and to that of Schiller before them. How do the Greeks, how does Shakespeare, relate to our own modern age? More specifically (and now Marx comes to a problem acute in Hegel's thoughts about art, from the *Phenomenology* onwards): what is the relation of specific genres—that of the epic, for instance—to specific periods of history? There have been many epics since Homer, but none of these, Marx believes, with Goethe and with Hegel, have ever attained the exemplary classical form, the epoch-making power, of Homer. Marx's vocabulary at this point again deserves closer scrutiny —for we now find him applying to the history of literature and the other arts terms central to his *economic* analyses, the terms *produzieren* and *Produktion*. The poet too is to be seen as a 'producer', the work of art as a 'product', though of a unique and special kind. Through his very way of speaking Marx is thus again reminding us that art must be seen in the context of other social relations, and more particularly that of the means and relations of material production. Having made this point, however, he can isolate and abstract; he can look, for a moment, at the realm of art by itself.

Even when a *Bereich der Kunst* has been isolated in such a way the puzzle with which Marx began his ruminations remains. Why is it that certain important and significant conformations of art—notably epic poetry—are possible only at an early stage of development, a stage at which full development of artistic potentialities has not, as yet, taken place? And if this is a puzzle within the realm of art taken in isolation, we should not be surprised that it remains one in a larger socio-historical context. There are 'contradictions' here (*Widersprüche*, a key term in Marx as it was in Hegel) which must be dialectically resolved. They can be explained, Marx declares, if one passes from a generalized formulation to specific instances—and that he now proposes to do.

Leaving Shakespeare aside, Marx concentrates on the differences between the literature of the Greeks and our own. Attention centres, as before, on the epic. Its basis is mythology— Greek mythology, as Marx had read in Hegel and again in

F. Th. Vischer's *Ästhetik*, is not only the store (*Arsenal*) from
which the Greek poets drew necessary equipment, but is the
very ground and soil of Greek art. The metaphoric term Marx
uses here, *Boden*, is a particularly useful one in his context: as
'ground' it goes well with the 'foundation' metaphor he had
used earlier, and as 'soil' it sorts no less admirably with the
'vegetation' metaphor of *Blütezeit*. *Boden* is at once the ground
on which something can be built and the soil in which something can grow. Yet this soil has been eroded, this ground cut
away, in the course of man's advance through history. Greek
mythology must be seen as the product of a specific kind of
imagination (*Phantasie*); and this imagination depended on a
view of nature, and on social relationships, that have gone for
ever, that cannot arise from human experience in a technological age. Marx sees the Greek gods, as many saw them in his
time, as hypostatizations of forces at work in the world that were
little understood and therefore regarded with awe: but, Marx
asks, how can we feel awe at the feats of Vulcan when we see
those of modern industrial machinery, or at Jupiter's thunder-
bolt when it can be rendered harmless by a lightning-conductor,
or at the speed and trickery of Hermes when they are outdone
by the operations of modern bankers? If mythology is indeed
(as Marx thought it was) a way of coming to terms with natural
forces, and thus dominating and shaping them in the imagination, then it must needs disappear when such forces have been
understood, tamed, and harnessed in reality.

Greek art presupposes a specific mythology; a mythology
which is already artistic in itself, for it is the way in which the
imagination of the Greek people (*Volksphantasie*—another Romantic concept, dear especially to the brothers Grimm!) transformed nature and social relations. This explains why mythology
cannot be simply taken over, transferred (like raw material of
another sort) from one society, one civilization, to another. As
Herder had insisted long before, a poet can work convincingly
only within the living traditions of his people; and at this point,
when he speaks of the impossibility that—say—Egyptian mythology could have fructified the art of the Greeks, Marx introduces
yet another organic metaphor. From *Boden*, soil as well as
ground, he passes to *Mutterschoß*, maternal womb, suggesting
the slow growth of one organism within another, and a birth

that results in the existence of two separate yet closely related beings.

Marx is now ready to sum up his argument so far. The epic poet needs a mythology, and cannot flourish in a society that precludes the kind of relation to nature which results in myths —'nature' being regarded here as the whole objective world and therefore including social relations. Once gunpowder and shot have been invented, one cannot introduce a hero like Achilles into the modern world; the *Iliad* represents an oral form threatened by the invention of the hand-press and even more by that of machine-printing; and what is the trumpet of Fame compared with a great newspaper like *The Times*? The conditions under which a meaningful mythology could flourish, and under which, therefore, epics like those of Homer could be produced, have gone for ever.

We have now watched Marx trying out, in this justly famous passage, various supplementary or alternative ways of speaking about the relationship between material and social conditions on the one hand and works of art on the other. He uses images of 'relationship' and 'proportion' (*Verhältnisse*; *Disproportion*); images of 'necessary development' (*notwendige Entwicklung*) and 'chance' (*Zufall*). He speaks, in the same breath, of a 'material basis', an 'organization' and a 'skeletal structure' of society (. . . *der materiellen Grundlage, gleichsam des Knochenbaus ihrer Organisation*). He uses metaphors from modern weapon-storage (*Arsenal*) side by side with a metaphor from the natural world (*Boden*, meaning 'ground' or 'soil' as well as 'foundation'). There are images of 'flowering', 'unfolding', 'ripeness', and 'growth' (*Blütezeit*; *entfaltet*; *unreife gesellschaftliche Bedingungen*; *zu der unentwickelten Gesellschaftsstufe, worauf sie wuchs*), but also more neutral images of 'coming into being' (*entstand, entstehen*). There are passages in which the imagination is said to 'rework' or 'work on' (*verarbeiten*) natural and social forms in an unconsciously artistic way. There are others that speak of art as 'tied to' particular forms of social development. All this is thrown out as a preliminary attempt to resolve troubling paradoxes, to find a way of speaking about vexatiously complex problems.

At the same time Marx has tried to see literature and art in a number of possible relations and from several different points of view. He has glanced at individual characters (Achilles) and

works (the *Iliad*) and genres (the Greek epic). He has looked at
the realm of art with its internal laws and relationships; but all
the while he has kept his readers alive to wider connections
through the very metaphors we have seen him use, which ranged
from the biological to the architectural, from the organic to the
economic. He has tried to see literature from the poet's point of
view. What materials does he find ready to hand? How far are
these pre-shaped by society or a social group? What can he, and
what can he not, use? What subjects, what themes, what forms
are removed from his grasp by historical, social, economic
progress?

Here, however, Marx reaches another crux. Granted that
certain literary forms can no longer be produced with artistic
success in later times—why should earlier achievements in these
forms still constitute for modern men (as they clearly did for
Marx) an ever-new source of artistic enjoyment, *Kunstgenuß*?
Why can men still regard them, in some respect at least, as
unerreichbare Muster, artistic norms, unattainable models of perfection?

Marx has now clearly turned from a consideration of the
poet's relationship to the work to that of the *reader*, and suggested
three aspects of it. First, that the relationship modern readers
have to Homer's work must differ, in important respects, from
that of Homer's contemporaries; second, that great literature
yields a specific kind of enjoyment, *Kunstgenuß*; third, that the
critical reader comes to recognize models and norms, to apply
what Matthew Arnold was to call 'touchstones'. No modern
attempt to write an epic, he suggests, could pass muster if touchstones derived from ancient Greek literature were applied. And
at this point he introduces yet another time-hallowed 'organic'
metaphor into the discussion: that which implies a parallel
between the ages of the world and the ages of man. Were we to
write mythological epics today, he argues, we would resemble
men who have returned to the ways of their childhood. But
though it would be wrong for grown men to regress in this way,
it would be no less wrong to cease taking delight in the naïvety
of the child; for such naïvety includes a degree of truth inevitably sacrificed amid the adaptations necessary to maturity, a
degree of truth we must strive to recapture and reproduce *at a
higher level*. In each and every historical epoch, children have

given the most natural and unforced expression to the character of that epoch. Marx is here reviving arguments Schiller had used in his famous essay on 'naïve' and 'sentimental' poetry; but he is also speaking out of his own experience. His love of children, his patience with them, his understanding of their ways, are attested by many competent observers.

Why then, Marx concludes, if this is true of individual human lives, should it not also be true of humanity as a whole? Childhood is a stage (*Stufe*) that has a value of its own; why should not the historical childhood of mankind, the stage at which it unfolded itself most beautifully (*wo sie sich am schönsten entfaltet*—another 'flower' metaphor!) exercise an eternal attraction? And now Marx tries again, at a crucial point of his argument, to compare and 'place'. If children have different dispositions and characters—they may be ill behaved and unruly, precocious, and so on—could not the same be true of the peoples of the ancient world? The Greeks, he concludes, were 'normal' children, and that is the ultimate secret of their attraction for us. There is thus *no* contradiction, no *Widerspruch*, between the strength of that attraction and the source from which it derives. Metaphors of growing and ripening (*wuchs, unreif*) come once more to the fore as Marx concludes his argument: that the admiration of Greek art is justified and that it owes much of its force to nostalgia for a beautiful state of humanity that can never return.

The equation of an early artistic period with the 'childhood' or 'youth' of mankind has a long history which runs from Plato to Hegel and Hölderlin. None the less there is something unsatisfactory about Marx's restatement of it. To speak of the Greeks, in their great period, as 'normal children', seriously undervalues their complexity and maturity, qualities of which Marx himself, in other texts, shows himself well aware. The valuation Marx explicitly makes here can all too easily be overturned if his metaphor is taken seriously. Heine, in fact, had already done just that in the 'Confessions' (*Geständnisse*) published three years before Marx's Introduction:

About the Jews . . . I have never spoken with adequate respect, probably . . . because my Hellenic nature was repelled by Jewish asceticism. Now I see that the Greeks were only youths while the Jews were always men, powerful, unbending men—and that not only in olden times, but right up to the present, despite eighteen centuries of persecution and misery.

Marx may well have had the Jews in mind when, in the Introduction, he described some of the peoples of the ancient world as 'precocious' children.

Marx has taken no account of the formal qualities of Greek poetry and drama; and his characterization of the Greeks as 'normal children' conflicts, as we have seen, with what he himself knew of the subtlety and sophistication of Greek art, as well as the more corrupt features of Greek society in post-Homeric times. The 'youthfulness' of an Aeschylus or a Sophocles appears, if at all, only in the provision of relatively simple models of general situations (conflict, fate, guilt); but such situations, as Marx well knew, are neither 'childlike' nor 'past'. Ernst Fischer, who has made this criticism, has also, however, pointed to what we may still recognize as a valuable and convincing part of Marx's otherwise imperfect answer: 'What matters is that Marx saw the time-conditioned art of an undeveloped social stage as a *moment of humanity*, and recognized that in this lay its power to act beyond the historical instant, to exercise an eternal fascination . . . Constant features of mankind are captured even in time-conditioned art.'[16] The word 'moment' in this passage, neuter in Fischer's original German, denotes 'an important element, stage or turning-point in an on-going process or course of events'; but the English translation usefully adds the sense of 'a definite point in time' ('*der* Moment' as opposed to '*das* Moment') to the total meaning.

Marx's observations on Greek art confirm Henri Lefebvre's description of the way in which he habitually distinguished between mythology and 'false consciousness'. 'Marx thought', Lefebvre has written, 'that Greek mythology, the soil that nourished Greek art, was an expression of the real life of the people, an ever fresh source of the "eternal" charm of this art. The Greek myths and the Greek gods were symbols of man or rather of his powers. They gave in magnified form a picture of how human beings appropriate their own nature—in the various activities of their own lives (warfare, metal-working), in games, love, and enjoyment. Cosmogonies, myths, and mythologies are

[16] E. Fischer, *The Necessity of Art. A Marxist Approach*, trans. Anna Bostock (Harmondsworth, 1963), pp. 12–13.

turned into ideologies only when they become ingredients in religion, especially in the great religions that lay claim to universality. Then the images and tales are cut off from the soil that nourished them, the beauty of which they represented to the eye and mind.'[17] Marx's admiration for the poetry, and the truth, embodied in myth never led him to abate one jot of his hostility to religion, which he continued to regard as a noxious (or, at best, irrelevant) compound of involuntary illusions and deliberate lies.

At the same time, however, as philosophers of religion have increasingly come to recognize, Marx is himself working out a system that draws a good deal of its strength, its grandeur, and its pathos, from a recollection of the eschatological pattern that underlies the great religions of Europe and Asia. No one has described this more clearly than Mircea Eliade.

Marx takes over and continues one of the great eschatological myths of the Asiatico-Mediterranean world—the redeeming role of the Just (the 'chosen', the 'anointed', the 'innocent', the 'messenger'; in our day, the proletariat), whose sufferings are destined to change the eschatological status of the world. In fact, Marx's classless society and the consequent disappearance of historical tensions find their closest precedent in the myth of the Golden Age that many traditions put at the beginning and the end of history.[18]

It is not difficult to discern in Marx's later work—with its demand for righteousness, its stern judgement of existing society, its vision of a battle between Good and Evil, its hope of an absolute end to historical processes as we now know them—a return to the traditions of the Hebrew prophets.

A later passage in the *Grundrisse* tries to show more precisely what attracted men in Marx's own nineteenth-century world to that 'moment of humanity' which Greek literature had captured for ever:

The ancient conception, in which man, though in various narrow national, religious, and political determinations, always appears as the aim of production, seems to be very superior to the modern world in which production appears as the aim of man and wealth as the aim of production. In fact, however, when the narrow bourgeois

[17] Lefebvre, *The Sociology of Marx*, p. 79.
[18] M. Eliade, *The Sacred and the Profane. The Nature of Religion*, trans. W. R. Trask (New York, 1959), pp. 206–7.

form is cast aside, what is wealth but the universality of the needs, capacities, enjoyments, productive forces etc. of individuals? The complete development of human domination of natural forces, those of so-called 'nature' as well as those of the individual's own nature? What is it but the absolute working-out of his own creative dispositions, without any preconception except that of previous historical development, which makes the totality of this development—i.e. the development of all human powers as such, not measured by any yardstick that is already given—an end in itself? What is this but a situation in which man does not reproduce himself in some predetermined form, but one in which he produces his totality? In bourgeois economics, and the epoch of production that corresponds to it, this complete elaboration of man's inner potential appears as complete depletion, this universal objectification as complete estrangement, and the demolition of all determined, one-sided aims as the sacrifice of autonomy to a wholly external aim. Thus on the one hand the childish ancient world *appears* to be the higher. On the other hand it *is* the higher world in everything that demands a finished shape, form, given limitation. The ancient world satisfied from a narrow point, while the modern world affords no satisfaction—or, where it does appear satisfied with itself, it is common and mean.[19]

What the works of the ancient world can give us, then, is a feeling of perfected structure and form, of totality, of the full development of human powers possible at what Marx here calls a 'childish' (*kindisch*) stage of social development. The modern world, Marx feels, has liberated far greater human potentialities through developments in the technical and economic spheres; but these have found expression mainly in forms that appear strange, alien to the very men who with their work have made the world and made themselves what they are. The ancient world, therefore, offers an image of wholeness and full development which cannot but attract those who long for such wholeness, for such development, in their own lives, and those who would seek to bring about a future state in which such wholeness may be known once more on a higher plane.

The contrast here drawn in the *Grundrisse* shows once again the continuity of Marx's aesthetics with those of the *Goethezeit*, with Weimar classicism and the German Romantics. His confrontation of the finished or closed shape (*geschloßne Gestalt*

[19] *G* 387–8 (*GM* 139–40).

Form, und gegebne Begrenzung) characteristic of the ancient world with the dissatisfied striving of the modern world towards a higher totality recalls Schiller's opposition of the 'naïve' and the 'sentimental' as much as A. W. Schlegel's contrast between a classical poetry of 'possession' and a modern literature which hovers between 'recollection' and 'divination', between *Erinnerung* and *Ahnung*.[20] Marx pours scorn, however, on all who would exalt the 'fuller' past at the expense of an 'emptier' present:

At earlier stages of development the isolated individual appears more complete just because it has not fully developed all possible relationships and has not confronted itself with them as independent social forces and conditions. It is just as ridiculous to yearn back to this original plenitude as it is to believe that one has to remain at the stage of total depletion. Bourgeois notions have never reached beyond opposition to that romantic view, and thus will be accompanied by it, as a legitimate antithesis, right up to its blessèd end.[21]

While having no truck with simple notions of straightforward, uniform, concurrent progress, while refusing, conversely, to exalt any past at the expense of the present, the *Grundrisse* look forward to a future which will combine the fullness of development made possible by modern modes of production with the unalienated satisfactions of an earlier, less complex world.

Here too Marx stands in a chiliastic tradition that begins with the Bible and passes through Schiller. Does not man, he asks, 'ever strive to reproduce his true being [*seine Wahrheit*] on a higher plane?'[22] Art does not come to an end with capitalism. There will be a new art, embodying a new truth, in the society of the future envisaged in *Grundrisse*: a society in which the exploitation of man (and, in particular, of class by class) will have ceased and machines will have reduced repetitive labour to a minimum. The corollary of such reduction, Marx proclaims, will be that 'all members of society will be able to develop their education in the arts, sciences etc., thanks to the free time and means available to all'.[23] This saving of labour-time, Marx adds, will mean not the *reduction* of pleasure, but the development of

---

[20] Cf. Schiller's essay 'On "Naive" and "Sentimental" Poetry' (*Über naive und sentimentalische Dichtung*), and the first of A. W. Schlegel's *Lectures on Dramatic Art and Literature.*

[21] *G* 80 (*GM* 82).

[22] Cf. M. Lifshits, *The Philosophy of Art of Karl Marx*, pp. 110–11.

[23] *G* 593 (*GM* 166).

power, of productive capacity, and hence the capacity for and the means of enjoyment.[24]

It will have been noticed that Marx has now returned to a theme which had figured prominently in the General Introduction considered earlier in this chapter. Works of art are not just passively consumed; they develop (and, in a way, create) the faculties by which they can be enjoyed:

Does not the pianist as he produces music and satisfies our tonal sense, also produce that sense in some respects?

The pianist stimulates production either by making us more active and lively individuals or (as is more commonly supposed) by arousing a new need whose satisfaction requires greater effort from directly material production.[25]

In this way material production can further improvements in the quality of life as well as increase the quantity of goods available. At the same time the artist can also show his fellow men how to make creative use of their free time—a lesson they will need to learn in the automated society of the future. He demonstrates, even in the less than satisfactory world of the nineteenth century, the meanness of regarding work as *necessarily* mere drudgery. Work *is* a burden when imposed on unwilling labourers by oppressive economic forces, by owners of capital who unjustly appropriate the surplus value created by their workers. Work freely chosen, however, is man's way of changing the world while also making, creating, himself. It is the surest means of self-realization. Here Marx parts company with Fourier, who saw freely chosen work as all enjoyment; his own vision of non-alienated labour, Marx claims indignantly, 'does not by any means imply that work is just a joke, a mere amusement as Fourier naïvely saw it in shop-girl terms. Really free work, the composing of music for example, is at the same time damned serious and demands the most intense effort.'[26] The artist can therefore teach an important lesson to sociologists, to economists, and to all mankind.

What the *Grundrisse* have to say about art thus bears a vital relation to their principal theme: labour in the modern world. This comes out particularly clearly in a key passage from the third notebook:

---

[24] *G* 599 (*GM* 171).   [25] *G* 212 (*GM* 94).   [26] *G* 505 (*GM* 146).

This economic relation—the character assumed by capitalist and worker as the two extremes of a relationship of production—develops, consequently, in a manner all the more pure and adequate in proportion to the extent that *labour loses its character of art*; that is, to the extent that its particular skill is converted into something increasingly abstract and undifferentiated, into an attitude that is more and more purely abstract, merely mechanical and, consequently, indifferent to specific form; into a purely formal activity or, what is the same thing, a purely material activity which is indifferent as to its form [my italics].[27]

As the italicized passage shows beyond doubt: Marx defined modern wage labour by its loss of artistic character and saw artistic creation as the type of labour to which all others aspire; the type of labour in which the individual can realize and develop his potentialities.

But how were the economic and social consequences which flowed from all this to be discussed in language accessible to non-specialists? The hated 'bellettrists', who 'colour everything green and chatter away into the blue', find no difficulty—they deal more in words than in facts, and happily 'smear their liquorice-sweet rubbish all over the sciences'.[28] Romantic theorists like Adam Müller, especially, compound confusion by reading deep mystical meanings into metaphoric expressions like 'dead capital'.[29] Yet as we have seen, Marx himself, when discussing cultural problems, is constantly driven back to metaphorical, analogical ways of speaking which invite exegesis and elaboration. No wonder, therefore, that he should devote some of his energies, in *Grundrisse*, to a consideration of the limitations as well as the uses of analogy:

To compare money with blood—a comparison occasioned by the word 'circulation'—is about as apt as Menenius Agrippa's comparison between patricians and the stomach. It is no less false to compare money with language. Ideas are not transmuted into language in such a way that their particular nature is dissolved and their social character exists alongside them in language, as prices exist alongside goods. Ideas do not exist apart from language. Ideas that have first to be translated from their mother tongue into a foreign language in order to circulate offer a somewhat closer

[27] *G* 204; cf. A. Sánchez Váchez, *Art and Society. Essays in Marxist Aesthetics* (London, 1974), p. 205.
[28] *G* 201. [29] *G* 413.

analogy; but here the analogy lies not in language itself, but in the foreignness of the language.[30]

It is notable that in this context even Shakespeare, who had prominently used the analogy between the patricians and the stomach in *Coriolanus* without ironizing Menenius Agrippa's views, is subjected—indirectly, it is true—to some necessary historical distancing.[31] So is William Cobbett, whose inadequate conception of the nature of money had allowed him, as Marx thought, to ask the right questions but not to supply the right answers.[32]

Marx continues, in *Grundrisse*, to follow his occasional practice of looking to the world's great poets for economic facts and insights where other sources fail. The works of Homer, Hesiod, and Lucretius are therefore searched for evidence of commercial and financial beliefs, practices, and conditions in the ancient world.[33] More often, however, Marx goes to the poets for confirmation of views independently formed; thus Pindar, Aristophanes, the author of Revelation, and Shakespeare's *Timon of Athens* are quoted in support of some aspects at least of Marx's own views on the nature and power of money.[34] As always, Marx's language is saturated with phrases from other writers, ranging from 'pleasant custom of existence' (*angenehme Gewohnheit des Daseins*) which recalls Goethe's *Egmont* to the term 'cash-nexus' taken over from Carlyle.[35] And—as if to supplement his warnings against false analogies with a demonstration of how valid analogies may abbreviate and illuminate an argument— Marx draws on the great writers of the past for images that vividly illustrate his contentions while suggesting, at the same time, an attitude to the problems raised. Don Quixote, for instance, is evoked when Marx speaks of vain efforts to oppose powerful historical forces;[36] but he also turns up in more surprising contexts:

When economists discuss existing relations of capital and wage-labour, profit and salaries; when they prove to the worker that he

---

[30] *G* 80 (*GM* 82).

[31] *Coriolanus*, I. i. A. O. Lovejoy, in *The Great Chain of Being*, and E. M. W. Tillyard, in *The Elizabethan World-Picture*, have described the larger context in which such analogies between the individual human body and the body politic must be seen.

[32] *G* 689.   [33] *G* 98, 679.   [34] *G* 871, 895.   [35] *G* 39, 874.

[36] *G* 77.

has no claim to a share in the chances of profit; when they try to reassure workers about the subordinate role they must play *vis-à-vis* the capitalists—then they all stress that unlike the capitalist the worker has a certain stability of income which makes him more or less independent of the great adventures of capital. Just so Don Quixote consoled Sancho Panza: Sancho had to take all the drubbings, certainly, but for that he had no need to be courageous.[37]

Here a literary analogy is used to ridicule fallacious arguments and expose the mechanisms of false consciousness or deliberate deceit.

(ii)

In August 1858 Marx began to prepare for publication part of the material he had collected and analysed in *Grundrisse*. The chapters on Money and Commodities were ready in January 1859, and were sent off to the publisher Franz Duncker, who brought them out that same year under the title *Towards a Critique of Political Economy* (*Zur Kritik der politischen Ökonomie*). The General Introduction Marx had written for *Grundrisse* was not, however, printed in this volume, or in any other that issued from the press in Marx's own lifetime. 'I omit', he explained, 'a general Introduction I had sketched out, because on closer reflection any anticipation of results yet to be proved appears to me disturbing, and the reader who wants to follow me at all must be resolved to ascend from the particular to the general.'[38] For this Introduction (*Einleitung*) Marx substituted a Preface (*Vorwort*) in which he briefly surveyed the course of his studies, mentioning jurisprudence, philosophy, history, and economics, but saying nothing of his literary and aesthetic investigations. This may well have been a deliberate, diplomatic omission; Marx did not want readers to confound him with economists who drew their evidence more from belles-lettres than from the study of economic theory and statistics. He then went on to speak of his critique of Hegel's *Philosophy of Right*, in which he correctly saw a watershed of his intellectual development:

My investigations led to the conclusion that legal relations as well as forms of state[39] could neither be understood by themselves nor

---

[37] *G* 851 (*GM* 67–8).   [38] *MEW* XIII, 7.
[39] The words 'Rechtsverhältnisse wie Staatsformen' could also mean: 'legal relations *such as* forms of state'.

explained by the so-called general progress of the human mind, but that they are rooted in the material conditions of life which are subsumed by Hegel, after the fashion of the English and French writers of the eighteenth century, under the name 'civil society' [*bürgerliche Gesellschaft*]; that the anatomy of this civil society is to be sought, however, in political economy. The study of the latter, which I had begun in Paris, I continued in Brussels where I had emigrated on account of an expulsion-order issued by M. Guizot. The general conclusion at which I arrived and which, once reached, continued to serve as the guiding thread of my studies, may be briefly formulated as follows: In the social production in which men engage they enter into definite relations that are independent of their will. These relations of production correspond to a definite state of development of their material powers of production. The totality of these relations of production constitutes the economic structure of society—the real basis, on which legal and political superstructures arise and to which definite forms of social consciousness correspond. The mode of production of material life conditions the social, political, and intellectual process of life as a whole. It is not the consciousness of men which determines their being, but, on the contrary, their social being which determines their consciousness. At a certain stage of their development, the material forces of production in society come in conflict with the existing relations of production, or—what is but a legal expression for the same thing—with the property relations within which they had been at work before. From forms of development of the forces of production these relations turn into their fetters. Then occurs a period of social revolution. With the change of the economic foundation the entire immense superstructure is more or less rapidly transformed. In considering such transformations, a distinction should always be made between the material transformation of the economic conditions of production which can be determined with the precision of natural science, and the legal, political, religious, artistic or philosophical—in short, ideological—forms in which men become conscious of this conflict and fight it out. Just as our opinion of an individual is not based on what he thinks of himself, so we cannot judge of such a period of transformation by its own consciousness; on the contrary, this consciousness must rather be explained from the contradictions of material life, from the existing conflict between the social forces of production and the relations of production.[40]

This famous passage elaborates what Marx and Engels had earlier maintained in the *Communist Manifesto*: 'What else does

[40] *MEW* XIII, 8–9; *BR* 67–8.

the history of ideas prove than that intellectual production transforms itself together with material production? The ruling ideas
of a period were never anything but the ideas of the ruling
class.'⁴¹ In the Preface, however, Marx specifically mentions *art*
along with law, politics, religion, and philosophy; and he introduces a significant metaphor: that of the material *basis* or *foundation* on which an intellectual *superstructure* rests. One may well
feel that this is an unhappy image, far too static for the constantly changing and evolving phenomena which it seeks to
evoke. Marx partly counteracts this by another image, that of
a ponderous turning-around and -over (*umwälzen*); and he tries,
at the same time, to allow for that lack of correlation between
economic/social *Umwälzungen* and aesthetic ones which had
played so prominent a part in the General Introduction:

Mit der Veränderung der ökonomischen Grundlage wälzt sich der
ganze ungeheure Überbau *langsamer oder rascher* um.

With the change of the economic foundation the entire immense
superstructure is *more or less rapidly* transformed [my italics].

In *Culture and Society 1780–1950* Raymond Williams has rightly
stressed the importance of the words 'more or less rapidly' in
the sentence just quoted:

Even if we accept the formula of structure and superstructure, we
have Marx's word that changes in the latter are necessarily subject
to a different and less precise mode of investigation. The point is
reinforced by the verbal qualifications of his text . . . The superstructure is a matter of human consciousness, and this is necessarily
very complex, not only because of its diversity, but also because it is
always historical: at any time, it includes continuities from the past
as well as reactions to the present . . . If . . . a part of the superstructure is mere rationalization, the complexity of the whole is further
increased.⁴²

The various forms of organic metaphor with which Marx had
experimented in the unpublished and abandoned Introduction
have a distinguished history in European cultural theory from

⁴¹ *MEW* IV, 480.
⁴² *Culture and Society*, 2nd edn. (Harmondsworth, 1961), p. 259. For Raymond
Williams's most sustained attempt to come to terms with Marx, see his article
' "Base and Superstructure" in Marxist Cultural Theory', *New Left Review*, 82
(Nov.–Dec. 1973), 3–16.

Plato and Aristotle to Goethe, but they were also to prove, in twentieth-century Germany, capable of distressing corruption. Marx may have perceived this latent possibility when he tried to substitute that of 'base' (or 'basis', or 'foundation') and 'superstructure'. I doubt, however, whether the new metaphor has yet proved as helpful in literary criticism as the old one. If one studies the history of its application after Marx's death, one may well come to feel that it has done more harm than good. In other respects too, as John Plamenatz has incisively demonstrated,[43] the formulations of the 1859 Preface are unhappy; not least because they take no account of that principle of 'interaction' (*Wechselwirkung*) which Marx and Engels had enunciated in *The German Ideology* and which Engels found himself forced to reassert after Marx's death. Ernst Fischer has cited some relevant passages from letters the aged Engels wrote to Joseph Bloch and Hans Starkenburg:

According to the materialist view of history, production and reproduction of real life are, *in the last instance*, the determining factor in history. Neither Marx nor I have asserted more than that. If anybody twists this into a claim that the economic factor is the *only* determining one, he transforms our statement into a meaningless, abstract, absurd phrase. The economic situation is the basis, but all the factors of the superstructure—political forms of the class struggle and its results, constitutions adopted by the victorious class after winning a battle, forms of law, and, more than that, the reflections of all those real struggles in the minds of the people involved, political, legal, and philosophical theories, religious views both in their early and their more developed, dogmatic form—all those factors also influence the course of historical struggles and in many cases play the dominant role in determining their *form*.

Political, juridical, philosophical, religious, literary, and artistic developments, etc., are based on economic development. But, in addition, they all react upon one another and also on the economic basis. The economic situation is not an *original cause* which alone is active while all else is merely passive effect. There is, rather, mutual action on the basis of economic necessity, which always proves the determining factor *in the last instance*.[44]

---

[43] J. Plamenatz, *Man and Society. A Critical Examination of some Important Social and Political Theories from Machiavelli to Marx* (London, 1963), vol. ii, pp. 325 ff.

[44] Quoted in Fischer, *The Necessity of Art*, p. 128.

The mixed metaphors of that last-quoted passage, in which 'developments' 'react upon' a 'basis', attest the inadequacy of the original metaphor in the Preface of *Towards a Critique of Political Economy*. That Preface had known no such qualification as Engels here seeks to introduce. Instead, its German text offers the interesting spectacle of Marx talking himself and his readers further and further into economic determinism. From two instances of 'correspondence':

Produktionsverhältnisse, die einer bestimmten Entwicklungsstufe ihrer materiellen Produktivkräfte *entsprechen* . . .

. . . die ökonomische Struktur der Gesellschaft, die reale Basis, worauf sich ein juristischer und politischer Überbau erhebt und welcher bestimmte gesellschaftliche Bewußtseinsformen *entsprechen*

we pass to an instance of 'conditioning':

Die Produktionsweise des materiellen Lebens *bedingt* den sozialen, politischen und geistigen Lebensprozeß überhaupt;

and from this we pass to 'determination', in the most famous sentence of all which echoes a similar sentence in *The German Ideology*:

Es ist nicht das Bewußtsein der Menschen, das ihr Sein, sondern umgekehrt ihr gesellschaftliches Sein, das ihr Bewußtsein *bestimmt*.[45]

This last uncompromising statement is not supplemented in the Preface by any suggestion that there might be interaction of the kind Engels envisaged in his letter to Starkenburg, or in a letter to Franz Mehring which sets out to clear up misunderstandings due to 'a common, undialectical conception of cause and effect as rigidly opposite poles'.[46] In this letter to Mehring Engels suggests that Marx may have omitted all mention of possible 'interaction' between basis and superstructure for diplomatic reasons:

In the first instance all of us laid the main stress, *had* to lay the main stress, on the *derivation* of political, legal, and other ideological conceptions, and the actions mediated [*vermittelt*] by such conceptions, from basic economic facts. In doing so we neglected the formal

[45] *MEW* XIII, 8–9. All italics are mine.
[46] Engels to Franz Mehring, 14 July 1893—*MEW* XXXIX, 96–100 (*ÜKL* I, 98).

side as against content: the manner in which these conceptions etc. came into being.[47]

In face of that German idealist tradition which culminated in Hegel, a tradition in which 'spirit' and 'idea' were seen as fundamental, ultimate reality, Marx may well have felt compelled to overemphasize the 'conditioning' power exerted by relations of production and the 'determining' power of man's social being.[48]

Marx never repudiated his 'base–superstructure' model—in *Capital* I, in fact, he defends it against its critics; but he never again used the term 'superstructure' when talking about literature and art.[49] It has, however, made a strong appeal to later Marxist critics, ranging from hack-journalists to the subtlest of them all, Walter Benjamin, who saw in it a challenge to his ingenuity, his delight in yoking the heterogeneous together by violence, and his constant endeavour to emulate those Talmudic scholars who sought (as Benjamin tells us) forty-nine levels of meaning in every passage of their sacred writings.

One further point must be made in this context, in face of persistent misunderstandings. Marx never thought that in seeking connections between man's economic life and his artistic

[47] *MEW* XXXIX, 96–100 (*ÜKL* I, 96).

[48] 'Marx's own account of what classes do politically, especially when they are revolutionary classes, gives the lie to the famous sentence so often quoted: "It is not the consciousness of men that determines their being but, on the contrary, their social being that determines their consciousness". Consciousness or ideology has a profound effect on social being, on the most important social relations. Indeed, if it were not so, there would be no point to the class conflicts and revolutions in which Marx believed so strongly. If it were really true that class ideologies only *reflect* class interests and do not also powerfully affect them, Marx would not be nearly as important a figure in world history as he actually is.' (Plamenatz, op. cit., vol. ii, p. 350.)

[49] *MEW* XXIII, 96. In his articles for the *New-York Daily Tribune* Marx associates the notion of 'superstructure' primarily with forms of the state, with political institutions (*MEW* XII, 420 and 591). In *Theories of Surplus Value* he attacks the view that 'conflicts or contrasts in material production necessitate a superstructure of ideological ranks and castes [*Superstruktur ideologischer Stände*], whose efficacy, be it for good or for ill, is good because it is necessary' (*MEW* XXVI (i), 259). In *Die Presse* Marx speaks, in July 1862, of a 'social substructure', *Unterbau*, which remains at rest while a constantly changing sequence of persons and tribes gains control of the political superstructure, *Überbau* (*MEW* XV, 514). In later notes and writings 'superstructure' describes systems of law, social and political views, and 'new financial, commercial, industrial, economic methods superimposed on an established, dominant way of production' (*MEW* XVI, 367; XVII, 336, 599, 551; XXXIV, 373–4). Cf. U. Erckenbrecht, *Marx' materialistische Sprachtheorie* (Kronberg, 1973), pp. 66–9.

achievements he might seem to be belittling those achievements. On the contrary: he firmly believed that his own conception of man was a nobler one than that of the fashionable bourgeois historians of his day. He thought the image of human endeavour, human achievement, and human possibilities which emerged from his own work far more consonant with man's dignity than that presented by Leopold von Ranke, for instance. In a letter to Engels dated 7 September 1864, Marx indignantly rejected 'what the bouncing little root-grubber Ranke regarded as the spirit of history—facile anecdote-mongering and the attribution of all great events to petty and mean causes'.[50]

In the passage quoted on pp. 293–4, art is only mentioned once. It is distinguished from the 'precision' of natural science and called, along with law, politics, religion, and philosophy an 'ideological' formation in which men 'become conscious' of an economically conditioned social conflict and 'fight it out'. This would seem to have three implications: (*a*) that the insights conveyed by art are different in kind from those derived from the sciences, and perhaps (if one remembers the many instances in which Marx and Engels associate 'ideology' with 'false consciousness'[51]) that they are more liable to distortion; (*b*) that art is not an autonomous realm—it is, rather, one of the ways in which men become conscious of, and express, conflicts and processes of change in the socio-economic world; (*c*) that art is a field in which battles or duels are fought (*ausfechten*); suggesting, probably, that art reflects, asserts, and confirms class-interests and class-positions. We may be sure, once again, that Marx did not want to belittle or devalue art by seeming to identify it with ideology in this way; but like so many other things in this contentious Preface, his formulation is liable to misunderstanding and abuse.

The Preface, it will have been noted, says little about the methods of approach appropriate to the arts. Marx had other

[50] *MEW* XXX, 432 ff.
[51] Plamenatz (op. cit., vol. ii, pp. 323–4) has usefully distinguished three connotations of the term 'ideology' in the works of Marx and Engels: (i) the entire system of ideas which men use to describe the world and to express their feelings and purposes; (ii) all theories and doctrines which are not scientific, and all normative concepts; (iii) normative concepts which serve the interest of some class or group.—All these connotations are relevant in our context if the notion of 'literary structures' is added to those of 'ideas' and 'normative concepts'.

fish to fry. It does assert, however, that a *distinction* must be made —that between changes in economic 'conditions of production' (which, Marx now believes, can be studied with the accuracy characteristic of the natural sciences) and ideological forms (among which, as we have seen, the arts are now included). When commenting on the arts, Marx tells us, we must guard against accepting at face value the interpretations of intentions and achievements offered by the artists themselves or their contemporaries; we must, above all, take into account economic and social factors of which authors and their first readers need not have been consciously aware but which have nevertheless entered into the literary and artistic works they produced and assimilated.

One other qualification needs to be made:

In broad outlines we can designate the Asiatic, the ancient, the feudal, and the modern bourgeois modes of production as so many epochs in the progress of the economic formation of society. The bourgeois relations of production are the last antagonistic form of the social process of production—antagonistic not in the sense of individual antagonism, but of one arising from the social conditions of life of the individuals. At the same time the productive forces developing in the womb of bourgeois society create the material conditions for the solution of that antagonism. This social formation, therefore, brings the prehistory of human society to a close.[52]

This passage, from *Towards a Critique of Political Economy*, demonstrates once again how powerfully Marx's early reading of Hegel continued to affect his view of historical sequence. What is important to note in our context, however, is its implications for the 'basis–superstructure' model of cultural dependence. Might not such a model be applicable only during a period of 'prehistory', before the advent of the socialist millennium? Is not Marx here looking forward to a state of society in which a model of this kind would be as obsolete as the economics of Adam Smith and Ricardo? To this, as to so many of the other questions and problems which it raises, neither the Preface nor the work it ushers in give any clear answer.

Literature is not specifically mentioned in the Preface which assigns the arts to an ideological superstructure; but it is not

[52] *MEW* XIII, 9; *SW* I, 504.

without significance that the Preface culminates in a quotation from Dante's *Inferno*:

This sketch of the course of my studies in the field of political economy is intended only to show that my views, however they may be judged and however little they may coincide with the interested prejudices of the ruling classes, are the result of conscientious investigation lasting many years. But at the entrance to science, as at the entrance to hell, there must stand the demand:

> Qui si convien lasciare ogni sospetto;
> ogni viltà convien che qui sia morta.

> Here you must abandon all division of spirit,
> and here all cowardice must perish.[53]

How characteristic of Marx that he should find what he felt to be the most adequate formulation of his own unwillingness to compromise *in the work of a medieval poet*—a poet with whom he shared the fate of exile, but whose social experience and world-view were as far removed from his own as any that can be imagined.

(iii)

Towards a Critique of Political Economy follows *Grundrisse* in searching literature for light on economic conditions, social attitudes, and beliefs—where *Grundrisse* had cited Homer, Hesiod, Sophocles, Aristophanes, and Lucretius, the *Critique* cites Euripides, Virgil, and Horace. One characteristic footnote begins with a passage from a Greek *historian*, Xenophon, sets this alongside a passage from a *philosopher*, Aristotle, and ends with remarks on the use of the terms δίκη and κέρδος in the Greek *tragic poets*, notably Euripides.[54] The passage in which Horace makes his appearance is particularly instructive:

Thus Horace shows no understanding of the philosophy of treasure-accumulation when he says (*Sermones*, Book II, Satire 3): 'A man who buys a quantity of lutes and heaps them up, knowing nothing

---

[53] *MEW* XIII, 11. It would not be appropriate in this context to translate 'ogni sospetto' as 'all mistrust', for mistrust was Marx's habitual attitude in the face of the writings of other economists and historians. I have therefore adopted John Ciardi's suggestion in *The Inferno. A Verse Rendering for the Modern Reader* (New York, 1954), p. 42: 'all division of spirit'.

[54] *MEW* XIII, 114–15.

of lute-playing, nothing of the Muses' art; or one who buys awls and lasts without being a shoemaker, sails without being a trader—such a man would rightly be thought, by the world, bereft of sense and reason. How, then, does such a man differ from one who buries silver and gold in his chest without knowing how to make use of his treasures, who treats them as though they were sacred and dares not touch them?' Mr Senior understands such things better . . .[55]

Horace, the reader is to suppose, could not have had the social experience of Nassau Senior, or H. F. von Storch, from whose economic analyses of accumulation Marx goes on to quote; yet Horace had much greater insight than these bourgeois scholars of a later day into absurdities of economic behaviour. Horace's words thus convey, in Marx's ironic note, not only information about past attitudes, but also correctives for the absurdities and inhumanities of the present.

A sentence from Peter Martyr Anghiera's *De orbe novo* (1530), quoted by Prescott in his *History of the Conquest of Mexico*, is made to perform a similar function.[56]

In the *Critique* of 1859 Marx also experiments with literary analogies. How could he convey to educated readers his sense of the insipidity of political economists who vulgarized the work of Adam Smith, together with his equally strong sense that such vulgarizers had acquired a reputation quite unwarranted by the quality of their thinking? Perhaps an analogy from literary history might help him perform this task adequately and concisely:

[Smith's] *vulgarisateur*, the insipid J. B. Say, whom the French named a *prince de la science* with the same right that Johann Christoph Gottsched named Schönaich a Homer or Pietro Aretino named himself *terror principum* and *lux mundi* . . .[57]

The nineteenth century's oblivion of Schönaich and its devaluation of Aretino are contrasted with those authors' reputation among their contemporaries, and with their self-estimate. The reader is thus prepared for a new perspective on the work of Jean Baptiste Say and enabled to predict the crumbling of Say's reputation under the combined onslaught of criticism and time.

Characters created by the great writers of the past are introduced into the *Critique* in three different ways. The first is the most straightforward: the father in Pushkin's *Eugene Onegin* is

---

[55] *MEW* XIII, 111.   [56] *MEW* XIII, 130.   [57] *MEW* XIII, 143.

regarded as the spokesman of economic views as yet unen-
lightened by Adam Smith:

> In his heroic poem Puskhin makes the hero's father fail to under-
> stand that commodities are money. The Russians have always
> understood, however, that money is a commodity . . .[58]

The second way is more oblique:

> Seller and buyer become creditor and debtor. Where the commod-
> ity-owner played a somewhat comic part as guardian of his treasure,
> he now becomes terrifying as he sees not himself but his neighbour
> in the guise of a sum of money, as he makes not himself but his
> neighbour the martyr of exchange-value. From a credulous be-
> liever he turns into a creditor, from religion he falls into juris-
> prudence: 'I stay there on my bond!'[59]

Shylock is here summoned up, through a quotation from *The
Merchant of Venice*, not only as a symbol of inhuman economic
behaviour, but also as an illustration of how nearly allied the
comic and the terrifying may be in men possessed by the rage
to accumulate. This clearly goes part of the way—though only
a small part—towards an account of Shakespeare's achievement
and possible intention. The contrasting 'inverted' use, which we
have seen to be so characteristic of Marx, is illustrated in the
Critique by an earlier reference to Chamisso's famous novella
Peter Schlemihl:

> It appears, therefore, as if the token of value represented the value
> of commodities *directly*, since it presents itself, not as a token of gold,
> but as a token of the exchange-value which is expressed in the price
> but which is actually present only in the commodity. This appear-
> ance is, however, deceptive. The token of value is *directly* a token only
> of price, and therefore of gold; only indirectly is it a token of the
> commodity's value. Gold has not sold its shadow, like Peter Schle-
> mihl; instead, it buys with its shadow.[60]

Peter Schlemihl, in Chamisso's tale, sold his shadow for gold,
but refused to sell his immortal soul. Here, by deliberate contrast, Marx shows us something soulless, gold, using its 'shadow'
(money as *Wertzeichen*, as token of value) to buy what men have
made or harvested. Which, we are meant to ask ourselves, is

[58] *MEW* XIII, 151.
[59] *MEW* XIII, 117; cf. *The Merchant of Venice*, IV. i.
[60] *MEW* XIII, 95.

more uncanny, which is more diabolic—Chamisso's Romantic original, or its economic variation? Marx has thus found a powerful way of conveying his sense of alienation, perversion, and inhumanity through what one might be tempted to call a 'meta-literature'; through varying and inverting the characters and incidents invented by earlier writers and using them— effectively—in ways their creators could never have foreseen.

Overtly, of course, *Towards a Critique of Political Economy* is not concerned with aesthetic values at all; it is concerned with com- modities and money, and the glimpses of art we are allowed in that context are made deliberately, and often amusingly, strange:

> Thus a volume of Propertius and eight ounces of snuff may have the same exchange-value despite the different use-value of tobacco and elegies . . . The exchange-value of a palace can be expressed in a definite quantity of boot-blacking. Conversely, London blacking manufacturers have expressed the exchange-value of their multi- plied tins in palaces.[61]

Such passages invite the reader to hold his own experience of Propertius against his own experience of snuff and feel the absurdity, the inhumanity, of any purely quantitative approach. The world of literature and art thus constitutes an implicit criticism of a world in which exchange-value—and, *a fortiori*, money-value—is the only value that counts.

And here we must remember the crucial insight of Mikhail Lifshits, who has shown that many of the terms and categories employed in Marx's economic works are, in fact, aesthetic in character. 'The issue of art', Terry Eagleton has rightly said, 'far from being a mere side-interest or embellishment . . . appears as a subordinate but significant factor in Marx's under- standing of social production, the division of labour and the product as commodity; its influence can be traced in the development of the concepts of fetishism, sensuousness and abstraction.'[62] It should therefore not surprise us to find in *Towards a Critique of Political Economy* one of Marx's rare remarks on the origins of the aesthetic sense and aesthetic 'use-value'. He elaborates here on reflections already introduced into the

---

[61] *MEW* XIII, 16.
[62] M. Lifshits, *The Philosophy of Art of Karl Marx*, p. 8 (Preface by Terry Eagleton).

Paris Manuscripts of 1844, reflections on the way different men will look at precious stones either as a commodity to be bought and sold or as an aesthetically pleasing adornment. *Towards a Critique of Political Economy* returns to this same point:

The great importance of metals in general in the direct process of production is connected with the part they play as instruments of production. Apart from their scarcity, the great softness of gold and silver, when compared with iron and even with copper (in the hardened state in which it was used by the ancients) makes them unfit for application to such purposes and therefore deprives them, in large measure, of that property on which the general use-value of metals is based. Useless as they are in the direct process of production, they are easily dispensed with as means of existence, as articles of consumption. For that reason any desired quantity of them can be absorbed into the social process of circulation without disturbing the processes of direct production and consumption. Their individual use-value does not come into conflict with their economic function. On the other hand, however, gold and silver are not just negatively superfluous, i.e. dispensable articles; their aesthetic properties make them the natural material of luxury, ornamentation, splendour, festive requirements, in short, the positive form of abundance and wealth. They appear, in a way, as pure light brought up from the underworld, since silver reflects all rays of light in their original combination and gold reflects only the colour of highest intensity—red. The sense of colour, however, is the most popular form of the aesthetic sense proper. Jacob Grimm, in his *History of the German Language*, has demonstrated the etymological connection between the names of the precious metals and colour-relationships in the different Indo-Germanic languages.[63]

The point Marx here makes about the derivation of terms for precious metals in the various Indo-European languages gains additional force if we remember how constantly Marx shows himself on guard against etymological tricks in the writings of Stirner, Proudhon, and others: against the trick, above all, of treating disparate things as equatable just because they stand in some real or fancied etymological relation to one another.[64] What the passage from *Towards a Critique of Political Economy* should serve to demonstrate, however, is that in the later economic works, no less than in the more obviously 'humanistic'

[63] *MEW* XIII, 130; *BM* 52–3.
[64] Cf. U. Erckenbrecht, op. cit., pp. 50 ff.

earlier ones, the whole of Marx, with his aesthetic, literary, and linguistic interests, constantly shows itself. His models and metaphors may not always be adequate to the complexities of art or, indeed, to his own deeper insights; but they are clearly animated by his desire to let the whole man move together while impelling his world towards a social order which would deny no man the chance to have his life enriched by aesthetic experience.

12 · Capital

'The realm of freedom truly begins only where
labour determined by necessity and mundane considerations ceases; in the very nature of things,
therefore, it lies beyond the sphere of actual
material production.'

(K III—MEW XXV, 828)

AFTER 1862 Marx's regular work as a journalist comes to
an end. Though he was never to be entirely free of money-
troubles, and though he still recorded as many crises in his own
economic affairs as in those of Europe, his financial position
improved in the course of the 1860s, thanks to some small
legacies and to Engels's generously increased support, and he
felt able to devote himself fully and wholeheartedly to his
economic studies until he was drawn—once again—into practical politics. The Working Men's International Association
was founded in 1864; Marx became a member of its central
council, wrote its inaugural address and provisional statutes,
and guided its fortunes until, in 1872, as a tactical move to
prevent further internal dissension, he had its headquarters
transferred to New York. The Council-meetings which he
attended regularly, and constant struggles against influences on
the international workers' movement which he thought pernicious, took a great deal of his energy and time, though his
renewed experience of practical politics also spurred him on to
greater efforts to complete his fundamental work on economic
theory. David McLellan has given an admirably concise account of the progress of that work:

At the time of writing the *Grundrisse*, Marx had thought of dividing
his *Economics* into six volumes, the first of which was to be entitled
Capital. The *Critique of Political Economy* published in 1859 was the
first instalment of this volume and was to be completed by a section

on 'Capital in General'. Marx's work on this section was interrupted
in 1860 by his dispute with Karl Vogt, and when Marx started to
work on it in 1861–3 he found—as usual—that he had produced an
enormous manuscript (around 3,000 printed pages) that was quite
unpublishable. Most of this manuscript was historical and dealt with
past theories of value; it was eventually published by Kautsky in
1905 under the title *Theories of Surplus Value*, as the fourth volume
of *Capital*. From 1863 onwards Marx was working directly on the
three books of *Capital* eventually published. Volume III was written
mainly from 1863 to 1865, thus before the final drafting of Volume I.
As for the manuscripts of Volume II, Marx worked on them both
before and after the final drafting of Volume I. Thus although
Volume I was completed, it was intended to be followed by Volumes
II and III which remained incomplete both in content and form;
and the whole was to be followed by further volumes.

The only part of this immense task that Marx managed to
complete in his lifetime [was] Volume I of *Capital*.[1]

It is clear, then, that much of the material edited by Engels
and Kautsky as *Capital* II and III and *Theories of Surplus Value*
antedates that which Marx himself published, in 1867, as
Capital I; though he continued to work on the as yet unpublished
material right up to the time of his death. This chapter will
therefore look briefly at *Capital* II and III and *Theories of Surplus
Value* before examining the role of literature in that first volume
of *Capital* of which Marx saw two German editions and one
French edition through the press and which has become one of
the most influential books in world history.

(i)

Capital III repeats a warning already sounded, more obliquely,
in *Towards a Critique of Political Economy*: 'We do not speak of
work which falls wholly into the domain of art, since that is,
by the nature of things, not part of our theme.'[2] Overtly, then,
these writings concern themselves with literature and the arts

---

[1] D. McLellan, *The Thought of Karl Marx*, pp. 84–5; cf. the same author's
Karl Marx. His Life and Thought (London, 1973), p. 422: 'Thus the manuscripts
for Volume Three of *Capital* remained virtually in the state in which they had been
since 1864–65. Marx had rewritten almost half of Volume Two in 1870, but there-
after made only minor additions and revisions—realising, as he said to Eleanor
shortly before his death, that it would be up to Engels "to make something of it".'
[2] *K* III—*MEW* XXV, 768.

only in so far as they touch directly on economic questions or enter into the economic sphere as commodities. The projected chapter VI of *Capital* I, which Marx did not, in the event, include in the volume published during his lifetime, speaks of literature and other fine arts as a 'non-material production' which none the less results in commodities and which therefore constitutes a 'transitional form':

It results in commodities which exist apart from the producer and therefore circulate in the interval between production and consumption—as books, paintings, all products of art which are distinct from the actual activity of the artist. Where they do not have journey-man-helpers (like sculptors etc.) or work independently, such people usually work for an entrepreneur's capital—for those engaged in the book-trade, for instance. This relationship constitutes a transitional form even in respect of a mode of production which is only formally capitalist. That the exploitation of labour is at its highest in precisely these transitional forms does not alter the case.[3]

The activities of publishers, printers, book-exporters, theatre-managers, actors, theatre-producers and artists' managers therefore enter, at various points, into Marx's analysis of 'productive' and 'unproductive' labour.

And so, of course, does the activity of authors. Here Marx agrees with Adam Smith's unsentimental constatation that in the capitalist system a writer can be called a 'productive' worker 'not in so far as he produces ideas, but in so far as he enriches the book-seller who publishes his works, or in so far as he is the wage-labourer of a capitalist entrepreneur'.[4] The product of science, scholarship, or any kind of mental labour, Marx maintains, 'always sells at a price far below its value, because the labour-time necessary to reproduce it stands in no sort of relation to the labour-time necessary to produce it in the first instance. The binomial theory, for example, can be learnt by a schoolboy in an hour.'[5] How this may apply to literature Marx explains in a passage which transfers the 'silk-worm'

---

[3] Karl Marx, *Resultate des unmittelbaren Produktionsprozesses* [= *Das Kapital* I: Der Produktionsprozeß des Kapitals. VI. Kapitel], Archiv sozialistischer Literatur, Verlag Neue Kritik (Frankfurt, 1969, 2nd edn., 1970), p. 74.

[4] *TM* I—*MEW* XXVI (i), 128.

[5] *TM* I—*MEW* XXVI (i), 329.

image from Goethe's *Torquato Tasso* (see above, p. 160) to an episode from the life of John Milton:

The same sort of work can be 'productive' or 'unproductive'. Milton, for instance, 'who did the *Paradise Lost* for £5', was an 'unproductive' worker. The writer, however, who turns out factory hack-work for his book-seller, is a 'productive worker'. Milton produced *Paradise Lost* for the same reason as that which makes the silk-worm produce silk. It was an activity wholly natural to him. He later sold the product for £5. But the cultural proletarian in Leipzig who churns out books (such as compendia of economics, for instance) under the direction of his book-dealer, is a 'productive worker'; for his product is from the first subordinated to capital and intended only to utilize capital. A singer who sells her singing on her own initiative, is an 'unproductive worker'. But if the same singer is engaged by an entrepreneur who lets her sing to make money for him, then she is a 'productive worker': for then she produces capital.[6]

This is the logic of Adam Smith's definition of 'productive' and 'unproductive', which Marx links with Hegel's 'cunning of reason' (how ubiquitous Hegel is in Marx's work right up to the end!) and wittily extends even to *crime*:

A philosopher produces ideas, a poet poems, a parson sermons, a professor compendia, etc. A criminal produces crime . . . The criminal produces . . . art too, *belles-lettres*, novels, and even tragedies: witness not only Müllner's *Guilt* [*Die Schuld*] and Schiller's *The Robbers*, but also *Oedipus* and *Richard III* . . .[7]

Marx defends Adam Smith's distinction against later theorists who jib at having to think great writers, artists, and thinkers less 'productive' than grub-street hacks. This merely shows, Marx maintains, how completely these later economists have accepted bourgeois over-valuation of 'productivity'; they are slavishly ready 'to portray all functions as serving to produce wealth for [the bourgeoisie]', and to accept 'that the bourgeois world is the best of all possible worlds, that everything in it is useful, and that the bourgeoisie is educated enough to recognize this'. Or again, a few pages earlier: 'These people are so dominated by their fixed bourgeois ideas that they would think

---

[6] *TM* I—*MEW* XXVI (i), 377.   [7] *TM* I—*MEW* XXVI (i), 363-4.

they were insulting Aristotle or Julius Caesar if they called
them "unproductive labourers". Aristotle and Caesar would
have regarded even the title "labourers" an insult.'[8]

The truth is, so Marx believes, that the modern bourgeois
world is not a favourable soil for art: 'Capitalist production',
we read in *Theories of Surplus Value*, 'is inimical to certain kinds
of intellectual production—to art and poetry, for instance.' He
therefore ranges himself with Lessing in holding fast to the heritage of the European Enlightenment yet ridiculing certain of
its cruder preconceptions: notably the notion of continuous
progress in the arts. Nothing is more ridiculous, he tells us,
than to suppose that a generation which has outstripped the
ancients in technological know-how must also be able to produce better poetry. As a result we have Voltaire's *Henriade* to
hold against the *Iliad*.

> Capitalist production is inimical to certain kinds of intellectual
> production—to art and poetry, for instance. [If this is not realized]
> one might fall into that illusion to which the French were prone in
> the eighteenth century and which Lessing ridiculed so beautifully.
> Because we have advanced further than the ancients in mechanics
> etc., why should we not also be able to produce an epic poem?
> And thus [we get] the *Henriade* instead of the *Iliad*![9]

This takes up again, in a new context, the theme which had
engaged Marx's attention at the end of the General Introduction of 1857: that technology is destructive of mythology, and
that without a living mythology no genuine epic poem is
possible.

There is, it must be admitted, something distinctly odd about
Marx's humorous use of the labels 'productive' and 'unproductive' in a literary context. If the distinguishing mark of 'productive labour' is that it serves to increase capital and bring profit

---

[8] *TM* I—*MEW* XXVI (i), 262, 259. Cf. M. Lifshits, *The Philosophy of Art of
Karl Marx*, p. 98: 'Marx subjected to severe criticism all "general, superficial
analogies between intellectual and material production". He ridiculed every attempt to represent artists, men of letters and economists as "productive workers in
Smith's sense" because they allegedly produce "not simply products *sui generis*,
but products of material labour and therefore, directly, wealth". All these attempts
show that "even the highest forms of spiritual production are recognised and
forgiven by the bourgeoisie only because they [= artists, men of letters etc.]
are represented and falsely labelled as indirect producers of material wealth".'

[9] *TM* I—*MEW* XXVI (i), 257.

to the owners of capital,[10] then the fact that Milton only received £5 for *Paradise Lost* proves no more than that he was
himself no capitalist. Publishers and book-dealers have made
a great deal more than £5 out of Milton's works! In the long
run, in fact, the Milton who wrote *Paradise Lost* has proved far
more 'productive' of capital than the Leipzig hacks with whom
Marx contrasts him in *Theories of Surplus Value*. But the general
point Marx is making remains clear enough. The true poet's
labour could remain—in Milton's time at least—unalienated to
the extent that he took no account of market value. Such a poet
writes what he has to, from the centre of his being, and leaves
it to others to convert his poem into a profit-bearing commodity. He thus prefigures that 'realm of freedom' which has
inspired the most eloquent and justly famous passage of
Capital III:

The realm of freedom truly begins only where labour determined by
necessity and mundane considerations ceases; in the very nature
of things, therefore, it lies beyond the sphere of actual material
production. Just as the savage must wrestle with nature to satisfy his
wants, to maintain and reproduce life, so must civilized man, and he
must do so in all social formations and under all possible modes of
production. With his development this realm of physical necessity
expands as a result of his wants; but, at the same time, the forces of
production which satisfy these wants also increase. Freedom in this
domain can only mean that socialized men, the associated producers, regulate their interchange with nature rationally, bringing it
under their common control, instead of being ruled by it as by the
blind forces of nature; and achieving this with the least expenditure
of human energy and under conditions most favourable to, and most
worthy of, their human nature. None the less this still remains a
realm of necessity. Beyond it begins that development of human

[10] 'The goal of capitalist production is not the production of commodities as such,
but profits. In this society labor is productive only to the extent it creates profits
for capital and the capitalists. It follows that in this society dominated by the
bourgeoisie the labor performed by the artist, the writer, the architect *qua* artist
is not (by contrast with the Middle Ages and the Renaissance) regarded as social
labor. What determines the value of works of art is a matter of psychological
chance, the money at the disposal of those who happen to feel a special need for
distraction, amusement, escape. For all that, a theater, for instance, remains an
enterprise in which capital is invested and which is expected to yield profits; the
spectators are offered a sort of "goods" which they consume and pay for with
income derived from over-all production and surplus value.' (Henri Lefebvre,
The Sociology of Marx, pp. 107–8.)

power which is its own end, the true realm of freedom, which, however, can blossom forth only with this realm of necessity as its basis.
The shortening of the working-day is its fundamental premiss.[11]

There is a clear line from Marx's visions of the conquest of
alienation in the Paris Manuscripts of 1844 to this stirring call
for a development of human powers that have not yet had full
play; for the advent of an order in which man will still, it is
true, have to toil to wrest his subsistence from nature and satisfy
his changing needs, but in which he will be liberated, at long
last, from 'commodity fetishism', economic injustice, and de-
bilitating greed.

The society of modern times, Marx believed, had created
vast wealth and an enormous potential for full human development; but it used its powers more to thwart such development
than to advance it. By transforming everything it could into
commodity, *Ware*, it limited and inhibited human responses to
nature and to art. Yet one of the great virtues of art, in Marx's
eyes, was precisely that through its very mode of being it offered
resistance to such 'fetishism'; just as a genuine artist would still,
even under modern conditions, resist transformation into a
wage-slave of the dominant social group. The production of
genuine art, even in unfavourable times, remains significantly
unlike that factory-labour which, as *Capital* tells us, deprives
the worker of his chance 'to enjoy work as the play of his own
mental and physical power'. It retains its affinity, even in the
age of machinery, to that medieval handicraft of which the
Grundrisse had said: 'it is still half artistic; it has its aim in itself'.[12]
That helps to explain why aesthetic categories remain so important in *Capital* as in other of Marx's later works. Literature
and the arts are a token of human capacity for free creation
and enjoyment which gives grounds for high hopes of man's
future.

One passage which is frequently adduced in support of such
claims is Marx's critique, in *Theories of Surplus Value*, of the
economist H. F. von Storch:

Storch, in failing to grasp the *historical* nature of material production—he sees it as production of material goods in general, not as

[11] *K* III—*MEW* XXV, 828; cf. I. Mészáros, *Marx's Theory of Alienation*, p. 216;
and M. Lifshits, op. cit., pp. 115–16.
[12] *BM* 16.

a definite form of production at a specific point in historical development—cuts away from under his own feet the ground on which alone the ideological components of the ruling class on the one hand, and the free intellectual [or mental or spiritual] production of this one given social formation on the other, can be understood. He cannot get beyond miserable generalities.[13]

In thus distinguishing between class-ideology (*die ideologischen Bestandteile der herrschenden Klassen*) and free intellectual production (*die freie geistige Produktion jeder gegebenen Gesellschaftsformation*), Marx, we are told, would seem to be suggesting once again that even amidst the restraints of an uncongenial social order art may constitute a realm of comparative freedom. The point is valid, even though we must recognize that the reading of this passage is in dispute. Marx himself never saw it through the press, and his handwriting is such that the phrase later editors read as 'free intellectual production' (*freie geistige Produktion*) could also be read as 'subtle intellectual production' (*feine geistige Produktion*).[14] In either case, however, the distinction between 'ideological components of the ruling class' and 'freer' or 'subtler' modes offers a welcome corrective to the implied identification of literature and ideology in the Preface of *Towards a Critique of Political Economy*.

Marx also shows his concern, in these later economic works, to dispel simplistic notions about the material 'basis' or 'base' whose importance for the arts he had so starkly stressed in this same Preface. *Theories of Surplus Value* contains his most direct pointer towards the interaction or interplay (*Wechselwirkung*) between material and intellectual production:

To study the connection between intellectual and material production it is necessary, above all, to deal with the latter not as a general category but in a definite historical form. Thus, for example, the kind of intellectual production which corresponds to capitalist methods of production is different from that corresponding to medieval methods of production. If material production itself is not grasped in its specific historical form, it is impossible to understand the concrete nature of the intellectual production corresponding to it and the interaction of both factors.[15]

[13] *TM* I—*MEW* XXVI (i), 257.   [14] *BM* 64.
[15] *TM* I—*MEW* XXVI (i), 256–7.

Capital III stresses even more unequivocally than the passages just quoted the axiom that historical truth is concrete. 'The same economic basis', Marx writes, 'the same, that is, in its principal conditions, can show—because of countless differences in empirical circumstances, natural conditions, racial constellations, historical influences working from outside etc.—an infinite number of variations and gradations in its appearance; and these can only be understood by means of the analysis of such empirically given circumstances.'[16] If vulgar Marxism sometimes makes things easy for itself, it can find little warrant for its simplifications in Marx's own writings.

It is entirely consonant with Marx's hatred of everything which gracefully skates over difficulties instead of facing them squarely, that the familiar denunciations of 'fine writing' in economics and sociology should now recur with new vehemence. 'Insipid belletrism', Marx thunders; 'purely belletristic elaboration, educated twaddle', 'dilettantes who write beautifully'.[17] He also shows himself more than ever hostile to German Romanticism. The theorist Adam Müller rarely appears in these pages without being characterized as a 'Romantic'; Marx's round condemnation of the cloudy mysticism and woolly thinking he finds in Müller's work thus reflects back on to the German Romantic movement as a whole:

Here follows some gibberish by the 'Romantic' Müller . . . It is impossible to cram more hair-raising nonsense into a few lines . . . their content is common prejudice skimmed from the most superficial semblance of things. This false and trivial content must then be 'heightened' and poeticized by a mystifying manner of expression.[18]

Less than ever can Marx now see reality in 'the superficial semblance of things'. The older he grew, the more he came to agree with Hegel and the German idealists that truth lay below the level of immediate empirical perception. It had to be dug for by well-informed men with a gift for theorizing and philosophic reflection, or seized by the intuition of great artists. In

---

[16] *K* III—*MEW* XXV, 800.

[17] *TM* I—*MEW* XXVI (i), 260, 271, 145.

[18] *K* III—*MEW* XXV, 410–11; cf. Marx's detailed critiques of Adam Müller in *Grundrisse*, *G* 413 and 694–5, and in *Towards a Critique of Political Economy*, *MEW* XIII, 56.

this belief, ironically enough, Marx and the German Romantics are at one.

The posthumously published economic works show us Marx once again raiding the Latin classics for phrases that sum up economic realities and attitudes in a memorable way: besides the familiar *fruges consumere nati* Marx now uses Virgil's *vos, non vobis* and Ovid's *materiam superabat opus* as formulations perfectly fitted to express what he himself wants to say.[19] Luther's pamphlets on usury supply models of striking imagery used for polemic purposes ('what a charming image for the capitalist', Marx exclaims at one point, after a long quotation from one of Luther's pamphlets; 'most picturesque—yet at the same time [Luther] has really caught the character of old-fashioned usury, and that of capital as a whole');[20] and the vocabulary, phrasing, rhythms, and characters of Luther's Bible are recalled again and again in Marx's own prose. In Shakespeare's history-plays Marx now finds images of a past that will bring home to nineteenth-century readers what aspects of the present need to be changed. The low wages of agricultural workers, he tells the General Council of the First International in 1865, constitute, when coupled with the English Poor Laws, 'a glorious way to convert the wages labourer into a slave, and Shakespeare's proud yeoman into a pauper'.[21] Schiller's *Wallenstein's Camp* provides two memorable images with which to characterize contemporaries. One of these is, once again, the capuchin preacher who thunders hell-fire and damnation at Wallenstein's soldiers in words Schiller took, in the main, from the sermons of a seventeenth-century divine who called himself Abraham a Santa Clara. The capuchin and his seventeenth-century model serve Marx to convey his attitude to Malthus:

Because the first edition of Malthus's *On Population* contains not a single new scientific word, it is to be regarded purely as an obtrusive capuchin's sermon, an Abraham a Santa Clara vision of the discoveries of Townsend, Steuart, Wallace, Herbert etc. Since in fact it only seeks to impress by its popular form, popular hate rightly turned against it.[22]

---

[19] *TM* I—*MEW* XXVI (i), 146, 197; *TM* II—*MEW* XXVI (ii), 117.
[20] *TM* III—*MEW* XXVI (iii), 525.
[21] *Wages, Price and Profit* (1865)—*SW* II, 72.
[22] *TM* II—*MEW* XXVI (ii), 113–14.

The other character Marx borrows from *Wallenstein's Camp* is a sergeant-major who tries to model himself on his great general, but manages to do so only in externals—he clears his throat and spits exactly like Wallenstein, but has none of Wallenstein's spirit or genius. Marx uses this character as a symbol to describe the relation of Ricardo's followers to David Ricardo himself.[23] Goethe supplies many formulas and snatches of quotation, and Heine's *Disputation* a characteristic Jewish joke.[24] It may well be, moreover, that Marx's witty juxtaposition of religious *belief* and commercial *credit* (*Glauben* and *Kredit*) was inspired by Heine's similar juxtaposition in chapter 7 of *Ideas. The Book of LeGrand.*[25]

Nor is it only the great writers who are used in this way. Nathaniel Lee's *The Rival Queens* supplies a tag Marx had probably picked up without ever having read the play in which it occurs: 'When Greek meets Greek, then comes the tug of war';[26] from Tom Taylor's *Our American Cousins* he takes the figure of an addle-pated aristocrat, Lord Dundreary, with whom he insists on comparing Malthus;[27] and Fritz Reuter's Low German novels yield the character of Inspector Bräsig, who allows Marx to caricature effectively the circular thought-processes and 'demonstrations' of dull-witted economists: 'Now we know one source of the capitalists' increase in wealth. It all comes down to Inspector Bräsig's secret: that great poverty derives from *la grande pauvreté*.'[28] Fritz Reuter here helps Marx to drive home the charge he constantly levels at 'belletrists' and 'literati' who have ventured into economics: they 'resolve' questions with purely linguistic tricks; they are long on words but short on logic.[29]

As has already been seen, William Cobbett inevitably appears to less advantage in these economic works than in Marx's newspaper articles on political affairs; for Cobbett's backward-looking economics, especially his total rejection of paper-money, could only make Marx smile. He continued, however, to quote Cobbett with approval, to commend at once his political insights and his forthright mode of expression. He loves him as

[23] *TM* III—*MEW* XXVI (iii), 171.   [24] *K* III—*MEW* XXV, 555.
[25] *TM* III—*MEW* XXVI (iii), 442.   [26] *K* II—*MEW* XXIV, 131.
[27] *TM* III—*MEW* XXVI (iii), 31.   [28] *K* II—*MEW* XXIV, 477.
[29] e.g. *MEW* XXVI (iii), 83–4, 86, 113, 134, 145 (*TM* III).

a true man of the people, and plays him off, in characteristic parentheses, against remote and ineffectual dons like W. G. F. Roscher of Leipzig University:

The hatred the English working class felt against Malthus—the *mountebank parson* as Cobbett rudely calls him (Cobbett, it is true, is the greatest political writer England produced in this century; but he lacked the education of a Leipzig professor and was the avowed enemy of 'learned languages')—is therefore wholly justified . . .[30]

Marx's conviction that great writers can have insights transcending their conscious convictions or attitudes becomes more and more obvious from the authorities he quotes. The clearest case is that of the conservative, royalist Balzac, for whose profound understanding of social realities Marx had the deepest admiration:

In his last novel *The Peasants* [*Les Paysans*], Balzac—who is altogether distinguished by his deep understanding of real conditions— depicts, with striking exactitude, how the small farmer, in order to keep his usurous creditor well disposed towards him, performs all sorts of services for that creditor and thinks he is not giving anything away because his labour costs him no cash. The usurer, for his part, kills two birds with one stone. He saves expenditure on wages and enmeshes the farmer, who is driven deeper and deeper into ruin by the withdrawal of labour from his own field, ever more inextricably in the spider's web of usury.[31]

Marx clearly delights in seeing his findings confirmed by the insights of a great novelist whose consciously held philosophy of life differed, in essential respects, from his own. How much deeper, he thought, the understanding of Balzac could delve than that of a modish author like Paul de Kock!

One of Paul de Kock's savants tells me that I cannot live without buying trousers, just as I cannot live without buying bread, and that I cannot, therefore, enrich myself without buying trousers, that the purchase of trousers is thus an indirect means, or at least a condition, of my enrichment in the same way as the circulation of my blood or the process of my breathing. But in themselves neither the circulation of my blood nor my breathing make me any richer . . .[32]

---

[30] *TM* II—*MEW* XXVI (ii), 113. For a cooler view of Cobbett see *MEW* XXIII, 784.

[31] *K* III—*MEW* XXV, 49.   [32] *TM* I—*MEW* XXVI (i), 378.

We know that Marx himself devoured Paul de Kock's novels in his leisure-hours;[33] he clearly found them useful as well as entertaining, for they mirrored the confusions of the readers who so eagerly bought them and to whose requirements they were tailored.

The great writers of the past appear, in these economic critiques, in one other characteristic context: the very mention of their names may help to 'place', and thus to diminish, the little writers of a later age. Thomas Hodgskin and other economists who stress 'the importance of past work in commodities as present *energeia*' are mockingly called 'Pindars of Capital'; and Professor W. G. F. Roscher, who had been rash enough to mention Thucydides in the Preface to his *Foundations of Political Economy* (*Die Grundlagen der Nationalökonomie*, 3rd edn. (Augsburg, 1858)) constantly appears, in *Theories of Surplus Value*, as 'Wilhelm *Thucydides* Roscher'.[34]

In his economic studies Marx follows Mandeville as well as Hegel in seeing *evil* as one of the mothers of the arts. We have already seen (p. 310 above) the beginning of this argument, Marx's witty disquisition on the 'productive' nature of crime; here is its culmination, which starts, characteristically, with a reference to the Bible:

Leaving the sphere of private crime, would there be a world market, would nations themselves exist, if there had not been national crimes? Is not the tree of evil also the tree of knowledge, since the time of Adam?

In his *Fable of the Bees* (1708) Mandeville already demonstrated the productivity of all the English occupations, and anticipated our argument: 'What we call Evil in this World, Moral as well as Natural, is the grand Principle that makes us sociable Creatures, the solid Basis, the Life and Support of all Trades and Employments without Exception: That there we must look for the true Original of all Arts and Sciences, and that the Moment Evil ceases, the Society must be spoiled if not totally dissolved.'

Mandeville simply had the merit of being infinitely more audacious and more honest than . . . narrow-minded apologists for bourgeois society.[35]

33 *METEC* 26 (Paul Lafargue).
34 *TM* III—*MEW* XXVI (iii), 271, 492–3 *et passim*.
35 *TM* I—*MEW* XXVI (i), 364 (*BR* 168).

Mandeville has here helped Marx to his fullest description of
the way Hegel's 'cunning of reason' may be thought to operate
in the cultural sphere.

One last lapidary sentence from *Theories of Surplus Value* deserves quotation in our present context. 'The man who seeks to
accommodate science not to standards derived from itself
(however much in error it might be) but from the outside,
from a point of view dictated by external interest foreign to
that science—such a man I call vulgar and common [*gemein*].'[36]
This accusation is flung at Malthus in the context of political
economy; but it has clear implications for Marx's literary
theory and criticism. Indeed, the contrast he draws between
Malthus's alleged 'sin against science' and the 'disinterested-
ness', 'scientific honesty', and 'scientific impartiality' he thinks
characteristic of Ricardo, bears a striking resemblance to his
implied contrast between Eugène Sue's subservience to the
prejudices of his bourgeois readership and the realistic impartiality Marx finds to be characteristic of Balzac.

(ii)

While he was writing *Capital*, Marx came to appreciate more
and more that the practice of sending parts of a work to the
printer while the rest was as yet unwritten—a practice described by Jacob Grimm in his *History of the German Language*
and necessarily adopted in bringing out his monumental dictionary—was not one that suited *him*. He wanted his works to
appear before their public as artistic wholes. 'Whatever shortcomings they may have', he therefore told Engels on 31 July
1865, 'the merit of my writings is that they are an artistic
whole, and that can only be attained by my method of never
having them printed until they lie before me as a whole. This
is impossible with the Jacob Grimm method, which is in general
more suited to works not dialectically constructed.'[37] It was not
given to him, however, to present all of *Capital* in this way;
only Volume I appeared in his own lifetime and in his own
final redaction.

In this one volume of *Capital* which Marx himself saw
through the press the fascination literature never ceased to

[36] *TM* II—*MEW* XXVI (ii), 112.   [37] *MEW* XXXI, 131 ff.

exert on him is evident on page after page. Here is a typical passage:

But original sin is at work everywhere. As capitalist modes of production, accumulation, and wealth develop, the capitalist ceases to be the mere incarnation of capital. He feels 'human stirrings of sympathy' [*ein 'menschliches Rühren'*] for his own Adam; and he acquires enough education to smile at the passion for asceticism as the mere prejudice of the old-fashioned miser. While the capitalist of the classical type brands individual consumption as a sin against his function and as 'abstinence' from accumulating, the modern capitalist is capable of seeing accumulation as a 'renouncing' of the impetus that drives him to enjoyment. 'Two souls, alas, reside within his breast/And each withdraws from, and repels, the other.'[38]

The passage begins, like so many others in Marx's economic works, with a theological phrase. This fulfils three main functions: (*a*) to point to a connection between 'religion and the rise of capitalism' which later sociologists and economists, notably Max Weber, Ernst Troeltsch, and R. H. Tawney, were to analyse in greater detail; (*b*) to convey Marx's feeling, shared with Heine and often expressed directly as well as indirectly, that in the modern world Money had moved into the place of God; and (*c*) to introduce a sense of incongruity, to remind men of values to which they paid lip-service but which they disregarded in practice. He likes to remind his readers that Christ drove the money-changers out of the temple; quotes with relish from Revelation 13: 17: 'And that no man might buy or sell, save he that had the mark, or the name of the beast, or the number of his name'; and frequently parodies biblical injunctions: 'Accumulate, accumulate! That is Moses and the prophets!'[39] But the passage we are considering is not content with recalling the Bible and the theology built upon it. It also quotes from Schiller's ballad *The Pledge* (*Die Bürgschaft*) and from Goethe's *Faust*. Schiller's ballad tells the story of Damon and Pythias; and the line to which Marx alludes comes from the climax of that story in which the tyrant Dionysius, struck with the fidelity of the two friends, remits Damon's punishment and entreats them to permit him to share their friendship. The allusion to the tyrant's 'human stirrings' of sympathy once again has a threefold effect in Marx's context: it suggests

that capitalists are tyrants; it holds the ancient tyrant's sudden
sympathy with *others* against the modern tyrants' sympathy
with *their own* old Adam; and it suggests the veneer of culture
which education has bestowed on wealthy citizens, who can
now quote their Schiller with the best of them and stylize their
selfishness accordingly. This last function is fulfilled by other
Schiller quotations in *Capital* I:

The great beauty of capitalist production consists in this: that it not
only constantly reproduces the wage-labourer as wage-labourer,
but also produces, always, a surplus population of wage-labourers
relative to the accumulation of capital. Thus the law of supply and
demand of labour is regulated along the right lines, the oscillation
of labour is kept within limits satisfactory to capitalist exploitation
and, lastly, the social dependence of the labourer on the capitalist—
that indispensable requisite!—is secured; an unmistakable relation
of dependence which mealy-mouthed political economists can
deceitfully transform, at home, in the motherland, into one of free
contract between buyer and seller, between equally independent
owners of commodities: the owner of the commodity 'capital' and
the owner of the commodity 'labour'. But in the colonies that fair
illusion tears asunder.[40]

Aber in den Kolonien reißt der schöne Wahn entzwei—the reference,
here, is to what was in the nineteenth century the most popular
of all Schiller's ballads, 'The Bell' (*Die Glocke*). Schiller's lines
refer to the wedding-night and the supersession of passion by
love:

> Mit dem Gürtel, mit dem Schleier
> Reißt der schöne Wahn entzwei.

> With girdle and veil
> The fair illusion tears asunder.

The fun in this quotation is to recognize the *unexpected* parallel,
the startling implications of juxtaposing behaviour in the
colonies with the sensations of the wedding-night. But there is
a serious point too; for the image of removing or tearing a veil
is a central one in Marx's mature work. It occurs elsewhere in
Capital I:

Great industry tore the veil which concealed from men the produc-
tion-processes of their own society;[41]

---

[40] *K* I—*MEW* XXIII, 796-7.   [41] *K* I—*MEW* XXIII, 510.

it occurs in Marx's *Mathematical Manuscripts*:

It is important here as elsewhere to tear the veil of mystery away from science;[42]

and it frequently occurs in other works, always with the implication that something hidden from the sight of the uninitiated is, at last, being revealed.

Marx frequently achieves such complex effects through allusions to popular classics. His description of the processes of appropriation, in *Capital* I, is another instance:

Commodities are things and cannot, therefore, resist men. If they be not willing, he can use force [*wenn sie nicht willig, kann er Gewalt brauchen*], in other words, he can take them.[43]

Once again Marx here recalls lines that no German reader could fail to recognize: lines from Goethe's eerie ballad 'The Erl-King' (*Erlkönig*) in which an uncanny, elfin spirit, threatens a feverish child:

> „Ich liebe dich, mich reizt deine schöne Gestalt,
> Und bist du nicht willig, so brauch ich Gewalt."

> 'I love you, your fair form allures me,
> And if you are not willing, I shall use force!'

As the original context of Marx's quotation flashes before us, we have a momentary vision of men themselves, in their rage to appropriate and accumulate, becoming uncanny beings like the Erl-King. But here the differences are, of course, as important as the parallel: commodities are made by and for men, men have a right to seize them . . . it only depends which men seize what, how they seize it, and when . . .

The passage with which we began (see above, p. 321) culminates in two lines from Goethe's *Faust*. These, Marx could again assume, would be known in their original context by most of his German readers; between their original context and their new one an interesting counterpoint might, therefore, be set up. The spiritual and intellectual impulsion to higher things represented by one of the two 'souls' of which Faust speaks contrasts starkly with the drive to enjoyment that

---

[42] Karl Marx, *Mathematische Manuskripte* (Moscow, 1968), p. 192.
[43] *K* I—*MEW* XXIII, 99.

parallels it in the world of the new capitalist so mercilessly scrutinized by Marx. Earlier quotations from Goethe had prepared this effect. Some lines from the *West–Eastern Divan*, for instance, which Marx had once appropriated to convey his sense of Hegel's 'cunning of reason' (see above, p. 248), are used in *Capital* I to characterize the heartlessness of unchecked capitalism:

Capital is reckless of the health or length of life of the worker, unless under compulsion from society. To the outcry about physical and mental stunting and crippling, about premature death, about the torture of over-work, it answers: 'Should this torture then torment us/Since it brings us greater pleasure?'[44]

'For *pleasure*', Marx adds, underlining the contrast within the parallel, 'read *profit*'. One might also cite that passage near the opening of *Capital* I in which Marx ironically likens the man who possesses marketable goods with Faust struggling to translate the opening of St. John's gospel. 'In their difficulty our commodity-owners think like Faust: "In the beginning was the Deed." They therefore acted and transacted even before they thought. Instinctively they conformed to the laws imposed by the nature of commodities.'[45] Here too contrast is important; but Faust's transformation of the Gospel's 'In the beginning was the Word' to 'In the beginning was the Deed' was always questionable, and it now looks doubly questionable in Marx's context.

One quotation from *Faust* which Marx carried over into *Capital* I from *Grundrisse* and which he also used in the notes for *Capital* III is of particular interest:

What used to be the activity of the living worker becomes that of the machine. Thus the appropriation of his labour by capital confronts the worker in a brutal fashion obvious to his senses: capital assimilates labour into itself 'as though it had love in its body' [*als hätt' es Lieb' im Leibe*].

In capital that bears interest the movement of capital has been abbreviated to the fullest extent; the mediating process has been omitted, and a capital of 1,000 becomes a thing which is $1,000^2$ in itself and is transformed, after a time, into 1,100, just as after

---

[44] *K* I—*MEW* XXIII, 285–6; cf. Goethe's *An Suleika* in *West–östlicher Divan* (Buch des Timur).

[45] *K* I—*MEW* XXIII, 101.

a certain period wine kept in a cellar improves its use-value. Capital is now a thing, but as a thing it is capital. Money now has love in its body [*Das Geld hat jetzt Lieb' im Leibe*].

By turning his money into commodities that serve as the material elements of a new product, or as factors in the labour-process, by incorporating living labour-power into their dead substance, the capitalist converts value—past, materialized, dead labour—into capital, into value big with value, a monster that has life breathed into it and begins to 'work' as if it had love in its body [*als hätt' es Lieb' im Leibe*].[46]

In all these passages the primary suggestion is clear: there is something obscene about reification, about money drawing living workers to itself and assimilating them to machines, or about money breeding money as though love were 'at work' in its body—either as sexual congress or as the child which is the fruit of such activity. The disgust is increased, however, and veiled threat is conveyed, if we remember the context of the line 'Als hätte sie Lieb' im Leibe' in *Faust*: for there the line refers to a *poisoned rat* that rages through the house, driven up and down by the poison working in its body, until it falls dead in the kitchen. And this song about the dying rat serves as a signal, in *Faust* Part I, for the entrance of the self-styled 'lord of rats and mice', Mephistopheles, who then dominates the scene and sings his own Song of the Triumphant Flea to cap Brander's Song of the Defeated Rat.

The majority of the quotations from *Faust* which enliven *Capital* I derive, in fact, from the speeches of Mephistopheles, or have some direct connection with that diabolic character. The writings of Proudhon and his disciples bring to Marx's mind Mephistopheles' ironic advice to a student:

> . . . wo Begriffe fehlen
> Da stellt ein Wort zur rechten Zeit sich ein.

> Where concepts are lacking
> A *word* will come to you at the right time.

A few pages later a table, an ordinary object perceived by the senses, is transformed—as commodity—into a 'sensual-supra-sensual' object. *Ein sinnlich übersinnliches Ding*: the conjunction

[46] *G* 592; *K* III—*MEW* XXV, 406; *K* I—*MEW* XXIII, 209.

is once again that of Mephistopheles, admonishing Faust for not
seizing his opportunities with Gretchen in the right spirit:

> Du übersinnlicher, sinnlicher Freier,
> Ein Mägdelein nasführet dich!

> You suprasensual, sensual wooer—
> A slip of a girl leads you by the nose!

Other instances abound. 'Our capitalist has had prevision of
the case that makes him laugh'—the phrase recalls Faust's
words about the first appearance of Mephistopheles in his study,
when the latter turns from a poodle into a travelling scholar:

> Das also war des Pudels Kern!
> Ein fahrender Skolast! Der Casus macht mich lachen!

> So that's what was hidden in the poodle!
> A travelling scholar! The *casus* makes me laugh.

Or again reverting to Mephistopheles' own words, near the end
of *Capital* I:

In fact, the misery of Ireland is once more the topic of the day in
England. At the end of 1866 and the beginning of 1867, one of the
Irish land magnates, Lord Dufferin, set about its solution in *The
Times*. 'How human of so great a lord!'[47]

'*Wie menschlich von solch großem Herrn*'—Marx's inverted commas
signal yet another reference to *Faust*: to Mephistopheles' words
about a greater 'Lord' than Lord Dufferin:

> Von Zeit zu Zeit seh' ich den Alten gern,
> Und hüte mich, mit ihm zu brechen.
> Es ist gar hübsch von einem großen Herrn,
> So menschlich mit dem Teufel selbst zu sprechen.

> I like to see the Governor now and then
> And take good care to keep relations civil.
> It's decent in the first of gentlemen
> To speak so humanly to the very devil.[48]

Mephistopheles, then, is a presence that looms large in
Capital I. Here one should remember that Hegel, in two works

---

[47] *K* I—*MEW* XXIII, 83, 85, 208, 737.
[48] *Faust* Part I ('Prolog im Himmel'). The translation is that of Philip Wayne.

of seminal importance for Marx's thought, had also quoted
Mephistopheles and called him 'a good authority'.[49] Above all,
there springs to mind one of Liebknecht's reminiscences of days
he spent with Marx and his family in London:

When he was in really high spirits, he would do us Seydelmann as
Mephistopheles. For [the actor Carl] Seydelmann, whom he had
seen and heard as a student in Berlin, he had a real passion, and
Faust was the work he liked best in the whole of German literature.
I cannot say that Marx recited well—he overacted grossly—but he
never missed the point of a quotation, he always expressed its sense
correctly; in short, he was effective, and the comic impression left
by his first violently declaimed words faded as soon as it became
obvious how deeply he had penetrated into the spirit of the part,
how fully he had grasped it and how thoroughly he knew it.[50]

Goethe's complex Mephistopheles is, among other things, a
spirit who exposes pretensions, who looks at the underside of
life, who points to rottenness that deserves to go under, who
mocks at grand gestures and fine words. No wonder that Marx
—ever aware, like the Lord in Goethe's 'Prologue in Heaven',
of the power of the negative to spur men to positive action—so
often speaks with Mephistopheles' voice.

Another literary figure that haunts the pages of *Capital* is,
once again, Shylock. Part of what he signifies had already been
suggested in *Towards a Critique of Political Economy* (see above,
p. 303): the inhumanity of money-transactions protected by
law; the mingling of the absurd and the horrible characteristic
of a world in which money has taken the place of God. It is
not surprising, therefore, that in *Capital* I capital itself takes
on the likeness and speaks with the very voice of Shylock. When
the question of child-labour in factories came up, Marx tells
us, and it turned out that there were no regulations forbidding
children to work, without interruption, from 2 until 8.30 p.m.,

Workmen and factory-inspectors protested on hygienic and moral
grounds, but Capital answered:

'My deeds upon my head! I crave the law,
The penalty and forfeit of my bond.'

[49] In the Preface to his *Philosophy of Right*, and in the *Phenomenology of the Spirit*,
C, AA, v, B. Hegel rarely quotes from a work of literature without garbling it
hideously; his quotations from Goethe are no exception.

[50] *ÜKL* I, 27–8.

Capital is then made to demand, not only that children drudge
from 2 until 8.30 p.m., but that they do so without the distraction of eating; and again it speaks with the voice of Shylock:

> 'Ay, his heart;
> So says the bond.'

Only then, after these unidentified quotations from the trial
scene of *The Merchant of Venice*, does Marx speak, explicitly, of
the British capitalist's 'Shylock-like clinging to the law of 1844'.[51]
Nor is Shylock only to be found among factory-owners; the
countryside too, we learn, holds 'aristocratic Shylocks' who
'pharisaically shrug their shoulders at building-speculators,
small landlords and "open" villages'.[52] Marx clearly takes a
malicious pleasure, once again, in charging High-Church aristo-
crats and Methodist or Quaker factory-owners with the vices
Shakespeare embodied in his Jew.

That point, we know, Marx had already made in his early
essay 'On the Jewish Question', where the all too prevalent
equation of Jewishness with money-grubbing and commercialism among men of any creed or race had been taken over
without qualification; where Marx had shown himself determined to ignore not only the deeper and truer spirit of Judaism,
but also the extent to which his own attitudes and arguments
embodied, and transmitted, the heritage of the Jewish prophets
and their Talmudic commentators. It is not surprising, therefore, that in *Capital* I it is the *exploiters* who speak with the voice
of Shylock. To this there is, however, one significant exception.
The technical necessities of modern industry, Marx explains,
and the social character inherent in its capitalistic form, stand
in a contradictory relationship which 'dispels all stability, repose, and security from the labourer's situation; . . . it constantly threatens to snatch his means of subsistence out of his
hands by taking away the very instruments he needs to work
with'; and he adds, in a footnote:

> 'You take my life
> When you do take the means whereby I live.'[53]

Here, for once, it is the *oppressed* who are made to speak with
the voice of Shylock; and consciously or unconsciously Marx

[51] *K* I—*MEW* XXIII, 304.   [52] *K* I—*MEW* XXIII, 713.
[53] *K* I—*MEW* XXIII, 511.

suggests a deeper, truer view of that complex figure than we might have expected from earlier identifications of Shylock with legalistic and bloody-minded exploiters.

Marx also quotes, once again, from Act IV, Scene iii, of Shakespeare's *Timon of Athens*, using Timon's speech on money as the 'common whore of mankind' to illustrate his contention that money is a radical leveller: 'Just as every qualitative difference between commodities is extinguished in money, so money, on its side, like the radical leveller that it is, does away with all distinctions.'[54] As in the Paris Manuscripts, where the same passage is quoted, Marx takes no account of the context of the passage in Shakespeare's play or the reliability of its speaker; nor is it relevant to his purpose to consider how far Timon utters views that were commonplaces in Shakespeare's day.

Two significant differences should be noted, however, between the form in which the quotation from *Timon of Athens* appears in the Paris Manuscripts and that in which they figure in *Capital* I. In the Paris version Timon is allowed to call on the gods:

Ha, you gods! why this? what this, you gods? . . .;

in *Capital* there is no such distracting reminder of the 'opium of the people'. In the Paris Manuscripts—written, we must remember, for Marx's own use and not for publication—the superannuated widow has suitors who bear the signs of what is clearly a venereal disease:

That makes the wappen'd widow wed again;
She, whom the spital-house and ulcerous sores
Would cast the gorge at, this embalms and spices
To th' April day again;

in *Capital* the spital-house and the ulcerous sores have vanished as completely as they have in Bowdler's Family Shakespeare. Marx was Victorian enough to feel that even in Shakespeare there are things which it might be better not to mention in public, even though, as is shown elsewhere in this book, he took a private interest in the presentation of sexual matters by such writers as Aretino and Régnier. His letters to Engels, moreover,

[54] *K* I—*MEW* XXIII, 146.

frequently speak with uninhibited frankness about sexual activities and sexually transmitted diseases.

The quotation from *Timon of Athens* is followed, in *Capital* I, by another from Sophocles' *Antigone*:

> Money! Money's the curse of man, none greater!
> That's what wrecks cities, banishes men from home,
> Tempts and deludes the most well-meaning soul,
> Pointing out the way to infamy and shame . . .[55]

Once again, no attempt is made to identify the situation in which these words are spoken with such powerfully ironic effect, or to point out that the speaker is Creon—hardly a character whose views would commend themselves to Marx in other respects. But this time Marx accompanies his quotation with a comment which shows clearly the purpose these excerpts from Shakespeare and Sophocles are designed to serve:

Money itself is a commodity, an external object, capable of becoming the private property of any individual. Thus social power becomes the private power of private persons. The ancients therefore denounced money as subversive of the economic and moral order of things. [Here follows, inserted as a footnote, the passage from *Antigone* that has just been quoted.] Modern society which, even in its infancy, pulled Plutus by the hair of his head from the bowels of the earth, greets gold as its Holy Grail, as the glittering incarnation of the very principle of its own life.[56]

What Marx looks for, in Shakespeare as in Sophocles, is the forceful expression, or suggestion, of an outlook which is the exact opposite of that which he attributes to the modern capitalist. Whether this is prompted by misanthropic despair (as in the case of Timon) or complete misapprehension of the real motives of an action (as in the case of Creon) is not to the point: it matters only that Shakespeare and Sophocles make their protagonists proclaim, or suggest, a view which may be presumed acceptable to many members of the society in which they lived and which constitutes a useful corrective of nineteenth-century capitalism. The whole of *Capital*, the whole of Marx's work,

[55] *K* I—*MEW* XXIII, 146. The translation of Sophocles which I have used is by E. F. Watling (Sophocles, *The Theban Plays* (Harmondsworth, 1947), p. 146).
[56] *K* I—*MEW* XXIII, 146-7.

shows clearly how far *he* was from any simplistic and unhistorical rejection of the capitalist outlook, how clearly *he* saw
that money had been not only man's curse and common whore,
but also a vital instrument of progress.

In the passage just quoted Marx goes on to support Creon's
attack on greed with a passage from a much later writer: from
the *Deipnosophistae* of the grammarian Athenaeus, compiled at
the end of the second century A.D. 'Greed', Marx quotes in a
footnote, 'seeks to draw Pluton himself from the bowels of the
earth.' He thus demonstrates how relevant Greek mythology
may still be even to the age of the printing-press, self-acting
mule spindles, locomotives, telegraphs, Roberts & Co., the
lightning-conductor, and *crédit mobilier*.

Capital I makes use of mythological characters and incidents
in various ways. The first may be called the 'straight' use:
Pluton or Plutus personifies wealth; the Medusa is a symbol for
something too horrible to be contemplated without comforting
illusions:

The social statistics of Germany and the rest of continental Western
Europe are, in comparison with those of England, wretchedly compiled. But they raise the veil just enough to let us catch a glimpse of
the Medusa's head behind it. We would be appalled by the state of
things at home if, as in England, our governments and parliaments
appointed periodically commissions of inquiry into economic
conditions . . .;

'cyclopian' serves as a vivid epithet for powerful machines;
and Prometheus—as always—is the archetype of a noble and
beneficent principle which has been shackled for a period by
a powerful tyranny:

The law, finally, that always holds in equilibrium the relative surplus population, or industrial reserve army, on the one hand, and
the extent and energy of accumulation on the other—this law rivets
the labourer to capital more firmly than Hephaestos wedged Prometheus to the rock.[57]

[57] *K* I—*MEW* XXIII, 146–7, 15, 405, 675. Cf. S. E. Hyman's comments on the
'metaphoric myths' and 'metaphoric rites' of *Capital* I: 'If the laborer is Sisyphus
and Prometheus, capital is not only Gorgon and Furies but a whole menagery of
supernatural horrors. It is a monster "that vampire-like only lives by sucking
living labor"; possessing a "vampire-thirst for the living blood of labour" . . .
It has a "werewolf's hunger for surplus labor". *Capital*'s machines are giants
and ogres: "a mechanical monster whose body fills whole factories, and whose

The second way in which classical mythology is used in *Capital* I may be termed 'inverted'. This, as we have seen so often, seems to be a particularly characteristic product of Marx's 'critical' cast of mind.

Perseus needed a magic cap that the monsters he hunted down might not see him. We draw the magic cap down over eyes and ears so as to be able to deny that there *are* monsters.[58]

Here the myth of Perseus serves as a counter-image to undesirable modern attitudes, as an encouragement to 'turn' things 'the right way up'. This is clearly related to the last use of mythology, as familiar in Marx as in Heine and Offenbach: the ironic or parodistic use. Thus division of labour is said to produce (with a glance at the fate of Orpheus) 'a poet's scattered limbs', *disiecta membra poetae*, while the clamour of British landowners during the great outbreak of foot-and-mouth disease in 1866 is said to prove 'that one does not have to be a Hindu in order to worship the cow Sabala, or Jupiter in order to turn into an ox'.[59]

Frequently the attitudes described and embodied in the poetry of the ancient world which Marx cites are held up to the nineteenth century, not as a model to emulate, but as a reminder of its own relative inhumanity. We do not want to return to a social order in which the full human development of one man depends on the slavery of another—but have we not evolved, Marx asks his contemporaries, in our 'Christian' society of 'free' men, a slavery worse than that of antiquity?

Antipatros, a Greek poet of the time of Cicero, hailed the invention of the water-wheel for grinding corn, an invention that is the elemen-

demon power, at first veiled under the slow and measured motions of his giant limbs, at length breaks out into the fast and furious whirl of his countless working organs". Two pages on machinery say "cyclopean", "cyclopean", "cyclopean", "gigantic", "monster", "such a weight that not Thor himself could wield it". The capitalists are ghouls . . . Everything is crystallized, congealed, petrified; commodities are "definite masses of crystallized labor-time"; "money is a crystal formed of necessity in the course of the exchanges"; . . . "money becomes petrified into a hoard"; and so on. But these dead will waken in Marx's world of fairy tale, where capital "has acquired the occult quality of being able to add value to itself. It brings forth living offspring, or, at least, lays golden eggs." Like the prince in *Sleeping Beauty*, "living labor must seize upon these things and rouse them from their death-sleep".' (*The Tangled Bank*, pp. 134–5.)

[58] *K* I—*MEW* XXIII, 15.   [59] *K* I—*MEW* XXIII, 602.

tary form of all machinery, as giving freedom to female slaves, and bringing on the golden age. Oh! those heathens! They understood, as the learned Bastiat, and before him the still wiser M'Culloch have discovered, nothing of political economy and Christianity. They did not, for example, comprehend that machinery is the surest means of lengthening the working day. They would excuse the slavery of one human being on the grounds that for another this was the means to develop his humanity to its full extent. But to preach the slavery of the masses in order that a few crude and half-educated parvenus might become 'eminent spinners', 'extensive sausage-makers', and 'influential shoe-black dealers'—for this they lacked the specific bump of Christianity.[60]

And Marx cites the relevant lines from Antipatros in the translation of an eighteenth-century German aristocrat, Count Christian von Stolberg, which Freiligrath had dug out for him.

At this point it may be recalled that Marx's quotation from Antipatros was to play a crucial part in William Morris's arguments for socialism in England. Morris had struggled manfully with *Capital*:

Well, having joined a Socialist body . . . I put some conscience into trying to learn the economical side of Socialism, and even tackled Marx, though I must confess that, whereas I thoroughly enjoyed the historical part of *Capital*, I suffered agonies of confusion of the brain over reading the pure economics of that great work. Anyhow, I read what I could, and will hope that some information stuck to me from my reading . . .[61]

Among the things which undoubtedly 'stuck' to William Morris was the quotation from Antipatros—as he demonstrates in his essay 'Art under Plutocracy':

Something must be wrong then in art, or the happiness of life is sickening in the house of civilization. What has caused the sickness? Machine-labour will you say? Well, I have seen quoted a passage from one of the ancient Sicilian poets rejoicing in the fashioning of a water-mill, and exulting in labour being set free from the toil of the hand-quern in consequence; and that surely would be a type of man's natural hope when foreseeing the invention of labour-saving machinery as 'tis called; natural surely, since though I have said that the labour of which art can form a part should be accompanied by pleasure, no one could deny that there is some necessary

[60] *K* I—*MEW* XXIII, 431.
[61] *Political Writings of William Morris*, ed. A. L. Morton, p. 242.

labour even which is not pleasant in itself, and plenty of unnecessary labour which is merely painful. If machinery had been used
for minimizing such labour, the utmost ingenuity would scarcely
have been wasted on it, but is that the case in any way? Look
round the world . . .[62]

This affords us a welcome illustration of the way in which the
quotations from literature introduced into *Capital* could bring
home Marx's arguments to minds that did not respond naturally
or easily to economic formulas and statistics.

Literature serves a documentary function in *Capital* I in two
related ways. The *Odyssey* is cited, alongside passages from
Plato, Thucydides, Xenophon, and Sextus Empiricus, for
evidence of the way in which division of labour may have
operated in the ancient world; Antipatros is cited to show
characteristic attitudes and expectations. The work of more
recent writers can also fulfil such documentary functions. Minor
authors may betray clearly the prejudices, preconceptions, and
outlook of the class that admires (and buys) their works: the
very name of the Reverend Martin Tupper, for instance, serves
Marx as a kind of shorthand symbol for Victorian sancti-
moniousness.[63] 'The imbecile flatness of the present-day bourgeoisie', Marx comments, in direct continuation, as it were, of
The German Ideology and *The Holy Family*, 'is to be measured by
the calibre of its "great intellects".'[64] Writers of the middle
rank, or of small literary pretension may, on occasions, speak
directly and movingly of the plight of the insulted and injured:
Marx cites with full approval some lines from Pierre Dupont's
poem 'Workmen' (*Ouvriers*, 1796) in which the urban poor
are made to detail their misery. Great writers, however, go
further than this: they can invent figures and incidents which
are particular and idiosyncratic, and which yet let us divine, or
recognize, general laws of character and social action. 'Thus,
for instance, Balzac, who so thoroughly studied every shade of
avarice, represents the old usurer Gobseck as already in his
second childhood when he begins to make himself a hoard of
accumulated goods.'[65]

Some writers have the ability to present in their works sim-

[62] *Political Writings of William Morris*, ed. A. L. Morton, p. 73.
[63] *K* I—*MEW* XXIII, 636.   [64] *K* I—*MEW* XXIII, 541.
[65] *K* I—*MEW* XXIII, 615.

plified models of social relations which can be used to illustrate facts that our more complex society obscures. Here the prime exhibit is *Robinson Crusoe*, which appears to better advantage in *Capital* I than it did in the General Introduction of the *Grundrisse*:

Since political economists love Robinson-Crusoe-stories [*Robinsonaden*], let Robinson appear before us on his island. Though he has been brought up to make only modest demands, there are yet some wants he has to satisfy; he must therefore do useful work of various sorts, such as making tools and furniture, taming goats, fishing, hunting, and so on. Of his prayers and the like we take no account, since our Robinson takes pleasure in them and regards such activity as recreation. In spite of the variety of his productive functions he knows that his labour, whatever its nature, is but the activity of one and the same Robinson, and that it therefore consists of nothing but different modes of human labour. Necessity itself compels him to apportion his time accurately between his different kinds of work. Whether one kind occupies a greater proportion of his general activity than another depends on the difficulties, greater or less as the case may be, to be overcome in attaining the useful effect he aims at. This our friend Robinson soon learns by experience, and having rescued a watch, ledger, pen, and ink from the wreck, he commences, as a true-born Englishman, to keep a book about himself. His inventory contains a list of useful objects that belong to him, of the operations necessary for their production, and (lastly) of the labour-time that given quantities of these different products tend to cost him. All the relations between Robinson and the things which form this wealth he has himself created are so simple and perspicuous as to be intelligible without special exertion even by Mr. M. Wirth. And yet these relations contain all that is essential to the determination of value.[66]

The story of Crusoe's lonely sojourn on his island, then, gives us a character-type of 'economic planners' in general and the 'true-born Englishman' of the eighteenth century in particular. It also affords a simple model of economic activities in a setting in which the value of an object can be directly proportional to the quantity of labour expended upon it, undistorted by market considerations.[67]

[66] *K* I—*MEW* XXIII, 90–1.

[67] Cf. the illuminating essay in which Ian Watt has used Marx's insights to analyse *Robinson Crusoe* more thoroughly than Marx: 'Robinson Crusoe as Myth', *Essays in Criticism* I (1951), pp. 95–119.

How such a model might be applied to the construction of a different world from any imagined by Defoe, to the visualization of a social Utopia, Marx demonstrates when he returns, a few pages later, to Crusoe's way of apportioning his labour and his time:

Finally, let us consider, by way of change, a community of free individuals, carrying on their work with the means of production in common, in which the labour-power of all the different individuals is consciously applied as the combined labour-power of the community. All the characteristics of Robinson Crusoe's labour are here repeated, but with this difference, that they are social, instead of individual. Everything produced by him was exclusively the result of his own personal labour, and therefore simply an object of use for himself. The total product of our community is a social product. One part serves as a fresh means of production and remains social. But another part is consumed by the members as means of subsistence, and has consequently to be distributed among them. The mode of this distribution will vary with the productive organization of the community, and the degree of historical development attained by the producers. We will assume, but merely for the sake of a parallel with the production of commodities, that the share of each individual producer in the means of subsistence is determined by his labour-time. Labour-time would, in that case, play a double part. Its apportionment in accordance with a definite social plan maintains the proper proportion between the different kinds of work to be done and the various wants of the community. On the other hand, it also serves as a measure of the individuals' share in the common labour, and of his share in that part of the total product destined for individual consumption. The social relations of the individual producers, both to their labour and to its products, are in this case perfectly simple and intelligible, and that with regard not only to production but also to distribution.[68]

That takes us far beyond Defoe, of course; but the analysis has been prompted by him and has become clearer and more communicable because of the model he has provided.

It is connected with their ability to create types and models in the ways just illustrated that great writers are so frequently shown, in *Capital* I, to 'anticipate' phenomena of a time later than their own. The word *schon*, 'already', often introduces such anticipations; as when Marx discusses the inability of modern

[68] *K* I—*MEW* XXIII, 92–3; *BR* 256–7.

economists to rid themselves of antiquated notions and categories: 'On the other hand Don Quixote already paid the
penalty for wrongly imagining that knight-errantry was equally
compatible with all economic forms of society.'[69] In the same
way Shakespeare's Dogberry is said to anticipate, not in detail
of course, but in the form of argumentation, nineteenth-century
professors of political economy: 'Who could fail to remember
here how our good friend Dogberry informs neighbour Seacoal
the night-watchman: "To be a well-favoured man is the gift of
fortune; but reading and writing comes by nature".'[70] Thus
Marx is able to characterize country-squires of his own day,
who justify their treatment of their labourers by a certain kind
of perverted logic, as 'the English Dogberries'. A letter in *The
Times* from Edmund Potter reminds Marx of some words by
Schiller's Hofmarschall Kalb in *Intrigue and Love*, while he finds,
in Dryden's reworking of the *Nun's Priest's Tale*, an 'anticipation' of Quaker employers of child labour:

> A Fox full fraught with seeming Sanctity,
> That fear'd an Oath, but like the Devil, would lie,
> Who look'd like Lent, and had the holy Leer,
> And durst not sin before he say'd his Pray'r.[71]

This chimes in well with Marx's approval of the way the English economist Henry Roy had used a passage from Boileau's
Satires to pinpoint contradictions in Gladstone's budget-speeches
of 1863 and 1864; and with the estimate of Balzac attributed to
Marx by Paul Lafargue, who recalled that his father-in-law
saw in Balzac not only the 'historian' of his own time, but also
the prophetic creator of character-types which were still in
embryo in the days of Louis-Philippe and did not fully develop
until after Balzac's death.[72]

The great writers, then, yield types, models, anticipations.
Their works are also, for the Marx of *Capital* I, a welcome
storehouse of *analogies*:

In order . . . that a commodity may, in practice, act effectively as
exchange-value, it must quit its natural shape, it must transform
itself from imaginary gold to real gold, although to the commodity

[69] *K* I—*MEW* XXIII, 96.   [70] *K* I—*MEW* XXIII, 98.
[71] *K* I—*MEW* XXIII, 628, 601, 257.
[72] *K* I—*MEW* XXIII, 682; *METEC* 20.

such transubstantiation may be more difficult than the transition
from 'necessity' to 'freedom' is to the Hegelian 'concept', or the
casting of his shell to a lobster, or putting off the Old Adam to St.
Jerome. Though side by side with its actual form a commodity (such
as iron, for instance) may take the form of gold in our imagination,
yet it cannot be both true iron and true gold at the same time. To
fix its price one need only equate it with imagined gold. It must be
replaced by gold in order to serve its owner as a universal equivalent.
If its owner were, for instance, to go to the owner of some other
worldly commodity and refer him to the price of iron (in order to
persuade him to an exchange), then the worldly owner of that other
commodity would give him the same answer that in heaven St.
Peter gave to Dante, after the latter had recited the Creed to him:

> 'Assai bene è trascorsa
> D'esta moneta già la lega e'l peso,
> Ma di mi se tu l'hai nella tua borsa.'

> 'We now have a sufficiently good idea
> Of this coin's alloy and weight;
> But tell me if you have it in your purse.'

A price therefore implies both that a commodity is exchangeable
for money, and also that it must be so exchanged.[73]

Marx clearly takes pleasure in the pecuniary metaphor Dante
puts into the mouth of the guardian of heaven, and reapplies
it—through his analogy—to the worldly affairs from which
Dante had taken it. But Dante supplies more serious analogies
too. In Canto 5 of the *Purgatorio* Virgil tells Dante to press on,
not to slacken his pace; 'what does it matter to you', Virgil is
made to ask, 'what they whisper here? Follow me and let the
people talk':

> Vien retro a me, e lascia dir le genti.

Marx, who has no Virgil to follow, appropriates this saying to
himself at the end of the Preface that accompanied the first
edition of *Capital* I, with one significant variation:

> Segui il tuo corso, e lascia dir le genti

Follow your own course, and let people say what they will.[74]

---

[73] *K* I—*MEW* XXIII, 117–18.   [74] *K* I—*MEW* XXIII, 17.

Finally, of course, the hell of Dante's *Inferno* holds horrors analogous to those in the modern world—if anything they fall too short. Victorian match-factories, for instance, with the terrible diseases unguarded handling of phosphorus could bring, go beyond anything the medieval writer pictured to himself and his readers: 'Dante will find the cruellest imaginings of his *Inferno* surpassed in this manufacture.'[75]

The hells imagined by earlier writers serve as analogies and illustrations of Victorian realities. Into his account of the conditions revealed in government Blue books Marx inserts a telling reminder of Odysseus' journey to the underworld:

From the motley crowd of labourers of all callings, ages, sexes, who press on us more avidly than the souls of the slain on Odysseus, on whom—without referring to the Blue books they carry under their arms—we see at a glance the marks of overwork, let us take two more figures, strikingly contrasted to show that before Capital all men are alike: a milliner and a blacksmith.[76]

The parody of Christian belief introduced into this passage ('that *before Capital* all men are alike') gives additional point to Marx's analogy between Victorian working-conditions and the hell imagined by the poets. What the poets can give us is a stimulus to emotional response and, at the same time, a kind of standard by which to measure the horrors Marx wishes to evoke. The insulted and injured of the Victorian world crowd into the writer's imagination 'more eagerly' than the souls of the slain; Victorian working-conditions 'surpass' Dante's infernal fantasies, just as they are later said to 'surpass the most revolting imaginings of our novelists'.[77] It is not irrelevant to remember that among the working-conditions whose squalor surpassed the most revolting imaginings of novelists Marx counted those obtaining in London's printing-works. Literature as commodity, literature as book, may enslave and degrade men as readily as other commodities in nineteenth-century society.

'Here, however', Marx tells his readers quite early on in *Capital* I, 'the analogy ceases to apply.'[78] Such perception of the *limits* of analogy may help to explain why Marx so often, in *Capital* I and elsewhere, modifies the creations of the great

---

[75] *K* I—*MEW* XXIII, 261. [76] *K* I—*MEW* XXIII, 268-9.
[77] *K* I—*MEW* XXIII, 488-9. [78] *K* I—*MEW* XXIII, 71.

writers, elaborates them for his own purposes. Dickens, for instance, would find it hard to recognize his own Bill Sikes in the voluble cut-throat who appears under that name in *Capital* I and *Herr Vogt*.[79] In the case of Heine Marx goes even further: after adapting lines from Heine's 'New Spring' and 'Heinrich', Marx begins to write in Heine's polemic style himself while ironically denying that he is doing so: 'If I had the courage of my friend Heinrich Heine I would call Jeremy Bentham a genius in the way of bourgeois stupidity.'[80]

Marx's treatment of Bentham, however, is well calculated to illustrate the uses of literary analogy rather than just its limits. 'Bentham', he writes, 'is among philosophers what Martin Tupper is among poets. Neither of them could have been manufactured anywhere but in England.'[81] That 'places' Bentham, Tupper, and the Victorian manufacturing spirit all at once. The sentimental (and covertly prurient) German novelist who called himself H. Clauren (= Carl Heun, 1771–1854) is invoked for a similar purpose:

One fine morning in the year 1836, Nassau W. Senior, renowned alike for his 'scientific' economics and his beautiful style, *the Clauren, as it were, among English economists*, was summoned from Oxford to Manchester to learn in the latter place the political economy he taught in the former [my italics].[82]

Analogies may hold for periods as well as for persons: such concatenations as 'economic storm-and-stress period' or 'storm and stress of the production-process' may lightly suggest limited parallels between the literary-cultural upheavals of the eighteenth century and the economic upheavals of the nineteenth. As always, however, Marx juxtaposes for contrast as much as for likeness:

With truly Gottschedian genius William Thucydides Roscher discovers that if the formation of surplus value, or surplus produce, is nowadays due to the thrift of the capitalist, it is the strong who compel the weak to economize in lower stages of civilization.[83]

Here Thucydides is clearly meant to 'place' Roscher by *contrast* while the eighteenth-century literary theorist Johann

[79] *K* I—*MEW* XXIII, 465; and *MEW* XIV, 431.
[80] *K* I—*MEW* XXIII, 637. [81] *K* I—*MEW* XXIII, 636.
[82] *K* I—*MEW* XXIII, 237. [83] *K* I—*MEW* XXIII, 231.

Christoph Gottsched, who often serves Marx as a butt, is meant to place Roscher by *analogy*.

The familiar metaphors from melodrama, farce, *Haupt- und Staatsaktionen*, and other dramatic entertainments recur in *Capital* I, in a new context and frequently with new implication. In the chapter on 'Circulation of Commodities' goods and money, alienated from the men who made them, play out a drama of their own which is even, by means of a quotation from *Romeo and Juliet*, given a Shakespearian flavour:

We see, then, that commodities are in love with money, but 'the course of true love never did run smooth' . . . The complete metamorphosis of a commodity, in its simplest form, implies four extremes and four dramatis personae. First a commodity comes face to face with money . . . In the first phase, sale, the commodity plays two parts . . . In the first instance, each new capital steps on to the stage (that is: the market) . . .[84]

In all three parts of *Capital* we find Marx personifying capital and landed property, transforming them into denizens of 'an enchanted, perverted, topsy-turvy world, in which Monsieur le Capital and Madame la Terre do their ghost-walking as social characters and at the same time directly as mere things'.[85] It has therefore been said, with some justification, that Marx has made his economic treatise a tragic drama played out between My Lord Capital and the Collective Worker, and that he has here given the world 'one of the most dramatic books of modern times'.[86]

[84] *K* I—*MEW* XXIII, 520, 770, 799; 122–6, 161.
[85] *K* III—*MEW* XXV, 838.
[86] R. C. Tucker, *Philosophy and Myth in Karl Marx*, 2nd edn. (Cambridge, 1972), pp. 204, 215, 221, 226. Cf. P. Stadler, *Karl Marx. Ideologie und Politik*, 2nd edn. (Göttingen, 1971), p. 129. The dramatic nature of Marx's work in general and *Capital* in particular has often been described. Some commentators have spoken of it as Victorian melodrama (on p. 146 of *The Tangled Bank* S. E. Hyman even suggests a title: *The Mortgage on Labor-Power Foreclosed*); others, more respectfully, as comedy and tragedy: 'Marx is at his best as a polemicist . . . when he reveals pious abstractions as a mask, and when he lifts that mask to show the homely and inglorious truth beneath . . . His method was one of the classic methods of comedy. And on top of that method there was also his recognition of the strange capacity of ideas to take over the command of human affairs. His historical analyses, in consequence, have a cumulative, relentless logic and a tragic quality. Like Oedipus, the actors in Marx's recounting of human history are in the grip of an inexorable necessity which unfolds itself no matter what they do. And yet all that links them to this fate is their own tragic blindness, their own *idées fixes*, which prevent them

That such dramatizations also drive home, in the most direct and forceful manner possible, Marx's point about 'reification', about the work of man's hand and brain confronting him as an alien presence, should need no further demonstration.

In view of the tragedy Marx sees played out in the economic and social life of nineteenth-century Europe, anything idyllic seems more than even irrelevant or dangerously misleading. 'In actual history it is notorious that conquest, enslavement, robbery, murder—force, in short—play the principal part. In the tender annals of political economy, the idyllic reigns from time immemorial.' Or again, with even heavier irony:

The spoliation of Church property, the fraudulent alienation of the State domains, the theft of common lands, the usurpation of feudal and clan property and its transformation into modern private property with unsparing terrorism, were just so many idyllic methods of primitive accumulation. They conquered the field for capitalistic agriculture, made the soil part and parcel of capital, and created for the town industries the necessary supply of a 'free' and outlawed proletariat.[87]

This supplies the necessary background for an understanding of Marx's frequently expressed dislike of literary phenomena like Gessner's pastoral poems and Auerbach's village stories.

The incidental literary references, analogies, and metaphors so far described are joined, in *Capital* I, by tags from the Bible, Virgil, Juvenal, and Horace; from Shakespeare's *King Henry IV* Part I (a characteristic inversion of one of Mistress Quickly's absurd sayings);[88] from More's *Utopia*, Butler's *Hudibras*, and Voltaire's *Candide*—and by allusions to horror tales (werewolf and vampire images!), German chap-books (especially *Fortunatus*), popular ballads, songs and jingles, legends, *Märchen*, mythological tales, and proverbs. And much of the liveliest prose quoted in *Capital* I comes from the work of writers who are not 'literary' in the usual sense. Marx loves, for instance, to

from seeing the facts until too late. In Marx's materialist interpretation of history we face the classic questions of Greek drama—the relation of ignorance to self-deception, and the relation of self-knowledge to freedom.' (C. Frankel, 'Theory and Practice in Marx's Thought', *Marx and Contemporary Scientific Thought*, p. 31.)

[87] *K* I—*MEW* XXIII, 742, 760–1.

[88] 'The reality of a commodity differs from Mistress Quickly in this respect: that we do not know where to have it.' (*K* I—*MEW* XXIII, 62.) Cf. *King Henry IV* Part I, iii. iii.

introduce his readers to the sustained metaphors and humorous analogies of the economist Sir William Petty (1623–87), whose rollicking description of money in terms of body-fat brings the first Section of *Capital* I to a close.[89]

At the same time, however, Marx shows once again his deep suspicion of 'fine writing' that goes with vapidity and lazy thinking. Such writing is occasionally even parodied in *Capital* I.[90] He attacks Proudhon once more for obliterating the frontier between tropes and realities (Proudhon, Marx says, regards the commodity 'work' as a 'grammatical ellipse'),[91] and shows constantly his distrust of economists who parade *literary* erudition:

They sought to conceal under a parade of literary-historical erudition, or by an admixture of extraneous material, their feeling of scientific impotence and the eerie consciousness of having to teach others what they themselves felt to be a truly strange subject.[92]

This makes Marx a little more lenient perhaps towards what he himself feels to be the 'literary deficiencies', deficiencies of style and exposition, in *Capital* I; it also makes him a harsh critic of learned stylists like Macaulay or the later Carlyle.[93]

Capital I leaves its readers in no doubt that all needs which go beyond the simplest biological ones are historically and socially conditioned:

Natural wants, such as food, clothing, fuel, and housing, vary according to the climatic and other physical conditions of a given country. The number and extent of so-called 'necessary wants' [*notwendige Bedürfnisse*], on the other hand, and the modes of satisfying them, are themselves the product of historical development, and therefore depend to a large extent on the stage of civilization [*Kulturstufe*] at which a given country has arrived—this includes, as an important element, the conditions under which the class of free workers, and consequently their habits and the demands they make on life, have been formed.

[89] *K* I—*MEW* XXIII, 160.   [90] e.g. *K* I—*MEW* XXIII, 241.
[91] *K* I—*MEW* XXIII, 559.
[92] *K* I—*MEW* XXIII, 19 (Preface to the second edition, 1873).
[93] *K* I—*MEW* XXIII, 22; 290, 270. In *Capital* I Macaulay appears as a 'Scottish sycophant and maker of fine phrases'; in a later letter, in company with Disraeli and Walter Savage Landor, as an 'innocent Englishman' prepared to preach what he would not practise (letter to Engels, 11 Apr. 1881). Burke and Ranke, predictably, also come in for their share of abuse in *Capital* I.

And again, in a key chapter entitled 'The Working-Day': 'The
worker needs time for satisfying his intellectual and social
wants; the extent and number of such wants are conditioned
by the general stage of development which civilization has
reached.'[94] Marx's glances, throughout *Capital* I, at the work of
the world's great writers must therefore be seen in the context
of his now fully developed views on specifically *human* labour:

We presuppose labour in the form which makes it specifically
human. A spider conducts operations which resemble those of a
weaver, and in the construction of its cells a bee puts to shame many
an architect. What distinguishes the worst architect from the best
bee is, however, this: that the architect has raised the cell in his
head before he constructs it in wax. At the end of the labour-process
stands a result which was already present ideally, in the worker's
imagination, at its beginning. He not only effects a change of form
in the material on which he works; he also realizes, in the world of
nature, his own purpose—a purpose of which he is conscious, which
determines, as a law, his way of going to work, and to which he
must subordinate his will. Nor is this subordination just a single,
isolated act. Besides the exertion of the bodily organs that perform
the work, the process demands that, during the whole operation, the
workman's will be steadily in consonance with his purpose—and
this expresses itself as close attention. His attention will have to be
the more strained the less he is carried along by enjoyment of the
content of his work and the way in which it is performed, the less,
therefore, he relishes it as something that calls into play his own
physical and mental powers.[95]

The creation of great literature and its assimilation enable those
fortunate enough to be able to devote themselves to it to relish
the play of their own mental powers in a way that is far beyond the animal. Of this satisfaction, as of so many others, the
nineteenth-century factory-worker has been deprived.

All this is clearly relevant to the concept of a 'realm of freedom' which has already been illustrated (see above, p. 312);
and it suggests many questions about the role of literature in
society, about the complex relationship between readers' demands and authors' response, that Marx never found time to
formulate fully, to argue out, and to answer. He leaves his
readers in no doubt, however, that he considers such questions

[94] K I—*MEW* XXIII, 185, 246.   [95] *K* I—*MEW* XXIII, 193.

important. His most withering contempt is reserved, in *Capital* I, for English utilitarians who think criticism of the arts 'harmful' because it disturbs honest citizens in their enjoyment of the works of Martin Tupper.[96]

The lives of the rich, *Capital* I shows its readers again and again, are in a spiritual sense as likely to be degraded in modern society as those of the poor. 'Commodity fetishism' drags down those who institute and practise it. In the civil society of the nineteenth century, commodities seem to acquire a life and empire of their own and to decree a general levelling-down of values:

What chiefly distinguishes a commodity from its owner is the fact that it looks on every other commodity as but the form of appearance of its own value. A born leveller and cynic, it is always ready to exchange not only soul but also body with any and every other commodity, even if the latter were more repulsive than Maritornes.[97]

After all we now know of Marx's uses of literature, we are not surprised to find that this portrait of Commodity preparing to assume its sway over men endowed with senses, feelings, and human needs should culminate in a reminiscence of *Don Quixote*.

The great writers of the past have their part to play in the development Marx envisages for the future—away from the one-sided cripples he saw all around him to a new 'total man' whose advent he desired as ardently as ever Schiller did, or Hölderlin:

It becomes a question of life and death to replace . . . the partial individual, the bearer of a partial social function, by the totally developed individual, for whom different social functions constitute successive modes of activity.[98]

To translate this vision into reality, however, so Marx believed, something more violent would be needed than Schiller's 'aesthetic education of man'. Literature could help to expose the deficiencies of an old order and prefigure a better, fuller life to come; it could alter men in subtle ways and prepare

[96] *K* I—*MEW* XXIII, 637. [97] *K* I—*MEW* XXIII, 100.
[98] *K* I—*MEW* XXIII, 512; cf. I. Fetscher, 'The Young and the Old Marx' in *Marx and the Western World*, ed. N. Lobkowicz (Notre-Dame and London, 1967), p. 38.

them for altering society; but it was no trumpet at whose mere sound the walls of the capitalist Jericho would fall down flat.

Nevertheless, enough has now been said to demonstrate that even in *Capital* aesthetic considerations were never far from Marx's mind. They were present, as has repeatedly been noticed, when he talked of social production, or of division of labour, or of the product as commodity, or of 'fetishism', or of a future 'realm of freedom'.[99] *Capital* I has therefore exerted a powerful fascination on literary theorists and critics prepared to brave its initial difficulties. They have found, and can still find, many things of interest there—not least the distinction, made explicit in the Postscript to the second edition of *Capital* I, between a *mode of investigation* that demands of its practitioners 'appropriation of the material in detail, analysis of its different forms of development, and the tracing of their inner connection', and a *mode of presentation* in which development is depicted in logical and temporal sequence and the 'life of the material' is 'mirrored in ideas'.[100]

The methodological fascination which Marx's economic writings have exercised in recent years has been most memorably described by Fredric Jameson in his book *Marxism and Form*. Marx's economic research, Jameson has argued with explicit reference to the opening chapter of *Capital* I, could be seen as 'a model of the way in which content, through its own inner logic, generates those categories in terms of which it organizes itself into a formal structure'. It thus provided 'a classic demonstration of dialectical thinking as a ceaseless generation and dissolution of intellectual categories'. Dialectical thinking, as Marx here demonstrates it, may be seen as 'doubly historical: not only are the phenomena with which it works historical in character, but it must unfreeze the very concepts with which they have been understood, and interpret the very immobility of the latter as historical phenomena in their own right.' 'This', Jameson adds, driving home the lesson which Adorno and Bloch, Benjamin and Sartre, in their different

---

[99] Cf. Terry Eagleton's Preface to M. Lifshits, *The Philosophy of Art of Karl Marx*, p. 8.

[100] *K* I—*MEW* XXIII, 27. Cf. Terrell Carver, *Karl Marx: Texts on Method*, pp. 4–5; and Martin Nicolaus's Foreword to *GN*: 'The *Grundrisse* and *Capital* I have opposite virtues of form. The latter is the model of the method of presentation, the former the record of the method of working' (p. 61).

ways, derived from Marx's practice, 'is why a genuinely dialectical criticism must always include a commentary on its own intellectual instruments as part of its own working structure.'[101] Marx, it is safe to assume, would have been anything but delighted by those who seek in his work a mode of operation, 'a form moving in time', rather than 'an objective and systematic body of ideas'.[102] This is one possibility, however, which was bound to appeal to those—and they are many—who find his work meaningful yet cannot share all his social and political beliefs; to those who have come to feel, as well they might, that he is too important to be left entirely to the Marxists.

[101] F. Jameson, *Marxism and Form. Twentieth-century Dialectical Theories of Literature* (Princeton, 1971), pp. 335–6.

[102] Jameson, op. cit., p. 362.

13 · Book-worming

'Your aversion . . . Martin Tupper
Favourite occupation . . . Book-worming
Favourite poet . . . Shakespeare, Aeschylus, Goethe
Favourite prose-writer . . . Diderot.'

(METEC, 179)

(i)

AFTER the first publication of *Capital* I Marx's efforts to carry on and complete the vast theoretical task he had set himself were constantly hampered by illness; but though he published little, he continued to read and make notes on what he read,[1] to correspond with friends and fellow intellectuals all over the world, to learn other languages (notably Russian), to comment on historic events (Bismarck's wars, the Paris Commune), to advise emergent socialist movements and parties, to work for unity and clear thinking among socialists and communists. He found many political battles to fight—against Lassallean state-socialism, for instance, and against the anarchist ideas of Bakunin and his followers. His fame grew steadily; but though he was pleased by the attention his work received, he grew very suspicious of readers who 'savoured' his writings without allowing them to influence their lives. He thought that he detected this culinary attitude in the many cultured Russians who admired *Capital* I: 'It's pure gourmandise with them', he wrote to Kugelmann on 12 October 1868, 'like that in which a part of the French aristocracy indulged in the eighteenth century. "It's not for our tailors and bootmakers" Voltaire said, at that time, about his own enlightenment. It doesn't prevent these

---

[1] 'He filled about fifty notebooks with excerpts from his readings—nearly 30,000 pages covered with his minuscule handwriting. The tons of material which he consumed and collected amazed Engels . . .' (M. Rubel and M. Manale, *Marx without Myth. A Chronological Study of his Life and Work*, p. 287).

same Russians from becoming blackguards as soon as they enter the service of their state.' But by the time he died, in March 1883, he must have had some inkling of the extent to which his ideas would reshape the world—though not, one hopes, of everything they would be made to justify.

When a second edition of *The Eighteenth Brumaire* became necessary in 1869, Marx accompanied the work with a new Preface in which he contrasted Victor Hugo's *Napoléon le petit* with his own portrait of Louis Napoleon:

> Victor Hugo confines himself to bitter and witty invective against the responsible editor of the *coup d'état*. The event itself appears in his work like a bolt from the blue. He sees in it only the violent act of a single individual. He fails to notice that he makes this individual great rather than little by ascribing to him a power of personal initiative such as would be without parallel in world history . . . I, on the contrary, demonstrate how the class-struggle in France created circumstances and relationships that made it possible for a mediocre, grotesque personage to play the part of the hero . . .[2]

Here the ubiquitous theatrical image is joined by a new one: Napoleon III is seen, not as the author, but as the *editor* of his *coup d'état*. It would be hard to think of a better literary analogy for the relation to history which Marx is here attempting to describe. At the same time, however, Marx is anxious once again to stress the limits of analogy as well as its uses:

> I hope that my work will contribute towards eliminating the stock phrase now current, particularly in Germany, of so-called Caesarism. In this superficial historical analogy the main point is forgotten, namely that in ancient Rome the class-struggle took place only within a privileged minority, between the free rich and the free poor, while the great, productive mass of the population, the slaves, formed the purely passive pedestal for these combatants. People forget *Sismondi's* significant remark: The Roman proletariat lived at the expense of society, while modern society lives at the expense of the proletariat. With so complete a difference between the material, economic conditions of the ancient and the modern class-struggles, the political figures they produce can likewise have no more in common with one another than the Archbishop of Canterbury has with the High Priest Samuel.[3]

[2] *MEW* VIII, 559–60; *SW* I, 394–5.
[3] *MEW* VIII, 560; *SW* I, 395.

Even in thus demonstrating, with the help of Sismondi, the dangers of unguarded arguing from analogy, Marx also demonstrates its uses: by adducing, as illustration of the contrast between the ancient Roman world and modern France, a parallel contrast between a biblical figure and an English dignitary of more recent times. Thus a glance at the Bible, at once great work of literature and indispensable historical source, rightly ends a Preface in which Marx had stressed again, as he did so often from the time of *The Communist Manifesto* onwards, the possibility of applying the term 'literature' to a wider field than mere belles-lettres:

Colonel Charras opened the attack on the Napoleon cult in his work on the campaign of 1815. Subsequently, and particularly in the last few years, *French literature has made an end of the Napoleon legend with the weapons of historical research, of criticism, of satire, and of wit.* Outside France this violent breach with traditional popular belief, this tremendous mental revolution, has been little noticed and still less understood [my italics].[4]

Historians, critics of every kind, satirists—they all find a place in the capacious mansion of 'French literature' as Marx now sees it. He made a similar point in the message he sent to the Russian section of the First International in 1870: he there praised the work of the Russian economist and sociologist 'N. Flerovsky (= V. V. Bervy) as that of 'a serious observer, a fearless worker, an unimpassioned critic, *a great artist*, and above all a man who is indignant about any kind of servitude' [my italics].[5] In the same way Marx expressed his delight at Sir William Petty's *Quantulumque concerning Money* by calling it, in the chapter he contributed to Engels's *Anti-Dühring*, 'a little masterpiece in content and form'.[6]

Of the many images that Marx borrowed from the Old Testament in his later works, one takes on particular prominence and importance. Here is an early example, taken from the speech with which he inaugurated the First International at a public meeting held at St. Martin's Hill in Long Acre on 28 September 1864:

Through their most notorious organs of science, such as Dr. Ure, Professor Senior, and other sages of that stamp, the middle class had

[4] *MEW* VIII, 560; *SW* I, 395. [5] *L* 239. [6] *MEW* XX, 218.

predicted, and to their heart's content proved, that any legal restriction of the hours of labour must sound the death knell of British industry, which, vampire-like, could but live by sucking blood, and children's blood, too. In olden times, child murder was a mysterious rite of the religion of Moloch, but it was practised on some very solemn occasions only, once a year perhaps, and then Moloch had no exclusive bias for the children of the poor.[7]

Two things are here worthy of remark. First, how Marx welds images and concepts from very different worlds—the vampire and Moloch images—into one amalgam of grotesque horror; second, that when he takes the biblical image over into his world, he is careful to stress points of contrast as well as similarity. Readers who see in the cult of Moloch chronicled in the Bible a *ne plus ultra* of horror and cruelty are to be rudely jolted by Marx's contention that respectable Oxford professors may, in the enlightened nineteenth century, be prepared to encourage and justify worse inhumanities than were ever thought of by Moloch's priests and worshippers.

Many other Old Testament images come to Marx's mind in his latter years—Esau selling his birthright for a mess of pottage suggests the proletariat before it has achieved class-consciousness as inevitably as Job smitten with sore boils suggests Marx himself afflicted with his eternal carbuncles. 'Plagued like Job', he called himself in 1868, 'but not so God-fearing'. L. S. Feuer, who quotes this passage, has also spoken of Marx's mellowing towards his Jewish ancestors in later life: he points to his cordial relations with Heinrich Graetz, the great historian of the Jewish people, whom he met in Carlsbad in 1877 and with whom he corresponded; and he recalls Marx's displeasure when he found that his wife and his daughter Eleanor wished to attend the 'secularist' services held by Charles Bradlaugh's National Secular Society. If they wanted to satisfy their metaphysical needs, he is said to have told them, they would do better to read the Jewish prophets.[8] Even if Marx's comments have been accurately reported here, they should not be thought to imply

---

[7] *SW* II, 16.

[8] L. S. Feuer, *Marx and the Intellectuals. A Set of Post-Ideological Essays* (New York, 1969), p. 49. Feuer quotes Max Beer and Frederick Lessner as authorities for Marx's alleged remarks on the Jewish prophets; the ultimate source is Eleanor Marx-Aveling.

any kind of 'return' to Judaism. He never recanted the interpretations he had given of the 'Jewish spirit' in 'On the Jewish Question', and felt little of that kinship with the Jewish people which others were so quick to detect in him. H. M. Hyndman's impression of Marx is wholly characteristic in this respect:

Marx, of course, was a Jew, and to me it seemed that he combined in his own person and nature, with his commanding forehead and great overhanging brow, his fierce glittering eyes, broad sensitive nose and mobile mouth all surrounded by a setting of untrimmed hair and beard, the righteous fury of the great seers of his race, with the cold analytical powers of Spinoza and the Jewish doctors.[9]

Marx himself continued to think, as Isaiah Berlin has rightly said, that the Jewish problem was an unreal subject, invented to screen more pressing questions, and that as far as his own person was concerned, he had not only scotched but killed the problem in his early essay.[10]

(ii)

In the light of subsequent history the most important work of Marx's later years was undoubtedly that series of three papers for the First International which appeared in 1871 under the title *The Civil War in France*. This described the end of the Franco-Prussian War and its aftermath, 'the Paris Commune, where the proletariat for the first time held political power for two whole months'.[11] The lessons that Marx drew from the Commune (which led him and Engels to regard some of the prescriptions contained in *The Communist Manifesto* as 'antiquated'[12]) were consciously learnt and applied by Lenin when he prepared and guided the Bolshevik Revolution in Russia.

The Civil War in France may be seen in many ways as the culmination and the continuation of *The Eighteenth Brumaire*; it is not surprising, therefore, that the literary imagery which we have seen dominating the earlier work should recur in the later.

---

[9] H. M. Hyndman, *The Record of an Adventurous Life* (London, 1911), pp. 270–1.

[10] I. Berlin, *Karl Marx. His Life and Environment*, p. 100. Marx alludes to his own Jewishness in two letters to Lion Philips: on 25 June 1864, when he speaks, ironically, of *unser Ahnenstolz* in connection with the Old Testament, and on 29 Nov. 1864, when he calls Disraeli *unser Stammesgenosse*.

[11] Preface to 1872 ed. of *The Communist Manifesto* (*MEW* IV, 573–4).

[12] Ibid., *MEW* IV, 574.

'The ferocious farce' of Napoleon III's Empire 'will end, as it began, by a parody'; Napoleon III himself appears as a 'senile mountebank', Thiers as Mr. Punch, or Pickelhäring; the 'monstrous gnome' Thiers adopts a 'pseudo-heroic style'; the Commune's more generous actions are a 'satire' on Thiers; Legitimists and Orleanists, 'ghouls of all defunct régimes', 'caricature 1789 by holding their ghastly meetings in the *Jeu de Paume*'.[13] Molière is present in the generic name Marx now gives to country-squires: 'all the *Pourceaugnacs* of France'; Shakespeare through Ancient Pistol (the nickname bestowed on the Marquis de Gallifet) and, once again, through Shylock:

To complete the ruin the Prussian Shylock was there with his bond for the keep of half a million of his soldiers on French soil, his indemnity of five milliards and interest at five percent on the unpaid instalments thereof.[14]

Marx's earlier drafts of *The Civil War in France* in fact suggest additional appearances of Shylock—always, however, in the guise of the Prussians, always insisting on his bond or his pound of flesh.[15]

Marx's deepest scorn is directed against Adolphe Thiers— that scholar-statesman whom Heine had treated critically, but not without sympathy and respect, in his accounts of French social and political life under Louis-Philippe, but whom the *Neue Rheinische Zeitung* had attacked as early as 1848. Now, in *The Civil War in France*, Marx proclaims his hatred of Thiers in a flurry of allusions to literature, play-acting, rhetoric, and folklore:

With the elated vanity of a parliamentary Tom Thumb, permitted to play the part of a Tamerlane, he denied the rebels against his littleness every right of civilized warfare, up to the right of neutrality for ambulances. Nothing more horrid than that monkey allowed for a time to give full fling to his tigerish instincts, as foreseen by Voltaire;

and again:

In sight of the impending municipal elections of the 30th April, Thiers enacted one of his great conciliation scenes on 27th April.

13 *SW* II, 192, 229; *MEW* XVII, 512; *SW* II, 205–6, 228, 229.
14 *SW* II, 209, 242, 209.   15 *MEW* XVII, 553, 599.

Amidst a flood of sentimental rhetoric, he exclaimed from the tribune of the Assembly . . .[16]

The career of Thiers, it seemed to Marx, provided a horrid example of what happens when a bourgeois littérateur is allowed to attain political power:

M. Thiers was never anything else but an 'able' journalist and a clever 'word fencer' . . . Vain, sceptical, epicurean, he has never written or spoken for things. In his eyes the things themselves are mere pretexts for the display of his pen or his tongue . . . The Roman historians finish off Nero's character by telling us that the monster gloried in being a rhymester and a comedian. But lift a professional mere journalist and parliamentary mountebank like Thiers to power, and he will out-Nero Nero.[17]

This comes from the first outline Marx sketched for his report on the Paris Commune; a second such outline adds: 'The so-called accomplishments of culture appear in such a man only as the refinement of debauchery and . . . selfishness.'[18] From here it is only a step to Marx's unforgettable denunciation, in the published version of *The Civil War in France*, of what may be called the 'aesthetic' attitude: an inclination, fostered by idle plays and novels, to regard the sufferings of others as a spectacle laid on for entertainment.

The Paris of M. Thiers was not the real Paris of the 'vile multitude', but a phantom Paris, the Paris of the *francs-fileurs*, the Paris of the Boulevards, male and female—the rich, the capitalist, the gilded, the idle Paris, now thronging with its lackeys, its blacklegs, its literary *bohème*, and its *cocottes* at Versailles, Saint-Denis, Rueil, and Saint-Germain; considering the civil war but an agreeable diversion, eyeing the battle going on through telescopes, counting the rounds of cannon, and swearing by their own honour and that of their whores that the performance was far better got up than it used to be at the Porte St. Martin. The men who fell were really dead; the cries of the wounded were cries in good earnest; and, besides, the whole thing was so intensely historical.[19]

---

[16] *SW* II, 216, 233. The allusion in the first of these quotations is to Voltaire's *Candide*, chapter 22, final paragraph, where France is called 'ce pays où des singes agacent des tigres'.

[17] Karl Marx and Frederick Engels, *On the Paris Commune* (Moscow, 1971), pp. 118–23.

[18] Ibid., p. 187.   [19] *SW* II, 230.

Theatrical spectacles that nourish a taste for sensation here combine with nineteenth-century historicism to bring about, or at least to foster, a terrifying dehumanization. Aestheticism and barbarism join hands.

It will have been noticed that the 'literary *bohème*' is included in the unflattering picture Marx here draws of 'the Paris of M. Thiers'. There is no connection, in Marx's mind, between a defiance of bourgeois conventions and revolutionary politics; the *bohème* advances the interests of the powers that be as inevitably as those overt apologists whom he calls in *The Civil War in France* 'penmen' of the middle class and 'the gentlemen's gentlemen with the pen and inkhorn'.[20] His letters of the time are full of denunciations of such 'penmen', particularly those that write for the newspapers. *The Civil War in France*, however, makes the important point that the British and French Press was well served, on occasions, by honest reporters who revealed without fear or favour the callousness of those who suppressed the Commune and of moneyed Parisians who continued to enjoy themselves as though nothing at all had happened:

> To find a parallel for the conduct of Thiers and his bloodhounds we must go back to the times of Sulla and the two Triumvirates of Rome. The same wholesale slaughter in cold blood; the same disregard, in massacre, of age and sex, the same system of torturing prisoners; the same proscriptions, but this time of a whole class; the same savage hunt after concealed leaders, lest one might escape; the same denunciations of political and private enemies; the same indifference for [*sic*] the butchery of entire strangers to the feud. There is but this difference, that the Romans had no *mitrailleuses* for the despatch, in the lump, of the proscribed, and that they had not 'the law in their hands', nor on their lips the cry of 'civilization'.
>
> And after those horrors look upon the other still more hideous face of that bourgeois civilisation as described by its own Press![21]

The quotations that follow, from 'the Paris correspondent of a London Tory paper', and from Edouard Hervé of 'the *Journal de Paris*, a Versaillist journal suppressed by the Commune', leave no doubt of the clear-sightedness and good faith shown by these journalists in their reports, although they fail to appreciate, according to Marx, that the cruelty and callousness they pillory are those of the class they serve rather than the whole

[20] *SW* II, 196, 224.   [21] *SW* II, 235–6.

community. This passing tribute to honest journalists writing
for conservative journals may be compared with the tribute
Marx had paid, in the Preface to *Capital* I, to the English
factory-inspectors and compilers of government-commissioned
Blue books from whose reports he culled most of the facts that
support his indictment of Victorian capitalism.[22]

On the whole, however, Marx's opinion of the journalism of
his time remained low. He never meant to compliment contemporary statesmen when he characterized their mentality—
as he liked to do—by mentioning journals for which they wrote
or with which they were in some other way associated. Bismarck
comes in for such treatment in *The Civil War in France*. In the
third section of that work Marx writes:

It could only enter into the head of a Bismarck, who, when not
engaged in his intrigues of blood and iron, always likes to resume
his old trade, so befitting his mental calibre, of contributor to
Kladderadatsch (the Berlin *Punch*), it could only enter into such a
head, to ascribe to the Paris Commune aspirations after that caricature of the old French municipal organization of 1791, the Prussian
municipal constitution which degrades the town governments to mere
secondary wheels in the police-machinery of the Prussian state.[23]

Marx himself had, of course, been an effective journalist
for many years, and he never forgot the lessons he had learnt
in that school. One of these was, as we have seen, that the
techniques of literary criticism could be used, with devastating
effect, on texts that were not 'literary' in any narrow sense. His
glosses on the 'Gotha Programme', the programme of the emergent social-democratic party in Germany, show that he continued to apply this lesson in the 1870s; the glosses contain
many condemnations of 'hollow phrases', 'obsolete phrases',
'meaningless humbug that comes fluently from the pen', and of
paragraphs as awkward in style as they are wide of the mark in
content (*stilistisch und inhaltlich verfehlt*).[24] The same critique
uses source-study to disparage Lassalle by referring Lassalle's
followers to a line in Goethe's poem 'Limits of Mankind': 'It is
well known that nothing of the "iron law of wages" belongs to
Lassalle except the word "iron" [*ehern*] which is borrowed from
Goethe's "great, eternal, iron laws" . . .'[25] In his analysis of

----

[22] *K* I—*MEW* XXIII, 15.   [23] *SW* II, 222.   [24] *MEW* XIX, 16–26.
[25] *MEW* XIX, 24. In a letter to Jenny Longuet dated 6 Apr. 1882 (*MEW*

the failings of the Gotha Programme Marx also makes parodistic use of technical terms normally reserved for discussions of the structure of Greek tragedy: 'The first strophe is taken from the introductory words of the Statutes of the International, but "improved" . . . In compensation the antistrophe is a Lassallean quotation of the first water . . .' Here suggestions of 'belletrism', plagiarism, and incompetence combine to discredit the prospectus of Social Democracy in Germany. It should not be thought, however, that Marx's critique is purely negative and destructive, for he frequently takes the formulations of the Gotha Programme as starting-points for his own elaborations and counter-suggestions. This is notably the case in a gloss that looks once again at the relation of labour, society, and culture, a gloss which therefore has implications for the role of literature in the society of Marx's own day:

'Labour only becomes the source of wealth and culture as social labour', or, what is the same thing, 'in and through society'.

This proposition is incontestably correct, for although isolated labour (its material conditions presupposed) can also create use-values, it can create neither wealth nor culture.

But equally incontestable is this other proposition:

'In proportion as labour develops socially, and becomes thereby a source of wealth and culture, poverty and neglect develop among the workers and wealth and culture among the non-workers.'

This is the law of all history hitherto. What, therefore, had to be done here, instead of making general phrases about 'labour' and 'society', was to prove concretely how in present capitalist society the material etc. conditions have at last been created which will enable and compel the workers to lift this historical curse.[26]

The implication, clearly, is that social organizations must be changed in such a way that literature, along with all other manifestations of cultural life, becomes available to all and not just to a leisure class.[27] Having restated this creed, Marx's critique of the Gotha Programme ends, appropriately, with yet another allusion to the Old Testament prophets. He quotes,

XXXV, 298) Marx traces Goethe's line, in its turn, to the *Antigone* of Sophocles. (The literal meaning of '*ehern*', the adjective used by both Goethe and Lassalle, is 'made of brass', 'brazen'.)

[26] *MEW* XIX, 17.

[27] In its most famous passage, the *Critique of the Gotha Programme* looks forward, in Marx's best eschatological vein, to a communist state of the future in which

in Latin, Ezekiel 3: 19: *Dixi et salvavi animam meam*—'I have spoken out and delivered my soul', a motto fit to go with that which Marx adapted from Dante at the end of his first Preface to *Capital* I: *Segui il tuo corso, e lascia dir le genti*—'Follow your course, and let people say what they will!'

Marx's critique of the Gotha Programme also contains the one lapidary sentence which may be said to sum up the spirit behind all the linguistic criticism to which Marx had subjected his opponents from his earliest days to his last. *Meinte man das, so mußte es gesagt werden*—'If that is what was meant, that is what should have been said.'[28] The maxim remains good, even if Marx was not always able to follow it himself.

(iii)

In other polemical works of his later years Marx continued to draw, gratefully, on such ammunition as the world's great writers could provide. Describing Gladstone's oratory to readers of the *People's State* (*Der Volksstaat*) (7 August 1872), he called it a 'Circumlocution-Office-style', explaining to an audience not acquainted with Dickens's *Little Dorrit* that Circumlocution-Office meant *Um-die-Sache-herumschreibungsbüro*.[29] The gentlemen of the German Manufacturers' Association, who had wrongly impugned his veracity and accuracy, are accused of rushing in where angels fear to tread; not in the words of Pope (whom they were not likely to know), but in those of Schiller (whose poems they would certainly have learnt at school):

> . . . was kein Verstand der Verständigen sieht
> Das übet in Einfalt ein kindlich Gemüt.

What the understanding of reasonable people fails to see
A childlike soul will practise in its simplicity.

all-round development will be possible for all and labour, whether physical or intellectual, will have become not only a means of life but a prime want: 'In a higher phase of communist society, after the enslaving subordination of the individual to the division of labour, and therewith also the antithesis between mental and physical labour has vanished; after labour has become not only a means of life but a prime want; after the productive forces have also increased with the all-round development of the individual, and all the springs of co-operative wealth flow more abundantly—only then can the narrow horizon of bourgeois right be crossed in its entirety and society inscribe on its banners: "From each according to his ability, to each according to his needs!" ' (*SW* III, 19.)

[28] *MEW* XIX, 31.　　　　　　　　　　　　　　[29] *MEW* XVIII, 114.

Marx ends his counter-attack with a literary puzzle embodying a final insult to the manufacturers who had challenged him (in a journal called *Concordia*, like the eponymous bell in Schiller's 'Die Glocke'): 'What were the wares peddled by, and what was the name of, the man who flung at an adversary at least as worthy as the *Concordia* the weighty words: "Asinus manebis in secula seculorum"?' He thus asserts again that these German manufacturers, who thought they had caught him out in a mis-quotation, 'are as fit to assess literary wares as a donkey is to play the lute'.[30]

In a later, more serious feud with Bakunin, Marx again called on Shakespeare for help—Bakunin is characterized by reference to Falstaff's saying that discretion is the better part of valour. He also inverted a famous saying of Chamfort's ('Peace to the palaces, war to the cottages') to pillory the logic of Bakunin's followers; and dismissed Nechaev's *Revolutionary Catechism* by branding its author as an amalgam of characters from Sue's *The Mysteries of Paris*, the elder Dumas's *Count of Monte Christo*, Schiller's *The Robbers*, and a play by Charles Antel and Frédéric Lemaître:

Such a masterpiece cannot be criticized. That would spoil the fun one can have with so grotesque a composition. Such criticism would take far too seriously this amorphic knocker-down who manages to combine in one person the characteristics of Rodolphe de Gérolstein, the Count of Monte Christo, Karl Moor, and Robert Macaire . . .[31]

French and German writers of the eighteenth and nineteenth centuries thus help Marx to convey what he thinks the essential characteristics of a Russian terrorist whose murderous exploits furnished some of the plot of Dostoevsky's *The Devils*. Other authors who aided Marx's polemics in these years include Defoe (whose *Memoirs of a Cavalier* suggest thoughts on French and German national psychologies);[32] Heine (whose telling coinage 'Konfusius' is used to characterize the economist H. D. Macleod);[33] and Saltykov-Shchedrin, who described

[30] *MEW* XVIII, 92, 115. Marx had already used the quotation from Schiller's poem 'Words of Faith' (*Die Worte des Glaubens*) for similar purposes in the *Rheinische Zeitung* (see above, p. 37).
[31] *MEW* XVIII, 431.
[32] Letter to Engels, 10 Aug. 1869—*MEW* XXXII, 360–1.
[33] *MEW* XX, 237.

capitalists and kulaks as 'new pillars of society'—a phrase
Marx marked in his copy of Shchedrin's works and introduced
into letters to Russian correspondents like N. F. Danielson and
Vera Zasulich.[34] In using that last phrase, he may also have
had Ibsen in mind; his daughter Eleanor, it will be recalled,
became one of Ibsen's earliest champions in Victorian England.

The polemic against Bakunin to which reference has just
been made is notable for a rare instance in which Marx seems
to venture a direct criticism of one of Schiller's works: he
speaks of the 'melodramatic' nature of Karl Moor, the hero of
The Robbers.[35] Marx had, of course, frequently expressed his
dislike of the form that admiration of Schiller tended to take—
schoolboys intoxicating themselves with *The Robbers*, Kinkel
stylizing his own life in a Schillerian mould, Ruge preferring
Schiller to Shakespeare because the former had a recognizable
philosophical system, Lassalle making dramatic characters into
megaphones for his own views or for his conception of the
Zeitgeist, Freiligrath using the metre of Schiller's 'Dithyrambe'
for a bad poem in Schiller's honour, liberal literati taking the
celebration of Schiller's centenary as an occasion for self-adver-
tisement and self-congratulation, merchants quoting Schiller's
more exalted verses while continuing to devote themselves to
their huckstering.[36] He had loved to tease Schiller's philistine
admirers by quoting, in ironical contexts, Schiller's lines about
the 'childlike spirit' which practises what the eye of reason
cannot even see and (on one memorable occasion) the lines
from the 'Ode to Joy' in which the poet offers to embrace the
whole world. At other times too he liked to use phrases from the
'Ode to Joy' to prepare a deliberate anticlimax; as when he
introduces an allusion to the often-quoted lines

> Wem der große Wurf gelungen
> Eines Freundes Freund zu sein . . .

> Whoever reached that highest goal
> To acquire a friend . . .

[34] *MEW* XIX, 389, 394; XXXV, 154 ff.; cf. L. I. Golman (and others), *Karl
Marx. Biographie*, p. 751.
[35] *MEW* XVIII, 404 ('Ein Komplott gegen die Internationale Arbeiter-
Assoziation').
[36] *MEW* II, 214; XXIX, 370; XXIX, 590–3; XXIX, 500; XVIII, 92.

into a sentence ridiculing the totally unknown and insignificant German ally Félix Pyat had found to back up his political views and ambitions: 'Pyat has reached his highest goal at last [*Pyat ist der große Wurf gelungen*]. He has found his German—Herr Weber from the Palatinate.' But from 1842, when he alluded with approval to a passage from 'On Naive and Sentimental Poetry', until 1870, when he commended Schiller as a 'competent judge' of philistinism on the strength of a poem in *Votive Tablets* (*Tabulae Votivae*),[37] Marx left his readers in little doubt that he respected Schiller as a great writer, even if his own tastes ran more to Goethe and (especially) Shakespeare, and even if he believed that imitation of Schiller—*das Schillern*—was leading nineteenth-century German dramatists into undesirable ways.

Most of the vast amount of reading that Marx continued to do in his last years was not 'literary' in the narrow sense: but it is important to notice in how many ways he tried to bring his literary and scientific-historical interests together. In the notes he made on Lewis H. Morgan's *Ancient Society, or Researches in the lines of Human Progress from Savagery through Barbarism to Civilisation* (London, 1877), Homer and Aeschylus are used as 'sources' of historical information with which to test, or confirm, Morgan's findings; and in the 'Ethnological Notebooks' which contain the record of further research into the structure of primitive societies we can observe again and again how critically Marx read, and how literature helped him to 'place' the authors he scrutinized. Sir Henry Maine's *Lectures on the Early History of Institutions*, for instance, provokes the following note (entirely in English except for one demonstrative pronoun):

If, then, (a nice 'If' only resting on Maine's own 'confident assertion') *then*, (dies 'then' Pecksniffian), at *any early period* [Maine transports his 'patriarchal' Roman family into the very beginning of things] the married woman had among the Hindoos *her property altogether enfranchised from her husband's control* ['enfranchised', that is to say, from Maine's 'confident assertion'], it is not easy to give a reason why the *obligations of the family despotism* [a principal pet-doctrine of block-headed John Bull to read in original 'despotism'] were relaxed in this one particular.*

* Square and round brackets and italics by Marx.

[37] *MEW* I, 6; XXXIII, 6 (letter to Engels, 20 July 1870).

This is not the only time Dickens's Pecksniff intrudes into these notes—Jeremy Bentham's 'greatest happiness of the greatest number' provokes the exclamation 'O you Pecksniff!' (*O du Pecksniff!*), applied impartially to Bentham and to Maine. An account of the ethics of Australian aboriginees copied from Sir John Lubbock:

> *So strictly is the amount of punishment limited*, that if inflicting such spear-wounds a man, either *through carelessness or from any other cause*, exceeded the recognised limits—if, for instance, he wounded the femoral artery—he would in turn become liable for punishment

brings a Shakespearian reminiscence: 'Shylock Affaire'. Lubbock's account of Brahmin practices (exhibiting divine images in chains in order to make worshippers relieve their plight by gifts of money) prompts Marx's note: 'Compare *Don Quixote*, Part II, ch. 23, where the good Don is in Montesinos' cave.' These notes also illustrate what one may call Marx's backstair-view of many great literary figures. Just as Jonathan Swift (whose works he read and studied carefully, as underlinings and annotations in the complete edition he possessed still testify) enters his ken principally because of his stand on Irish affairs, so Edmund Spenser and Sir John Davies are not, for him, the authors of enduring poems, but rather the contemptible instruments of oppressive policies:

> The lousy Sir John Davis [*sic*] was King James's Attorney-General for Ireland, and for this post, of course, a right kind of rascal was chosen—a similarly 'unprejudiced' and disinterested fellow as Elizabeth's arse-kissing poet Spenser ('State of Ireland'). His remedy for the ills of Ireland, the employment of large masses of troops 'to tread down all that standeth before them in foot, and lay on the ground all the *stiffnecked people of that land*.' That war was to be waged, not only in summer, but in winter too; he continues: 'the end will be very short' and he describes in proof what he himself had witnessed 'in the late wars of Munster' etc. For further cannibalism of this poet see Haverty [=M. Haverty, *History of Ireland, Ancient and Modern* (Dublin, 1860)].[38]

---

[38] *The Ethnological Notebooks of Karl Marx*, ed. L. Krader (Assen, 1972), pp. 324, 351, 305. An account of Marx's underlinings and annotations in copies of the works of Swift, Defoe, and Cobbett can be found in B. Kaiser and I. Werchan, *Ex Libris Karl Marx und Friedrich Engels. Schicksal und Verzeichnis einer Bibliothek.*

These ethnological and political studies, lastly, make constant appeals to ancient myths and ancient literature, of which the following comment on a speech from the *Iliad* is the most elaborate but by no means the only example:

Odysseus is here not giving a lecture on a form of government, but demanding obedience to the supreme commander in war. Since they are appearing before Troy only as an army, the proceedings in the *agora* secure to the Greeks all necessary democracy. When Achilles speaks of presents—that is, the division of the booty—he always leaves the division, not to Agamemnon or any other *basileus*, but to the 'sons of the Achaeans,' that is, the people. Such epithets as 'descended from Zeus,' 'nourished by Zeus,' prove nothing, for *every* gens is descended from a god, that of the leader of the tribe being already descended from a 'superior' god, in this case Zeus. Even those without personal freedom, such as the swineherd Eumaeus and others, are 'divine' (*dioi* and *theioi*), and that too in the *Odyssey* which is much later than the *Iliad*; and again in the *Odyssey* the name *Heros* is given to the herald Mulios as well as to the blind bard Demodocus. Since, in short, council and assembly of the people function together with the *basileus*, the word *basileia*, which Greek writers employ to denote the so-called Homeric kingship (chief command in the army being the principal characteristic of the office), only means—military democracy.[39]

It is worth remembering in this connection that the old Marx continued to find classical myths useful and meaningful in his discussions of the modern world. His contrast between the 'heaven-storming' French *communards* and German 'slaves of heaven' recalls the contrasts he had drawn in earlier years between the Prometheus and the Hermes of Aeschylus: 'Just compare', he wrote to Ludwig Kugelmann on 12 April 1871, 'these heaven-storming Parisians with the heaven-slaves of the Germanico-Prussian Holy Roman Empire with its posthumous masquerades . . .'[40]

When Marx looked up from his ethnological studies, however, to survey how *others* were using myths in the last quarter of the nineteenth century, he confessed himself appalled. Engels quotes a letter from Marx, written in the spring of 1882, in which

[39] Quoted in Engels's *The Origin of the Family, Private Property and the State*, ed. E. B. Leacock (London, 1972), pp. 168–9.
[40] *MEW* XXXIII, 206.

Marx charges the text of Wagner's *The Ring of the Nibelungs* with grossly titillating misuse of Germanic legend:

' "Was it ever known that a brother embraced his sister as his bride?" These "gods of lechery" [*Geilheitsgötter*], who, quite in the modern fashion, spice their amours with a dash of incest, are answered by Marx: "In primitive times [*in der Urzeit*] the sister *was* the wife, and that was moral." '⁴¹

Marx found old myths maltreated, then—but he also found new kinds of 'myth' being produced in his own day. Eleven years before the protest against Wagner, on 27 July 1871, he had written to Ludwig Kugelmann:

It has hitherto been believed that Christian myth-making was possible only because printing had not yet been invented. Quite on the contrary! The daily Press, and the telegraph that in a moment spreads its inventions over the whole earth, fabricated more myths in a single day (and the bovine bourgeois believes and propagates them) than could have been produced by earlier times in a century.⁴²

It goes without saying that to Marx such lying 'myths' as these would seem more ephemeral than those he found in Homer and Aeschylus; that from them a new florescence of epic and drama was not to be expected.

Besides the entries in his 'Ethnological Notebooks' Marx made other jottings in his later years which show him continually trying to bring his literary experiences into a relation with his historical and political research. In notes on J. R. Green's *History of the English People*, for instance, Marx seeks clarification about class-feeling in fourteenth-century England by confronting Langland's *Piers Ploughman* with what he sees as the more 'courtly' *Canterbury Tales*; and in the excerpts he made from F. C. Schlosser's *History of the World* (*Weltgeschichte für das deutsche Volk*) he sought once again to come to grips with the

---

⁴¹ *MEW* XXI, 44. Marx's references to Wagner are invariably unfriendly. After being introduced by Wilhelm Pieper to the 'music of the future', he writes to Engels: 'C'est affreux, and makes one fear for the future and its *Poesiemusik*' (12 Feb. 1856—*MEW* XXIX, 11). In later life he shows himself at once scandalized and amused by what he learnt of the relations between Wagner, v. Bülow, Liszt, and Cosima: 'It is hard to imagine a better libretto for an Offenbach opera than this family-group with its patriarchal relationships. The events connected with this group could be depicted in a tetralogy—just like the Nibelungen.' (To Jenny Longuet, Aug.–Sept. 1876—*MEW* XXXIV, 193.)
⁴² *MEW* XXXIII, 252.

discontinuity or disproportion between political and cultural history: 'In this wild, unquiet time Italy [experienced] the finest flowering of its culture (e.g. Dante, the philosopher Guido Cavalcanti etc.).'⁴³ Elsewhere literature served him for analogies of various kinds. Thus, in a letter written before the publication of *Capital* I, Marx tried to convey what he thought were the nature and importance of Proudhon's work on the nature of property by means of a parallel from German philosophy as well as from literary history:

[Proudhon's] first work, *What is Property?*, is undoubtedly his best. It is epoch-making not because it contains anything new, but because of the new and bold way in which it restates what is already known . . . In this work Proudhon bears to Saint-Simon and Fourier about the same relation that Feuerbach bears to Hegel . . . In a strictly scientific history of political economy this work would hardly deserve a mention. But sensational writings of this kind have a part to play in the sciences just as they have a part to play in literature, in the novel . . .⁴⁴

In drafts for *The Civil War in France*, Marx likened the officials of the Paris Commune, conscientiously performing public offices without claiming great rewards, to Milton selling *Paradise Lost* for £5.⁴⁵ Such analogies work the other way round too. The history of mistranslations is illuminated by the history of errors in geology (see below, p. 387). Palaeontology throws light on the history of ideas.⁴⁶ A term learnt from the physiologists—*regressive metamorphosis*—describes Marx's feelings about the intellectual history of Europe from Diderot via Hegel to Jules Janin.⁴⁷ Crystallography supplies a term for writers who imitate, consciously or unconsciously, the style and manner of thinking of a class to which they themselves do not fully belong: the term *pseudomorph*.⁴⁸

'This work of Proudhon's', Marx said of *What is Property?* (*Qu'est-ce que la propriété*), 'is characterized, if I may so express myself, by a certain muscularity of style. And it is this style which I consider Proudhon's main merit.'⁴⁴ That, needless to

⁴³ *ÜKL* I, 380, 355.
⁴⁴ Letter to J. B. von Schweitzer, 24 Jan. 1865—*MEW* XVI, 25–6.
⁴⁵ *MEW* XVII, 544.
⁴⁶ Letter to Engels, 25 Mar. 1868—*MEW* XXXII, 51.
⁴⁷ Letter to Engels, 15 Apr. 1869—*MEW* XXXII, 303–4.
⁴⁸ *The Secular Chronicle*, 1878—*MEW* XIX, 146.

say, was not meant as an unalloyed compliment; but Marx goes on, in this same letter to J. B. von Schweitzer, to characterize what he admires about Proudhon in terms that might apply, word for word almost, to Marx himself:

Challenging defiance which does not shrink from touching the economic Holy of Holies, with paradoxes to tease the bourgeois understanding, incisive judgements, bitter irony, now and then glimpses of a deep and true anger at the infamy of the existing order, revolutionary seriousness . . .

Marx adds to this something he feels to be lacking in Proudhon's 'sentimental' publication: a view of society and political economy backed up by serious scientific research. He hopes to have made, through constant and devoted study, a contribution that deserves to be mentioned (unlike Proudhon's!) in a 'strictly scientific history of political economy'. And as soon as he has said this, a literary analogy again comes to his mind.

But sensational publications like these [i.e. like Proudhon's *What is Property?*] have a part to play in the sciences *just as they do in the history of the novel*. Take Malthus's work on Population: its first edition is nothing but a 'sensational pamphlet', and plagiarized to boot from beginning to end. And yet how stimulating this 'satire on mankind' has proved! [my italics].

In practice as in theory, Marx never compartmentalizes his history—the development of the novel and that of economic thought exhibit analogies which make for mutual illumination.

If Marx found much to admire in Proudhon's early work, he thought his later writings irredeemably bad in content as in style:

The style is what the French call *ampoulé*. Pompous speculative jargon, a would-be German-philosophical manner, takes over whenever Gallic acuity of understanding fails. Bombastic self-advertizing, a boastful tone, and in particular that constant babbling about 'science', and false parade of 'scientific' learning which, always so unprofitable, sound unceasingly in one's ears. Instead of exhibiting the true warmth characteristic of his first pamphlet Proudhon systematically talks himself, in certain passages of his later work, into a flushed and fugitive heat. Add to this the clumsy and revolting pretence of learning characteristic of the self-taught man whose pride in thinking everything out for himself has already been broken and who now believes himself obliged—as a parvenu of science—to preen himself on precisely those things which he neither is nor has.

With his love of hollow phrases, his philistine imagination, his burlesque grumblings and rantings, his vanity, his 'scientific' charlatanism, and his political compromises the later Proudhon appears, in Marx's eyes, the typical petty-bourgeois intellectual of his country and his time:

Like the historian Raumer this petty-bourgeois is composed of 'on the one side' and 'on the other'. This is true of his economic interests and *therefore* [the italics are Marx's] of his religious, scientific, and artistic views, of his morality, of everything.

'Perhaps', Marx concludes this new blast against *The Philosophy of Poverty*, 'posterity will view the latest phase of French life as characterized by the fact that Louis Bonaparte was its Napoleon, and Proudhon its Rousseau–Voltaire.'[49]

While his remarks on Proudhon show the later Marx bringing his literary and stylistic interests to bear on the analysis of economic texts, his remarks on the novelists he admired show him looking to them for light on men's economic actions and motives. In a letter of 14 December 1868 he copies out a passage from Balzac's *Village Priest* (*Le Curé de village*) and asks Engels to confirm or deepen, from his own knowledge and experience of practical economics, what Balzac there shows of the motives that swayed his contemporaries.[50] That he also turned this light on to his own inner life is attested by Paul Lafargue, who tells us that Balzac's *The Unknown Masterpiece* (*Le Chef-d'œuvre inconnu*) made a deep impression on Marx because it was in part a description of his own feelings.[51]

As the letter about Proudhon has already served to demonstrate, Marx remained ever conscious, in these his later years, of the importance of style—the importance, above all, of clear, forceful, and accurate expression. When he looked into German newspapers he was frequently horrified by what he found.[52]

[49] *MEW* XVI, 31–2. Marx's respect for Rousseau's political and social thought is well attested: see *MEW* I, 103, 370; III, 387, 513; IV, 353; XIII, 280. For a more critical perspective see *MEW* I, 78; III, 75; XIII, 615.

[50] P. Demetz, *Marx, Engels und die Dichter*, pp. 168–9.

[51] *Karl Marx: His Life and Work. Reminiscences by Paul Lafargue and Wilhelm Liebknecht* (New York, 1943), p. 16.

[52] See letter to Engels, 28 Apr. 1862—*MEW* XXX, 227–8.

Nor were his experiences with translators of his own non-German works calculated to restore his faith in the ability of his German contemporaries to write their own language with elegance and accuracy. He hated with equal fervour the 'pseudo-philosophical and pseudo-scientific jargon' which he found in many *English* writings on political economy: 'The art consists in puzzling and mystifying the reader until he discovers, with relief, that all these hard words were nothing but masks assumed by commonplaces.'[53] This observation comes from a letter to Engels, whose own early work *The Condition of the Working Class in England* Marx reread in the 1860s with a sense of discovery allied to sadness:

Reading your book again I felt, with regret, that we are growing old. How freshly and passionately, in what a bold, anticipating way, how free of learned, scientific scruples, you here go straight to the heart of the matter! And the illusion that tomorrow, or the day after tomorrow, history will clearly show what is to come of all this lends the whole work a warmth, a *joie de vivre*, a humour, against which all that comes later seems all the more unpleasantly 'grey in grey'.[54]

It comes as no surprise, therefore, to find Marx stressing, during the composition of *Capital* I, the literary and artistic side of his own works. Whatever shortcomings they may have, he writes to Engels on 31 July 1865 'my writings have this merit: they are an artistic whole'. The texture of style, and the proportion of the parts within the whole structure, are carefully considered and worked over, with 'artistic considerations' (*artistische Rücksichten*) very much in mind—though these must always, of course, go together with a search for truth. He feels at times that all his striving after a form that is as elegant and popular as his difficult subject permits is wasted on German readers who tend to judge books more by their cubic capacity than by their weighty content and pleasing construction. He is conscious that his illnesses prevent him from giving *Capital* I quite the polish he would like

[53] Letter to Engels, 23 May 1868—*MEW* XXXII, 91.
[54] Letter to Engels, 9 Apr. 1863—*MEW* XXX, 343. 'Grey in grey' is an allusion to a famous passage in Hegel's Introduction to his *Philosophy of Right*: 'Wenn die Philosophie ihr Grau in Grau malt, dann ist eine Gestalt des Lebens alt geworden, und mit Grau in Grau läßt sie sich nicht verjüngen, sondern nur erkennen; die Eule der Minerva beginnt erst mit der einbrechenden Dämmerung ihren Flug.'

to have given it, but he writes, again to Engels, on 20 February 1866:

You will understand, my dear fellow, that in a work like mine there must be many shortcomings in detail. But the composition of the whole, the way it all hangs together, is a triumph of German science and scholarship to which an individual German may confess since the merit belongs not to him but to the whole nation.[55]

In the Postscript (*Nachwort*) appended to the second edition of *Capital* I (dated 24 January 1873) Marx conceded the 'literary shortcomings' of his work, but pointed with pride to reviews in England and Russia that commended his lively manner of writing, and the ease and charm with which he conveyed the most difficult and abstruse matters.[56] He also took pains to explain to his readers how and why his method of presentation had necessarily to differ from his method of inquiry:

The latter has to appropriate the material in detail, to analyse its different forms of development, to trace out their inner connection. Only after this work is done can the actual movement be adequately described. If this is done successfully, if the life of the subject-matter is ideally reflected as in a mirror, then it may appear as if we had an *a priori* construction before us.[57]

In a famous passage from this same Postscript Marx explains, too, why he still found it appropriate to use Hegelian terminology in *Capital* I:

The mystifying side of Hegelian dialectic I criticized nearly thirty years ago, when it was still the fashion of the day. But just when I was working at the first volume of *Capital*, the peevish, arrogant, and mediocre epigones who now set the tone among educated Germans were pleased to treat Hegel as the good Moses Mendelssohn treated Spinoza in Lessing's day—as a 'dead dog'. I therefore openly confessed myself a pupil of that great thinker, and even coquetted here and there, in the chapter on the theory of value, with the modes of expression peculiar to him. The mystification which dialectic suffers in Hegel's hands by no means prevents him from being the first to present its general form of working in a

[55] *MEW* XXXI, 132; XXX, 368; XXX, 248; XXXI, 183.
[56] *K* I—*MEW* XXIII, 22.   [57] *K* I—*MEW* XXIII, 27.

comprehensive and conscious manner. With him it is standing on its head. It must be turned right side up again, if the rational kernel is to be discovered in the mystical husk.[58]

This passage reveals Marx's concern with methods of presentation and adequate expression; his use of imagery as an instrument of thought and persuasion ('kernel' and 'husk', something 'standing on its head' which has to be turned 'right side up'); his deliberate 'coquetting' with Hegelian terminology; and, it must be added, the strength of his prejudices against certain writers and thinkers of the past. On 7 July 1780 Lessing had indeed said to F. H. Jacobi that their contemporaries tended to talk of Spinoza 'as of a dead dog'; but there is no evidence whatever that he included Mendelssohn in this category. Lessing knew, in fact, that though Mendelssohn thought Spinoza's philosophy mistaken in many respects, he had been at great pains to show its supposed influence on the Leibnizian philosophy Mendelssohn admired, and that he had consistently praised Spinoza the man.[59] But Moses Mendelssohn was one of Marx's *bêtes noires*; he is therefore predisposed to entertain unfavourable notions about Mendelssohn's opinions and to belittle him in ways that can only be called unfair.

(iv)

Marx was all the more conscious of the necessity to cultivate what might be called the 'literary' virtues because so many of his friends showed themselves unable to convey, with any degree of accuracy and effectiveness, such insights as they had. Karl Siebel, for instance, who did so much to make Marx's works better known in Germany, seemed to lose all sense and reason as soon as he put pen to paper. 'What do you say', Marx wrote to Engels on 5 August 1865, 'to Siebel's "achievements" in the patriotic-liberal-poetic domain? All that stuff seems to have been written under the influence of a terrible hangover. It is

[58] *K* I—*MEW* XXIII, 27.
[59] Marx had already brought the same charge against Mendelssohn in *Towards a Critique of Political Economy* (*MEW* XIII, 142) and in a letter to Ludwig Kugelmann dated 27 June 1870. Cf. A. Altmann, 'Moses Mendelssohn on Leibniz and Spinoza' in *Studies in Rationalism, Judaism and Universalism in Memory of Leon Roth*, ed. R. Loewe (London, 1966), pp. 13–45.

stupid nonsense, and beats everything our friend has so far permitted himself.'[60] Even sadder was the case of S. L. Borkheim, whom Marx respected as an *homme d'esprit*, an able talker and an interesting thinker, but whose writings he found wholly deficient in clarity, taste, and tact: 'He resembles those savages who think they are beautifying their face when they tattoo it in all the colours of the rainbow.'[61] At the same time, Marx remains as suspicious as ever of belles-lettres. His chapter in the *Anti-Dühring* expresses detestation of 'bellestristic tricks' (*belletristische Mätzchen*) in works of economics, and his context leaves no doubt that when he calls Alexander Herzen a 'Russian belletrist', he means to dismiss him as irrelevant.[62] In similar vein he shrugs off Renan's *Life of Jesus* as 'a mere novel, full of pantheistic-mystical stupor' and uses the word *Poesie* as a euphemism for lies.[63] 'I do not read bellestristic German rubbish', he had written to Freiligrath on 20 July 1867; and his letters to Engels at this same period leave little doubt that Freiligrath's own poems belong, in his eyes, to the same rubbish-heap.

> I had rather be a kitten and cry mew,
> Than one of these same metre ballet-mongers

he quotes from Shakespeare's *Henry IV* Part I in an indignant epistle about Freiligrath which he sent to Engels on 22 August 1870.[64] Many other men of letters who sympathized with some, at least, of his views and aspirations aroused Marx's suspicion and ire in these later years: the 'boastful, confused, pushful literary *flaneur*' M. A. Kertbény, for instance, or the prominent Social Democrat Eduard Lasker, who had written a novel that Marx characterized (without even reading it) as a 'milksop's Odyssey'.[65] Marx distrusted and hated the *flaneur*-type, described by Baudelaire and later celebrated by Marx's self-styled disciple Walter Benjamin, as much as he loathed the

[60] *MEW* XXXI, 135.
[61] Letter to L. Kugelmann, 11 Oct. 1867—*MEW* XXXI, 560.
[62] Letter to *Otechestvennye zapiski*, 1877—*MEW* XIX, 107; *Anti-Dühring*, *MEW* XX, 215.
[63] Letters to Engels, 20 Jan. 1864 and 14 May 1869—*MEW* XXX, 386, and XXXII, 318.
[64] *MEW* XXXI, 554; XXXIII, 47.
[65] Letters to L. Kugelmann, 26 Oct. 1868, and Engels, 19 Aug. 1876—*MEW* XXXII, 573, and XXXIV, 25.

'bohemian' literati for whom he now found the forceful and untranslatable term *Lumpenliteratenpack.*[66]

'Though it is easy', Marx had written to Engels on 10 December 1864, 'to convince English workers of the necessity of what is rational, great caution becomes necessary as soon as literati, bourgeois, or semi-literati [*Literaten, Bürger oder Halbliteraten*] participate in our movement.'[67] A month later he professed himself horrified by the stuff the Lassallean journal *Der Social-Demokrat* published in the columns it set aside for contributions from worker-poets; *beliebiger Knotenblödsinn* he called it, any old nonsense written by men without proletarian class-consciousness or revolutionary ardour.[68] Working-class origin, then, is not enough to save literati from corruption—especially if they take up writing full time. 'The workers themselves', Marx writes to F. A. Sorge in the late 1870s, 'when, like Herr Most & Co., they give up work and become *professional literary men*, always breed "theoretical" mischief and are always ready to join muddleheads from the allegedly "learned" caste.'[69]

That poets make unreliable party-men Marx had learnt to his cost from his dealings with Herwegh and Freiligrath; indeed, Freiligrath had spelt it out for him in his dignified letter of 28 February 1860. 'The party', Freiligrath had said, 'is a cage; and even *for* the party it is better to sing outside it than within it.'[70] It would be quite wrong, however, to conclude that the later Marx wanted literature to be overtly propagandist. He was angry with Freiligrath because of his association with Gottfried Kinkel and his friends during the Schiller centenary celebrations of 1859, and because of Freiligrath's refusal to stand by him openly during his quarrel with Karl Vogt; but the charges he levelled against his later poetry were charges against its hollow bombast (*Pomp und Schall*), its 'Schillerizing', its stuffy family atmosphere, its patriotic trumpetings after 1870 (particularly in the poem which begins 'Hurra, du stolzes, schönes Weib, / Hurra, Germania!'), and its lack of humour. 'If only',

[66] Letter to Engels, 13 Apr. 1867—*MEW* XXXI, 288.
[67] *MEW* XXXI, 39.
[68] To Engels, 30 Jan. 1865—*MEW* XXXI, 48. Marx suspects Sophie von Hatzfeld of being directly or indirectly responsible for the appearance of these effusions in praise of Lassalle.
[69] Quoted in D. McLellan's *Karl Marx. His Life and Thought*, p. 435.
[70] Cf. Demetz, *Marx, Engels und die Dichter*, pp. 92–101.

he had written to Freiligrath before their relations soured, 'you would make the effort to bring into your art the humour which Your African Majesty shows in private life, you would, I am sure, make a contribution to the humorous genre too.'[71] Marx ever remained as suspicious as Engels of literary works that had too palpable a design on their readers.

Nor did Marx demand of literature a direct and unmediated reflection of social and historical circumstance. In the late 1860s he sent Engels a copy of Hoffmann's fantastic tale *Little Zaches (Klein Zaches genannt Zinnober)* along with some factory-reports;[72] he sent another copy of the same tale to the Kugelmann family;[73] and among other works he read with appreciation in his later years are Balzac's *Unknown Masterpiece* and *Melmoth Reconciled*. 'I advise you to read ... *Le Chef-d'œuvre inconnu* and *Melmoth réconcilié*', he writes to Engels on 25 February 1867. 'These are two little masterpieces, full of the most delightful irony.'[74] He clearly responded to such works for personal reasons (was he not himself driven, like the hero of the *Unknown Masterpiece*, to elaborate and over-elaborate what he felt to be the principal work by which posterity ought to remember him?)[75] and because he felt important problems of the time were powerfully symbolized in them. Hoffmann's *Klein Zaches*, the tale of a mis-shapen dwarf to whom is attributed, because of some potent spell, everything good and worthwhile said and performed by other people, is as apt a symbol of alienation as may be found in world literature; while Balzac's *Melmoth* has been described, with some justification, as 'a masterfully ironic reflection on the state of a totally secularized society in which "even the Holy Spirit has its quotation on the Stock Exchange"'.[76] But as the letter to Engels which has just been quoted

---

[71] Letters to Engels, 3 Nov. 1859 and 2 Sept. 1870; to Sigfried Meyer, 21 Jan. 1871; to Freiligrath, 10 Jan. 1850—*MEW* XXIX, 501; XXXIII, 50, 173; XXVII, 596.

[72] Letter to Engels, 20 Feb. 1866—*MEW* XXXI, 183.

[73] *Mohr und General. Erinnerungen an Marx und Engels*, p. 316.

[74] *MEW* XXXI, 278.

[75] Cf. *Gespräche*, 307, 559; and Demetz, op. cit., pp. 169–70.

[76] I. Mészáros, *Marx's Theory of Alienation*, p. 33. Cf. J. Smulkstys, *Karl Marx*, pp. 93–4: 'It is conceivable that he read into [*Melmoth réconcilié*] a prediction of doom for the bourgeoisie in its mad rush to amass wealth without regard for basic human values. Balzac seems to hint at this in a reference to the French bourgeois society as "a civilization which, since 1815, has been moved by the spirit of gain rather than the principle of honour". It is also possible that Marx was impressed

makes quite clear, Marx responded not only to the overt or
latent theme of such stories, but also to their tone—delighting
particularly in the irony with which the author told his tale.

Marx continued to stress that an author's intention and his
achievement were two different things. 'A writer must distinguish', he told Maxim Kovalevsky in April 1879, 'between what
an author in fact says and what he thinks he is saying. This is
true even of philosophical systems.'[77]

Ever since his early poems about Pustkuchen's readings of
Goethe, and with renewed fervour after the antics of Gottfried
Kinkel and his friends during the Schiller centenary of 1859,
Marx had used men's understanding of great literature as a
touchstone by which to judge their intellectual and spiritual
capacity. He was horrified, he tells Engels in a letter dated 19
April 1864, to read in the London *Athenaeum* that 'Mr Karl
Blind has joined the Shakespeare Committee'; for he knew this
liberal *émigré* sufficiently well, he thought, to be able to say 'the
fellow does not understand a line of Shakespeare'.[78] The same
was true of that prolific writer of comedies Roderich Benedix:
'If he and his like understood Shakespeare, how could they have
the courage to produce their own manufactures before the
public?'[79] What is true of individuals is true of whole epochs.
In April 1869 Marx sent Engels a copy of one of his favourite
works, Diderot's 'unique masterpiece' *Rameau's Nephew*. In an
accompanying letter he copied out what Hegel had to say of
this classic confrontation of 'honest soul' and 'disintegrated
consciousness' in the *Phenomenology of the Spirit*, and then adds
a few remarks on Jules Janin's interpretation of the same work.

Janin deplores the want of a moral 'point' in Diderot's *Rameau*, and
remedies this defect through his discovery that the nephew's
perversity stems from his chagrin at not being born a *gentilhomme*.
The Kotzebuean rubbish he has smeared on this cornerstone is

by the author's success in combining a contemporary social message with a variation on a Faustian theme, which had fascinated him since his school days. Finally,
it could not have escaped Marx's attention that the story was presented in dialectical contrasts between phenomena such as power and impotence, idealism and
cynicism, emotion and intellect—a method of writing certainly close to his heart.'
Smulkstys's point that *Melmoth réconcilié* appealed to Marx as a variant of the Faust
legend is well taken.

[77] Apr. 1879—*MEW* XXXIV, 506.   [78] *MEW* XXX, 390.
[79] Letter to Engels, 11 Dec. 1873—*MEW* XXXIII, 102.

being melodramatically performed in London at this very moment.
The passage from Diderot to Jules Janin illustrates, I suppose, what
the physiologists call 'regressive metamorphosis'. There you have your
French mind *before* the French Revolution and *under* Louis-Philippe.[80]

What is particularly instructive in this passage is Marx's condemnation of seeking a directly expressed 'moral', a 'moral
"point"', in great works of literature; his use of a term from
physiology to describe a phenomenon in the history of literature; the continuing respect in which he held Hegel in his later
years (for all the fun he occasionally made of his style and his
manner of thinking); and his attempt to see writers as representatives of the *Geist*, the mind and spirit, of their nation and
their time.[81] This last endeavour provided Marx with a new
perspective from which to see his old *bête noire* Chateaubriand.
A letter to Engels dated 30 November 1873 shows that he has
been reading Sainte-Beuve's book on Chateaubriand (*Chateaubriand et son groupe littéraire sous l'Empire* (Paris, 1860)). He
speaks of Chateaubriand as 'a writer I have always found repulsive', and continues:

If this man became so famous in France, it was because he incorpor-
ates, in every respect, French *vanité*: not in its easy, frivolous eighteenth-century garb, but romantically dressed-up, strutting along
with newfangled phrases, false profundity, Byzantine exaggeration,
coquettish sentiment, garish irridescence, word-painting, theatricality, 'sublimity'—in short, a mishmash of lies which is unpre-
cedented in form and in content.[82]

Even the quality of *vanité*, it would seem, has declined between
the eighteenth and the nineteenth centuries. Wherever Marx
looks in his later years, he finds little to foster an easy faith in the
progress of taste; the capitalist order, he clearly thought, had
led to 'regressive metamorphosis' in the cultural life of Europe.
'That windbag Bodenstedt' we read in one of his last letters to
Engels, 'and the pansy aesthetician Friedrich Vischer—these
are the Horace and Virgil of the Emperor William I.'[83]

[80] Letter to Engels, 15 Apr. 1869—*MEW* XXXII, 303–4.
[81] In one of his *NYDT* articles Marx had looked to Dante and Machiavelli
for help in understanding the 'Italianness' of Garibaldi (*MEW* XV, 185).
[82] *MEW* XXXIII, 96.
[83] *MEW* XXXV, 54; the letter is dated 8 Mar. 1882, but was in fact written
on 8 Apr. of that year.

(v)

Marx's letters continue to be permeated by literary reminiscences that come, almost unbidden, to his mind. Guilt-feelings
brought on by a failure to answer his correspondents as
promptly as he would have liked remind him of a fable from
Luther's *Table Talk*. Charles Bradlaugh's 'distortion' of his,
Marx's, views leads him to recall the plaint of Cacciaguida in
Canto XVII of Dante's *Paradiso* about the 'vicious and ill
company' men are forced to keep in exile, while men in protec-
tive rubber clothing, taking a course of sulphur-inhalations in
the baths at Enghien, seem to be enacting an 'innocent scene
from Dante's *Inferno*'. He likes to dub an opponent *vir obscurus*,
thus comparing him, by implication, to obscurantist monks
ridiculed in a famous humanist satire of the sixteenth century,
Epistolae obscurorum virorum. An embarrassing illness brings to
mind the poems of Mathurin Régnier; the activities of Wilhelm
Liebknecht are glossed with an adaptation of a famous sentence
from Voltaire's *Candide*; a casual glance into the *Maxims* of La
Rochefoucauld brings vividly before him a passage from
Sterne's *Tristram Shandy* to which he had alluded in the *Neue
Rheinische Zeitung*, and again in *The Class Struggles in France*,
many years before; and the very mention of Lizzy *Burns* conjures up the co-presence of her namesake, 'the great poet'.[84] At
the opposite end of the literary scale Marx finds himself reminded, by the behaviour of the Freiligrath family, of sentimental novels by the writer who anagrammatized his name
Carl Heun into 'H. Clauren'; other absurdities recalled for
him the writings of Kotzebue and Berthold Auerbach.[85] Some
of Marx's literary references, in these later years, are so fleeting
and obscure that only readers well attuned to his way of thinking can even hope to catch them. When on 11 April 1868 he
writes one of his charming family letters to his daughter Laura,
he says of his new son-in-law Paul Lafargue (who had non-
European ancestry): 'As to that said helpmate, his sending

[84] *MEW* XXXIV, 245 (Luther); XVII, 482, and XXXV, 75 (Dante); XIX,
371 (*vir obscurus*); XXXI, 368–9 (Régnier); XXXII, 534 (Voltaire); XXXII,
326 (Sterne); XXXI, 72 (Burns).

[85] *MEW* XXXII, 10 (Clauren); XXXV, 12 (Kotzebue); XXXIV, 25 (Auerbach). Berthold Auerbach had just written a preface to Eduard Lasker's anony-
mously published *Erfahrungen einer Mannesseele*, and this brought back all Marx's
old antipathies.

books to me, at such a critical juncture, speaks volumes for the innate kindness of the "young man". This simple fact would go far to prove that he must belong to a better than the European race.'[86] That last sentence alludes, slyly, to J. G. Seume's once famous poem 'The Savage' (*Der Wilde*), whose hero (an aborigine horrified by the sham politeness of Europe, *Europens übertünchte Höflichkeit*) retreats into the bushes with the words:

Wir Wilden sind doch bessre Menschen

We savages, after all, are better men.

The extent and variety of Marx's literary allusions is well exhibited by another letter, written (again in English) to his daughter Jenny on 10 June 1869, which describes a visit to a Yorkshire farm belonging to the geologist J. R. Dakyns. Here successive sentences allude, in a wholly natural and unforced way, to the novels of Charlotte Brontë, to Goethe's *Faust*, and to George Eliot's *Felix Holt*:

We had dinner on his farm—on Sunday last—in the room directly lying over the chapel. The room had evidently formerly served as an assembly room of the monks, big walled (ich meine, mit dicken Mauern umgeben),* with a look out to magnificent trees, and to an amphitheatrical group of mountains, the one overtopping the other, and wrapt in that blue veil Currer Bell is so delighted with. During the very merry, and in spite of its rusticity comfortable dinner, the sing-song of the youth in the chapel, coming from the depths, and sounding as from a far-away place, reminded me somewhat of the Christian song in Faust.

Well, our friend Dakyns is a sort of Felix Holt less the affectation of that man, and plus the knowledge.[87]

From this it is clear that Marx had read Charlotte Brontë's *Shirley* to good purpose—at the back of his mind are landscape-celebrations like that in chapter XII:

. . . the distant hills were dappled, the horizon was shaded and tinted like mother-of-pearl; silvery blues, soft purples, evanescent greens

---

* 'I mean "surrounded by thick walls".'

[86] *KMP* 120.
[87] I am indebted to Professor Dr. Rolf Dlubek of the Institut für Marxismus-Leninismus (Marx-Engels Abteilung) for a photocopy of this letter and permission to quote from it.

and rose-shades, all melting into fleeces of white cloud, pure as azury snow, allured the eye with a remote glimpse of heaven's foundations. The air blowing on the brow was fresh, and sweet, and bracing.

'Our England is a bonnie island', said Shirley, 'and Yorkshire is one of her bonniest nooks.'

or in chapter XXXII:

The hills wore a lilac-blue; the setting sun had purple in its red; the sky was ice, all silvered azure . . .

We learn from Marian Comyn's reminiscences of visits to the Marx household in the last years of Marx's life[88] that the whole family professed its admiration for the works of Charlotte and Emily Brontë and ranged them above those of George Eliot.

But if Marx's mind was increasingly full of English literary association, German ones were never driven out. Again and again we find the words and music of German songs he had known in his youth coming to his lips and to his pen. A noteworthy scene described by his daughter Jenny in a letter to the Kugelmann family shows him and Engels singing Max Schneckenburger's 'Watch on the Rhine' (*Die Wacht am Rhein*) to the tune of the students' drinking-song *Krambambuli*; and he cannot so much as mention Schleswig-Holstein without hearing, at once, the epithet with which a famous ditty by M. F. Chemnitz and K. G. Bellmann had graced that region—'girt by the sea', *meerumschlungen*. Such reminiscences include, right up to the end, snatches from plays that were popular when Marx was a student in Berlin. The words

> Löse mir, o Örindur,
> Diesen Zwiespalt der Natur!
>
> O Oerindur, solve for me
> This contradiction in nature!

which occur in a letter of 7 October 1876, represent a not quite accurate recollection of Adolph Müllner's fate-tragedy *Guilt* (*Die Schuld*). German jingles are increasingly joined by—not

---

[88] *The Nineteenth Century*, xci (1922), 151–69. A usefully annotated German translation has recently been published: Marian Comyn, *Meine Erinnerungen an Karl Marx*, übersetzt und annotiert von Frank T. Walker. Mit einem Vorwort von Hans Pelger (Trier, 1970).

always correctly remembered—English ones: 'I cannot sing with the Miller of Dee: "I care for nobody and nobody cares for me".'[89] Certain favourite quotations from Goethe (Mephistopheles' words to the student about grey theory and the golden tree of life, the *West–Eastern Divan* lines about 'torment' bringing 'greater pleasure') recur in the letters as well as the works,[90] and are joined by other, less familiar ones. Even the carbuncles that tortured him in his later years bring Goethe to mind—when one of these prevents his sitting down, he reminds Engels of the final lines of Goethe's poem 'Totality' (Totalität):

> Und wenn er keinen Hintern hat,
> Wie soll der Edle sitzen?

> And if he has no behind,
> How can the noble fellow sit down?

Nor can Marx enjoin discretion on one of his correspondents without at once remembering Mignon's lines in *Wilhelm Meister's Apprenticeship*: 'Do not bid me speak—bid me be silent.'[91]

Heine, as always, runs Goethe close. Marx adopts or adapts Heine's contentious verbal compounds, once again taking *Menschenkehricht* ('human garbage') from No. 44 of the *New Spring* cycle, or transforming the *Vorschußlorbeerkronen* ('advance laurel crowns') of 'Plateniden' into *Zukunftslorbeerkronen* ('future laurel crowns').[92] At the time of the Gotha Programme he recalls Heine's lament: 'I have sown dragons and harvested fleas.'[93] In a letter from Margate to his daughter Laura, dated 20 March 1866 and written in English, he cannot talk of regulations about foot-and-mouth disease without remembering first a stanza from Heine's *Homecoming* (*Die Heimkehr* 45), which

---

[89] *Gespräche*, 373. Letters to Engels, 4 Dec. 1863 (*MEW* XXX, 378); to Wilhelm Liebknecht, 7 Oct. 1876 (*MEW* XXXIV, 209); to Engels, 24 Mar. 1866 (*MEW* XXXI, 193); and to his daughter Laura, 20 Mar. 1866 (*KMP* 110). The Müllner quotation should have read: 'Und erklärt mir, Örindur, / Diesen Zwiespalt der Natur' (*Die Schuld*, I. v).

[90] e.g. *MEW* XXX, 280, 653; and *KMP* 83.

[91] Letter to Engels, 17 Dec. 1867—*MEW* XXXI, 412; letter to W. Liebknecht, 13 Apr. 1871—*MEW* XXXIII, 207.

[92] Letters to Engels, 14 Aug. 1879 and 5 Aug. 1865—*MEW* XXXIV, 89, and XXXI, 134.

[93] Quoted by S. E. Hyman in *The Tangled Bank*, p. 161.

he translates into English doggerel, and then a song from *As You Like It*, IV. ii, which Laura—'discreet By Bye'—loved to sing:

Withdrawing somewhat from the seaside, and roaming over the adjacent rustic district, you are painfully reminded of '*civilisation*' by large boards, staring at you everywhere, headed 'Cattle Disease', and placarded over with a government proclamation, the result of the wild rush which the horned cattle gentry, lords and commoners, made at the government, on the opening of parliament.

> Oh, oh King Wiswamitra,
> What fool of an oxen art thou,
> That thou so much wrangle'st and suffer'st,
> And all that for a cow.

But if honest Wiswamitra, like a true Indian, tormented himself for the salvation of the cow Sabala, those English gentry, in the true style of modern martyrs, bleed the people for their cows' ailings. The horn plague upon them! The horn, the horn, as discreet By Bye sings it lustily.[94]

Even this does not end the flurry of literary allusions—the letter continues with a reference to a pun by Thackeray and to the title of Chaucer's *Canterbury Tales*.

Snatches from Heine's verse and prose seem to float continually into Marx's mind. In a letter to Paul Lafargue, written in a characteristic mixture of English and French, he alludes to a passage from *Lutetia*: 'Bakounine . . . understands la réclame almost as well as Victor Hugo qui, comme Heine dit, n'est pas simplement égoiste, mais Hugoïste.'[95] And even when writing about the defeat and glory of the Paris Commune Marx found Heine's words more adequate than any others to convey his feelings: 'This Parisian uprising—even though overcome by the wolves, pigs, and common dogs of the old society—is the most glorious deed of our party since the June insurrection in Paris.'[96] *Wenn auch unterliegend vor den Wölfen, Schweinen und gemeinen Hunden der alten Gesellschaft*—that phrase superimposes on the defeat of the Commune the defeat of another series of uprisings, those of 1848, which Heine had celebrated in a powerful poem entitled 'In October 1849':

[94] *KMP* 111–12; *MEW* XXXI, 507.   [95] *KMP* 128–9.
[96] *MEW* XXXIII, 206.

. . . Es muß der Held nach altem Brauch
Den tierisch rohen Mächten unterliegen.

Und diesmal hat der Ochse gar
Mit Bären einen Bund geschlossen —
Du fällst; doch tröste dich, Magyar,
Wir andern haben schlimmre Schmach genossen.

Anständge Bestien sind es doch,
Die ganz honett dich überwunden;
Doch wir geraten in das Joch
Von Wölfen, Schweinen und gemeinen Hunden.

Das heult und bellt und grunzt — ich kann
Ertragen kaum den Duft der Sieger . . .

. . . The hero must—it is a time-honoured custom—
Succumb to bestial, coarse powers.

And this time the [Austrian] ox has even
Allied himself with Russian bears—
You fall, Hungarians; but take comfort:
Our fate is more disgraceful than yours.

You, after all, were worsted by decent beasts,
In a fight that was not too unfair;
But we come under the yoke
Of wolves, pigs, and common curs.

Such howling and barking and grunting—I can
Hardly bear the victors' smell . . .

Franziska Kugelmann remembers conversations about Heine
in 1867 in which Marx quoted Heine's poems about the sentimental young lady admiring the sunset (*New Poems*—'Ver-
schiedene' 10) and the laughing, faithless woman (*New Poems*—
'Romanzen' 1) with approval, but spoke scathingly of Heine's
personal character.[97] And H. M. Hyndman, who visited Marx
at the very end of his life, in 1880 and 1881, recalls that Marx
thought Heine one of the greatest masters of language, and
that he took a keen interest in attempts to translate his works
into English:

He told me much about Heine, with whom he had a long correspondence which has never even yet been published . . . One evening

[97] *Gespräche*, 316–17; *METEC* 182.

I recall when discussing Freligrath [*sic*], Heine, Hervegh [*sic*] and other great German men of letters of the modern era, he insisted on my reading out . . . Thompson's (B.V.'s) translation of some of Heine's smaller pieces, which he said were the best that had ever been done in any language.[98]

When measured against Heine, other nineteenth-century poets paled into insignificance. This did not apply only to poets whose interests and outlook were as remote from his own as those of Johann Peter Hebel, one of whose dialect-poems Marx encountered with something less than enthusiasm. It applied even to Georg Weerth, with whom he had closely collaborated in the days of the *Neue Rheinische Zeitung*, whose political and social views had never become suspect to him, and whose passing he mourned, in a letter to Engels dated 13 February 1864, as that of an 'old comrade'. Of all Weerth's many writings, only two lines from just one poem ever came to Marx's mind:

> Kein schöner Ding ist auf der Welt
> Als seine Feinde zu beißen . . .

> There is nothing finer in the world
> Than biting one's enemies.[99]

No one who reads Marx's works and letters, or accounts of his conversation, can have any doubt why it should have been this pugnacious formulation which hooked itself into his memory. Weerth thus joins the many now forgotten figures who have left traces in Marx's writings because of one remembered couplet— the mocking jingle, for instance, with which Marx liked, throughout his life, to deflate pretentious writings and actions:

> Wenn das nicht gut für die Wanzläus ist,
> Dann weiß ich nicht, was besser ist

> If that's not good for bedbugs
> I don't know what's better,

or lines from a poem by Wilhelm von Merckels, written in

---

[98] H. M. Hyndman, *The Record of an Adventurous Life*, pp. 279–80.
[99] Letter to L. Kugelmann, 11 Jan. 1868 (*MEW* XXXII, 533); cf. *Gespräche*, 421. Marx does not quote Weerth's poem quite accurately. For J. P. Hebel, see *MEW* XXXI, 148 (letter to Engels, 22 Aug. 1865).

1848, which Marx recalls in a letter to Engels dated 18 November 1861:

Gegen Demokraten
Helfen nur Soldaten.

Only soldiers can help
Against democrats.

The letters Marx wrote in his last years demonstrate constantly how natural he found it to move from one field of knowledge to another. An uncomprehending reviewer of *Capital* I brings to his mind the work of an eighteenth-century philosopher, Moses Mendelssohn, whom he always regarded (somewhat unfairly) as the quintessence of shallow rationalism; that leads him to the psychology and aesthetics of G. Th. Fechner (1801–87) who had tried to find a correlation between stimulus and response which could be expressed mathematically, by means of a 'logarithm of stimulus' (*Logarithmus des Reizes*); and he then sums up his feelings about all these disparate instances of what he sees as shallow thinking by referring his correspondent to a little-known poem in Schiller's *Votive Tablets* (*Tabulae Votivae*):

... philosophical tripe worthy of Moses Mendelssohn, the nagging of a would-be clever, disgruntled know-all. And now, Political Economy is to be dissolved into some nonsense about 'Concepts of Right'! That beats even the 'logarithm of stimulus'. Philistines, as Schiller— a competent judge in this field—has already remarked, resolve all questions by shoving them off into 'conscience'.[100]

This is only one example, taken at random, of the wide context in which Marx constantly places his allusions to literature.

The linguistic and cultural range of Marx's quotations and allusions also continues to be wide. We find him searching for Dutch and Frisian books in Amsterdam; preparing to grapple, at the very end of his life, with Langland's Middle English;[101] reading Appian in Greek for recreation, Dante in Italian, Cervantes and Calderón in Spanish. As a young man he had

[100] Letter to Engels, 20 July 1870—*MEW* XXXIII, 6. Schiller's poem is entitled *Moralische Schwätzer*.
[101] A letter to Eleanor Marx, dated 10 Nov. 1882, asks her to procure a copy of *Piers Plowman* (*MEW* XXXV, 398).

told his father (in the famous letter dated 10 November 1837) of his vain efforts to learn English and Italian out of grammars; but when, in later life, he engaged his literary interests in the service of language-learning, his progress was astonishing. He learnt English from Shakespeare and Cobbett, Italian from Dante and Machiavelli, Spanish from Cervantes and Calderón —and when, in his last years, his newly awakened desire to know more of economic and social conditions in Russia made him want to gain access to the Russian language, he tried to do so by way of Pushkin's *Eugene Onegin* and a volume of Alexander Herzen's memoirs which had already served Engels for the same purpose.[102] His proficiency in Russian never became very great; but he learnt enough to make out Russian economic and statistical works, and he acquired a library of Russian books which numbered between 120 and 200 titles by the 1880s. Among these were the satiric writings of M. Y. Saltykov-Shchedrin, in which he marked several passages in a way that indicated interest and comprehension. In 1873 we find him reading Saltykov's *Diary of a Provincial in St. Petersburg* and *The Gentlemen from Tashkent*, and later other works by the same author, including *Journey to Paris* and *Monrepos*. He also read N. G. Chernyshevsky's *Letters without Address* at least twice, once in the 1870s and a second time in the 1880s; whether he also read Chernyshevsky's novel *What's to be Done?* is not certain, although Jenny Marx mentions it with high praise in one of the articles she contributed to the *Frankfurter Zeitung* in May 1877. Marx's Postscript to the second edition of *Capital* I praises Chernyshevsky as 'a great Russian scholar and critic'. Franziska Kugelmann thought—some thirty years after the event— that she remembered Marx praising Turgenev and Lermontov:

He found Turgenev had depicted especially faithfully the idiosyncrasies of the Russian folk-soul [*Volksseele*] with its veiled Slav excitability; and he thought that Lermontov's depictions of nature could hardly be surpassed and could seldom be equalled;

while Paul Lafargue seemed to recall Marx speaking of the pleasure he took in the works of Gogol as well as those of

---

[102] This did not mitigate his dislike of Herzen. In a letter to Engels (10 Feb. 1870) he speaks of 'Citizen Herzen's fantastic lies' (*die Phantasielügen des Bürger Herzen*) (*MEW* XXXII, 437).

Pushkin and Saltykov. A recent Soviet biography of Marx, which contains a full survey of Marx's Russian readings, adds that he patently did not seek just aesthetic pleasure in these works. He tried, through them, to feel himself into the social conditions within which they were produced and to learn of social facts and attitudes in a country he would never visit.[103]

It was this same endeavour to come a little closer to an understanding of the Slavonic cultures which sent Marx to F. G. Eichhoff's *Histoire de la langue et de la littérature des Slaves*, where the Russian *Song of Igor* aroused his interest because of the 'pagan elements' he discerned beneath its 'Christian-heroic' surface; and to various anthologies of Slavonic folk-poetry (or pseudo folk-poetry) in German translation. Among the volumes on his 'Russian' shelves were works like M. P. Dragomanov's *The Persecution of Ukrainian Literature by the Russian Government*; his markings in that work indicate an interest in the Ukrainian poet Taras Shevchenko. Peter Demetz, surveying the evidence, has concluded, however—rightly, I think—that Marx's Slavonic studies never amounted to much.[104] Marx continued to feel much more at home with the Latin classics (his later letters yield a good crop of tags from, and allusions to, Horace, Virgil, Juvenal, and Cicero) and with the later writings of Western Europe. We find, in the letters of his final years, snatches of Middle High German as well as a passage in sixteenth-century French—a boldly sexual passage from the writings of Mathurin Régnier, which he sends to Engels with the characteristic comment: 'Although I am very well read in this region of literature [*Trotz meiner Belesenheit auf diesem Gebiet*], I do not think that the chaude pisse has ever been so poetically described.'[105] We also find allusions to European plays from Calderón's *The Prodigious Magician* onwards, and to the European novel, at various levels of excellence and appeal, from *Rameau's Nephew* to *Felix Holt*, *Harry Lorrequer*, and *Peter Simple*.[106]

[103] Cf. *ÚKL* I, 33, 596–600, and Demetz, op. cit., pp. 123–5. For Marx's sole reference to *Eugene Onegin*, see above, p. 303 and *MEW* XIII, 151. A good survey of Marx's Russian readings appears in L. I. Golman (and others), *Karl Marx. Biographie*—see esp. pp. 488, 701, 751, 752–5.

[104] Cf. Demetz, *Marx. Engels und die Dichter*, p. 124.

[105] Letters to Laura Marx, 25 Sept. 1869, and to Engels, 19 Oct. 1867—*MEW* XXXII, 632, and XXXI, 369.

[106] Letters to Jenny Marx, 10 June 1869, and to Engels, 7 May 1870—*MEW* XXXII, 612–13, 498.

The author of *Peter Simple* played an important part in the education of Marx's children, where he kept some very distinguished company. Marx's daughter Eleanor recalls how her father would read to her:

To me, as to my sisters before me, he read the whole of Homer, the whole *Nibelungen Lied*, *Gudrun*, *Don Quixote*, the *Arabian Nights*, etc. As to Shakespeare he was the Bible of our house, seldom out of our hands or mouths. By the time I was six I knew scene upon scene of Shakespeare by heart.

On my sixth birthday Mohr [=Marx] presented me with my first novel—the immortal *Peter Simple*. This was followed by a whole course of Marryat and Cooper. And my father actually read every one of the tales as I read them, and gravely discussed them with his little girl . . . [Then] the Scott mania had set in, and the little girl heard to her horror that she herself partly belonged to the detested clan of Campbell . . . I should add that Scott was an author to whom Marx again and again returned, whom he admired and knew as well as he did Balzac and Fielding. And while he talked about these and many other books he would, all unconscious though she was of it, show his little girl where to look for all that was finest and best in the works, teach her—though she never thought she was being taught, to that she would have objected—to try and think, to try and understand for herself.[107]

There are few more powerful and convincing testimonies to Marx's love and veneration of literature than the reminiscences of his children.

His interest in the writings and the languages of many countries led Marx, not unnaturally, to a continuing interest in the art of translation. The watch he kept on the progress of the French translation of *Capital* is illustrated by a letter to Paul and Laura Lafargue, dated 18 October 1869 and written in English:

Tell Mr. Keller that he shall go on. On the whole I am satisfied with his translation, although it lacks elegance and is done in too negligent a way . . . The changes I have made in his chapter II need not be maintained, but they show the direction in which I want corrections to be made . . . In German we use the word 'Prozess' (procès) for economical movements, as you say chimical procès, si je ne me trompe pas. He translates by phenomena which is nonsense. If he

[107] *BM* 147-8.

can find no other word, he must always translate by 'mouvement' or something analogous.[108]

As Louis Althusser and others have shown in detail, a good deal of interest in fact attaches to this French version of *Capital* I: for Marx accepted, in some crucial cases, a French text that modified (or clarified) the meaning of the German original. Marx himself pointed to this when he wrote in the Postscript to the French edition, dated 28 April 1875: 'Whatever the literary defects of this French edition may be, it possesses a scientific value independent of the original and should be consulted even by readers familiar with German.'[109]

In April 1877 we find Marx highly critical of Isolde Kurz's attempts to render into German a French work he greatly admired: P. O. Lissagaray's *History of the Commune of 1871* (*Histoire de la Commune de 1871*, Brussels, 1876). To his detailed objections he adds a characteristic generalizing comment: 'Where it is not absolutely wrong, this translation is frequently clumsy, philistine and tedious. Perhaps this corresponds, in some degree, to German taste in such matters.'[110] He is fascinated particularly by the way in which a translator's socially conditioned preconceptions may affect the wording and tenor of his translations. Jacob Grimm, for instance, for whose philological work Marx had the greatest respect,[111] is taken to task for lending the force of his authority to a rendering of a disputed passage in chapter 26 of Tacitus's *Germania* which fails to bring out, in Marx's opinion, the absence of private property and social privilege among the ancient Germans.

Just as geologists, even the best of them (like Cuvier) interpreted certain facts quite wrongly, so philologists as powerful as Jacob

---

[108] *KMP* 124–5; cf. *Gespräche*, 454.

[109] *For Marx*, trans. B. Brewster (Harmondsworth, 1969), p. 89; *K* I—*MEW* XXIII, 32.

[110] Letter to W. Bracke, 26 May 1877—*MEW* XXXIV, 277.

[111] See especially Wilhelm Liebknecht's reminiscences, *ÜKL* I, 24. The knowledge of, and respect for, Jacob Grimm's work which Liebknecht here attests is borne out by several references in Marx's writings to Grimm's etymologies. Cf. H. Kolb, 'Karl Marx und Jacob Grimm', *Archiv für das Studium der neueren Sprachen*, ccvi (1969–70), 96 ff., and P. Ganz, *Jacob Grimm's Conception of German Studies* (Oxford, 1973), p. 7: 'Karl Marx placed him high above his romantic medievalizing contemporaries as a man who was moving, albeit unconsciously, and unaware, in a socialist direction.' Cf. also letter to Engels, 25 Mar. 1868—*MEW* XXXII, 51.

Grimm mistranslated the simplest Latin sentences because they were
under the influence of people like Justus Möser (who was delighted,
as I remember, by his discovery that 'liberty' had never existed
among the Germans) . . . For instance: the well-known sentence in
Tacitus 'arva per annos mutant, et superest ager', means 'they
exchange their fields (*arva*) by lot, and common land (*ager*, as
opposed to *arva*, in the sense of *ager publicus*) remains'. Grimm, however, translates this as follows: 'They cultivate new fields every year,
and still there remains (untilled) land'![112]

Marx does not, however, take his occasional criticism of
Grimm's social attitudes and preconceptions as a cue for im-
pugning either Grimm's scholarship or his good faith. 'The
first reaction against the French Revolution and the Enlightenment attitudes connected with it', he writes to Engels on 24
March 1868, 'was, of course, to see everything in a medieval,
romantic light; even men like Grimm are not free from this.
The second reaction, however, corresponds to the direction
taken by socialism, although the scholars concerned look beyond the Middle Ages to the earliest beginnings [*die Urzeit*]
of every people. There, to their surprise, they find in the oldest
what is newest, they even find egalitarians *to a degree* . . .'[113]
His concern with Grimm's exploration of German antiquities
through the history of the German language and through records left by ancient historians thus causes Marx to revalue
German Romanticism and the scholarship to which it gave rise.
By continuing its thrust backwards *beyond* the Middle Ages,
the Romantic generation of scholars unconsciously fuelled, so
Marx now believes, the forces of social progress. In our own day,
tradition-conscious literary critics of the German Democratic
Republic have found this view predictably congenial and have
been able, with its help, to take up a more positive attitude to
the Romantic movement in Germany than might otherwise
have been the case.

---

[112] Letter to Engels, 25 Mar. 1868—*MEW* XXXII, 52. Most modern English
translators agree with Grimm rather than Marx. In Marx's own day, however, we
find English scholars not committed to socialism or communism surmising that
the ancient Germans assigned land-portions *by lot* and seeing *ager* as a short form
of *ager publicus* in Tacitus's chapter 26. See A. J. Church and W. J. Brodribb,
The Agricola and Germany of Tacitus and the Dialogue on Oratory, rev. edn. (London,
1877), p. 130.
[113] *MEW* XXXII, 51. The words 'to a degree' are in English in the original.

Marx's suspicion and dislike of the common run of profes-
sional literati extended to bluestockings too. His portrait of
Ludmilla Assing, in a letter he wrote (in English) to his cousin
Nannette Philips, is one of the most malicious he ever penned:

This Fräulein, who really swamped me with her benevolence, is
the most ugly creature I ever saw in my life, a nastily Jewish
physiognomy, a sharply protruding thin nose, eternally smiling and
grinning, always speaking poetical prose, constantly trying to say
something extraordinary, playing at false enthusiasm and spitting
at her auditory during the trances of her extasis. I shall today be
forced to pay a visit to that little monster which I treated with the
utmost reserve and coldness, giving her to understand by friend
Lassalle that the power of attraction works upon myself always in a
centrifugal direction and that, when I happen to admire a person very
much, I am apt to steal altogether out of its presence.

In a later letter to this same correspondent, again written in
English, he complained that during the visit to Germany which
brought him Ludmilla Assing's acquaintance 'half an army of
antiquated beauties and detestable blue stockings did their
best to transform me into an ass'. 'Old Circe', he added, 'as
you are aware, metamorphosed the companions of Ulysses into
pigs. These modern Circes have so far civilized themselves as
to take the asinine line.'[114] When, however, Marx encountered,
in the feuilleton columns of the *Cologne Gazette* (*Kölnische Zeitung*)
for 1879, a novel by one Bertha Augusti, of whose narrow circle
and straitened circumstances he knew from a common acquaintance, he felt moved to write to the authoress in warm
terms, commending her 'great talent' and encouraging her to
go on. To give more force to his praise Marx added that in
respect of German novels he was 'a great heretic'. 'I don't much
care for them', he writes; 'I have been too thoroughly spoilt by
reading the best French, English and Russian novelists.'[115]

No account of Marx's dealings with literature is complete
which fails to take note of the playful element which comes so
delightfully to the fore in his letters to his family—which makes
him, for instance, report to his daughter Eleanor on a new
cosmetic aid by reminding her of a little-known poem by

[114] Letters of 24 Mar. and 13 Apr. 1861, in W. Blumenberg, 'Ein unbekanntes
Kapitel aus Marx' Leben', *International Review of Social History*, i (1956), 84, 85.
[115] Letter to Berta Augusti, 25 Oct. 1879—*MEW* XXXIV, 416.

Goethe: 'When Goethe praises a man for being able to "cast his old snake-skin", he does not, probably, count artificially produced "fausses peaux" as part of that process of rejuvenation.'[116] The family is always playing literary games, on which Marx frequently reports to Engels. In May 1869, for instance, he passes on to Engels a riddle composed by his daughter Jenny: 'Why did Mr. "Excelsior" of the Alpine Club not marry "Lady Clara Vere de Vere"'[117]—a riddle which Engels could answer only if he was sufficiently acquainted with the verse of Longfellow and Tennyson. Five years later, Marx shares another joke about Tennyson with Jenny, and asks her to pass it on to 'Tussychen' (= Eleanor Marx).[118] To these family games we also owe the answers to a questionnaire which his daughters submitted to Marx (as well as to Engels and other visitors) in 1865:

CONFESSIONS

Your favourite virtue . .	Simplicity.
Your favourite virtue in man .	Strength.
Your favourite virtue in woman	Weakness.
Your chief characteristic . .	Singleness of purpose.
Your idea of happiness . .	To fight.
Your idea of misery . .	Submission.
The vice you excuse most .	Gullibility.
The vice you detest most .	Servility.
Your aversion . . .	Martin Tupper.
Favourite occupation . .	Book-worming.
Favourite poet . . .	Shakespeare, Aeschylus, Goethe.
Favourite prose-writer . .	Diderot.
Favourite hero . . .	Spartacus, Kepler.
Favourite heroine . . .	Gretchen.
Favourite flower . . .	Daphne.
Favourite colour . . .	Red.
Favourite name . . .	Laura, Jenny.
Favourite dish . . .	Fish.
Favourite maxim . . .	*Nihil humani a me alienum puto.*
Favourite motto . . .	*De omnibus dubitandum.*

Karl Marx[119]

---

[116] 28 May 1882—*MEW* XXXV, 328. The poem in question may be found in Goethe's *Zahme Xenien*.   [117] 8 May 1869—*MEW* XXXII, 315.
[118] 19 Apr. 1874—*MEW* XXXIII, 623–4.
[119] *METEC* 179. 'Gretchen' is, of course, a character in Goethe's *Faust*; Laura and Jenny are the names of two of Marx's daughters; Jenny is also the name of Marx's wife.

For all their levity (in the answer to 'Favourite virtue in woman', for instance,[120] or in that to 'Favourite name') these 'Confessions' offer valuable confirmation for the image of Marx's literary taste which has emerged from the preceding pages. Even in play Marx was wholly himself.

'The name of a thing', Marx had written in *Capital* I, 'is quite distinct from the qualities of that thing. I know nothing of a man by knowing that his name is Jacobus.'[121] Small wonder, therefore, that one of the most prominent forms Marx's playfulness continues to take in his letters is the conferring of new names on his family and acquaintances. As often as not these derive from his reading and thus bring literary figures into his daily life. The clumsy radical Karl Heinzen appears, as before, in the guise of 'Heinecke the mighty drudge'. S. L. Borkheim, merchant and would-be revolutionary, is transmogrified into Balzac's *Illustre Gaudissart*. The radical geologist John R. Dakyns is described, as has already been seen, as 'a sort of Felix Holt, less the affectation of that man, and plus the knowledge'; and parodying the full title of George Eliot's novel Marx ever afterwards refers to Dakyns, affectionately, as 'Felix Holt the Rascal'. His son-in-law Paul Lafargue, whose non-European ancestry was ever in Marx's thoughts, becomes 'the strange Caliban boy'. He calls his daughters 'Miss Lilliput' after Swift, and 'Master Kakadu' after a tailor in some now forgotten novel. Beset by debts, he sees himself as Mercadet in Balzac's comedy *Le Faiseur*, and when he signs letters to his children 'Old Nick', as he so frequently does in his last years, is he not playfully assuming, once again, his favourite role of Mephistopheles?[122] Nor is it only Marx's immediate circle which is thus 'invaded' by figures from world literature. Napoleon III appears as a *picaro*, an 'imperial Lazarillo de Tormes'; Lassalle before King William of Prussia recalls Heine's portrait of Herwegh before

---

[120] This particular jest has a serious background, however: Marx's listing of Gretchen as his favourite heroine, and 'weakness' as the virtue he most favoured in women, derives ultimately from masculine-patriarchal attitudes which he shared with many a more conservative Victorian contemporary.

[121] *K* I—*MEW* XXIII, 115.

[122] *MEW* XXX, 584, and XXXII, 516 ('Heinecke'); XXXII, 136, 156 (Gaudissart); XXXII, 613 (Felix Holt); *KMP* 121 (Caliban); XXXI, 477 (Lilliput); *METEC* 183 (Kakadu); XXXI, 278 (Mercadet). For 'Old Nick' see the letters to Jenny Longuet dated 22 July 1881, 9 Aug. 1881, 18 Aug. 1881, and 17 Dec. 1881 (*MEW* XXXV, 206, 208, 219, 251).

King Frederick William IV, and Schiller's Marquis Posa
before King Philip of Spain; the French branch of the First
International reminds Marx, collectively, of the rascal Spiegelberg in Schiller's *Robbers*; Friedrich Zabel, editor of the Berlin
National-Zeitung, reincarnates Wackford Squeers; Louis Blanc
and Ranke appear as Rumpelstiltskin and other mis-shapen
dwarfs from fairy-tale and folklore;[123] while elsewhere in Marx's
letters, Ulysses and Calypso, Frankenstein's monster, Gulliver
and his Lilliputians all walk again. When P. Robin decided to
break with him in September 1871, in order to follow Bakunin
instead, Marx reports the fact in one of his bilingual letters to
Paul and Laura Lafargue and adds a characteristic comment:

I did not think it worth my while to answer to R. R. R. Robin
mouton. (Rabelais le connaît déjà sous ce nom et l'emmène spéciale-
ment parmi les moutons de Panurge). Maintenant je retourne à nos
autres moutons.[124]

Here the mechanism by which literary nicknames are created
in Marx's world may be seen particularly clearly. He remembers
that Robin is one of the traditional French names for a sheep;
that triggers off the reminiscence of a famous passage in Book
IV, chapter 6, of Rabelais's *Pantagruel*, which in turn reminds
Marx of the phrase 'Revenons à ces moutons' from *Maistre
Pierre Pathelin*. Henceforward the 'renegade' Robin will always
be Robin Mouton for Marx, and his behaviour in following
Bakunin will always recall that of the stupidly suicidal creatures described by Rabelais.

The creations of Cervantes had become, as we know by now,
even more indissolubly part of Marx's world than those of
Rabelais. Here it is striking to notice that after seeing, all
through his life, his *opponents* in the guise of Don Quixote—
particularly if he felt them to be, in some essential way, out of
tune with what he conceived to be the spirit of their time—he
comes to feel in his last years that the great Don is in some

---

[123] *MEW* XXX, 369 (Lazarillo); *MEW* XXXI, 10 (Marquis Posa); *MEW*
XXXII, 131 (Spiegelberg); *MEW* XXX, 31–2 (Squeers); *MEW* XXXI, 432
(dwarf, mandrake). Leopold v. Ranke's way of writing history displeased Marx
because of its 'anecdotage' and its 'way of deriving all great events from petty
causes' (to Engels, 7 Sept. 1876). Eleven years later he distanced himself no less
emphatically from the Prussian nationalism and militarism he detected in Heinrich
v. Treitschke (*MEW* XVIII, 571).
[124] *KMP* 156.

respects akin to *himself.* 'Sleepless, without appetite, coughing badly, a little perplexed, and not without occasional attacks of a profound melancholia, like the great Don Quixote.' That self-characterization, from a letter written in March 1882,[125] shows that as Marx himself changes he stresses new aspects of his old literary favourites.

The incidents and scenes he witnesses remind him no less surely of literary prototypes than do the characters of his acquaintances. As he writes to his wife on 17 September 1878,

> I cannot resist telling you of one incident which, in its originality, reminds one of Balzac and Paul de Kock at the same time. When Tussy, Mrs. Renshaw, and Pumps (she is knighted now—Engels calls her Pumpsia from now on) went through the deceased's effects, Mrs. Renshaw found, among other things, a small packet of letters (about eight, six of them from the Marx family, two from Williams in Ramsgate) and was on the point of handing them to Mr. Chitty, who was present during this operation. 'No', said he, 'burn them! I need not see her letters. I know she was unable to deceive me.' Could Figaro (I mean the real Figaro, the one by Beaumarchais) have trouvé celà?[126]

The bizarre incident Marx had witnessed (Engels's reactions after the death of his mistress Lizzie Burns) triggers off three literary reminiscences at once: Balzac, de Kock, Beaumarchais. By mentioning these to his wife, he helps her to recapture something of the experience which he himself had had, and to relate it to other shared experiences in their literary-minded family.

We know from many sources that Marx remained to the end a fascinating story-teller—his daughter Eleanor remembers in particular a fantastic yarn in the manner of E. T. A. Hoffmann which her father would spin out from week to week, from month to month:

> It went on for months and months; it was a whole series of stories. The pity no one was there to write down these tales so full of poetry, of wit, of humour! Hans Röckle himself was a Hoffmann-like magician, who kept a toy-shop, and who was always 'hard up'. His

---

[125] To Engels, 1 Mar. 1882—*MEW* XXXV, 44.

[126] *MEW* XXXIV, 344; cf. 'Pends-toi, Figaro, tu n'aurais pas inventé celà', quoted in *Revelations about the Cologne Communist Trial*, *MEW* VIII, 425.

shop was full of the most wonderful things—of wooden men and women, giants and dwarfs, kings and queens, workmen and masters, animals and birds as numerous as Noah got into the Ark, tables and chairs, carriages, boxes of all sorts and sizes. And though he was a magician, Hans could never meet his obligations either to the devil or the butcher, and was therefore—much against the grain—constantly obliged to sell his toys to the devil. These then went through wonderful adventures—always ending in a return to Hans Röckle's shop. Some of these adventures were as grim, as terrible, as any of Hoffmann's; some were comic; all were told with inexhaustible verve, wit and humour.[127]

This story has been ingeniously linked, by L. S. Feuer, to Marx's own experiences as a penurious exile and as a maker of history. Röckle's shop, we have just heard Eleanor recall, was full of wooden men and women, giants and dwarfs, kings and queens, workmen and masters; precisely, Feuer comments, like Marx's *Capital* and the materialist conception of history. And while the fact that Röckle could never meet his obligations either to the devil or to the butcher have an autobiographical foundation patent to anyone who knows the shifts to which the Marx family was reduced during their penurious earlier years in London, the eventual return of the toys to the shop, after horrendous adventures, may well be thought to symbolize more than just a return from the pawnshop. 'The ordeals of history', Feuer comments, not unreasonably, 'had their triumphant culmination.'[128]

Occasionally we catch a glimpse of this yarn-spinning side of Marx in his letters—he ghoulishly proposes, for instance, as he tells Engels in December 1863, to convert the carbuncles that plagued him into the heroes of his next short story. 'In the foreground stands someone who regales his Inner Man with port, bordeaux, stout, and huge quantities of meat . . . But behind him, on his neck, sits the Outer Man, that damned carbuncle.' 'But it is your own flesh!', Eleanor is said to have exclaimed when he faced her with this story of the Outer Man or Second Frankenstein.[129]

Marx continued to evince interest in what one might call

---

[127] *BM* 147. Eleanor Marx wrote these reminiscences in English.
[128] L. S. Feuer, *Marx and the Intellectuals*, pp. 141–2.
[129] 4 and 27 Dec. 1863—*MEW* XXX, 378, 382.

'literature as performance'. He not only liked to read novels aloud and to declaim verse, but he also criticized the declamations of others: Ferdinand Lassalle, especially, came in for some cruel mockery on this account.[130] We know that he disliked theatricality in ordinary life;[131] but this did not prevent him from frequenting the London theatres and delighting, along with his family, in the acting of Phelps, Irving, and Salvini. Eleanor Marx even claimed, when sending Carl Hirsch a eulogy of Henry Irving written by her mother:

If Papa had had time, he would have written a review on Mr. Irving himself, since we are very interested in him, although we do not know him personally; first, because he is a man of rare talents, and then because the English press has fallen upon him as a result of a miserable intrigue and has let loose a real campaign against him.[132]

The Shakespeare-cult rife in the Marx household was noted by many observers—it brought about regular meetings of a Shakespeare-reading society called 'The Dogberry Club' in Marx's house, which Marx is known to have attended and enjoyed, as well as contacts with Furnivall and the English Shakespeare Society.[133] No wonder that the aged Marx impressed his Russian visitor Maxim Kovalevsky as 'an exceedingly cultured Anglo-German gentleman'.[134]

The testimony of many other visitors who sought Marx out in his later years confirms such impressions. A Spanish member of the First International, whom Marx received in his house in September 1871, confessed himself astonished at his host's wide knowledge of the works of Calderón, Lope de Vega, Tirso de Molina, and Cervantes, and at his ability to express his insights in fluent and grammatically accurate (if not always correctly pronounced) Spanish.[135] A correspondent of the *Chicago Tribune*, who visited Marx seven years later, noted the works in many

[130] *Gespräche*, 335, 521.
[131] *METEC* 61–2.
[132] Bruno Kaiser, 'Jenny Marx as a Theatre-Critic—A Remarkable Discovery', in *Cross-Section. Anthology of the PEN Centre, German Democratic Republic* (Leipzig, 1970), pp. 125–6.
[133] e.g. *Gespräche*, 275, 482–3, 566, 568, 575.
[134] *Gespräche*, 486.
[135] *Gespräche*, 386.

languages that stood on his shelves, including volumes of Shakespeare, Dickens, Thackeray, Molière, Racine, Voltaire, and Goethe; Marian Comyn, at the same period, glanced at the volumes of poetry and prose on his writing-table and noted that these included novels by Bulwer-Lytton.[136]

(vi)

The many reminiscences of Marx which went into print after his death do little, on the whole, but confirm what we have already gleaned from an examination of his works and his correspondence. Only in two respects can such reminiscences significantly augment our knowledge of Marx's relation to world literature. One of these is that they may apprise us of literary plans which Marx never had time to put into execution: to write a play on the subject of the Gracchi, for instance, or a critical study of Balzac.[137] The other is that they offer testimony to Marx's reading of authors and books which have left no trace in his writings at all. He is said to have greatly admired Fielding's *Tom Jones* and Scott's *Old Mortality*, and to have been altogether an enthusiastic reader of Scott,[138]—yet if either Fielding or Scott is ever quoted or mentioned in his writings, I have missed the reference. The same is true of Chamisso's social poems and—more significantly—of the writings of Emily Brontë.[139] A good deal of caution is necessary, however, if one wishes to use such evidence. A notorious case in point is the contrast between Shelley and Byron that Edward Aveling, in a pamphlet entitled *Shelley's Socialism* on which Eleanor Marx collaborated and which was published in 1888, attributes to Marx:

The true difference between Byron and Shelley is this: those who understand and love them think it fortunate that Byron died in his thirty-sixth year, for if he had lived longer, he would have become a bourgeois reactionary; they regret, however, that Shelley died at twenty-nine, for he was a revolutionary through and through, and would always have been in the vanguard of socialism.[140]

---

[136] *Gespräche*, 575.
[137] Paul Lafargue, *METEC* 33, 26.
[138] Eleanor Marx-Aveling and Paul Lafargue, *METEC* 26, 156.
[139] *Gespräche* 575 (Marian Comyn).   [140] *ÜKL* I, 536–7.

Despite Marx's hostility to Romanticism (a hostility, be it noted, that does not seem—in his later years—to have included the writings of E. T. A. Hoffmann), I cannot believe in the authenticity of this remark. Nothing in Marx's published writings confirms it. Shelley is never mentioned there at all, and Byron rarely—but when Marx does mention Byron, it is with evident approval. He commends his own early collection of folk-songs to Jenny with a reference to *Childe Harold's Pilgrimage*; he ridicules a common acquaintance, in a letter to Engels written in 1854, because he dares to see himself as a cross between Byron and Leibniz; in an article in the *Neue Oder-Zeitung* (1855) he refers with a nod of complicity to a line from *English Bards and Scotch Reviewers*:

> A turn for punning, call it Attic Salt;

and in *Herr Vogt* (1860) he alludes, with relish, to Byron's 'Epitaph' on Castlereagh:

> Posterity will ne'er survey
> A nobler grave than this;
> Here lie the bones of Castlereagh:
> Stop, traveller, and piss.[141]

What we know of Marx's literary sensibilities and political understanding does not suggest that he was obtuse enough to see a potential 'bourgeois reactionary' in the author of *Don Juan*. We know a good deal, on the other hand, of Edward Aveling's 'propensity to falsify facts' (Yvonne Kapp). The baneful role Aveling played in Eleanor Marx's life has been distressingly documented; and C. Tsuzuki's description of the circumstances in which, and the polemical purposes for which, *Shelley's Socialism* was written is not calculated to strengthen our faith in the reliability of the information it contains.[142]

[141] *MEGA* I, 1 (2), 96; *MEW* XXVIII, 348 (22 Apr. 1854); *MEW* XI, 30 (2 Feb. 1855); *MEW* XIV, 600. The ascription of Leporello's 'Let him go, he is not worth your anger' to Byron's *Don Juan* in *Surveys from Exile* (Pelican Marx Library (Harmondsworth, 1973), p. 344) is an error: Marx is referring to Da Ponte's libretto for Mozart's *Don Giovanni*.
[142] Y. Kapp, *Eleanor Marx. Vol. I: Family Life (1855–1883)* (London, 1972), p. 248; C. Tsuzuki, *The Life of Eleanor Marx, 1855–1898. A Socialist Tragedy* (Oxford, 1967), p. 171.

In other cases memory may well have played tricks on informants called upon to recollect encounters with Marx that had taken place many years earlier. Did Marx really know the works of Gogol? Did he really—as Franziska Kugelmann tells us some thirty years after the event—talk knowledgeably of Lermontov and Turgenev?[143] Was he really in the habit of quoting 'Chamisso's touching poem "The Beggar and his Dog"'?[144] Until further documents appear such cases must be held 'not proven'; but there is enough cumulative evidence to convince us that Marx's enthusiastic 'book-worming' went deeper even and wider than would appear from his published writings and his letters.

---

[143] *METEC* 26 (Lafargue); *METEC* 185 (Franziska Kugelmann).
[144] *METEC* 184 (Franziska Kugelmann).

Conclusion

'Books were tools for his mind, not articles of
luxury. "They are my slaves and they must serve
me as I will", he used to say.'
(Paul Lafargue—*METEC* 24)

MARX never wrote a complete aesthetic treatise, nor did he
ever publish a sustained piece of formal literary criticism—his
analysis of Sue's *Mysteries of Paris* is incidental to his exposure of
Szeliga and the Young-Hegelian followers of Bruno Bauer, and
his remarks on *Franz von Sickingen* are dashed down in a private
letter. Yet from the first he shows a passionate interest in literature, an interest which never abates and which leads to a multitude of incidental critiques, allusions, and quotations. Literature
embellishes his personal life and private affairs; his doctoral
thesis is shot through with references to literary works; literature
becomes a potent weapon in his early battles as a journalist; as
his own *Weltanschauung* gradually emerges from an early amalgam of Hegel and Feuerbach, the help of literature is sought to
confirm and formulate his new views; the system the mature
Marx tried to construct would have been incomplete, he felt,
without a secure and prominent place for literature and the
other arts; and the old Marx constantly turns to literary works
for spiritual sustenance, material for playing games, and polemical ammunition. He felt at home in the literature of classical
antiquity, German literature from the Middle Ages to the Age
of Goethe, the worlds of Dante, Boiardo, Tasso, Cervantes, and
Shakespeare, the French and English prose-fiction of the eighteenth and nineteenth centuries; and he showed himself interested in any contemporary poetry which might help—as that of
Heine had certainly done—to undermine respect for traditional
authority and arouse hopes of a socially juster future. On the
whole, however, his gaze was directed more to the past than to

the present, more towards Aeschylus, Dante, and Shakespeare than towards the writings of his own contemporaries. In this as in many other things his later interpreter Lukács has followed the master's own example.

If one traces Marx's dealings with literature chronologically, as this book has tried to do, one must become aware of certain changes. An early sympathy with a Fichtean brand of Romanticism[1] soon disappears, to give way to a view which sees the aesthetic beauty of Romantic literature as a veil drawn over a harsh and oppressive reality—if the reality is to be changed, the veil must be torn or removed. An early admiration for Schiller is soon tempered by an increasing feeling that Schiller's plays and poems lend themselves to misuse in a way that Shakespeare's do not—that they idealize too much, that they provide too much ready material for those who want to deceive themselves and others about the true nature of the social world and of their own motives, and that Schiller's influence on dramatists of lesser genius is likely to be disastrous. The opposition of a Schillerian to a Shakespearian mode, lightly suggested in *The Holy Family*, finds its most uncompromising statement in the 'Sickingen' letter of 1859. Marx becomes more guarded, after 1845, in speculating about the effect an ultimate resolution of class-conflict would have on literature and the arts; the later work does not indulge in Utopian visions of a society in which everybody will be (amongst other things) an artist, though Marx continues to believe that a fundamental alteration of modes of exchange and production will be necessary to allow everyone the chance to develop artistic and appreciative faculties which are stunted and starved in a capitalist society. The later Marx considers changes in some of his more contentious formulations; the famous statement of 1859

Die Produktionsweise des materiellen Lebens *bedingt* den sozialen, politischen und geistigen Lebensprozeß *überhaupt* [my italics]

The mode of production of material life conditions the social, political, and intellectual life process altogether

appears in the French version, over which Marx kept a close watch, as

[1] Cf. M. Lifshits, *Karl Marx und die Ästhetik*, pp. 43–4.

Le mode de production de la vie matérielle *domine en général* le développement de la vie sociale, politique et intellectuelle.

Maximilien Rubel, who points out this difference, adds that an exact French translation of the German 'bedingt' would be 'détermine' or 'conditionne', and that by accepting 'domine' Marx stresses the role of human *Praxis* in the genesis of forms of consciousness without introducing the notion of a mechanical causality between such *Praxis* and mental attitudes.[2] One notices also other changes of vocabulary—after 1857 Marx does not use Romantic organic metaphors like *Blütezeit* and *Mutterschoß* in a literary-critical context, while showing himself more ready to apply to authors and their works terms drawn from economics (an author *liefert* [= supplies] or *produziert*); in his last period he brings his literary and scientific interests together by applying terms from the physical and biological sciences—'regressive metamorphosis' for instance—to the history of literature. There are also constant additions to Marx's canon of literary excellence: Homer, Aeschylus, Ovid, Lucretius, Shakespeare, Cervantes, Goethe, and Heine are joined, successively, by Dante, Diderot, Cobbett, Balzac, Dickens, and many others. In the same way his list of literary *bêtes noires* grows steadily: Gottsched, Gessner, Lamartine, Chateaubriand are joined by such lesser figures as Kinkel, Daumer, the later Freiligrath, Gustav Freytag, and Martin Tupper.

The most striking result, however, of our chronological scrutiny of Marx's references to and uses of literature is the realization that his development is steady and consistent, and that Marx had to alter remarkably few of his earlier views on literature as he worked out his revolutionary conception of society. René Wellek has therefore spoken truly when he said that even if Marx's scattered pronouncements on literature do not amount to a fully unified theory of literature, they do not lack coherence; they are held together by a general philosophy of history (itself gradually evolving) and show a comprehensible evolution. I would not, however, agree with Wellek's contention that this evolution passed, in Marx's case, 'through a stage of rigid economic determinism to a more mellow and tolerant attitude in

---

[2] M. Rubel, *Karl Marx. Essai de biographie intellectuelle*, rev. edn. (Paris, 1971), pp. 297–8.

the framework of late realism and naturalism'.[3] Such economic determinism as there was (notably in the Preface of *Towards a Critique of Political Economy*) coexisted with the 'realist' theory most fully stated in Marx's letter about Lassalle's *Franz von Sickingen*, a letter written only a few months after the Preface; there is nothing to suggest that Marx was sympathetic to literary Naturalism; and on the whole Marx's literary attitudes and opinions do not become more 'mellow and tolerant' as he grows older.[4]

One concept the older Marx used more sparingly and cautiously than the younger is that of 'alienation'—though the notion does still play a significant part in the *Grundrisse* of 1857–8 and in *Capital*.[5] Marx never had to revoke, however, his early analysis of the manner in which literature functioned in the context of alienation and reification. In the Paris Manuscripts of 1844 he tried to show some of the ways in which literature may be pressed into the service of a ruling class, and some of the ways in which an age given over to commerce and acquisition may prove as unfavourable to the appreciation as to the creation of great literature. He there attempted to demonstrate how imaginative literature may become an instrument of class hegemony or fall victim to modern alienation—how it may become a casualty of the state of affairs in which man is estranged from nature, from himself and his own activity, from his human essence or 'species-being', and from his fellow men.[6] But literature, the young Marx believed, may also help us to gain insight into the mechanics of alienation and reification (passages from Goethe and Shakespeare are adduced in support of this view); it may project images that make us more conscious of our dehumanized state or of what we might be in more favourable circumstances (the earlier Marx adduces Aeschylus' *Prometheus Bound*, the later will cite Dante's *Divine Comedy*); it may be used as a weapon in the class-struggle (witness the song of the Silesian weavers that Marx admired so much); and like the other arts

[3] René Wellek, *A History of Modern Criticism 1750–1950*, vol. iii, p. 239.

[4] In *The Record of an Adventurous Life* H. M. Hyndman recalls one of several visits to Marx's London home: 'I remember saying to him once that as I grew older I thought I became more tolerant. "Do you", he said, "*do* you?" It was quite certain he didn't.' (p. 271.)

[5] The relevant passages have been collected by I. Mészáros in *Marx's Theory of Alienation*.

[6] Cf. Mészáros, op. cit., p. 14.

it will play its part in man's cultural rehabilitation (Marx uses the example of music to show how the arts help to create the very taste by which they are enjoyed).

The view of literature projected in the Paris Manuscripts never had to be denied by Marx, even though his growing absorption in economic analysis and the growing definition and complexity of his materialist outlook caused him to modify many of his other views. It is supplemented in the later writings by suggestions of further functions and uses, and by aesthetic formulations wrung from Marx by some practical necessity (like that of being asked to judge a specific work). These, as the present book should have helped to show, interlock to such a remarkable extent that a summary of Marx's literary beliefs and attitudes need not seem a totally hopeless undertaking.

After the period of his early poems, in which there is some play with Romantic religiosity, Marx sees literature as belonging wholly to this our terrestrial world. It is not produced by supernatural inspiration, nor does it speak of any transcendent realm, any numinous or uncanny Beyond. Literature speaks of man in a definite socio-historical setting, and is produced as well as received by individual, socially conditioned men.

The creators of literature, then, are, discernibly, individual human beings—Marx will have no truck with 'impersonal' theories. At the same time, however, they are, in various ways, representative: of their country and its developing and changing national spirit, of their time, and of the class to which they belong or with which they identify themselves. Marx seeks to distinguish many different ways in which authors may relate to the social classes of which their society is composed. They may belong to an opportunistic intellectual *Lumpenproletariat*. They may be 'paid hirelings' of a dominant class or group. They may be conscious or unconscious spokesmen for such a group, reflecting or proclaiming its interests, its ideals, its world-view, its political positions, its self-images, its illusions, its hatreds, and its fears. They may choose to adopt the point of view of a class or group to which they do not themselves belong by birth or by upbringing. They may, while consciously identifying themselves with one class or group, present reality so faithfully and with such insight that their works will tell against that group and transcend the author's own conscious allegiances or creed.

Marx believed, then, that though many authors are spokes-men for a dominant class, great literature is able to rise above a prevalent ideology. When this happens, it may constitute an area of relatively unalienated labour, a realm in which an author can express himself—to a considerable extent—as a total human being. In this respect the poet is more favoured than the factory-worker—although in a 'capitalistic' society the products of both are subject to the laws of the market, which all too often force an author to write to live instead of living to write. There are limits, however, to the extent to which a work of literature can be transformed into an object of mere utility, something to acquire and possess. It fully exists only in 'consumption', yet when it has been 'consumed' it is still there, an object created by one historically conditioned human being to be enjoyed by another. And when, in *Grundrisse*, Marx says of medieval handi-craft: 'This work is still half artistic, it has its aim in itself [*Selbstzweck*]', he in fact equates the artistic and the autotelic in a way which would have commended itself to Kant.

The ultimate significance of this view of literature and the arts in Marx's world-picture has been justly summed up by Adolfo Sánchez Váchez in *Art and Society*:

The more the artistic nature of labour is affirmed, the more it approximates art, that is, the more it approximates an activity through which man deliberately realizes and objectifies his human essence. The more labour loses its artistic character, the more it moves away from art, until it becomes a purely formal and mechani-cal activity which is radically opposed to art. Art then appears as the proper sphere for the spiritual richness which the sphere of labour has lost.[7]

Literature, for Marx, is not simply a means of *expression*—it is also, to a significant degree, a means of *self-constitution*. One of the great differences between man and beast is that man not only labours to satisfy his physical needs and urges, but also forms 'according to the laws of beauty'. Literature, therefore, answers a human need and like the other arts creates and shapes the senses by which it is enjoyed. It is thus possible to speak of 'productive consumption'. Producing and enjoying works of art

[7] A. Sánchez Váchez, *Art and Society. Essays in Marxist Aesthetics*, p. 206. Originally published in Mexico in 1965 as *Las ideas estéticas de Marx: ensayos de estética marxista*. The English translation is by Maro Riofrancos.

helps to make us fuller human beings. In some notes on Bakunin, penned towards the end of 1874 and the beginning of 1875, Marx lists literature among 'acquired forces of production, material and spiritual, language, literature, technical skills etc. etc.'[8] He sees in literature and the other arts what Gajo Petrović has described as 'a universal-creative, self-creative activity by which man transforms and creates his world and himself'.[9] In this way it is intimately bound up with man's progress towards a juster society.

Marx was fully aware, however, that representativeness, expressiveness, and acceptable ideas about society and history are not enough to ensure artistic merit. Everything he says on this topic, from his disquisition on 'authorized' and 'unauthorized' (or 'competent' and 'incompetent') authors in the *Rheinische Zeitung* to his letter on Lassalle's *Franz von Sickingen*, shows him alive to the need for artistic talent coupled with intellectual and moral insight.

Works of literature are products, authors are producers, and literature cannot remain unaffected by the modes of production and consumption prevalent in the society within which and for which it is produced. There are many pages, in *Capital* and elsewhere, in which Marx shows what happens when literature takes shape as a book or a play, as a commodity to be ordered and paid for by an entrepreneur, printed, advertised, and sold on the open market. He glances at the manipulations of fame made possible by newspapers and other means of communication. Neither from the author's nor from the reader's point of view can literature be seen as an autonomous realm. Its import and its forms are not independent of the economic organization and the modes of production characteristic of a given society; but the degree of such dependence and its kind are differently described in different works. Such differences are frequently due to the specific purpose Marx has in mind: the Preface of *Towards a Critique of Political Economy*, for instance, is much more starkly and deliberately polemic than the ruminations of the abandoned Introduction to *Grundrisse*, in which Marx tries to take fuller account of the complicated nature of the relationship. Many of his theses are designed to have what Walter Benjamin called

[8] *MEW* XVIII, 620.
[9] G. Petrović, *Marx in the Mid-twentieth Century*, pp. 78–9.

Kampfwert, combat-value. Overemphasis of economic factors—comprising all men's efforts to master and exploit nature, relations of production and distribution, and property-relationships —may be seen as an antidote to German idealist philosophies, or as a weapon against those who tried, consciously or unconsciously, to deflect attention from the way in which property was distributed, and goods and services were exchanged, in nineteenth-century Europe.

Allowing for such fluctuations and shifts of emphasis, the material collected in this book tends to confirm Stefan Morawski's description of the 'historicist' perspective on art which Marx shared with Engels:

Aesthetic phenomena are to be regarded as a cultural activity of *homo sapiens* in his slow progress to self-realization within the matrix of the socio-historical processes. The non-isolate [*sic*] phenomena of the arts, which variously depend on other manifestations of culture, social, political, moral, religious and scientific, influence in turn these other spheres of activity. Moreover, the system of mutual dependencies and complex interrelations is in each case twofold. It is synchronic, occurring across the structure of society within a given moment, and diachronic, occurring as an aspect of historical process influenced by the past, and exercising possible influence on the future nature of culture. The continual dynamic flux and change in aesthetics and the arts derive chiefly from the rise and decline of the always complex ideological outlooks which, in the final analysis, are conditioned by the general contradictions and evolutions of class society. But the dynamism arises also from the contradiction between crystallized ideological outlooks and emergent attitudes.[10]

As we have seen, however, the later Marx is more apt to talk of the way in which the economic organization of society affects the arts than of that in which the arts affect other spheres of being and activity; just as he is more ready to point to what Morawski calls the 'allogenetic' aspect of art (the way the various arts are dependent on extra-artistic factors) than to its 'idiogenetic' aspect (the way in which art may be said to have a history of its own, in which one work affects another). In his eagerness to assert the importance of 'allogenetic' factors Marx even denies, in one place, that there can be any history of art

[10] S. Morawski, 'The Aesthetic Views of Marx and Engels', *Journal of Aesthetics and Art Criticism,* xxviii (1970), 303.

at all—meaning, no doubt, a history of art which fails to take into account the social and economic history of the country and time within which it is produced.

Though Marx was fully aware of the uniqueness of each historical period, aware too that a given economic 'base' was capable, in empirical reality, of an infinite number of variations, he nevertheless believed that there were historical parallels which could lead to similar developments in literature and the arts. His account of German 'booby-literature' (see above, pp. 126–7) is designed to show how a historical constellation parallel, in some respects, to an earlier one may lead to a revival of interest in the literature of that earlier period, and suggests that it may also call into existence similar literary works. No direct 'influence' need be involved; similar historical parameters may result in similar works of art. Both the appreciation and the production of art must therefore be seen as social, dynamic processes, marked not only by changes but also by recurrences in varying forms and at varying levels. In the end, however, differences prove to be at least as important as resemblances; the comparative method which Marx so frequently practises implies his awareness of both.

Marx knew as well as Hegel that not all literary genres could hope to benefit from progress in man's economic, social, and political relations. The Introduction to *Grundrisse*, which talks so vividly of the decline of the epic since Homer's day, makes this plain beyond any doubt. Marx also believed, as we have seen, that a 'capitalist' society is on the whole inimical to literature. In *Grundrisse*, however, the older Marx repeats the younger one's prophecies about the place of the arts in a regenerated and juster society; and there is nothing to suggest that he ever came to share what George Lichtheim has called 'Hegel's pessimism concerning the fate of art in a world rendered transparent by philosophy and science'.[11] He continued to believe, on the contrary, that the talent for creating, and for appreciating, works of literature was much more widespread than the organization of nineteenth-century European society would lead one to suspect. The social reorganization for which he worked was therefore designed to have, as one of its aims, the liberation of such talent. It was designed to give all men the chance to express

[11] G. Lichtheim, *Lucáks*, Fontana Modern Masters (London, 1970), p. 118.

what they had it in them to express, to develop tastes stunted
and thwarted by the daily struggle for existence. In this respect
his vision of a classless society differed markedly from that of the
older Heine, who more than once expressed his fears that a communistic society would not be favourable to poetry. Since the
ultimate communistic society so hopefully envisaged by Marx
—'an association that will exclude classes and their antagonism'
where 'there will no longer be a political power properly so
called, since political power is precisely the official resumé
of the antagonism within civil society'[12]—has not, so far,
appeared on this imperfect earth, the issue still awaits its full
empirical test.

Even the depressed condition of literature in the age of Martin
Tupper, however, an age in which (as Marx saw it) millions of
those who had a potential for creating and enjoying literature
were prevented, by an unjust social system, from developing
their talents—even this was not an unmitigated disaster for
literature and the cultural future of mankind. On the contrary.
Through its development of technology which held an ultimate
promise of lightened toil and possibilities of leisure, through its
development of modes of traffic and exchange which necessi-
tated the crossing of frontiers and the overcoming of national
narrowness, the bourgeoisie of the nineteenth century was preparing the ground for a future literature whose greatness might
well rival, and in some ways (though never in all) might even
surpass, that of ancient Greece. The very frustrations experienced
by those who felt themselves prevented, by the social order of
the nineteenth century, from developing their humanity to the
full had a positive function—they made men wish to hasten the
advent of that juster society in which, Marx believed, literature
and the arts would develop along new and delightful lines.

Marx does not often speculate on the precise form literary and
artistic development would take in the better future he desired;
for he was ever conscious of the many incalculable particularities which make up any given historical situation and render
precise predictions impossible. He rested content with pointing

[12] *Misère de la philosophie*, *MEGA* I, 6, 227. Marx preserves this vision of a future
stateless society in his later years (*Critique of the Gotha Programme*, 1875) but also
states his belief that it can be attained only by way of a changed system of power
involving what he calls 'the revolutionary dictatorship of the proletariat'.

out the necessity for liberating thwarted talents and thus necessarily increasing the amount of literary and artistic activity. He
stressed the role co-operative human labour would play in
bringing about this goal: labour which would once again hold
delight and not just frustration, and which would be done by
human beings no longer compelled to deny themselves the full
development of their many-sided powers. This emphasis on
human labour is crucial and distinctive. 'Whereas Feuerbach',
Lifshits has rightly said, 'whenever he dealt with the subject of
art, always started with contemplation, Marx invariably stressed
the importance of the productive factor, which determines
aesthetic needs and evolves them, through practice, out of their
initial crudeness.'[13]

For all his trust in the cultural self-development of mankind
Marx never forgot, however, that one does not have to live in
a socialist Utopia to produce great literature. His theory of the
'unequal development' of the economic and cultural, the material and intellectual spheres, sketched out in the Introduction
to *Grundrisse*, saved him from crude notions of unilinear and
necessarily concurrent progress; and his love of the literature
produced in slave-holding Greece, in the feudal Christendom
of the European Middle Ages, and in that very nineteenth century whose social organization he did his best to subvert, saved
him no less surely from confusing artistic merit with social
equality. His belief in the class-basis of literature never prevented him from discovering still applicable truths, authentic
models of recurring human situations, in the imaginative works
of great writers of all climes and times, from Homer to Dante,
Shakespeare, and Goethe. At the same time he believed, despite
his hatred of moral trumpetings as of all other forms of sentimentality and bombast, that in the last analysis great literature
would always show concern with truth and a humane sense of
moral values.

Marx never uses the image of 'mirroring' or 'reflecting' when
speaking about literature—though he does occasionally use it,
as we have seen, when speaking about language and philosophy.[14]

[13] M. Lifshits, *The Philosophy of Art of Karl Marx*, p. 83.

[14] 'In ... der Verbrechersprache spiegelt sich der Charakter des Verbrechers ab'
(*MEW* II, 59); 'Der Zustand Deutschlands am Ende des vorigen Jahrhunderts
spiegelt sich vollständig ab in Kants "Critik der practischen Vernunft" ' (*MEW*
III, 176).

Nevertheless his programmatic and constant focus on what he called 'actual' men in 'actual' social situations based on 'actual' property-relationships necessarily leads him to scrutinize literature for documentary information. He clearly believed that literature can speak to us of the society within which it came into being, its organization, institutions, modes of production, and modes of thinking and feeling. He looks to the world's great writers, from Homer and Aeschylus to Pushkin and Balzac, as well as to lesser lights from Antipatros to Paul de Kock, for information about the countries within which and the audiences for whom they wrote, and about the classes whose values they more or less consciously adopted. But he clearly never mistakes the writer's world for a *plain* mirror-image of the life he knew. The writer selects and heightens, and thus allows his readers to see distinctly and vividly processes obscured in real life by the sheer profusion of contingent detail. What appears in literature must be significant and representative—but this, as the letter to Lassalle about *Franz von Sickingen* so clearly shows, does not mean abstraction. The plays and novels he admires tend to be 'true to life' in the sense that their characters exhibit individuality, even quirkiness, and are yet typical of their kind and situation. They must not become megaphones through which their authors proclaim their own convictions; they must exhibit an inner logic or consistency which is based on the mental functioning and social action of similar characters in actual societies. 'Individuality and specificity are an integral aspect of typicality.'[15] In this way a novel by Balzac or Dickens may become a 'concrete universal'—it may reveal more of the dynamic of nineteenth-century life in France and England, and of the workings of human nature in its general as well as its temporally and sociologically particular aspect, than the writings of most historians, economists, and sociologists.

It should be clear, therefore, that although Marx never uses the word 'realism', or any of its derivatives, in a literary-critical context, the aesthetic of fiction and drama which emerges from his writings after 1844 may, without distortion, be called a 'realist' aesthetic. Not, however, a 'naturalist' one—he never showed any liking for raw slices of life served up as literature. Nor did it exclude fantasy: he found apt symbols for human

[15] *BM* 31.

experience in such 'fantastic' works as the tales of the *Arabian Nights*, Chamisso's *Peter Schlemihl*, Hoffmann's *Little Zaches*, and Mary Shelley's *Frankenstein*.

Besides its documentary and symbolizing functions, literature may also fulfil a 'critical' function in Marx's cultural universe. A writer like Eugène Sue will, for the most part, reflect or flatter the prejudices of his potential readers; but even he may occasionally rival the achievement of greater writers by presenting, in fictional form, truths about society which run counter to his own consciously adopted political or social stance. Diderot and Goethe, through the speeches of Rameau's Nephew and Mephistopheles respectively, enunciate cynical views about social attitudes and institutions which usefully expose the *partie honteuse* of European 'civil society'. The labouring classes, though largely cut off from the enjoyment of literature and unable to develop freely such talent for its creation as they possess, may also occasionally find a potent critical voice: witness, for instance, that song of the Silesian weavers which Marx so admired for its insight and maturity.

The literary aesthetic implicit in Marx's work owes a great deal to the aesthetics of Herder, Goethe, Schiller, August Wilhelm Schlegel, and Hegel.[16] His assumptions about the need to unite the individual and the general, the particular and the representative, the specific and the symbolic stem directly from Weimar classicism; and for all his avowed anti-Romanticism, his ideal of the 'all-round' man—his vision of a future in which men would 'hunt in the morning, fish in the afternoon, rear cattle in the evening, criticize after dinner, just as they have a mind, without ever becoming hunter, fisherman, shepherd or critic'—has a good deal in common with the image of the 'free and cultivated man' projected by Friedrich Schlegel.[17] His

---

[16] S. Pazura, in *Marks a klasyczna estetyka niemiecka*, has shown the continuity between Marx's aesthetics and those of K. P. Moritz and Kant. An admirable summary of Marx's aesthetic 'debts' appears in *BM* 40–5.

[17] Cf. E. E. W. Kux, *Karl Marx — Die revolutionäre Konfession*, Diss. (Zürich, 1966), p. 74; and F. J. Raddatz, *Karl Marx. Eine politische Biographie*, pp. 362–3. M. H. Abrams, discussing Marx in the context of the Romantic movement in England, comes to the conclusion that Marx's 'ideal for mankind embodies the essential values of Romantic humanism', but adds: 'The difference is that the reconciling and integrative role which, in their various ways, Schiller, Schelling, Hegel, Coleridge, Wordsworth and Blake had assigned to the imaginative work of the artist, Marx expands to include all the work of men's hands—provided, that is,

critical vocabulary too is much influenced by the German writers already named—like them, he experiments a good deal with various kinds of biological or organic metaphor, though he adds the famous metaphor of 'base' and 'superstructure' and uses a key notion like *Schein* (aesthetic semblance) in ways which would not have satisfied Schiller. The present book should, however, have demonstrated beyond doubt that in his actual dealings with literature Marx never makes mechanical and rigid use of the 'base–superstructure' model, and that it does not, in fact, figure at all prominently in his appreciations of existing literary works.

In one of his earliest essays Marx had asserted that the mind was not an examining magistrate taking down depositions; that literary objects of perception were refracted differently in the minds of different readers, and that each literary object called for a particular and specific mode of approach. His dismissive remarks about G. Th. Fechner, the German pioneer of experimental aesthetic psychology, suggest that he had little sympathy with aesthetic schemes that directed attention away from the literary work of art and its creator to the psychology of its readers. Yet he did show himself able, in comments on Sue and Kinkel, to peer into the psychological processes that go on when a literary work is written and when it is read. In his later years he showed himself alive, in particular, to the changing aspects that literary works, and literary theories, present to successive generations of readers. New social experiences, fresh needs, may reveal dimensions and meanings in a work of art which were not suspected by its first admirers. This is one aspect of the permanent appeal made by works of literature; another, dialectically related to the first, is that the great works of the past represent a unique 'moment' of humanity which in life has passed away for ever, but which has been preserved for the delight of posterity in its artistic embodiment and expression. Marx also speaks, in his earlier works, of 'laws of beauty' which the artist observes. The observance of such 'laws' distinguishes man from the beasts, who are credited with no aesthetic sense; just as the poorest human architect is distinguished from the

that his work is performed in the social ambience of free communal enterprise.'
(*Natural Supernaturalism. Tradition and Revolution in Romantic Literature* (New York, 1973), pp. 314, 316.)

Conclusion

Conclusion 413

most perfect bee or spider by the fact that he has built his
edifice in imagination before he constructs it in reality.

Marx does not often deal with questions of form. His literary
aesthetic, like that of Hegel, recognizes the primacy of *Gehalt*,
of theme and import; his early dictum that 'form is of no value
unless it is the form of its content' remains constantly at the back
of his mind when dealing with specific literary works. The dictum implies the necessity of harmony between what a work says
and how it says it; but it implies also Marx's impatience with
artists who knew how to use the bridle but had no horse, with
formalisms and aestheticisms of all kind, with a *Belletrismus*
which hides conventional thinking, sentimentality, or plain
ignorance under fine words. This made him, only half ironically, commend Lassalle for *not* writing correct blank verse; but
he showed at other times how much he was aware of the writer's
need, not only to think and feel, but also to learn his craft. He
scourges halting verses and sloppy use of language in some of
his most trenchant and amusing pieces. In Marx's view it was
precisely in his use of language, and in the rhythms of his verse
and prose, that a poet's deficiencies of thought and feeling were
likely to betray themselves. And as we have seen, he admired
as much as any eighteenth-century classicist what he called, in
Grundrisse, the compact structure, the 'closed shape and form
and given limitation', of Greek art.[18]

His own response to literature, Marx wrote to Lassalle in
1859, was predominantly intellectual; but he kept himself conscious, as this same letter about *Franz von Sickingen* showed, of the
emotional and visceral appeal works of imaginative literature
make and should make. Men respond to certain themes, structures, images, sounds, and rhythms with an immediate excitement, a shock of recognition, for which criticism tries to account
after the fact. They respond as whole beings, with their eyes,
their ears, their emotions, as well as their intellect. Like earlier
German aestheticians, from Baumgarten onwards, Marx saw in
art a sensuous form of consciousness, distinct from abstract
thought—and nothing amused him more than to hear critics
like Ruge commend their favourite writers because their works
yielded a fully formed and articulated philosophic system.

[18] *Geschloβne Gestalt, Form und gegebne Begrenzung* (*G* 388); cf. Morawski, op. cit.,
p. 305.

Everything depends, for Marx, on who responds and to what. Men betray themselves by their literary tastes. Marx's characterization of such minor but representative figures as Pustkuchen, Daumer, and Kinkel therefore proceeds to a not inconsiderable extent by way of the literary works such men admire or dislike; the aspects of such works which they single out for praise or blame; and the way in which they seek to stylize their own lives and works in conformity with literary heroes or ideals. The same is true of Marx's judgement of Carlyle: he believed that Carlyle's admiration of the quirky fictions of Jean Paul reveals an important aspect of his nature.

Marx tended to trust the tale more than the author. Implicit in his dealings with literature is the belief which was to find its best-known formulation in Engels's letter to Margaret Harkness of April 1888: that an author's performance may conflict with his intention, his latent involvement with his overt opinion.[19] Marx would occasionally talk as though the characters an author had devised existed in real life and had a history that extended beyond the novel or play in which they appear. This 'How many children had Lady Macbeth'-mentality is not as obtrusive, however, as is sometimes claimed; and when it does appear we find it soon corrected by passages in which Marx shows precisely that the author has perverted the logic of the characters he has himself created, that he has failed to allow them to unfold their full potentiality, or that he speaks all too obviously through their mouth. 'According to Marx, Lassalle ought to have allowed the heroes of his tragedy the possibility of being faithful to their own selves, of testing their capabilities to the very limit, of exploring the internal, organic dialectic of their own personalities.'[20] At the same time it must be admitted that Marx does not always choose his terms so carefully as to avoid another imputation: that he fails to distinguish sufficiently rigorously between the views of a dramatic character (Shakespeare's Timon of Athens, for instance) and the views of an author. Careful scrutiny of the words actually quoted and their context in Marx's argument will often reveal, however, that Marx is aware of the distinction and expects his readers to be aware of it too.[21]

[19] Cf. Wellek, *A History of Modern Criticism, 1750–1950*, vol. iii, p. 238.
[20] Cf. Henry Arvon, *Marxist Esthetics*, trans. Helen Lane (Ithaca and London, 1973), p. 37.
[21] There are exceptions. A quotation from *Timon of Athens* in *The German Ideology*

We have seen Marx reject the idea that literature is valuable in proportion to the abstract thought or the formulated morality it contains; but this does not mean that he saw aesthetic experience as 'apractical'. On the contrary: for him literature had a multitude of 'uses', some of which the present book has tried to describe. He saw its enjoyment, like its creation, as a form of *Praxis*, raising man above the animals, enhancing the realizable potential of mankind,[22] offering visions of past and present realities and future possibilities. Literature achieves all this, however, in Marx's view, by means wholly different from those appropriate to philosophy, appealing to the 'total' man in a manner no philosophical system could rival. To confuse literature with philosophy or abstract thinking is no less fatal to writers than it is to readers; for this is likely to make them proclaim their own opinions directly—as did so many of the political *Tendenzdichter* of Marx's day, or as Lassalle did in *Franz von Sickingen*—instead of bodying forth, in the heterocosm of their art, a concrete, complex, and formed vision of reality.

In his private life Marx constantly demonstrates the way in which literature may embellish, enliven, and heighten existence. He at first writes and later adopts or adapts poems in order to pay delicate compliments. He reads tales and poems with his children, and invents tales of his own based on folklore or German Romantic literature but given substance by his own nature, his own problems, his own social experience. He declaims aloud poems and dramas in several languages, delighting in their sound and rhythm as well as their sense. He characterizes his acquaintances by means of literary nicknames culled from the works of Shakespeare or Dickens or George Eliot. He reads imaginative works in Greek, in Latin, in Spanish, in Russian, in French, in English, and in German for refreshment and for enlightenment. As a public figure too, as author and as orator, Marx constantly draws on the writers of past and present whose work he admires. He adopts, for polemical purposes, the voice of Aeschylus' Prometheus, Shakespeare's Thersites, and Goethe's

(*MEW* III, 212) does seem to equate Timon's views with those of Shakespeare himself. The passage from Act IV which Marx quotes has been so curtailed that Timon's misanthropic delight in the state of affairs he chronicles disappears from view.

[22] Cf. Henry Arvon, op. cit., p. 26.

Mephistopheles. He uses quotations from the world's great writers—either in as accurate a form as his memory will allow, or deliberately adapted—to convey his argument in the most concentrated and memorable way possible. At times, remembering the original context of such quotations is harmful to the intended effect—as when Marx wrests a saying with which he clearly agrees from one of Shakespeare's most unpleasant characters, Cornwall in *King Lear*. At other times the original context counts for little: it is perfectly possible, for instance, to respond adequately to Marx's 'straight' or ironic use of his favourite lines from Goethe's *West–Eastern Divan* without remembering that they come from the book devoted to Tamburlaine and are part of a love-poem in which the lover describes the wealth of roses that had to die in order to make a few drops of perfume for his beloved. In such cases—and they are in the majority—a recollection of the original context does, however, enhance the contrast or parallel Marx wants us to draw. At yet other times, where particularly well-known works of literature are involved, our failure to recognize the earlier text seriously weakens the intended effect. We have to remember that certain words quoted by Marx are originally spoken by Shakespeare's Shylock, and that the failure to control the spirits he summoned was originally that of the sorcerer's apprentice and not (as in *The Communist Manifesto*) that of the sorcerer himself.

Marx likes to refer his readers to literary creations (Don Quixote, for instance, or Falstaff, or Pecksniff) as types to which his opponents may be said to conform or from which they may be said to deviate in essential respects. He uses incidents from specific literary works to show, as in a model, the actual or perverted logic of events in the real social world (as when the Hegelian Left directing its energies against religion reminds him of Don Quixote attacking a funeral procession.[23] Economic processes which are 'opaque' in real life may be made 'transparent' in literature—*Robinson Crusoe* is therefore a prime exhibit in *Capital* I. Marx finds the structures of men's arguments and their actions clearly revealed in literary structures: either in those of individual works like the *Jockellied*, or in those of specific scenes of specific plays, like Falstaff's ever-growing magnification of the number of men in buckram and Kendal green, or in those

[23] *MEW* III, 216–17.

typical of a whole genre, be it tragedy, comedy, farce, or parody. Alternatively, he brings out the logic of actions and events in the actual world by *contrasting* them with those in literature—when he speaks, for instance, of 'inverted Peter Schlemihls' who buy shadows with gold. He uses a tissue of allusions to a particular literary work—Boiardo's *Roland in Love*, Shakespeare's *King Henry IV*, *Don Quixote*—as leitmotivs that bind his own essays and pamphlets together. He may himself deliberately imitate literary structures in order to make his points more effectively: the dramatizations characteristic of *Capital* I provide a telling but not isolated example. He constantly employs metaphors derived from literature and literary criticism to characterize men and events. And last but not least: he found in some of the techniques of literary criticism—metrical and rhythmic analysis, scrutiny of imagery, scrutiny of sentence-structures—a powerful means of discrediting his opponents' opinions along with their style. He charges his opponents, in critiques of this kind, with a multitude of offences against sound and sense: discrepancies between what is actually said and what the writer thinks he is saying, empty verbiage, tautologies, unrealized abstractions, euphemisms, attempts at specious transcendence of obstinate contradictions, linguistic equivocations that mirror equivocations of thought, lack of reflection on the historical ambience of words and phrases, semantic and etymological tricks, mixed metaphors, jingles, grammatical errors, and incompetent use of metrical schemes. Such analyses help Marx's own argument forward while covering his enemies with that 'contempt and mockery' of which Engels speaks in a letter to Eduard Bernstein dated 2 February 1881:

As you have the *Neue Rheinische Zeitung* you would do well to read it occasionally. The contempt and mockery with which we treated our opponents was just what brought us in nearly 6,000 subscribers in the six months ending with the declaration of martial law, and although we started again from the beginning in November we had the same number and more by May 1849.

Many of Marx's quotations, as the foregoing pages will have shown, alter the wording of the original. Such alterations are often deliberate: he uses his authors for his own purposes, and does not hesitate to adapt their words, if necessary, to his requirements. Sometimes, indeed, the very contrast between his wording and that of the original is part of the intended effect. At other times, however, it is simply Marx's memory that is at fault—as he says, with engaging frankness, in a letter to Kugelmann dated 13 October 1866: 'I frequently quote from memory, without looking up the original.' But even then the distortions he introduces are never as disturbing as those we find in the works of Hegel; Marx had a remarkable ear, and a retentive memory, for linguistic cadences, and would have been incapable of garbling his Schiller, for instance, in the distressing way Hegel does in the final sentence of the *Phenomenology of the Spirit*.

Like other educated men of his time, Marx found his mind increasingly stocked with *Bildungsgut*, phrases from the world's great writers which could be used ornamentally, without full intellectual and emotional assent. That he occasionally employed literary quotations and allusions in this way cannot be doubted. More often, however, they constitute an appeal to authority. The words of writers whom Marx can respect, and to whom his readers may be thought to owe some of their finest cultural experiences, give additional weight to his own views and may, on occasions, relieve him of the necessity to furnish rigorous proof. Beyond that, however, such material helps Marx to make connections to establish complex associations, between man's economic and his cultural activities. The vivacity of his intelligence, the sheer range of his varied yet unified interests, are nowhere more apparent than in this bringing-together of so many diverse contexts; even if, at times, he overdoes it, even if (in parts of *The German Ideology*, for instance, or in *Herr Vogt*) the plethora or the repetitiousness of the allusions becomes wearisome and loses its intended effect.

In the section of the Paris Manuscripts that is headed 'Private Property and Communism', Marx had inveighed against a system of private property which 'made us so stupid and partial that an object is only *ours* when we have it—when it exists for us as capital, or when it is directly possessed, eaten, drunk, worn, inhabited etc., in short, when it is *used* by us'. Great literature, as we have seen, was valuable to Marx not least because it resisted crude 'utility-' and 'consumption'-thinking. At the same time, however, his literary quotations and allusions act as constant warning-signals against the economistic reduction of Marx which Karl Korsch and others have noted in some of his latter-day disciples: against the view that only the economic and social struggle matters and that a concern with literature is a dance along the superstructure which can only distract the workers of the world from their revolutionary task. In the context of earlier political struggles Ludwig Börne had once charged Heine with exactly this kind of distracting irrelevance; and in that quarrel, one remembers, Marx had firmly ranged himself alongside Heine.

Marx was very much aware, from his earliest days with the *Rheinische Zeitung* onwards, of the great service writers of poetry or fiction can render to a cause by espousing it, by producing works which pillory injustice, urge the necessity of change, and ridicule opponents. He was therefore deeply hurt when writers with whom he had collaborated drifted away from him, or showed themselves unable to give wholehearted allegiance to his own social and political views. This does not mean, however, as has been shown, that he judged a writer's work solely or even principally by the degree to which its 'message' corresponded to his own beliefs and hopes, or by its usefulness as a weapon in the immediate struggle. He never denigrated the later work of Heine, or those earlier works written before his own views and Heine's were most in harmony—even though he was clearly out of sympathy with Heine's professed return to monotheism. Nor, conversely, did he ever exalt the works of Georg Weerth, even though Weerth was one of the most valued contributors to the *Neue Rheinische Zeitung* and (unlike Freiligrath) never became a renegade in Marx's eyes. He loved Dante and Goethe as much as Shakespeare, even though he knew enough of the *Weltanschauung* of the two former writers to be sure that in important respects it conflicted with his own. Here the historical imagination had also to be called into play: Marx had nothing but scorn for those of his contemporaries who condemned Klopstock's poetry, for instance, because the attitudes to life implicit in it differed from neo-Hegelian attitudes.

There are cases, however, in which Marx felt such strong antipathies to a writer's political stance and activities that he seems not even to have tried to redress the balance by reading —or responding sympathetically—to the imaginative works that writer left behind him. His judgement of Edmund Spenser and Sir John Davies rests on their involvement in Irish affairs and is unmitigated by *The Faerie Queene* and *Orchestra*. His judgement of Chateaubriand is based on that author's political activities and historical writings, and remains unaffected (as far as one can see) by any serious response to *René*. He is also impatient with *idyllic* literature of all kinds—his dislike of Gessner, of the hero of Goethe's *Hermann und Dorothea*, and of Auerbach's village stories all point in this direction. One may regret, of course, that this led to occasional unfairness—unlike Börne and Heine, Marx was never able to respond at all adequately to the work of Jean Paul; but we have no right to expect apples from a pear-tree. He came to literature as a whole man; and a Marx who could sympathize with bourgeois idylls would have had to cease being Marx.

Inevitably, his taste was partial and his reading highly selective; he could not spend days and weeks lingering over literary delicacies, savouring them, and sampling the critical opinion of others in the hope that it might correct and direct his own. Nor could he muster either the time or the money to 'keep up' with the literary production of his own day. He built up, over the years, a stock-company of favourite quotations and allusions which could be assigned different roles in different contexts. But when all this has been said, it is still remarkable how wide his range turns out to be, and—given the strength of his opinions—how comparatively rare patent misjudgements are in his comments on literature.

'Misjudgements' should not be confused, however, with 'personal appropriation'. Marx's writings exemplify to perfection the way in which a man of strong personality, opinions, and tastes appropriates the work of great writers in accordance with his own particular needs. The case of Dante may serve as a convenient illustration. It is clear that the mature Marx felt *The Divine Comedy*—the *Inferno* in particular—to be relevant to his own life and concerns, despite its metaphysical orientation; in this respect it joins such other works with supernatural elements as Goethe's *Faust*, Balzac's *Melmoth Reconciled* and—of course—Luther's translation of the Bible, which has left an indelible mark on Marx's imagery and style. The examples of Marx's consistently secularizing use of *The Divine Comedy* adduced in earlier chapters of this book suggest that there are six well-defined situations in which Dante springs to his mind. An unusual sight or new experience, like his first glimpse of sulphur baths, triggers off a literary reminiscence—what he sees becomes an 'innocent scene from Dante's *Inferno*'. Or he will search for some way of describing the unswerving path through life which he has himself taken and which he wants his followers to take: Virgil's admonition to Dante to 'follow me and let the people talk' comes to his mind; but since he has had no Virgil to follow he amends it to read: 'Follow your own course and let people say what they will.' He also finds, however, that in certain situations Dante's lines fit his own feelings exactly, without the need for verbal tinkering. What Dante makes Cacciaguida say about 'climbing the hard stairs of exile', and about the bad company exiles are forced to keep, seems to Marx as well fitted to describe his own experiences as the same passages from the *Paradiso* always seemed to Heine; and his journeyings into the 'dismal science' of economics appear to call for the same intrepidity and determination that Dante's hell demands of those who would enter its portals. At other times he will find in *The Divine Comedy* a humorous way of conveying some economic point—as when he puts into the mouth of a commodity-owner, challenging an opponent to come down to brass tacks and cut the cackle, a pecuniary metaphor used by Dante's St. Peter: 'We now have a sufficiently good idea of this coin's alloy and weight; but tell me if you have it in your purse.' In the *Inferno* Marx finds, again like Heine, a repertoire of punishments that fit the crime, along with insults to hurl at his opponents; *Herr Vogt* yields several telling examples of this. And lastly: what Marx found most important of all in his reading of Dante was that the *Inferno* could provide points of comparison with which to characterize, standards against which to measure, the hell on earth which, he thought, the Victorians had created for the urban and rural poor.

As we have seen, Marx does not use the words *Literatur* and *literarisch* with sole reference to imaginative compositions; he applies such terms readily to the whole body of written and printed material, whether artistic or not, or to the writings pertaining to a given field of investigation. This is merely one outward manifestation of his belief that imaginative literature and other kinds of writing are not wholly distinct and discrete, which is itself the corollary of his deepest conviction of all: that all the ways in which men express themselves, all the institutions they call into being, all the social relations they form, are intimately related, and that their study should form an integral whole, a 'science of man'. One may, of course, disagree with the ways Marx saw and formulated such interconnections, or with the means he thought necessary to overcome social injustice and inequalities. One may regret that he did not pay enough overt attention to literary structures and to the 'literariness' of literary works. His constant insistence, however, in theory and in practice, that man and his works need to be seen as a whole may be found salutary even by those who most disagree with him in other respects.

Marx's delight in literature and eagerness for literary experience must be seen as part of his endeavour to know the best that has been thought and uttered in the world; an endeavour as constant with him as with Matthew Arnold. In the year of Marx's death Arnold found himself stimulated, by his controversy with T. H. Huxley, to set down the following confession of faith:

I talk of knowing the best which has been thought and uttered in the world; Professor Huxley says this means knowing *literature*. Literature is a large word; it may mean everything written with letters or printed in a book. Euclid's *Elements* and Newton's *Principia* are thus literature. All knowledge that reaches us through books is literature. But by literature Professor Huxley means *belles lettres*. He means to make me say, that knowing the best which has been thought and said by the modern nations is knowing their *belles lettres* and no more. And this is no sufficient equipment, he argues, for a criticism of modern life. But as I do not mean, by knowing ancient Rome, knowing merely more or less of Latin *belles lettres*, and taking no account of Rome's military, and political, and legal, and administrative work in the world; and as, by knowing ancient Greece, I understand knowing her as a giver of Greek art, and the guide to a free and right use of reason and to scientific method, and the founder of our mathematics and physics and astronomy and biology—I understand knowing her as all this, and not merely knowing certain Greek poems, and histories, and treatises, and speeches—so as to the knowledge of modern nations also. By knowing modern nations, I mean not merely knowing their *belles lettres*, but knowing also what has been done by such men as Copernicus, Galileo, Newton, Darwin . . . To know Italian *belles lettres* is not to know Italy, and to know English *belles lettres* is not to know England. Into knowing Italy and England there comes a great deal more, Galileo and Newton amongst it. The reproach of being a superficial humanism, a tincture of *belles lettres*, may attach rightly enough to some other disciplines; but to the particular discipline recommended when I proposed knowing the best that has been thought and said in the world, it does not apply. In that best I certainly include what in modern times has been thought and said by the great observers and knowers of nature.[24]

The later Marx would have insisted more strongly on the importance of 'doing' as well as 'knowing'; and for all his love of Homer and Aeschylus, for all his admiration of Epicurus, he would hardly have thought of ancient Greece as 'the guide to a free and right use of reason and to scientific method' in the unequivocal way Arnold does in this passage; but it contains nothing else with which he could not have wholeheartedly agreed.

When Marx thinks about literature, then, he does so in a wide economic, social, historical context. When he thinks about a particular author, or a particular body of literary compositions, he does so in relation to other authors, other compositions, in many languages. His formulation in *The Communist Manifesto*— that 'national one-sidedness and narrow-mindedness become more and more impossible, and from the numerous national and local literatures there arises a world literature'—was true of himself. The tissue of references to the literature of many nations which we have traced in Marx's works show the extent to which he had made his prophecy become reality in his own life, and in his own writings. He remained ever aware of local and temporal differences, of course, and more than once tried to show how a particular author (Lucretius, say, or Dante) might be said to be 'representative' of his nation, his time, his social circumstances; and he no more thought of 'world literature' as standardized and undifferentiated than Goethe did in *his* pronouncements on *Weltliteratur*. In his life and in his writings Marx showed how a man could be at home in many literatures at once, relishing their idiosyncrasies and diversities, letting his

[24] Matthew Arnold, 'Literature and Science'—a lecture delivered during Arnold's tour of America in 1883. It answers a lecture on 'Science and Culture' which T. H. Huxley had delivered in Birmingham in 1880.

knowledge of one enrich and deepen his understanding of the other. He was as deeply committed to a comparative and historical approach to literature as Herder. Despite his interest in the politics and social organization of India and China, however, and despite his occasional references to North American writers like Fenimore Cooper and Mrs. Beecher-Stowe,[25] 'world literature' means, for Marx, essentially the literature of Western Europe. There is little in his work which corresponds to Goethe's reception of Persian, Chinese, and Indian literature—if one excepts the fascination which the tales of the *Arabian Nights* held for him as for his children, the interest in Arabian fables which he acquired in the very last year of his life,[26] and his occasional glances at Rückert's translations from the Persian or at Indian tales about Hanuman the monkey and Sabala the cow.

This study has confined itself, deliberately, to Marx's own dealings with literature. It has not inquired into later applications of dialectical thinking to literature—'thought', as Jonathan Culler has said, 'to the second power, thought which turns back upon itself in a movement of self-transcendence and, reversing itself, finds that what at one level was believed a limitation or deficiency becomes at a higher level a strength or advantage'.[27] It has not tried to look beyond Marx himself to the late Engels, Lenin, Plekhanov, Mehring, Caudwell, Lukács, Brecht, Benjamin, Goldmann, Fischer, Gramsci, della Volpe, Macherey, and the many, many others who have developed what is now known as Marxist literary theory and criticism. Such developments have frequently proceeded from hints that Marx's works may give when their author is not overtly talking about literature at all. His observations on ideology and mythology, on

[25] Harriet Beecher-Stowe is mentioned in Marx's *NYDT* article of 18 September 1861 (*MEW* XV, 304, 306); and like so many of his contemporaries he uses the phrase 'Uncle Tom' as a generic term for the suffering slaves in the Southern states of the U.S.A. (e.g. the *People's Paper*, 30 Apr. 1853—*MEW* IX, 80). Marx also alludes more than once to Benjamin Franklin (for whose theory of value he had great respect) and, in a letter to N. F. Danielson, to some unspecified American writers: 'The best writers among the Yankees [*die besten Yankee-Schriftsteller*] loudly proclaim the stubborn fact that the war against slavery has burst asunder the bonds of the blacks but has enslaved the white producers.' (*MEW* XXXIV, 359; *ÜKL* I, 609–10, 665.)

[26] See his letter to Laura Lafargue dated 13–14 Apr. 1882—*MEW* XXXV, 310–11.

[27] Review of Fredric Jameson's *Marxism and Form*, *Mod. Lang. Review*, lxix (1974), 599.

'commodity-fetishism', on 'productive consumption', on contradiction and totality, on *Praxis* and hegemony—all of these could, like the dialectic method itself, be adapted, elaborated, and incorporated into systems which differ as widely from Marx's own conceptions as from one another. But that is another story, and subject for many another book.

Chronology

1858–9   Articles for the *New American Cyclopaedia*
1859   *Zur Kritik der politischen Ökonomie*
          Articles in *Das Volk*
1860   *Herr Vogt*
1861–2   Articles in *Die Presse*
1864   *Address and Provisional Rules of the International Workingmen's Association*
1865   Address to the General Council of the International Workingmen's Association, later published under the title *Value, Price and Profit*
1867   *Das Kapital. Kritik der politischen Ökonomie*, vol. I. (Marx's drafts and notes for subsequent volumes were published posthumously under the titles *Das Kapital* vols. II and III, and *Theorien über den Mehrwert*)
1867–73   Manifestoes, Programmes, and Declarations of the General Council of the International Workingmen's Association
1870–1   *The Civil War in France*
1875   Critique of the *Gotha Programme* [*Gothaer Parteiprogramm*] of the German Social Democratic Party
1877–8   Contribution to Part II, chapter 10, of Engels's *Herrn Eugen Dührings Umwälzung der Wissenschaft*
1880   'Enquête ouvrière' in *Revue socialiste*

Select Bibliography

A. EDITIONS

Marx, Karl, and Friedrich Engels, *Historisch-kritische Gesamtausgabe*, ed. D. B. Ryazanov and V. Adoratski (Frankfurt–Berlin–Moscow, 1927–35) (*MEGA*). A new *MEGA* is being prepared for the Dietz Verlag, Berlin.

—— —— *Werke*. Herausgegeben vom Institut für Marxismus-Leninismus beim ZK der SED (Berlin, 1956–68) (*MEW*).

—— —— *Collected Works* (Moscow, New York, and London, 1975 ff.) (*MECW*).

—— —— *Selected Works in Three Volumes* (Moscow, 1969) (*SW*).

—— —— *Selected Correspondence 1846–1895*, transl. and annotated by Dona Torr (London, 1936).

The Pelican Marx Library. General Editor: Q. Hoare:

Early Writings. Translated by R. Livingstone and G. Benton, introduced by L. Colletti (Harmondsworth, 1975).

Grundrisse. Foundations of the Critique of Political Economy (Rough Draft). Translated with a Foreword by Martin Nicolaus (Harmondsworth, 1973).

The Revolutions of 1848 (Political Writings I). Edited and Introduced by David Fernbach (Harmondsworth, 1973).

Surveys from Exile (Political Writings II). Edited and Introduced by David Fernbach (Harmondsworth, 1973).

The First International and After (Political Writings III). Edited and Introduced by David Fernbach (Harmondsworth, 1974).

Ruge, Arnold, and Karl Marx, *Deutsch-Französische Jahrbücher*, (*1844*), ed. J. Höppner (Leipzig, 1973).

Marx, Karl, *Manuskipte über die polnische Frage*, ed. W. Konze and D. Hertz-Eichenrode (The Hague, 1961).

'Lettres et documents de Karl Marx, 1856–1883', *Annali* (Feltrinelli, Milan), i (1958).

The Ethnological Notebooks of Karl Marx, ed. L. Krader (Assen, 1972).

Freiligraths Briefwechsel mit Marx und Engels, ed. M. Haeckel (Berlin, 1968).

Marx, Karl, and Friedrich Engels, *Über Kunst und Literatur*, ed. M. Kliem (Berlin, 1967) (*ÜKL*).

—— —— *On Literature and Art*, eds. L. Baxandall and S. Morawski (St. Louis, Milwaukee, 1973).

Mohr und General. Erinnerungen an Marx und Engels (Berlin, 1970).

An edition of Marx's articles for the *New-York Daily Tribune*, ed. Ferguson and O'Neill, was announced for publication in 1973 but had not appeared when the typescript of the present book was completed.

For other editions used in this book see List of Abbreviations on pp. 11–12.

B. COMMENTARIES AND INTERPRETATIONS

Adams, H. P., *Karl Marx in his Earlier Writings* (London, 1940).

Adorno, T. W., *Ästhetische Theorie* (Frankfurt, 1970).

Althusser, L., *For Marx*, trans. B. Brewster (Harmondsworth, 1969).

—— (and others), *Lire le Capital* (Paris, 1965).

Aptheker, H. (ed.), *Marxism and Alienation. A Symposium* (New York, 1965).

Arvon, H., *Marxist Esthetics*, trans. H. R. Lane, Introduction by F. Jameson (Ithaca, 1973).

Avineri, S., 'Marx and the Intellectuals', *Journal of the History of Ideas*, xxviii (1967).

—— *The Social and Political Thought of Karl Marx* (Cambridge, 1968).

Barth, H., *Wahrheit und Ideologie* (new edition Frankfurt, 1974).

Baxandall, L., *Marxism and Aesthetics. A Selective Annotated Bibliography* (New York, 1968).

Bell, D. R., 'Marx, Sartre and Marxism', *Memoirs and Proceedings of the Manchester Literary and Philosophical Society*, civ (1961–2).

Benjamin, W., *Schriften*, ed. T. W. and G. Adorno (Frankfurt, 1955).

Berlin, I., *Karl Marx. His Life and Environment*, 3rd edn. (Oxford, 1963).

Bernstein, R. J., *Praxis and Action* (London, 1971).

Blackburn, R. (ed.), *Ideology in Social Science. Readings in Critical Social Theory* (London, 1972).

Bloch, E., *Das Prinzip Hoffnung* (Frankfurt, 1959).

—— *Über Karl Marx* (Frankfurt, 1968).

Blumenberg, W., *Karl Marx in Selbstzeugnissen und Bilddokumenten* (Reinbek, 1962).

Bober, M. M., *Karl Marx's Interpretation of History* (Cambridge, Mass., 1927) (new edn. New York, 1965).

Böhme, S., *Grundlage und Methodik der Literaturbetrachtung bei Karl Marx und Friedrich Engels*, Diss. (Berlin, 1954).

Bottomore, T. B., *Introduction to Karl Marx: Early Writings* (London, 1963).

——(ed.), *Karl Marx*, Makers of Modern Social Science (New Jersey, 1973).

Breuer, K. H., *Der junge Marx: Sein Weg zum Kommunismus* (Cologne, 1954).

Burns, E. and T. (eds.), *Sociology of Literature and Drama*. Selected Readings (Harmondsworth, 1973).

Calvez, J.-Y., *La Pensée de Karl Marx* (Paris, 1956).

Carr, E. H., *Studies in Revolution* (London, 1950).

Carver, T., *Karl Marx: Texts on Method* (Oxford, 1975).

Clecak, P., *Marxism and American Literary Criticism* (Ann Arbor, 1964).

Cornu, A., *Karl Marx et la pensée moderne* (Paris, 1948).

—— *Karl Marx et Friedrich Engels, leur vie et leur œuvre* (Paris, 1955 ff.).

Cwojdrak, G., 'Karl Marx, die Phantasie und die Kinderliteratur', *Der Bibliothekar*, xxii (Leipzig) (1968).

Delfgaauw, B., *The Young Marx*, trans. F. Schütz and M. Redfern (London and Melbourne, 1967).

Demetz, P., *Marx, Engels and the Poets. Origins of Marxist Literary Criticism*, 2nd edn. revised and enlarged by the author and translated by J. L. Sammons (Chicago, 1967).

—— *Marx, Engels und die Dichter. Ein Kapitel deutscher Literaturgeschichte* (Frankfurt–Berlin, 1969).

Dymschitz, A., 'Zur Sickingen-Debatte', *Weimarer Beiträge*, vi (1960).

—— 'Marx und Literatur — Antwort an Hans Mayer', *Sinn und Form*, xxi (1969).

Elvin, H. L., 'Marx and the Marxists as Literary Critics', *Journal of Adult Education*, x (1938).

Erckenbrecht, U., *Marx' materialistische Sprachtheorie*. Mit einem selektiven Sachregister zu den Marx-Engels-Werken (Kronberg, 1973).

Feuer, L., *Marx and the Intellectuals. A Set of Post-Ideological Essays* (New York, 1969).

Fischer, E., *The Necessity of Art. A Marxist Approach*, trans. Anna Bostock (Harmondsworth, 1963).

Fischhof, H. (ed.), *Karl Marx, Friedrich Engels: Über Kunst und Literatur* (Vienna, 1948).

Freville, J., Introduction to *Karl Marx/Friedrich Engels sur la littérature et l'art*. Textes choisis (Paris, 1954).

Fridlender, G. M., *Karl Marks i Fridrikh Engels i voprosy literatury* (Moscow, 1962).

Fügen, N., *Die Hauptrichtungen der Literatursoziologie. Ein Beitrag zur literatur-soziologischen Theorie* (Bonn, 1964).

Gallas, H., *Marxistische Literaturtheorie. Kontroversen im Bund proletarisch-revolutionärer Schriftsteller* (Neuwied and Berlin, 1971).

Garaudy, R., *Karl Marx* (Paris, 1964).

Gemlow, H. (and others), *Karl Marx. Eine Biographie* (Berlin, 1968).

Glaser, H. A. (and others), *Literaturwissenschaft und Sozialwissenschaften. Grundlagen und Modellanalysen* (Stuttgart, 1971).

Glicksberg, C. I., 'Literature and the Marxist Aesthetic', *University of Toronto Quarterly*, xviii (1949).

Goffenshefer, V. Ts., *Iz istorii marksistskoi kritiki: Pol Lafarg i borba za realizm* (Moscow, 1967).

Goldmann, L., *Le Dieu caché* (Paris, 1955).

—— *Pour une sociologie du roman* (Paris, 1964).

—— *Marxisme et sciences humaines* (Paris, 1970).

Golman, L. I. (and others), *Karl Marx. Biographie*. Institut für Marxismus Leninismus beim ZK der KPdSU (Berlin, 1973).

Goux, J.-J., 'Marx et l'inscription du travail', *Tel quel. Théorie d'ensemble* (Paris, 1968).

Gramsci, A., *Prison Notebooks* (London, 1970).

Harstick, H.-P., 'Zum Schicksal der marxschen Privatbibliothek', *International Review of Social History*, xviii (1973).

Hauser, A., *Philosophie der Kunstgeschichte* (Munich, 1964).

Hillmann, G., *Marx und Hegel. Von der Spekulation zur Dialektik* (Frankfurt, 1966).

Hinderer, W., 'Der ritterliche Adam und die Bauernrevolte. Die Debatte über die historische Tragödie "Franz von Sickingen" von Ferdinand Lassalle', *Germanisch-romanische Monatsschrift*, NF xxiii, 1973.

—— *Sickingen-Debatte. Ein Beitrag zur materialistischen Literaturtheorie* (Darmstadt and Neuwied, 1974).

Hirth, F. E., 'Heine und Marx' in *Heinrich Heine. Bausteine zu einer Biographie* (Mainz, 1950).

Hook, S., *From Hegel to Marx. Studies in the Intellectual Development of Karl Marx* (New York, 1938) (new edn. Ann Arbor, 1962).

Hyman, S. E., *The Tangled Bank. Darwin, Marx, Frazer and Freud as Imaginative Writers* (New York, 1966).

Israel, J., *Alienation. From Marx to Modern Sociology* (Boston, 1971). (Swedish edn., Stockholm, 1968).

Jackson, T. A., 'Marx and Shakespeare', *International Literature*, vi (1936).

Jameson, F., *Marxism and Form. Twentieth-century Dialectical Theories of Literature* (Princeton, 1971).

Jay, M., *The Dialectical Imagination. A History of the Frankfurt School and the Institute of Social Research, 1823–1950* (London, 1973).

Johnson, Pamela Hansford, 'The Literary Achievement of Marx', *The Modern Quarterly*, New Series, ii (1946–7).

Johnston, W. M., 'Marx's Verse of 1836–7 as a Foreshadowing of his Early Philosophy', *Journal of the History of Ideas*, xxviii (1967).

Karbusicky, V., *Widerspiegelungstheorie und Strukturalismus. Zur Entstehungsgeschichte und Kritik der marxistisch-leninistischen Ästhetik* (Munich, 1973).

Koch, H., *Marxismus und Ästhetik. Zur ästhetischen Theorie von Karl Marx, Friedrich Engels und W. I. Lenin*, 3rd edn. (Berlin, 1962).

Kolakowski, L., *Marxism and Beyond*, trans. J. Z. Peel (London, 1969).

—— 'Marx' anti-utopische Utopie', *Merkur*, xxviii (1974).

Kolb, H., 'Karl Marx und Jacob Grimm', *Archiv für das Studium der neueren Sprachen und Literaturen*, ccvi (1969–70).

Korsch, K., *Marxismus und Philosophie* (Leipzig, 1930).

Kosik, K., *Dialektik des Konkreten. Eine Studie zur Problematik des Menschen und der Welt* (Frankfurt, 1971).

Kux, E. E. W., *Karl Marx — Die revolutionäre Konfession*, Diss. (Zürich, 1966).

Lang, B., and F. Williams (eds.), *Marxism and Art. Writings in Aesthetics and Criticism* (New York, 1972).

Lapin, N. J., *Der junge Marx im Spiegel der Literatur* (Berlin, 1965).

Laurenson, D., and A. Swingewood, *The Sociology of Literature* (London, 1972).

Lefebvre, H., *Contribution à l'esthétique* (Paris, 1953).

—— *Pour connaître la pensée de Karl Marx* (Paris, 1956).

—— *The Sociology of Marx*, trans. N. Guterman (Harmondsworth, 1972).

LeRoy, G. C., and U. Beitz (eds.), *Preserve and Create. Essays in Marxist Literary Criticism* (New York, 1973).

Lichtheim, G., *Marxism. An Historical and Critical Study*, 2nd edn. (London, 1961).

Lifshits, M., *The Philosophy of Art of Karl Marx*, trans. R. B. Winn (New York, 1938, reprinted London, 1973).

—— *Karl Marx und die Ästhetik*, 2nd edn. (Dresden, 1967).

—— *Karl Marks. Iskusstvo i obschchestvennyi ideal* (Moscow, 1972).

Livergood, N. D., *Activity in Marx's Philosophy* (The Hague, 1967).

Lobkowicz, N. (ed.), *Marx and the Western World* (Notre Dame and London, 1967).

Löwith, K., *Von Hegel zu Nietzsche* (Zürich–New York, 1941).

Lukács, G., *Geschichte und Klassenbewußtsein* (Berlin, 1923).

—— *Karl Marx und Friedrich Engels als Literaturhistoriker* (Berlin, 1948).

—— 'Marx und Engels über dramaturgische Fragen', *Aufbau*, ix (1953).

—— *Beiträge zur Geschichte der Ästhetik* (Berlin, 1954).

—— *Probleme des Realismus* (Berlin, 1955).

—— *Wider den mißverstandenen Realismus* (Hamburg, 1958).

—— *Probleme der Ästhetik* (Neuwied, 1969).

Macherey, P., *Pour une théorie de production littéraire* (Paris, 1971).

MacIntyre, A. C., *Marxism. An Interpretation* (London, 1953).

—— *Marxism and Christianity* (New York, 1968).

McLellan, D., *The Young Hegelians and Karl Marx* (London, 1960).

—— *The Thought of Karl Marx* (London–New York, 1971).

—— *Marx's Grundrisse* (London, 1971).

—— *Karl Marx: Early Texts* (Oxford, 1971).

—— *Marx before Marxism*, rev. edn. (Harmondsworth, 1972).

—— *Karl Marx. His Life and Thought* (London, 1973).

Maguire, J., *Marx's Paris Writings* (Dublin, 1972).

Marcuse, H., *Negations. Essays in Critical Theory* (Boston, 1969).

—— *The Philosophy of Aesthetics* (New York, 1972).

Marcuse, L., 'Marx und das Tragische', *Der Monat*, iv (1952).

Marx and Contemporary Scientific Thought, Publications of the International Social Science Council, xiii (The Hague and Paris, 1969).

Mayer, H., 'Karl Marx und die Literatur', *Merkur*, xxii (1968).

Mehring, F., *Aus dem literarischen Nachlaß von K. Marx, F. Engels und F. Lassalle* (Stuttgart, 1902).

—— 'Karl Marx und das Gleichnis', *Ges. Schriften*, vol. xii (Berlin, 1963).

—— *Karl Marx. Geschichte seines Lebens*, 2nd revised edn., *Gesammelte Schriften*, vol. iii (Berlin, 1964).

Mende, G., *Karl Marx' Entwicklung vom revolutionären Demokraten zum Kommunisten*, 3rd edn. (Berlin, 1960).

Mészáros, I., *Marx's Theory of Alienation* (London, 1970).

Miller, S., and B. Sawadzki, *Karl Marx in Berlin* (Berlin, 1956).

Mills, C. W., *The Marxists* (New York, 1962).

Miranda, J. P., *Marx and the Bible. A Critique of the Philosophy of Oppression*, trans. J. Eagleson (New York, 1974).

Mönke, W., *Die heilige Familie. Zur ersten Gemeinschaftsarbeit von Karl Marx und Friedrich Engels* (Glashütten im Taunus, 1972).

Morawski, S., 'The Aesthetic Views of Marx and Engels', *Journal of Aesthetics and Art Criticism*, xxviii (1970).

Nechkina, M., 'Shakespeare in Karl Marx's "Capital"', *International Literature*, No. 3 (1935).

Ollivier, R., *Marx et Engels, poètes* (Paris, 1935).

Pascal, R., *Karl Marx. His Apprenticeship to Politics* (London, 1942).

—— *Karl Marx. Political Foundations* (London, 1943).

Payne, R., *The Unknown Karl Marx* (New York, 1971).

Pazura, S., *Marks a klasyczna estetyka niemiecka* (Warsaw, 1967).

Petrović, G., *Marx in the Mid-twentieth Century* (New York, 1967).

Plamenatz, J., *Man and Society. A Critical Examination of some Important Social and Political Theories from Machiavelli to Marx* (London, 1963).

—— *Karl Marx's Philosophy of Man and its Legacy of Ideas*, Oxford, 1975.

Popitz, H., *Der entfremdete Mensch. Zeitkritik und Geschichtsphilosophie des jungen Marx* (Basle, 1953).

Popper, K. R., *The Open Society and its Enemies*, vol. ii: *The High Tide of Prophecy: Hegel, Marx and the Aftermath* (London, 1945).

Prévost, C., *Littérature, politique, idéologie* (Paris, 1973).

Raddatz, F. J. (ed.), *Marxismus und Literatur. Eine Dokumentation* (Reinbek, 1969).

—— *Karl Marx. Eine politische Biographie* (Hamburg, 1975).

Rader, M., 'Marx's Interpretation of Art and Aesthetic Value', *British Journal of Aesthetics*, vii (1967).

Raphael, M., *Proudhon, Marx, Picasso* (Paris, 1933).

Reeves, N., 'Heine and the Young Marx', *Oxford German Studies*, vii (1973).

Rubel, M., *Bibliographie des œuvres de Karl Marx* (Paris, 1956). (Supplement volume Paris, 1960).

—— *Karl Marx. Essai de biographie intellectuelle*, revised edn. (Paris, 1971).

—— 'Les cahiers de lecture de Karl Marx', *International Review of Social History*, ii (1957) and v (1960).

—— *Marx-Chronik. Daten zu Leben und Werk* (Munich, 1968).

—— *Marx critique du Marxisme. Essais* (Paris, 1974).

—— and M. Manale, *Marx without Myth. A Chronological Study of his Work* (Oxford, 1975).

Sánchez Váchez, A., *Art and Society. Essays in Marxist Aesthetics* (London, 1974).

Sander, H.-D., *Marxistische Ideologie und allgemeine Kunsttheorie* (Basle and Tübingen, 1970).

Sanwald, R., *Karl Marx und die Antike* (Zürich, 1957).

Schiel, H., *Die Umwelt des jungen Marx* (Trier, 1954).

Schiller, F., 'Marx and Engels on Balzac', *International Literature*, iii (1933).

Schmidt, A., *Geschichte und Struktur. Frage einer marxistischen Historik* (Munich, 1971).

—— *The Concept of Nature in Marx*, trans. B. Fowkes (London, 1971).

Schuffenhauer, W., *Feuerbach und der junge Marx* (Berlin, 1965).

Sebag, L., *Marxisme et structuralisme* (Paris, 1964).

Smulkstys, J., *Karl Marx*, Twayne's World Author Series, 296 (New York, 1974).

Solomon, M., *Marxism and Art. Essays Classic and Contemporary* (New York, 1973).

Sommer, C. (ed.), *Karl Marx — Friedrich Engels: Über Literatur* (Stuttgart, 1971).

Stadler, P., *Karl Marx. Ideologie und Politik*, 2nd edn. (Göttingen, 1971).

Stein, E., 'Karl Marx — ein Meister der Sprache', *Der Deutschunterricht* (Berlin) vi (1953).

Steiner, G., 'Marxism and the Literary Critic', *Language and Silence, Essays 1958–1966* (London, 1967).

Strelka, J. (ed.), *Literary Criticism and Sociology. Yearbook of Comparative Criticism*, v (1973).

Strey, J. and G. Winkler, *Marx und Engels 1848–49. Die Politik und Taktik der 'Neuen Rheinischen Zeitung' während der bürgerlich-demokratischen Revolution in Deutschland* (Berlin, 1972).

Teller, J., *Karl Marx und Friedrich Engels zu Fragen des künstlerischen Volksschaffens*, Diss. (Berlin, 1967).

Thier, E., *Das Menschenbild des jungen Marx* (Göttingen, 1957).

Thomson, G., *Marxism and Poetry* (London, 1946).

Trilling, L., *Sincerity and Authenticity* (London, 1972).

Trofimov, P. S., *Ocherki istorii marksistskoi estetiki* (Moscow, 1963).

Tucker, R. C., *Philosophy and Myth in Karl Marx*, 2nd edn. (Cambridge, 1972)

Victor, W., *Marx und Heine. Tatsache und Spekulation in der Darstellung ihrer Beziehungen* (Berlin, 1951).

della Volpe, G., 'Methodologische Fragen in Karl Marx' Schriften von 1843 bis 1859', *Deutsche Zeitung für Philosophie*, vi (Berlin, 1958).

Walton, P., and S. Hall (eds.), *Situating Marx. Evaluations and Departures* (London, 1972).

Weber, P., 'Die Einheit von politischer und ästhetischer Kritik in Marx' und Engels' Stellungnahme zu Lassalles Drama "Franz von Sickingen"', *Weimarer Beiträge*, xii (1966).

Wellek, R., *A History of Modern Criticism 1750–1950*, vol. iii: *The Age of Transition* (New Haven, 1965, London, 1966).

Williams, R., *Culture and Society 1780–1950*, 2nd edn. (Harmondsworth, 1961).

—— '"Base and Superstructure" in Marxist Cultural Theory', *New Left Review*, 82, (Nov.–Dec. 1973).

Wilson, E., 'Marxism and Literature' in *The Triple Thinkers* (New York, 1938).

Wintermeier, J., *Um das Wesen der Kunst. Studien zur marxistischen Ästhetik*, Diss. (Münster, 1971).

Wolff, A. v. Schmidt, 'Heine und Marx', *Archiv für Kulturgeschichte*, liv (1972).

Yezuitov, A. N., *Voprosy realizma v estetike Marksa i Engelsa* (Moscow–Leningrad, 1963).

Žmegač, V. (ed.), *Marxistische Literaturkritik* (Bad Homburg, 1970).

Index